MORE PRAISE F[...]

"Reading *Autobiography of a Yogi* by Paramhansa Yogananda was a transforma-tive experience for me and for millions of others. In *The New Path: My Life with Paramhansa Yogananda*, Swami Kriyananda carries on this great tradi-tion. Highly recommended."
—**Dean Ornish, M.D.**, founder and president, Preventive Medicine Research Insti-tute, Clinical Professor of Medicine, University of California, San Francisco, author of *The Spectrum*

"Swami Kriyananda has written a compelling and insightful account of his own life, as well as revealing his remembrances of Paramhansa Yogananda. Com-pletely revised and updated, *The New Path* is filled with profound reflections, insights, experiences, challenges, and spiritual wisdom. Required reading for every spiritual seeker. I heartily recommend it."
—**Michael Toms**, founder, *New Dimensions Media*, and author of *True Work* and *An Open Life: Joseph Campbell in Conversation with Michael Toms*

"[T]he teaching, the message, and the life of Paramhansa Yogananda are illumi-nated in a way that makes it possible for us to not only easily access his timeless wisdom, but—through the elegantly easy-to-follow explanations and the liv-ing example of one of Master's most devoted disciples—actually apply Eternal Truth to our present-day life. It is impossible for me to think of a greater gift that humanity could receive at this critical time in our evolution as a species, and I am personally and forever grateful to Swamiji for this blessed offering."
—**Neale Donald Walsch**, author of *Conversations with God*

"Not only did Kriyananda walk in the footsteps of an enlightened master, *The New Path* makes it obvious that he himself became an embodiment of Yoga-nanda's teachings."
—**Michael Bernard Beckwith**, founder of Agape International Spiritual Center, author of *Spiritual Liberation—Fulfilling Your Soul's Potential*

"By following the disciplines in this book, we can experience the realization that we are not our mind, thoughts, or feelings but are actually the pure es-sence of God. . . . Swami Kriyananda's great work on his life with Paramhansa Yogananda will inspire each person on the journey from avidhya [ignorance] to vidhya [spiritual knowledge]."
—**Dr. Vasant Lad**, BAM&S, MASc, author of *The Complete Book of Ayurvedic Home Remedies* and "Textbook of Ayurveda" series

"Yogananda was one of the towering figures who first brought the wisdom of the East to Western shores. We are incredibly fortunate to have Kriyananda's personal account of his experiences with this great master. A highly readable—at times even magical—book, *The New Path* chronicles Kriyananda's indefati-gable quest for authentic spiritual insight."
—**Linda Johnsen**, author of *Daughters of the Goddess: The Women Saints of India*

"For nearly thirty years the life and teachings of Paramhansa Yogananda have deeply resonated a truth within us as we have read daily from his works. We have felt a great debt to his devoted disciple Swami Kriyananda who has labored so diligently to make his Master's teachings known to the world. How thrilled we are to learn that after thirty years of memories and additional insights, Swami Kriyananda has given his book *The Path* a rebirth as *The New Path*. Our great and earnest wish is that another generation of students will find their own paths greatly illuminated by this deeply moving book."
  —**Brad and Sherry Steiger**, authors of *Revelation: The Divine Fire* and 170 books of metaphysics and mysticism

"*The New Path* is a true masterpiece, a valuable guide for the sincere seeker of truth and spirituality. It addresses the common problems faced by everyone on the spiritual path. . . . [E]very page is a piece of supple, clear, elevating, spiritual literature. . . ."
  —**D. R. Kaarthikeyan**, former Director, Central Bureau of Investigation and National Human Rights Commission, former Director General, Central Reserve Police Force, India

"*Autobiography of a Yogi* literally changed my life. It was the first book I read when I began my spiritual journey, and now *The New Path* has reignited my passion for Yogananda and the journey itself. This is a book with rare insights and profound truths."
  —**James Twyman**, author of *The Moses Code* and *Emissary of Light*

"It is not easy to describe this remarkable work with mere words—only time itself can reveal the importance of its ageless message. *The New Path* gives us a glimpse of Paramhansa Yogananda, one of the most beloved saints of modern times, through the eyes of a direct disciple—and what a view! Lucid, inspiring, and life changing, Swami Kriyananda takes us on a journey of tears, laughter, and joy. This is a good book!"
  —**Walter Cruttenden**, author of *Lost Star of Myth and Time*

"[T]his book is . . . a great boon to mankind, as great as the *Autobiography of a Yogi* which [Yogananda, Kriyananda's guru] wrote. Kriyananda Swamiji's mission in life is to bring the glories of his master to the eyes of this new age, and he has indeed succeeded in this wonderful work, which gives us an intimate glimpse into the life of that great and noble soul, a true avatar of the rishis of old. I have no doubt that it will inspire as many people in this 21st century as *Autobiography of a Yogi* did in the 20th century."
  —**Mata Devi Vanamali**, Vanamali Ashram, Rishikesh, author of *The Play of God: Visions of the Life of Krishna* and *Sri Lila Devi: The Play of the Divine Mother*

"Insightful, inspiring, and uplifting. A gift, not only for everyone who has been touched by Yogananda and his teachings, but to every seeker on the path."
  —**Deva Premal and Miten**, musicians, composers of *The Essence*, *Soul in Wonder* and other works

"Amazing! *The New Path* is a wonderful twinning of Swami Kriyananda's autobiography and Paramhansa Yogananda's biography! The openness and the honesty of the author are captivating. In deceptively simple words he tells an incredible story. It is hard to believe, but good to know, that such deep and sincere spirituality can flourish in today's America. *The New Path* also shows Hindu-Christian dialogue practiced at a depth hardly paralleled anywhere else. This is a wonderful book: a joy to read and a true inspiration!"
—**Klaus K. Klostermaier**, FRSC, University Distinguished Professor Emeritus, Former Head of Department of Religion and Director of Asian Studies, The University of Manitoba, Canada, author of *A Concise Encyclopedia of Hinduism*

"The words of Swami Kriyananda lead us to a fearlessness that is without anger, hate, and terror. Swami Kriyananda gives us inspiration for introspection. It is like the fearlessness of Gandhi that only inspired love and trust in others."
—**Tara Gandhi**, granddaughter of Mahatma Gandhi, Vice Chairperson, Kasturba Gandhi National Memorial Trust

"*The New Path* gives voice to why Americans—or modern people of any nationality—become attracted to the path of spirituality set forth in the Yoga tradition. Yoga suggests—even shouts—that the world of the spirit goes far beyond the obvious, the mundane, the trivial. Through stories of personal inspiration, and with great honesty, Swami Kriyananda narrates his relationship with his guru, Paramhamsa Yogananda, and his selfless service within the Self-Realization Fellowship and beyond. Having had the gift of personal transformation through direct transmission from the guru, Swami Kriyananda's memoir inspires the reader to strive for personal and social betterment, searching for truth, and finding truth in selfless service."
—**Christopher Key Chapple**, Doshi Professor of Indic and Comparative Theology, editor of *Worldviews: Global Religions, Culture, and Ecology*, Loyola Marymount University

"In *The New Path* we can find the divine wisdom which allows us to understand and heal our lives."
—**Bernie Siegel M.D.**, author of *365 Prescriptions for the Soul*

"*The New Path* is a godsend for anyone seeking enlightenment. Every page shines with deep wisdom and integrity, beautifully revealing the timeless principles for finding God. If you enjoyed reading *Autobiography of a Yogi*, you will find *The New Path* a deeply moving sequel. Swami Kriyananda shares hundreds of stories from his life as a close disciple of the great master, Paramhansa Yogananda, artfully including the reader, so that we, too, can be blessed by the great master's life and counsel."
—**Joseph Bharat Cornell**, founder of Sharing Nature Worldwide, author of *Sharing Nature with Children*

"Truly a 'Gospel of Paramhansa Yogananda,' *The New Path* makes readers feel that they are living with Yogananda, experiencing his guidance and blessings, basking in his divine radiance. I am deeply grateful to Swami Kriyananda for bringing to life the personality and nature of this great man of God. Just as the disciples of Christ captured in words their spiritual master for the benefit of millions, Swami Kriyananda has perfectly depicted his guru for the ages. What a blessing to encounter a disciple/biographer with such deep attunement and a keen understanding of his teacher's nature and mission, along with a profound gift of words. *The New Path* is a masterpiece, a modern spiritual classic, and one of the best-kept secrets of New Age literature."
  —**Richard Salva**, author of *The Reincarnation of Abraham Lincoln* and *Walking with William of Normandy*

"Kriyananda has done it again—that is, he has succeeded in writing a book (*The New Path*) about his guru, Paramhansa Yogananda, that inspires us about the guru-disciple relationship. . . . A must-read for spiritual afficionados."
  —**Amit Goswami**, quantum physicist and author of *God Is Not Dead, Creative Evolution,* and *The Self-Aware Universe*

"*[The New Path]* gives to the reader a rare insight [into] Yogananda's spiritual journey through . . . stories and anecdotes. The book is full of dialogues between the Guru and [disciple]. As one reads from . . . page to page, one feels as if one is in the company of both Yogananda and Kriyananda. The book makes . . . fascinating reading."
  —**Dr. S. B. Mujumdar**, Chancellor, Symbiosis International University, Pune, India

"Swami Kriyananda's narrative is a uniquely American and human story. It affords us a rare firsthand account of the history and development of the religious movement that brought the tradition of Yoga to the West. It is, at the same time, a profound personal memoir of the special relationship of nurture and demand that exists between teacher and student in this tradition. Paramhansa Yogananda's impact on the religious landscape of the United States is significant and enduring. Swami Kriyananda's chronicle deepens our understanding of the early origins of this movement and the powerful religious appeal of its founder."
  —**Anantanand Rambachan**, Professor and Chair, Religion Department, Saint Olaf College

"*The New Path* completes the spiritual content of *Autobiography of a Yogi.* Swami Kriyananda reveals the innermost teachings from the wisdom attained by being a close disciple of the Master Paramhansa Yogananda. The inner circle experiences, the Western adaptation to the ancient yogic science, the insightful stories, and the presence of Paramhansa Yogananda's energies make the book the ultimate read for those who are on the path of Light."
  —**Nandhi**, yogi, artist, musician, and spiritual teacher, Ariven Turiya Sakti Temple

THE NEW PATH

swami Kriyananda
J. Donald Walters

THE NEW PATH

My Life with Paramhansa Yogananda

by Swami Kriyananda
(J. Donald Walters)

Crystal Clarity Publishers
Nevada City, California

Crystal Clarity Publishers, Nevada City, CA 95959
© 2009 Hansa Trust
All rights reserved. Published 2009

Printed in China
3 5 7 9 10 8 6 4 2
ISBN-13: 978-1-56589-242-2
ISBN-10: 1-56589-242-9

Cover Design by Tejindra Scott Tully
Interior Design and layout by Madhavi Eby, Crystal Clarity Publishers

Special thanks to the many photographers that have given their contributions.

Library of Congress Cataloging-in-Publication Data

Kriyananda, Swami.
 The New Path : My Life with Paramhansa Yogananda / by Swami Kriyananda. — 1st ed.
  p. cm.
 Originally published: 1996.
 ISBN-13: 978-1-56589-733-5
 ISBN-10: 1-56589-733-1
 1. Kriyananda, Swami. 2. Ananda Cooperative Village—Biography. 3. Spiritual biography. I. Title.

 BP605.S38A5255 2008
 294.5092—dc22
 [B]   2008030552

www.crystalclarity.com
clarity@crystalclarity.com
800-424-1055

*To the sincere seeker,
whatever his chosen path*

A group of Paramhansa Yogananda's disciples had gone with him to see a movie about the life of Gyandev, a great saint of medieval India. Afterwards they gathered to hear the Master explain a few subtler aspects of that inspiring story. A young man from India mentioned another film he had seen years earlier about the life of Mirabai, a famous woman saint.

"If you'd seen *that* movie," he exclaimed, "you would have *hated* this one!"

"Why make comparisons?" the Guru rebuked him. "The lives of all saints manifest in various ways the same, one God."

PREFACE to *The New Path*

by Dharmaraj Iyer, M.S. Computer Science, M.I.T.
CEO, Harmony at Work, Pvt Ltd, Gurgaon, India

IN 1946, THE GREAT INDIAN MASTER, Paramhansa Yogananda, published his famous *Autobiography of a Yogi*. His book has sold over a million copies, has been named one of the top 100 spiritual books of the last century, and has become the most widely read spiritual autobiography of all time. Yogananda's story has inspired many millions of readers to seek God and divine joy within themselves.

The New Path: My Life with Paramhansa Yogananda, written by his close disciple, Swami Kriyananda, is a much-needed sequel to *Autobiography of a Yogi*. It is really the only account ever written by someone who lived with the Master, whom the Master commissioned personally to share with the public his words, teachings, and message.

The reader of *Autobiography of a Yogi* is likely, after finishing that inspiring book, to wonder what it was like to live with its author. For Yogananda wrote much less about himself than about the great saints he had met. Though his book is an autobiography, he manages to give the impression that he was only a humble devotee seeking wisdom at the feet of those great saints. The truth is, however, that he was born already fully enlightened, and was wiser than most of the saints about whom he wrote. In his last years he told his disciple Kriyananda, "I went to those saints for guidance, but they kept looking for answers to *me*!" Such, evidently, was his life-role. It was similar in this respect to that of Arjuna, the already-enlightened soul who played the role of humble seeker of truth from Lord Krishna, in the Bhagavad Gita.

What, the reader is left wondering also, was Yogananda's experience of America? What was his mission to the West? How did he present the ancient yoga science to modern audiences? How did he train his disciples? And finally, a burning question for the reader who has been deeply moved by his life story: *What was it like to live with him?*

Two or three other disciples of Yogananda have written sweet and uplifting accounts about him. Their books lack the insight, however, born of many years' experience with the public: while describing how Yogananda affected them, personally, they tell little about the vast scope, and omit the countless subtle details of the Master's life and mission. The reader, after finishing those books, is left thinking only, "How lucky the authors were to have known Yogananda!"

In *The New Path*, Swami Kriyananda addresses the many questions that naturally occur to anyone who has read Yogananda's autobiography. Indeed, this book gives the reader a feeling that he has actually *lived* with the Master. *The New Path* tells from the point of view of every disciple what it was like—and what it would have been like for the reader—to have lived with the Master. This book shares Yogananda's teachings directly, in the Master's own words. And it serves as a handbook for every truth-seeker, by addressing the common problems everyone faces on the spiritual path. Full of fascinating stories, humor, and insight, *The New Path* conveys high teachings and deep, but simply stated, truths with illustration after illustration.

As one reader exclaimed, "After reading this book I felt as if *I too* had lived with Yogananda!"

Kriyananda has written here a true masterpiece, captivating in its depth, power, and clarity. Yet one of the charms of his book is that he does not presume to "explain" Yogananda, nor to "reveal" his guru's inner nature. He writes, "The task that Infinity places squarely on the shoulders of every human being is just this: 'Understand thyself—*know* thyself.'" He adds that wise discrimination leads one "to study the life of a master with the purpose, not of understanding *him*, but of obtaining deeper insight into *one's own* true nature, and into *one's own* potential for divine unfoldment."

The New Path differs from *The Path*, its predecessor, primarily by offering an additional thirty years of reflection on the nuances of meaning in the Guru's life.

A final comment regarding the book's title. *The New Path* is of course a revision of the previous edition, *The Path*. That edition sold widely, and was translated into seven languages. This new version, however, is like a new book: it contains thousands of changes, and many new stories. There is a deeper meaning to the title also, indicated at the end of Chapter 39, where Kriyananda writes, of Yogananda's teachings: "And though I always say that what I want most deeply is to convert you to your own highest Self, I don't hesitate to add that, if you are still seeking your own path to truth, it may well be worth your while to explore the possibilities offered by this new dispensation, which is, truly, a new path to God."

FOREWORD to The Path, 1977

by John W. White, M.A.T., Yale University
author, *Everything You Want to Know about TM*;
editor, *The Highest State of Consciousness,*
Frontiers of Consciousness, What Is Meditation?;
associate editor, *New Realities Magazine*

WHEN ONE HAS been moved to laughter and tears, deep contemplation and joyful insight, as I have been while immersed in *The Path*, it is hardly possible to find a word or a phrase sufficient to encompass the enriching experience. "Deeply inspiring"—though hardly adequate—is the best way I can find to describe it.

Briefly, *The Path* is a story of one man's search for God through the path of yoga. It tells how American-born Donald Walters became universally-born Swami Kriyananda. At the same time, it serves as a practical manual of instruction for others in search of God-realization, no matter what tradition or path they follow. As an exceptionally lucid explanation of yogic philosophy, *The Path* will also be a valuable resource for those intellectually curious, but not consciously committed to spiritual growth.

The catalyst in Kriyananda's transformation was his guru, the well-known yogi, Paramhansa Yogananda, author of *Autobiography of a Yogi*. In fact, it is accurate to say that *The Path*, subtitled *"Autobiography of a Western Yogi,"* is as much about Yogananda as about Kriyananda. For, in truth, the two are one. That is part of the inspirational quality of *The Path*—the selfless devotion to guru which Kriyananda displays throughout the book. At the same time, he makes clear that Yogananda did not want devotion for himself. Rather, he would lovingly redirect his disciples' devotion to God.

This brings me to another element of the book which helped produce my feeling of inspiration—its abundant wisdom. Kriyananda's commentaries on spiritual unfoldment and his lucid explanations of yogic concepts are profoundly instructional. Moreover, like a true teacher he blends theoretical presentations and practical advice with personal anecdotes and illustrative stories in a way that is altogether engaging. Last of all, he presents us with much previously unpublished conversation from Yogananda, whose words are always enlightening.

Kriyananda's freedom from sentimentality is still another appealing aspect of his account. In creating this self-portrait, he speaks frankly about his failings, his ignorant shortcomings, his periods of doubt and depression, his moments of thralldom to spiritual pride. He doesn't attempt to romanticize the path he followed nor gloss over the difficulties he encountered within himself and in relation to others.

I have mentioned devotion, honesty, and wisdom as three characteristics of *The Path*, that give it an uplifting quality. There are others just as important—transpersonal love, for example, and the constant emphasis on attunement to God as the solution to all our problems. However, it is also important to note that *The Path* is not only spiritual—it is spiritual *literature*. The literary style with which Kriyananda reveals himself is worthy of study by authors as well as spiritual seekers. It is by turns elegant, graceful, supple, delicate and always clear—a verbal elixir that would work powerfully on the consciousness of readers even if the theme were profane instead of divine.

The final quality of *The Path* which I want to note is its planetary vision of society. Yogananda encouraged his followers—and I quote him here—"to spread a spirit of brotherhood among all peoples and to aid in establishing, in many countries, self-sustaining world brotherhood colonies for plain living and high thinking."

Today, Ananda World Brotherhood Village, established by Kriyananda and dedicated to human upliftment in accordance with Yogananda's teachings, is part of a growing global network of spiritual communities that are linking together ever more intensively to become the seedbed for a new world—rooted in a vision of humanity's oneness rather than in the warfare and competition that has characterized this century heretofore.

The Path chronicles the establishment of Ananda.* In so doing, it provides useful instruction in still another dimension that the dedicated spiritual seeker must come to face—his or her relation to society in general. The solution proposed in the life and teaching of Paramhansa Yogananda, as carried forward by Swami Kriyananda, is still another reason why *The Path* is so worth reading. The integral relation between spiritual practice and worldly affairs becomes abundantly clear through Kriyananda's words and deeds.

Not only is *The Path* inspirational—urging you to "go and do thou likewise"—it also gives the pragmatic technical instruction needed to put principle into action. Moreover, it does so with a beauty and simplicity that is the verbal embodiment of the yogic approach to God-realization. I trust that you will find *The Path* to be a major resource in your life and that you will, in accord with yogic tradition, lovingly share it with others as part of your service to the world. For an inspired work such as this, that is the only proper response.

Cheshire, Connecticut
June 1, 1977

---

* Ananda has long since grown to a point where its story really requires, and has received, books of its own for the telling. So I have removed much of the limited material about Ananda included in earlier editions. Interested readers may enjoy reading *Cities of Light* and *A Place Called Ananda* (which I wrote in 1988 and 1996, respectively), or any of a number of other books written about Ananda by its members. —S.K., 2009

Contents

Part III

List of Illustrations

Part III

INTRODUCTION

SINCE THE PUBLICATION of *The Path* over thirty years ago, it has appeared in several editions and languages. Recently I reread it, and decided that, after so many years, it could do with revision. And though the same number of years of my own life have passed also, bringing me now to the age of eighty-two, I decided not to bring the reader comparably up to date on my own life. Essentially, indeed, this book was never intended to be an autobiography so much as an account of my life with Paramhansa Yogananda. My basic purpose was to tell about his life from the perspective of a disciple. This would, I felt, fill a much neglected need.

I've written here about the deep humility which caused him, in his autobiography, to relate more about other great saints he had known than about himself. Indeed, the average reader might receive the impression from that autobiography that the author himself was not even a master, but simply a devout, earnest spiritual seeker who had had the good fortune to meet all those saints.

What I have done here, then, is complete the story of his life from an objective point of view. In this sense, I might indeed have titled this book *A Gospel of Paramhansa Yogananda*, were it not for the fact that I have also written other books, containing hundreds more of his sayings.

This book is also, and primarily, a sequel to Yogananda's autobiography, which, I am told, has become the best-selling spiritual autobiography of all time, and is still, after more than sixty years, among the ten best-selling spiritual books in the world.

The underlying saga of my own life has been universal in that it has been mostly a search for truth. Thus, this book is really more concerned with principles than with persons or events.

My story—detailed in Part I of this book—begins with my boyhood search. I sought by many paths: scientific, political, artistic, literary, dramatic, religious, philosophical, and (finally) spiritual. My hope is that this book will touch a receptive chord in others, for what I have dealt with here is a search that is central to the life of every man.

THE NEW PATH

PART I

CHAPTER 1

The Pilgrim Whittles His Staff

THERE ARE TIMES when a human being, though perhaps not remarkable in himself, encounters some extraordinary person or event that infuses his life with great meaning. My own life was blessed with such an encounter more than sixty years ago, in 1948. Right here in America, of all lands the epitome of bustling efficiency, material progressiveness, and pragmatic "know-how," I met a great, God-known master whose constant vision was of eternity. His name was Paramhansa Yogananda. He was from India, though it would be truer to say that his home was the whole world.

Had anyone suggested to me prior to that meeting that so much radiance, dynamic joy, unaffected humility, and love might be found in a single human being, I would have replied—though perhaps with a sigh of regret—that such perfection is not attainable by man. And had anyone suggested to me, further, that divine miracles have occurred in this scientific age, I would have laughed outright. For in those days, proud as I was in my intellectual, twentieth-century "wisdom," I mocked even the miracles of the Bible.

No longer. I have seen things that made a mockery of mockery itself. I know now from personal experience that divine wonders do occur on earth. And I believe that the time is approaching when countless men and women will no more think of doubting God than they doubt the air they breathe. For God is not dead. It is man only who dies to all that is wonderful in life when he limits himself to worldly acquisitions and to advancing himself in worldly eyes, but overlooks those spiritual realities which are the foundation of all that he truly *is*.

Paramhansa Yogananda often spoke of America's high spiritual destiny. When first I heard him do so, I marveled. *America?* All that I knew of this country was its materialism, its competitive drive, its smug, "no-nonsense" attitude toward anything too subtle to be measured with scientific instruments. But in time that great teacher made me aware of another aspect, an undercurrent of divine yearning—not in our intellectuals, perhaps, our self-styled cultural representatives, but in the hearts of the common people. Americans' love of freedom, after all, began in the quest, centuries ago, for *religious* freedom. Their historic emphasis on equality and on voluntary cooperation with one another reflects principles that are taught in the Bible. Americans' pioneering spirit is rooted in these principles. And when no frontiers remained to our people on the North American continent, and they began exporting their pioneering energies abroad, again it was the spirit of freedom and willing cooperation that they carried with them, setting a new example for mankind everywhere. In these twin principles Paramhansa Yogananda saw the key to mankind's next upward step in evolution.

The vision of the future he presented to us was of a state of world brotherhood in which all men would live together in harmony and freedom. As a step toward this universal fulfillment, he urged those people who were free to do so to band together into what he called "world brotherhood colonies": little, spiritual communities where people, living and working together with others of like mind, would develop an awareness of the true kinship of all men as sons and daughters of the same, one God.

It has been my own lot to found the first such "world brotherhood colonies," examples of what Yogananda predicted would someday become thousands of such communities the world over.

Because the pioneering spirit is rooted in principles that are essentially spiritual—implying the perennial quest for a higher as well as a better way of life—that spirit has not only expanded men's frontiers outwardly: in recent decades, especially, it has begun to *interiorize* them, to expand the inward boundaries of human consciousness, and to awaken in people the desire to harmonize their lives with truth, and with God.

It was to the divine aspirations of these pioneers of the spirit that Paramhansa Yogananda was responding by coming to America. Americans, he said, were ready to learn meditation and God-communion through the practice of the ancient science of yoga.* It was in the capacity of one of modern India's greatest exponents of yoga that he was sent by his great teachers to the West.

In my own life and heritage, the pioneering spirit in all its stages of manifestation has played an important role. Numerous ancestors on both sides of my family were pioneers of the traditional sort, many of them ministers of the Gospel, and frontier doctors. My paternal grandparents joined the great land rush that opened up the Oklahoma Territory in 1889. Other ancestors played less exploratory, but nonetheless active, roles in the great adventure of America's development. Mary Todd, the wife of Abraham Lincoln, was a relative of mine. So also was Robert E. Lee, Lincoln's adversary in the Civil War. It pleases me thus to be linked with both sides of that divisive conflict, for my own lifelong inclination has been to reconcile contradictions—to seek, as India's philosophy puts it, "unity in diversity."

My father, Ray P. Walters, was born too late to be a pioneer in the earlier sense. A pioneer nevertheless at heart, he joined the new wave of international expansion and cooperation, working for Esso as an oil geologist in foreign lands. My mother, Gertrude G. Walters, was a part of this new wave also: After graduating from college, she went on to study the violin in Paris. Both my parents were born in Oklahoma; it was in Paris, however, that they met. After their wedding, Dad was assigned to the oil fields of Rumania, where they settled in Teleajen, a small Anglo-American colony about three kilometers east of the city of Ploeşti. Teleajen was the scene of my own squalling entrance onto the stage of life.

My body, typically of the American "melting pot," is the product of a blend of several countries: England, Wales, Scotland, Ireland,

---

* Yoga: a Sanskrit word meaning "union," or, more exactly, self-integration. Yoga is also a system of psycho-physical techniques for helping man to achieve conscious union with the Infinite Spirit, God. The yogi, a practitioner of the yoga science, acquires outwardly also a vision of the underlying unity of all life.

Holland, France, and Germany. It was little Wales, the smallest of these seven, that gave me my surname, Walters. For Kriyananda is a monastic appellation that I acquired only in 1955, when I was initiated into the ancient Swami order of India.

The human body, through the process of birth, is a new creation. Not so the soul. I came into this world, I believe, already fully myself. I chose this particular family because I found it harmonious to my own nature, and felt that these were the parents who would best afford me the opportunities I needed for my own spiritual development. Grateful as I am to my parents for taking me in, a stranger, I feel less indebted to them for making me what I am. I have described them, their forebears, and the country from which they came to show the trends with which I chose to affiliate, for whatever good I might be able to accomplish for myself, and—I hoped—for others.

Everyone in this world is a pilgrim. He comes alone, treads his chosen path for a time, then leaves once more solitarily. His is a sacred destination, always dimly suspected, though usually not consciously known. Whether deliberately or by blind instinct, directly or indirectly, what all men are truly seeking is Joy—Joy infinite, Joy eternal, Joy divine.

Most of us, alas, wander about in this world like pilgrims without a map. We imagine Joy's shrine to be wherever money is worshiped, or power, or fame, or good times. It is only after very distant roaming that, disappointed at last, we pause in silent self-appraisal. And then we discover, perhaps with a shock, that our goal was never distant from us at all—indeed, *never any farther away than our own selves!*

This path we walk has no fixed dimensions. It is either long or short, depending only on the purity of our intentions. It is the path Jesus described when he said, "The kingdom of God cometh not with observation: Neither shall they say, Lo here! or, lo there! for, behold, the kingdom of God is within you."* Walking this path, we yet walk it not, for the goal, being inward, is ours already. We have only to claim it as our own.

The principal purpose of this book is to help you, the reader, to make good that claim. I hope in these pages to help you to avoid,

* Luke 17:20,21.

among other things, a few of the mistakes I myself have made in my own search. For a person's failures may sometimes be as instructive as his successes.

I was born in Teleajen on May 19, 1926, at approximately seven in the morning. James Donald Walters is the full name I received at christening in the little Anglican church in Ploești. Owing to a plethora of Jameses in the community, I was always known by my second name, Donald, in which I was the namesake of a step-uncle, Donald Quarles, who later served as Secretary of the Air Force under President Eisenhower. James, too, was a family name, being the name of my maternal grandfather. It was my ultimate destiny, however, to renounce such family identities altogether in favor of a higher and more spiritual one.

Mother told me that throughout her pregnancy she was filled inwardly with joy. "Lord," she prayed repeatedly, "this first child I give to Thee."

Her blessing may not have borne fruit as early as she had hoped. But bear fruit it did, gradually — one might almost say, relentlessly — over the years.

For mine is the story of one who did his best to live without God, but who — thank God — failed in the attempt.

My parents, Ray and Gertrude Walters, in Teleajen, Rumania, a few days after my appearance on the scene, May 1926.

My mother, my brothers Dick and Bob, and I *(right)*. If Dick was one year old at the time, I was five.

CHAPTER 2

He Sets Out from Home

J OY HAS ALWAYS een my first love. I have longed to share it with others.

My clearest early memories all relate to a special kind of happiness, one that seemed to have little to do with the things around me, that at best was only reflected in them. A lingering impression is one of wonder to be in this world at all. What was I doing here? Intuitively I felt that there must be some higher reality—another world, perhaps, radiant, beautiful, harmonious, in relation to which this earthly plane represented mere exile. Beautiful sounds and colors thrilled me almost to ecstasy. Sometimes I would cover a table down to the floor with a colorful American Indian blanket, then crawl inside and fairly drink in the luminous colors. At other times, gazing into the prism formed by the broad edge of a mirror on my mother's dressing table, I would imagine myself living in a world of rainbow-colored lights. Often also, at night, I would see myself absorbed in a radiant inner light, and my consciousness would expand beyond the limits of my body.

"You were eager for knowledge," Mother told me, "not a little willful, but keenly sympathetic to the misfortunes of others." Smiling playfully, she added, "I used to read children's books to you. If the hero was in trouble, I would point pityingly to his picture. When I did so, your lips quivered. 'Poor *this*!' you exclaimed." Mother (naughty *this*!) found my response so amusing that she sometimes played on it by pointing tragically to the cheerful pictures as well—a miserable ploy which, she informs me, invariably succeeded.

As I grew older, my inner joy spilled over into an intense enthusiasm for life. Teleajen gave us many opportunities to be creative in our play. We were far removed from the modern world of frequent movies, circuses, and other contrived amusements. Television was, of course, unknown at that time even in America. As a community composed mostly of English and American families, we were remote even from the mainstream of Rumanian culture. Our parents taught us a few standard Anglo-American games, but for the most part we invented our own.

Our backyard became transformed into adventure lands. A long stepladder laid sideways on the snow became an airplane soaring us to warmer climes. A large apple tree with hanging branches served a variety of useful functions: a schoolhouse, a sea-going schooner, a castle. Furniture piled high in various ways in the nursery would become a Spanish galleon, or a mountain fortress. We blazed secret trails through a nearby cornfield to a cache of buried treasure, or to a point of safety from the pursuing officers of some unspeakably wicked tyrant. In winter, skating on a tennis court that had been flooded to make an ice rink, we gazed below us into the frozen depths and imagined ourselves moving freely in another dimension of wonderful shapes and colors.

I remember a ship, too, that I set out to build, fully intending to sail it on Lake Snagov. I got as far as nailing a few old boards together in nondescript imitation of a deck. In imagination, however, as I lay in bed at night and contemplated the job, I was already sailing my schooner on the high seas.

Leadership came naturally to me, though I was unwilling to exert it if others didn't spontaneously share my interests. The children in Teleajen did share them, and enthusiastically embraced my ideas. More and more, however, as I grew older, I discovered that many people considered my view of things somewhat peculiar.

I noticed it first in some of the newly arrived children in Teleajen. Accustomed as they were to the standard childhood games of England and America, they would look puzzled at my proposals for more imaginative entertainment—like the time we gazed into unfamiliar dimensions in the ice while skating over it. Unwilling

A typical scene of rural Rumania as it was when I lived there.

Me, at four years old . . . . . . and at ten in Bucharest.

to impose my interests on them, I was equally unwilling to accept their imposition in return. I was, I suppose, eccentric, not from any conscious desire or intent, but from a certain inability to attune myself to others' norms. What was important to me seemed to them unimportant, whereas, frequently, what they considered important seemed to me incomprehensible.

Miss Barbara Henson (later, Mrs. Elsdale), our governess for a time, described me years later in a letter the way she remembered me as a child of seven: "You were certainly 'different,' Don—'in the family but not of it.' I was always conscious that you had a mystic quality which set you apart, and others were aware of it, too. You were always the observer, with an extraordinarily straight look in those blue-grey eyes which made you, in a sense, ageless. And in a quiet, disconcerting way, you made funny little experiments on other people as if to satisfy your suspicions about something concerning them. Never to be put off by prevarication or half-truths, you were, one felt, seeking the truth behind everything."

Mildred Perrot, the wife of our Anglican minister in Ploeşti at the time, once told me, "I can go through a keyhole."

"You *can*?" I exclaimed. From then on I kept pestering her to perform this miracle, until finally she relented. Writing the letter *i* on a small piece of paper, she folded it up and shoved it through a keyhole! I still remember my disappointment, for I *wanted* miracles to belong in the realm of the possible.

Cora Brazier, our next-door neighbor, a kind, sympathetic Rumanian lady, once remarked to Miss Henson, "I always try to be especially nice to Don, because he's not like the others. I believe he knows this, and is lonely."

Although this knowledge was not to dawn on me fully until after I left Teleajen, there was even then a certain sense of being alone. It was held in abeyance, however, by the presence of good friends, and by a harmonious home life.

My parents loved us children deeply. Their love for each other, too, was exemplary and a strong source of emotional security for us. Never in my life did I know them to quarrel, or to have even the slightest falling out.

My father was especially wonderful with children. Rather reserved by nature, he yet possessed a simple kindness and a sense of humor that enabled him to appreciate young minds. At bedtime he would invent hilarious stories for us that were continued night after night, frequently with additions from his enthusiastic listeners. Then, as my brothers and I were ready to fall asleep, he would arrange us at one end of the bed or the other depending on whether we said we wanted to travel in sleep to Australia, America, or to some other distant land.

He taught us much, by example as well as words. Above all what we learned from him came from observing in him a nature always humble, honest, truthful, honorable, kind, and scrupulously fair. I would go so far as to call him, in his quiet, rather reserved way, a great man.

But in my own relationship with him there was always a certain sadness. I could not be to him the kind of mirror a man naturally hopes for in his sons, especially his first-born. I tried earnestly to share his interests, but where he was attracted to the "hows" of things, I was attracted to the "whys." He was a scientist, and I, instinctively, a mystic and philosopher. He tried to interest me in the way things worked. (I still remember one dusty expedition under

My parents, taken outside their home in Atherton, California, 1976.

the house, where he showed us boys what made the front doorbell ring. I at least *tried* to feel grateful!) But I was only interested in what things meant. My inability to communicate with him on those subjects which most deeply interested each of us was the first indication I had that his world—which I considered, by extension, the normal world—could never truly be mine.

Mother and I understood one another intuitively; ours was a communication of souls, less so one of speech. Though she never spoke of praying for us children, I know that her prayers and love for me were my greatest blessing during the formative years of my life.

Rumania was still a feudal land. Its people, gifted artistically, tended otherwise to be somewhat inefficient and unhurried. The country was an anachronism in the busy twentieth century. Its workmen could spend fifteen years with picks and shovels digging a tunnel under the railway tracks at the main station in the capital. One summer, eager to follow the example of the rest of the modern world, the whole nation, by official mistake, went on Daylight *Losing* Time! Drivers' tests included such penetrating questions as "What goes on the front of a car?" (Headlights, naturally.) Years later, Indra Devi, the well-known yoga teacher,* told me that while traveling by train through Rumania she had once been asked by the conductor what she was doing in a second-class compartment.

"Why, can't you see? I have a second-class ticket!"

"Oh, that doesn't matter in *Rumania*! Please, just go sit in first class where everyone else is."

Inattention, however, to the petty details of modern commerce and efficiency seemed somehow appropriate in a land that inspired thoughts of music and poetry. Rumania was one of the most fascinatingly beautiful countries I have ever seen: a land of fertile plains and soaring mountains; of colorfully clad peasants and musically gifted gypsies; of hay carts on the highways vying with automobiles for the right of way; of giggling, naked children; of gay songs and laughter. Frequently, outside our colony in the evenings, we would hear bands of gypsies conversing, singing, or playing the violin: the sad, haunting melodies of a people forever outcast from their true home, in India.

* Author of *Forever Young, Forever Healthy* and other books.

These gypsies were my first contact with the subtly subjective moods of the Orient—moods that, I was to learn, are reflected in many aspects of life in Rumania. For centuries Rumania had been under Turkish rule. Now a proud and upcoming Western nation, there still clung to her something of the aura of the mystical East.

Rumania was a kingdom. King Carol II had his summer home about sixty kilometers (forty miles) northwest of us, in Sinaia, a lovely hill station in the Transylvanian Alps. Though I never saw him there, we, too, spent many vacations in Sinaia, and in other quaint towns and villages nearby: Buşteni, Predeal, Timiş, Braşov. In winter we often skied; in summer we hiked, or waded and swam in friendly, chuckling brooks, or played in fragrant meadows. Many times these mountain trips were taken because of my health, which was precarious. I was skinny as a pencil, and forever coming down with a variety of obscure ailments. Timiş was my favorite spot. There we always stayed at a guest lodge run by a German lady, Frau Weidi, whose husband kept bees that produced the best honey I have ever tasted.

Sixty kilometers to the south of Teleajen was Bucharest, Rumania's capital: a clean, modern city that rose like a prophetic dream in the mind of a nation still asleep in the Middle Ages. Ploeşti remained, however, for the first nine years of my life, the Big City: a not-very-attractive jumble of dirty streets and uninteresting houses. My recollections of it are few: visits to Ghiculescu, the grocer; Sunday services at the Anglican church; and very occasional outings to the movies—Walt Disney cartoons, mostly, and comedies featuring Laurel and Hardy, whom the Rumanians had renamed fondly, Stan and Bran (*Stan si Bran*).

The church served as a focus for Mother's piety. In this area of her life Dad played the role of disinterested spectator. Though he respected Mother's religious inclinations, and went with her to church more or less regularly, I never observed that liturgy held any attraction for him. His own natural concept of reality was more abstract. Nothing, I think, so inspired him as the contemplation of vast eons of geologic time. The thought of a God sitting somewhere on a heavenly throne, bestowing favors on special groups of worshipers, struck him, I suspect, as faintly barbaric.

My own natural bent lay somewhere between these two: the pious and the abstract. Like Dad, I was not greatly attracted to the church worship services. The hymns seemed to me rather dull and sad. The minister I considered a good man, but certainly not an inspired or inspiring one. I suppose I accepted the rituals as good things to do; beyond this pale recognition, however, they held little meaning for me. I wish I could report that the life of Jesus, at least, made a strong impression on me. I am moved by it now. But then it reached me through a barricade of wooden traditionalism, robbed of immediacy. I'm sure I couldn't have defined my feelings at the time, but I think what I missed most of all in our church services were love and joy. Mother had these qualities. What impressed and touched me about her was not religion as she defined it, but as she lived it.

Like Dad, I found it difficult to believe in a God who loved each human being personally. That God was impersonal seemed to me self-evident, when I considered the vastness of the universe. How, then, I thought, could He be interested enough to listen to us mortals when we prayed to Him? It was only many years later, in the teachings of India, that I found reconciliation of these seemingly incompatible concepts of a God both personal and impersonal. For the Infinite Spirit, as my Guru was to explain with perfect simplicity and clarity, though impersonal in its vastness, has become personal also in creating us individual beings. Infinity, in other words, implies infinitesimal smallness as well as infinite immensity.

Though I found it difficult to address God personally, I always felt that reality must be *spiritual*, that it must have some high meaning and purpose. I remember a discussion I had once with Dad. I was about six years old at the time; we were standing on the terrace of our Teleajen home, watching the birds twitteringly at play in the large apple tree.

"In the hundreds of millions of years," Dad said, "since the world was created, every species has had its turn at being the master of this planet, except the birds. First there were the fishes, then the insects, then the reptiles, and now man, representing the mammals. Perhaps, millions of years from now, man, too, will be pushed aside, and the birds will get their turn at being the earth's masters."

How appealing I found this picture of vast reaches of time! But then a doubt occurred to me: Is there no *meaning* to it all? Is life nothing but a process of endless variety, with different species ruling for no better reason than that their turn has come? Surely there must be some higher purpose—hidden, perhaps, but divine.

My questioning mind must have made me something of a trial to my parents. Mother, on a visit to Italy in 1933, wrote to Miss Henson: "Please tell the boys that I want them to try to be very good and that will help both them and me to have a good time. (Donald is sure to find a flaw in that argument, but you might try it!)"

Fortunately for me, Mother and Dad never discouraged my questioning. I remember one day, at the age of five, standing in the bathroom, watching Dad shave. I was pondering one of the deep mysteries of childhood: How can Santa Claus reach every home on earth in a single night? Suddenly the answer dawned on me.

"Daddy, there isn't really a Santa Claus, is there?"

Dad, too honest to insist that there is, but too considerate of the sweet myths of childhood to admit that there isn't, hedged his reply. I understood him perfectly. Then and there I decided that it would really be much more fun to go on believing in Santa Claus anyway. In that spirit I believe in him still.

Myths are an important part of life. Paradoxical as it seems, they are important to man's search for truth as well, for they help to give his mind the elasticity it needs to imagine new solutions to old problems.

Myths (in fact!) formed a large part of my education. I loved Greek mythology, the adventures of King Arthur and his knights of the Round Table, the legends of Robin Hood and Peter Pan, Grimm's fairy tales, stories from the Old Testament—myths, all, in which goodness, courage, and honor win in the end. One's life experiences may not always endorse these moral preachments, but wise men and women have ever insisted that justice does prevail eventually, even if the time of reckoning stretches to distant horizons. "*Yato dharma, tato jaya,*" proclaim the Indian scriptures: "Where there is righteousness, there is victory." Fact may well, as people claim, be stranger than fiction, but fiction is very often, in a deeper sense, truer than fact. I think it a pity that the ancient myths are not given more emphasis in modern education. Certainly they enriched my own upbringing.

But then, the culture of Rumania was more conducive to legend-telling than that of pragmatic America. As children, my brothers and I got periodic opportunities to compare these two countries. Every three or four years Dad received a three-months' vacation, all expenses paid, in America. My first journey was when I was six months old, then three years, seven, ten, and thirteen. It was after I turned thirteen that we settled here.

I still recall my amazement, at the age of three, on arriving in London to find waiters, taxi drivers, the man in the street—all speaking English! I'd supposed English was spoken only by parents and their friends. Nurses, of course, spoke German. But wasn't it a law of life that practically everyone else spoke Rumanian? I suppose by so compartmentalizing these languages I managed to keep from confusing them—a further example, perhaps, of the value of the myth-making process. Once Mother addressed me in Rumanian, and I replied to her in shocked tones, "Mother, don't talk to me like that!

Looking at America with a mentality that was partly Rumanian, I received insights that sometimes conflicted with my pride in being an American. I deeply loved America. I admired its dynamic energy, and stood almost in awe of its constant emphasis on common sense: The Americans I met seemed to know exactly what to do in every situation. I loved them, too, for their kindness—whenever they took the time from constant, driving activity to be kind. But on the other hand, I found myself puzzled by what often struck me in their conversation as "big talk." I'd noticed it in a few of the Americans in Teleajen, especially in the newcomers. In America even the children, it seemed, were always trying to show how grown-up they were, how sophisticated, how important. It was as though they had no patience with childhood. What, I wondered, was all that *important* about being important?

Compared to America, Rumania is a little country. Though independent in spirit, its people have a less exalted self-image. Americans, with their four million territorial square miles (the U.S. is the third largest country in the world, after Russia and Canada), fall more easily into the thought of self-importance, a temptation which seems to accompany bigness whether in nations, institutions, or individuals.

Vacations in America entailed visits to our various relatives. My earliest memories include Mother Ella, my maternal grandmother, who died while I was still young. I remember best her sweet smile, so loving it seemed almost saintly. My paternal grandparents, who lived longer, were simple, good people also. It was in these relatives, and in many other people like them, that I caught my first glimpse of the special spiritual genius of America: childlike innocence and simplicity, a predisposition to see goodness in others, a love of freedom tempered by a desire to live in harmony with man and God.

Granddad introduced me also to another American trait: the tendency to dignify inconsequential matters by humorously pretending that serious issues were at stake. It is a trait that can, and sometimes does, lead to misunderstandings.

Once in Tulsa Dad paid a minor traffic fine. Granddad remarked straight-facedly to me afterwards, "Well, I guess your Dad escaped prison this time." I took him literally. Several days later our family was eating in a crowded restaurant. As sometimes happens in a crowd, there occurred a brief interlude when, without apparent reason, everyone in the room stopped talking—everyone, that is, but young Donald. Heedlessly, I chose that moment to pipe up in a loud voice:

"Daddy! Tell us about the time you escaped from prison!"

There ensued a still-more-silent hush of shock. Then, suddenly, everyone was laughing. (Why, I wondered, was Dad blushing so furiously? It seemed to me such a brave thing for him to have done.)

Trips to and from America must have been something of an ordeal for our poor parents. We were three brothers. Dick, the youngest, wasn't old enough to engage in much fraternal rivalry, but Bob and I were close to the same age, and when we weren't

cooperating in some misadventure (like the time we upset a traveling prince and his retinue by scrambling their shoes, left overnight
in the corridor to be shined), we often wrestled each other to work
off excess energy.

Bob was born a year and a half after me, but soon grew to my
height, and occasionally surpassed it. He felt little hesitancy in
challenging a seniority which I had no intention of relinquishing.
Temperamental differences existed between us, too. Bob was impulsive, outgoing, fond of popularity, demonstrative of his feelings.
I was in many ways quite the opposite: reserved, pensive, forever
questioning. Bob once picked up a caterpillar from a path with the
loving cry, "There, there, you poor little worm! I'll put you over
here so no one can step on you." He then ran off gaily, quite forgetting the incident. Had I helped the same caterpillar, I would have
pondered the incident for days, wondering what it was that made
certain creatures defenseless, and why this particular insect, out of
millions, should have received help.

Beside Bob I'm afraid I sometimes felt myself rather a lump. As
a matter of fact, that thought sometimes seemed to bother him,
too. His spirit of rivalry was, I think, rooted partly in unconscious
disapproval of me for not being more like others. But for all that we
managed to be good friends. And always, where the rest of the world
was concerned, we stood together in brotherly solidarity, never more
so than when either of us was being threatened.

Fighting is, I suppose, inextricably a part of the process of growing up, particularly so for boys. I recall what might be considered
my fair share of boyhood scraps, though I don't remember ever
instigating one. (In this respect I was unlike my cousin Ed, who made
full, aggressive use of nature's gift to him of a strong body. "Eddy,"
his mother once admonished him, "don't you know that when another boy hits you, you shouldn't hit back?" "Oh, but Mother," Ed
remonstrated self-righteously, "I *never* hit back. I always hit first!")

Though I myself never "hit first," if ever it seemed important to
me to demonstrate to others, or to myself, that I was no coward
I was not one to turn the other cheek. Several fights, in fact, far from

stirring me now to repentance, stand out in memory as having helped me to learn worthwhile lessons.

It was because of a fight that I first learned something of the fickleness of human loyalties. I was seven or eight at the time. Alvin, a big boy who was visiting Teleajen with his parents, determined to impose his command on our group. Brawn, fortunately, was not important to our "group dynamics." I knew that the support I had from my friends was born of mutual affection, not of fear. But when Alvin challenged me, his victory seemed so much a foregone conclusion that most of the children, fearing later retribution, sided with him. Bob was the sole exception. I was indignant at the rest of them for their fickleness, and determined to teach them a good lesson by beating Alvin.

It was a long, somewhat bloody battle. Every shout for Alvin only goaded me to renewed efforts. Gradually his strength flagged. As it began to look as if I might win after all, first one of the children, then another, joined Bob in rooting for me. At last Alvin's courage crumbled altogether. By this time everyone was enthusiastically on my side.

Victory was bittersweet for me that day, however. I knew my friends had really wanted me to win all along. But I also understood a little bit of what an unreliable thing is the support of one's fellow creatures.

Wise indeed is he who discovers that God's friendship *alone* can never fail him.

Disappointment, however, is a good teacher; it helps us to take our first, faltering steps out of childhood toward maturity. For the world is frequently at odds with our desires. The sign of maturity is a willingness to adjust to realities broader than one's own. It is how we react to disappointment that determines whether our development will be a shrinking inward towards bitterness and cynicism, or an expansion outward towards acceptance and wisdom.

CHAPTER 3

Storm Clouds

IT WAS SUMMER, 1935. I WAS nine years old. Vacationing in the quaint mountain village of Buşteni, I was enjoying a happy season of games, picnics on grassy meadows, and carefree laughter.

One afternoon I went to my room to read a book. Sitting in a chair, I suddenly felt dizzy. I lay down on the bed, but even from this position the room seemed to be spinning. I cried weakly for help, but no one came. At last, summoning all my strength, I struggled to the door, leaning against the wall for support. There, I called again. This time I was heard.

A doctor was hastily summoned. A large, loud-voiced, overconfident lady, she was evidently determined to prove that I had appendicitis. (*Prod.* "Does it hurt here?" *Prod again.* "How about here?") Minutes of this diagnostic predetermination made me hurt all over. Finally, deciding, perhaps, that it would be no use operating on my entire abdomen, she gave up.

I came near dying in that little village. As it was, though I survived, the happy world I had known for the first nine years of my life died for me with this illness. Back home in Teleajen, all I remember "clearly" are long stretches of delirium: Dad reading to me from Mark Twain's *Huckleberry Finn*, and the drunken fits of Huck's father, returning to mind at night in terrifying garb.

"I don't *want* to be a drunkard!" I cried, wrestling with my own delirium. "I don't *want* to be a drunkard!"

At last I came to associate *any* unusual mental state with delirium. The very soul-expansion which, until this time, had visited me so normally at night now filled me with a nameless dread.

Because of this fear, I now began making a conscious effort to adjust to the norms of others. For the better part of a decade, insecurity and self-doubt left me anxious to prove to myself that I was not, in some indefinable way, abnormal and inferior.

Dr. Stroyei, a pediatrician in Bucharest, finally diagnosed my illness as colitis. He forbade me all dairy products, and put me on a bland diet of soft-cooked foods that almost robbed me of my interest in eating. When I'd recovered sufficiently, my parents decided, on Dr. Stroyei's recommendation, to send me to the salubrious climate of Switzerland. Dr. Winthrop Haynes, my godfather, recommended a small Swiss-English boarding school where his own sons had studied for a time, in Chesières, a mountain village in French Switzerland. The school was named, perhaps a trifle pretentiously, *L'Avenir* ("The Future").

My own future here, eighteen long months of it, was somewhat bleak. Only nine years old when I arrived, never before away from my family, and ignorant of French (the language commonly spoken at L'Avenir), I was homesick much of the time. Throughout my stay, moreover, I was afflicted with a series of fairly serious illnesses stemming from the colitis. Mostly it was my kidneys; I had to live for days at a time on zwieback (a kind of dried bread) and Vichy water.

L'Avenir was owned and run by a kindly couple, Mr. and Mrs. John Hampshire. Mr. Hampshire was English; his wife, whom we children knew affectionately as Tante Béa (Aunt Beatrice), was French-Swiss. The students themselves were a mixed bag of Swiss, English, American (me), Italian, and French.

Unhappy though I was, my stay there did have its compensations. The scenery, for one thing, was stunningly beautiful. Across the valley from us loomed the famous Alp, Les Dents du Midi. In winter we skied daily. In warmer weather, frequent walks led us through flowered pastures and quiet, discreet woods—all very properly Swiss. I still recall the herds of cows passing our chalet school in the early mornings, with dangling bells ringing melodiously.

Gradually, too, as I learned to speak French, adjustment became easier for me. The teachers, able to communicate with me now, grew quite fond of me. (Grownups were touched, generally, because

Chesières, Switzerland, where I went to school in 1935 and 1936.

With schoolmates at L'Avenir, my school in Switzerland. Skiing was our favorite winter pastime. I am standing third from the right.

I treated them like *people*.) Even our frosty German teacher, to whom I'd seemed merely stupid as long as I couldn't speak French, eventually thawed. Teaching her German class in the French language, which I didn't know, she had remarked, "Donald, *tu ne sais pas comme tu es bête*! (Donald, you don't know how stupid you are!)" In reporting this interchange in a letter to my parents, I concluded, "I stuck my tongue out at her!"

My long illness coincided with the growing political malady of Europe. In Vienna, where Mother and I stopped on our way to Switzerland, we were warned by friends not to criticize Nazi Germany except in places that were safe, and then only in whispers. Austria had not yet been annexed to Germany, but one saw Nazi officers everywhere, marching about, challenging people with their Nazi salute and shouting sternly, "*Heil Hitler!*" ("Hi," I would reply, waving a nonchalant hand.) Storm clouds were gathering. In the bluster of bullies everywhere one saw the arrogance of men newly justified in their own eyes. And, growing in the hearts of peace-loving people everywhere, there was fear.

One of the students at L'Avenir was an Italian boy, larger by a head than most of us, and a braggart. Guido tried to ingratiate himself with us by laughing loudly at everything, and at nothing. But he was a bully, and nobody liked him. He was also—naturally enough, considering his own insensitivity—an ardent supporter of Italy's dictator, Mussolini. We were never allowed to forget his country's "glorious" conquest of poor, backward Abyssinia.

Little cogs in a big wheel! But it took those little cogs to make the wheel turn. Individual bullies, each one insignificant in himself, were banding together on the stage of history and imagined in their swelling ranks that fate had given them the power to change the world. For them it was a heady hour. Such, indeed, is the influence of mass hysteria that, ere long, many others, too, formerly peace-loving, were striding about behaving like petty dictators.

An Austrian friend of ours in Teleajen, pleasant enough when he first came there, caught the bully fever. From then on, normal conversation with him was impossible; all he ever spouted was a succession of proud boasts. "We Germans," it seemed, would soon be marching in to subjugate everyone and his dog.

This man's chief weakness was only, I think, that he lacked a sense of humor. I've never known a bully to possess one. I don't mean they can't laugh *at* people; *that* they do readily enough. It's that they can't laugh *with* others. Humor certainly was conspicuous by its absence among those who succumbed to the disease of Naziism.

I even wonder whether the evolution of tyranny isn't reducible to some kind of law, in which humorlessness plays an essential role. First in the line of converts to tyranny, it seems, come the true bullies—the sadists, the mentally crippled and vengeful, the criminal. Then, as the spirit of arrogance spreads, well-meaning but essentially humorless people enter to swell the tide. Finally come the well-meaning, but stupid. At this point, anyone with any true values has little choice but to flee, go underground, or maintain a resolute silence in the face of general insanity. Or—he can laugh.

One evening in Germany a famous comedian appeared on stage before a large audience. Clicking his heels together, he raised a straight right arm high above his head. Several people in the audience leapt to their feet and returned the Nazi salute.

"That," said the comedian, "is how high my dog jumped yesterday."

This man knew the probable consequences of his brave gesture, but his sense of humor in the face of those probabilities revealed that indomitable spirit in human nature before which tyranny must ever succumb in the end.

In the summer of 1936 we traveled through Germany on our way to America. A stranger sharing Bob's train compartment was arrested at the German border by the Gestapo. Perhaps he was Jewish. Or perhaps, like thousands of others, he was merely trying to flee despotism. But, young as we were at the time, we knew the likely outcome of his arrest: imprisonment, and then death.

In Bucharest I had a governess for a time who, like our friend in Teleajen, was an Austrian Nazi. Also like him, she was quite devoid of any sense of humor. Miss Annie assured us constantly, whenever our parents weren't there to hear her, that Japan would never lose in any war against America, having never lost one in its long history. The German people, moreover, in league with the Japanese and the Italians, were destined to rule the whole world. It seemed peculiarly fitting to us when it was discovered that Miss Annie was a kleptomaniac. She was dismissed.

Whenever we traveled through Germany, however, all the people we met were exceedingly kind and hospitable, eager to help us in every way they could. Were *these* people Nazis? Some, I suppose, must have been; the worst bully, after all, is still a child of God, and cannot but reflect something of the Divine Goodness. But I think most of them were simply normal, good people caught up in the flood of a national tragedy. We loved them almost the more, I think, for the sadness of their plight. What country, after all, is in a position to be able to say honestly, "*Our* people would never sink to such depths"?

The plight of Europe affected me deeply. Why, I wondered, can people not learn to live together in harmony? What is it in human nature that courts, that seems almost to *demand*, tragedy?

Perhaps my gloomy reflections were aggravated by my own unhappiness. One day I was standing alone on the balcony of our chalet school. Mr. Hampshire came out to find me weeping silently.

"What's the matter?" he inquired gently.

"I'm homesick!" I sobbed.

Kindly, he wrote that day to my parents. Soon it was decided that I should return home.

During my stay in Switzerland Dad had been transferred to Bucharest. Our new residence was on the outskirts of the city, at Strada Capitan Dimitriade No. 10. Here I got six months' respite before resuming my formal education. It was during this period that Miss Annie tutored me.

My health through this winter of 1936–37 was still precarious. Occasionally the pain was intense, though I remember now, more clearly than the pain, the tears in Mother's eyes as she suffered with me in her love.

Sometimes, when I was well enough, I played football (soccer, we call it in America) on an empty lot with the neighborhood children. One of these was a boy from a slum area across Boulevard Bușteni. His family were so poor they couldn't even afford window panes, but covered up the openings in winter with newspapers. I took intense pity on him, invited him frequently to my home, and gave him freely of my toys. I was his friend. He, I assumed, was my friend.

One day he and a few of the boys in our own neighborhood taught me a hard lesson. Dissembling camaraderie, they invited me to join them in the nearby courtyard of one boy's home. The gate was closed quietly behind me; someone locked it. Then, to my surprise, they backed me against a fence and began to kick a football at me, trying to hit me with it. Obviously, they were working up the courage for an attack.

I stood my ground and quietly waited, struck the football aside whenever it came too near, and affected an attitude of indifference. Minutes passed. At last the boys changed their minds about the merits of this afternoon's entertainment. The gate was opened, and I was allowed to walk out unscathed.

Though physically unhurt, I thought my heart would break. Back home, I wept inconsolably. Why, I asked Mother through tears, had my "dearest" friend, and my other good companions, so betrayed my love for them? It was small comfort to reflect that war hysteria had by now made Rumanians suspicious of *all* foreigners.

Painful though this experience was, it proved an excellent lesson. From it I learned that it isn't enough to give to others, even with love. If one would not beggar them in their own eyes, one must make it possible for them in some way also to reciprocate.

My absence in Switzerland, which had relieved Bob of the restraining presence of an older brother, had left him by no means languishing in his new freedom. Gleefully in fact, from then on, he insisted that every important event in our family must have occurred "while you were in Switzerland."

My absence from home had had its effect on me, too. Whether I liked it or not, I now was a little less dependent on the home for which I had so recently been pining. God was weaning me from dependence on earthly security. My illness; my consequent absence, in that condition, in a distant land; my growing sense of aloneness: these were, I think, meant only to help me realize that my true home is not here, on earth, but in God.

Indeed, this is, for all men, an eternal truth: God is our reality. Ineluctably we are led, quickly or slowly, by one path or another, towards this divine understanding.

In this thought I am reminded of a brother disciple who once asked our Guru, "Will I ever leave the spiritual path?"

"How could you?" the Master answered. "Everyone in the world is on the spiritual path."

CHAPTER 4

A Temporary Haven

PERHAPS THE DIVINE Fisherman was thinking this poor fish had better not be pulled in too forcibly, lest he break the line. At any rate, the process of dragging me out of my little pond of earthly security became for me, temporarily, much more pleasant. After six months in Bucharest my health was greatly improved. I was eleven years old now, and my parents were anxious to see me resume my formal education.

A Quaker boys' school in England had been highly recommended to us. Nestling snugly in the heart of the Malvern Hills near the village of Colwall, The Downs School was surrounded by verdant, rolling fields, and by narrow country roads that wound their way carefully between clipped, very *English* hedges. The buildings were attractive, and the grounds spacious. I was steeled to the idea, which months earlier had been so painful to me, of living away from home. The Downs seemed a better place than most in which to spend my exile.

The English have many wonderful traits: honor, loyalty, a sense of duty and fair play. Since this is a chronicle of my spiritual search, however, I cannot in good conscience ignore what comes across to me also as a certain blind spot in their national temperament: a reliance so complete on the ordinary that it gives almost no credence to the extraordinary. Something there is about the religious spirit of England that tries to mold Jesus Christ himself into the very proper image of an English gentleman, and casts the Old Testament prophets as fellow club members with him, perhaps writing occasional letters to the *Times* in protest against the lamentable want of good

The Downs School, Colwall, England, where I studied from 1937 to 1939. (*insert*) I, during my days at The Downs.

form in a few of their countrymen. Whether members of the Church of England or of any other sect, the English give one the impression of having neatly clipped and trimmed their religion, like a hedge, to protect values that are primarily social. I refer not to the courageous, free-thinking few, but to the many whose worship seems to close, rather than open, windows onto infinity.

I hope I am wrong. At any rate, the only memorable religious event for me during my two years at The Downs occurred one Sunday evening when the father of one of our students, an Anglican minister, delivered a sermon. This man's body, almost perfectly round, was surmounted by a face that was dangerously suggestive of a pig's — dangerously, I say, because his porcine appearance, combined with an attitude of immense dignity, reduced me and a friend beside me to fits of helpless, though silent, merriment. All I remember clearly now is looking up at one point through tears to see "the pig" describing a wide circle with his arms. "And the whole world . . ." he cried feelingly. His gesture so perfectly outlined his own global figure that fresh paroxysms of suppressed mirth overwhelmed us. The row directly behind ours was filled with faculty members, but to my surprise none of them endeavored to discipline us. Perhaps they, too, were finding self-control difficult!

The Downs was easily the best school I ever attended. Religious teaching there may not have been exactly ponderous, but in other respects the teachers knew how to draw the best out of their students. Character building is more basic to the English educational system than to the American. At The Downs, honor, fair play, truthfulness, and a sense of responsibility were given strong emphasis. To tell a lie was considered almost outside the realm of possibility. A boy was once caught stealing sixpence and a little candy from another boy's locker, and so shocked everyone that he was expelled from the school.

In sports, too, though we did our best to win, we were taught that the game itself, not its outcome, was what really mattered. After rugby matches with other schools, the members of both teams dined together, rivalry forgotten, new friendships affirmed. I have sometimes wondered what would happen if opposing teams in America were to dine together after a game. Given our national emphasis on winning, I suspect there might be a free-for-all.

Once, in punishment for some peccadillo, a group of us were told to run several miles around a course of country roads. No one checked up on us to make sure we didn't spend that time lying under some tree instead. Mr. Hoyland, the headmaster, knew it wouldn't occur to us to break our word to him. He only told me to report in to him again when we returned.

Another time, as punishment for some infraction, I was told not to go swimming on three occasions when I really wanted to. The trust implied in this condition helped me to live up to it, though I must admit that on one of those occasions it was raining, so I wouldn't have been able to go anyway!

Needless to say, idealism didn't always win out over basic human weaknesses, nor propriety over boyhood's natural exuberance. But on the whole I am impressed with what the English school system was able to accomplish.

The Downs School had a number of innovative features of its own: two kinds of marks, for example, one of them in Greek letters (alpha, beta, gamma, delta), to show how well (or badly) we'd done in the subjects themselves; the other in colors, to show how earnestly we'd applied ourselves to those subjects. Those bright colors seemed somehow even more worth striving for than the letter grades.

Wednesday afternoons were hobby time. We were allowed, on approval, to select our own hobbies, and were given qualified instructors for them. My first year there I studied sculpture; my second, painting. For what would have been my third year, a group of us generated enough interest to get astronomy approved. For me, however, as will become clear later on, that year was not to be.

In addition to sculpture and painting I studied piano and also sang in the choir. Our choir instructress, a puffy-cheeked, solemn, but good-natured lady, would peer at us myopically as she waved her baton. With great earnestness she taught us to sing:

> Bach and Handel, as you know
> Died and were buried long ago.
> Born in the year one-six-eight-five,
> Still they're very much alive.

If this ditty fell short of the musical standards it celebrated, we had no quarrel with the sentiment it expressed. For we loved classical music. Actually, I seldom heard modern popular music until we moved to America. My parents and their friends occasionally threw parties and danced to records, but to us boys this was just "grown-up nonsense." I remember how we shook with merriment the time I imitated for my brothers a recording I'd heard in England of "*Bei Mir Bist Du Schön*," sung in extravagantly nasal American accents by the Andrews Sisters. At The Downs, too, tastes ran generally to classical music, except perhaps among the older boys. It was quite unselfconscious on our part; we simply liked it.

Too many people treat the classics like something to be bolted down with water and a wry face. But if children's tastes weren't conditioned otherwise by their sexually awakened elders, I think most of them might grow up loving great music.

Life in England exposed me also to another kind of sound: the British accent. Not that I was unfamiliar with it; many of our friends in Rumania were English. But there at least we mixed with them on neutral ground. Here I alone was a foreigner. Placed at such a disadvantage, I worked hard to overcome it. By the time I returned home for my first vacation I was already saying "ne-oh," and "shahn't" with the best of 'em—much to my parents' dismay.

At first I tried awkwardly to cloak my reserve under a somewhat ill-fitting mantle of jocularity. A boy named Randall decided my behavior lacked proper dignity for a Downs boy. When I passed off his scolding with another joke, he became so irritated that he challenged me to a fight. Randall was the accepted leader of our form,* and was accustomed to being obeyed.

Grudges at The Downs weren't supposed to be settled on the spot. To win time for a possible reconciliation, the rule was to submit a formal challenge, after which a boxing match was arranged in the gym, complete with seconds and a referee.

I accepted Randall's challenge. The date for the match was set. As the days passed and Randall observed in me no sign of apprehension, his attitude toward me gradually changed.

* The English equivalent of *grade*.

"Let's be friends," he suggested one day. I assured him I'd never felt we were enemies. In time our friendship developed into one of the happiest I have ever known.

Randall was good-natured, highly intelligent, sensitive, yet practical, and intensely earnest in everything he did. His friendship opened for me the door to acceptance by the other boys. Once accepted, I brought to them a lighter spirit—the ability, for example, to laugh at oneself. Our Latin teacher, Mr. Days, a formidable man whose bluff I somehow managed to penetrate, wrote to me years later, "Yours wasn't, perhaps, the brightest class I ever had, but it was certainly the happiest."

The months passed in study, good fellowship, and sports. A fast runner, I managed to play wing three-quarter (the principal running position) in several of the rugby games with other schools. Cricket, however, I considered an utter waste of a sunny afternoon. In practice sessions, which were obligatory, I would lie down in the outfield and wait comfortably for someone to shout, "Walters, get up! The ball's coming your way!"

Sometimes there were inter-form "wars"—in fun, not in anger. One form would "board" the other, perhaps through windows that hadn't been secured quickly enough. Fights at The Downs, even those initiated in anger, commonly strengthened the spirit of friendship. This was an outcome that, to my surprise, I never encountered in the schools I attended later in America.

But while we scrapped and competed merrily in classrooms and on playing fields, another more serious conflict was developing in Europe. The relentless approach of World War II made a somber backdrop to our school days, one that was never very far from our thoughts. Many of us, we realized, might have to fight in the next war. Many of us, probably, would be killed.

The pride of the English is intense. One boy, dignifying with the label, patriotism, what was really only a mean nature, once called me a "dirty foreigner." I was inured to the second half of this role, so wasn't offended. "If I'm a dirty foreigner," I replied with a smile, "perhaps you're a dirty Englishman." Outraged, the boy leapt at me. I was stronger than he, and had no difficulty in holding him down while he writhed and spat up at me till he tired of hurling imprecations and cooled off. Later I related the incident to Randall and one or two other friends, and was impressed by the depth of their patriotism. Their laughter at the outset was generous; none of them liked the boy, and all of them liked me. But their laughter subsided when I reached the point where I'd said, "Perhaps you're a dirty Englishman." Sympathy returned only when I explained that it was purely a question of whether or not the other boy had bathed recently.

England's Prime Minister, Sir Neville Chamberlain, went to Germany in 1938, returning with the welcome proclamation, "Peace in our time." Much was made in the press of his glad tidings, though I don't think people put much faith in them. At any rate, gas masks were soon passed out to each of us at school. On a trip to Rumania with Roy Redgrave, the son of family friends of ours there, we sang the English national anthem loudly in the streets of Hamburg, feeling very brave, though I don't suppose the Gestapo felt particularly threatened by a couple of skinny English schoolboys. What children do, however, reflects the spirit of their elders. Throughout Europe, defiance was now in the air. It could only be a matter of time before open conflict broke out.

My two years in England gave me much for which to be grateful. The friendships I formed there, and the good times we had, left me with many happy memories. Though circumstances prevented me from returning for my third and final year, Mr. Hoyland had selected me for the second half of that year to be the head boy. My gain, moreover, was not only in the form of memories. I also learned many worthwhile lessons, particularly on the correctness or incorrectness of different patterns of behavior. Such teaching contains an important spiritual principle. For, as my Guru was to emphasize later, it is not enough to be guided by high ideals: One must also "learn to behave." That is to say, one must know how to relate properly to every reality on its own level.

This balance of the inner and outer aspects of life is not easy to achieve. My two years in England helped me toward its fulfillment. Partly for this reason, England has always held a warm place in my heart. So great is my regard for the fine characteristics of her people, and so loving were the friendships I formed there, that I think I shall always remain, in part, an Englishman.

CHAPTER 5

The Storm Breaks

IT WAS SPRING, 1939. Dad, after fifteen years in Rumania, had risen to become head geologist for Esso in Europe. Now he was being transferred to Zagreb, Yugoslavia, there to become Esso's exploration manager. All our belongings were packed and stored in Bucharest, ready for shipment. In March, Dad rented an apartment in The Hague, Holland, on Koninginnegracht. We spent our Easter vacation there. (Fond memories of picturesque streets, acres of tulips, and smiling, friendly people!)

Summer came, and with it another visit to America. The weeks passed quietly for us as we visited relatives in Ohio and Oklahoma. August was about to close its ledger; it was time for us to return to Europe, so we entrained at Tulsa for New York.

As we stepped out onto the station platform in Chicago, the headline struck us with all the force of a massive ocean wave: *WAR!* Hitler had invaded Poland. Hopes for peace had been smashed on rocks of hatred and nationalistic greed. To return now to a war-ravaged continent would be foolish. Dad was transferred to the head offices of Esso at Rockefeller Center, in New York City. Our belongings, packed and ready for shipment to Zagreb, had only to be rerouted to America.

We settled eventually in the New York suburb of Scarsdale, at 90 Brite Avenue, in the Foxmeadow section. For the next nine years this was to be my home, or rather my point of perennial departure.

While I was still a small child my parents had enrolled me at Kent School, in Kent, Connecticut. This was a church school for boys, run by Episcopalian monks. I was not scheduled to enter

Kent for another year, however. Meanwhile I was placed at Hackley, a boys' school near Tarrytown, New York.

And now the Divine Fisherman began once again to reel in His line determinedly. Looking back after all these years, it is easier for me to summon up a certain proper sense of gratitude to God for holding me so closely in check. At that time, however, I'm afraid gratitude was not my uppermost sentiment. A month earlier my expectations had been bright. I was returning to The Downs for a happy final year there, surrounded by good friends. Now, suddenly, I found myself at thirteen the youngest boy in the lowest grade of a high school where the only familiar feature was my own perennial status as a "foreigner," a status which, as a born American returning to live in his own country, I found particularly difficult.

Even my accent, now English, set me apart from others. But whereas formerly, in England, my American accent had occasioned little more than good-natured chaff, here, my English accent marked me for derision. It took me at least a year to learn to "talk American" once again. I have never learned to do so perfectly.

Heretofore I had never in my life heard a dirty word. At Hackley it seemed, once I'd been initiated into the new vocabulary, that I heard little else. In the past, swing music had been only an amusing pastime. Here, it was practically a religion. Sex had never before figured in our conversations. Here, it was virtually an obsession. Aggressive behavior, rudeness, insensitivity to others as affirmations of one's own independence from them—these seemed to be the norms. School "wisdom" included such precious advice as "Silence is golden—and also healthy."

The fact that I was just entering puberty made the problem of adjustment all the more difficult. In truth, I could see no good reason to adjust. Rather, I tended to enclose myself defensively within psychic walls, like a medieval town under siege. One or two of the boys were friendly to me, but to the others I seemed merely an import, dumped on American soil quite unnecessarily, and, considering the solid worth of the domestic article, even presumptuously.

In the room next to mine there was a boy of fifteen, named Tommy Maters, who weighed two hundred and twenty pounds to

At age fourteen, when I was attending Kent School.

Our home at 90 Brite Avenue, Scarsdale, New York.

my one hundred and seven. Tommy was a bully. My "English ways" were, to him, an insult to the flag of America. It wasn't long before, dissatisfied with merely voicing his disapproval, he advanced to open threats.

I'm not sure he was quite sane. One morning I awoke to see him peering in my window, an air pistol in his hand. As I leapt to safety behind my desk, a bullet struck the other side of it with a thud.

What bothered Tommy about me, I think, was not only the implied insult of my un-American ways, but the fact that I wouldn't acknowledge my self-evident inferiority by cringing before him. Later that day he made it a point to sit next to me at lunch, the better to express his opinions. Throughout the meal he criticized my appearance, my vocabulary, my table manners. ("Don't you know you should spoon your soup toward the *far* side of the bowl?— peasant!") I paid no attention to him. Finally he muttered, "Boy, am I going to get you!"

I knew he meant it. Back in my room after lunch I pushed the dresser up against the door, which was without a lock. Tommy arrived shortly afterward, breathing threats. He rattled the doorknob, then leaned heavily against the door, puffing dire predictions with mounting fury. At last he succeeded in shoving the door open, rushed into the room like an enraged bull, and proceeded to beat me with such uncontrolled rage that it really seemed as if he wanted to kill me.

"I'm going to throw you out that window!" he panted again and again. (We were three storeys above the ground.) Throughout the beating he kept his voice low for fear of attracting the attention of others on our floor. Somehow the ferocity of his whisper sounded more threatening than an angry shout.

What could I do, small as I was? I lay motionless on the bed, face down, waiting for him to exhaust himself.

"Why didn't you cry for help?" a friend asked me the next day.

"Because I wasn't afraid."

Interestingly, the fact that I took Tommy's beating calmly, and never thereafter altered my attitude toward him, left him without another weapon to use against me. People commonly see physical victory as conclusive, but true victory is always mental. One's conqueror may feel conquered in turn by a spirit that he finds he cannot reach with physical weapons. Tommy, from this time on, gave me a wide berth.

Though I was released now from his bullying, in other respects my life at Hackley grew no happier. I sought escape in the music room, where I practiced the piano for hours together. My unhappiness stirred me also for the first time to a longing for religion. Perhaps, I thought, I would become a missionary. I expressed these aspirations, somewhat hesitantly, to my cousin Betty when both of us were at my parents' home in Scarsdale. She was horrified.

"Not a missionary, Don! There's too much to *do* in this world. You wouldn't want to bury yourself on some primitive island!"

The vigor of her reaction shook me in my still-frail resolution. What, after all, did I really know about the missionary calling? Self-doubt was in any case becoming my own private hell.

After a year at Hackley School, the time came for me to enter Kent.

Kent is an Ivy League prep school; it ranks high, scholastically and socially. I entered it with high hopes. But I soon found that the general interests of the boys here were essentially what they had been at Hackley, with the addition of a sort of "All for God, Country, and Our School Team" spirit in which arrogance played the leading part. The Kent student was expected by his peers to embrace every social norm, to like or dislike all the "right" people, and to boast of his proficiency in all the "right" activities, particularly those related to sex and drinking. Woe betide that hapless youth who danced to a different piper. To laugh with the loudest, tell the dirtiest jokes, shout boisterously when merely passing the time of day, smile expansively at everyone ("Oh, *hi*, Don!") in a bid to get *others* to like *you*: These were the banners of success. Conformity made one eligible for that supreme reward: popularity. Nonconformity exiled one to a limbo of disapproval and contempt.

Experience had shown me that I had the ability to make friends. But what was I to do when, try as I might, I simply couldn't share the enthusiasms of my fellow students? It was not a question, as it had been in England, of relating to new realities on their own level. In England, principles at least had been concerned. Here I could find none—only egotism, selfishness, and self-interest. I might have been able to stand my ground firmly had I been able to out-shout, out-boast, and out-laugh others. As it was, being somewhat reserved by nature, I was unwilling to offer my ideas where I felt they were unwelcome.

Instead I became intensely introverted, miserable with myself, certain that my life was already, at its outset, a failure. In an environment that demanded absolute conformity, my inability to conform seemed like failure indeed. Gradually it became as evident to others as it was already to me that I was simply one of that unfortunate breed, of which the human race will ever produce its allotted few: a misfit, a general embarrassment, a creature of subnormal ability.

Yet in my heart I knew this judgment was false.

I tried my best to enter into the life of the school. I joined the school paper, reporting sports events with a hopeful heart. My first two articles, however, spelled my undoing; my humorous touch on so sacred a subject as *sports* was considered almost blasphemous. When I wrote that the fatness of the goalie was fortunate, for it made it more difficult for the ball (or the puck; I'm not sure which) to pass, the editor smiled with amusement, then appeased his conscience by withholding further assignments from me. I joined the debating society, but found I couldn't speak in defense of issues to which I wasn't sincerely committed. I became a member of the French club, but my fellow members were for the most part lonely outcasts like me. I played football. I rowed. I sang in the glee club.

Nothing worked. There was almost a kind of shame in the few friendships I did form, a tacit understanding that ours was a companionship in rejection.

At times I was actually afraid to leave a roomful of boys, lest my departure give them the opportunity to talk against me. Nor were my fears groundless: I knew, from the times when I stayed, what uncomplimentary things they had to say about those less popular boys who happened to be absent. One day, after passing a couple of classmates on the stairway in our dormitory, I overheard one of them, who obviously didn't care whether I heard him or not, laugh derisively, "What a sad case!"

The worst of it was, I had no clear grounds on which to refute him.

During this gloomy period, religion might have been the comfort for me that it had been at Hackley. Kent was, after all, a church school, and most of the boys there were moderately religious; at least, I recall none of them grumbling over the required attendance at worship services. But religion at Kent seemed as though preserved in formaldehyde. With the exception of one jolly, elderly brother who taught no classes, and who was, I think, a little foolish, the monks seemed a joyless lot, uninspired and uninspiring in their calling. The church services were heavy with the consciousness that one went through all this simply because it was *done*. Religion at Kent inspired me to look almost anywhere but to God for solace and enlightenment.

Soon I was seeking both of these fulfillments in the realm of ideas. Always a bookworm, I began diving into the worlds of James Fenimore Cooper, Sir Walter Scott, Keats, Shelley, Shaw, and other famous writers.

At fourteen I began writing a novel of my own. The influence of Cooper was evident in my setting: A pioneer family living on an isolated farm in Oklahoma was attacked by red Indians. Only two boys escaped massacre by fleeing during the confusion. Earnestly, at this point, I counseled the reader not to think harshly of the Indians, "for they had been oppressed by the white man ever since he came to this continent, and had had their hunting grounds taken away and changed into towns and places of civilization. . . . Nor must you think ill of their scalping methods, for that was just the coustom [*sic*] among the indians, and though we may think it cruel or repulsive, surely some of the things we do are just as bad, if not more so."

The two boys escaped into a nearby forest, pursued by Indians. Deep in the forest they discovered a cliff, scaled it to a high ledge, and there rested, thinking they'd arrived unobserved. Minutes later, one of them happened to look down from their ledge, "and drew back in astonishment, for there, not five feet below him, was an Indian, and following him came three more, the last two carrying guns, but the others without them for greater agility. Just then the foremost one heard him and uttered a word that would correspond to our word 'Shucks!' For they had planned on a surprise." (How often I've chuckled over that Indian's disappointed exclamation!)

The boys, having nowhere else to go, fled into a nearby cave. It led them down, down, deep beneath the surface of the earth, past unspeakable obstacles including huge spiders in a stream that tried to block their progress and devour them. At last, to their amazement, they emerged into another world, inexplicably sunlit and beautiful. Here Indians and white men lived happily together in perfect brotherhood: hence the title of the novel, *The Happy Hunting Grounds*.

All this was, of course, pure escapism. Yet it also reflected a feeling which I think comes to many people from time to time in their lives: the deep, inner certainty that their true home *is* elsewhere, that they belong in heaven, and that the present world is only a proving ground for the soul. As Jesus said, "No man hath ascended up to heaven, but he that came down from heaven."* This certainty is born not of speculation, but of deep astral memories that have become dimmed by more recent, earthly experiences.

Unhappiness and suffering are necessary for the soul's unfoldment. Without them we might remain satisfied with petty fulfillments. Worse still, we might remain satisfied with *ourselves*.† My personal unhappiness at Kent School inspired me to ponder the sufferings of mankind everywhere. Could anything be done, I wondered, to improve the human lot?

Surely, if all men would truly accept one another as equals they would be much happier. I worked out a laborious system of government in which no man possessed any personal property, all things being owned in common. Though I don't think I realized it at the time, my ideas were similar in several respects to those preached, though hardly practiced, under modern communism. But as I pondered the matter more deeply, I came to realize that most men are not capable of living in a voluntary state of nonpossession. A few

* John 3:13.

† "Because thou sayest, I am rich, and increased with goods, and have need of nothing; and knowest not that thou art wretched, and miserable, and poor, and blind, and naked: I counsel thee to buy of me gold tried in the fire . . . and anoint thine eyes with eyesalve, that thou mayest see." (Revelation 3:17,18)

people—monks, for instance—might be non-attached enough to consider nothing their own, but to *force* nonpossession on humanity at large would be tyranny. Dictatorship, even in the name of the common weal, would inflict more abuses than it could alleviate.

At this time also I wrote a one-act play, titled *The Peace Treaty*. Its subtitle was, "Every Man for Himself." It was about a group of cave men, tribal chieftains, who got together after a war to determine the conditions for peace. One of them who, like all visionaries, was ahead of his time, proposed an idea that he claimed would banish war forevermore. His plan demanded a generous spirit of international cooperation among the different tribes to replace the inter-tribal rivalries and selfishness that had prevailed hitherto. The other chieftains professed great admiration for his ideas. It soon became clear, however, that they understood him not at all, for when it came to the question of what sacrifices each would have to make to ensure peace, each suggested a few "minimal" improvements in the original plan, with a view to getting as many concessions as possible for himself. The peace treaty was finally thrown out, as chieftains scrambled for whatever booty they could grab for themselves.

At the close of the play the hero soliloquized: "If God existed, would He allow all this? . . . But—of course He exists! How could life have come to this earth without Him? Ah! I see it all now. Yes, God exists, but He wishes mankind to live under hard conditions, for it is only under such that Man can prove himself worthy of the Kingdom of Heaven." God cares, I concluded, but wants man to *earn* His blessings, for without victory over greed, paradise itself would become but another battleground. Man, I was saying, is not perfectible through mere systems, but only by working conscientiously on himself.

The play ended with blows and shouts offstage, followed by gunshots, then cannonades, then bombs, and finally one bomb, mightier than all the rest. And then: *silence.*

The harsh reality of human greed was the stumbling block on which all my dreams of political salvation became shattered. At fifteen I began writing another novel, about a man who foresaw the destruction of modern civilization, and decided to do what he could to preserve its most constructive elements. Far out into the wilderness he went, and there built a utopian community. Aiding him were experts in various fields, men and women who understood that expertise must be rooted in wisdom and love, not in mere knowledge. This little community kept the lamp of civilization burning while the rest of humanity bombed itself back to the caves. The group then returned to their fellow men to teach them a better, more constructive way of life.

The more I thought about my visionary community, the more compellingly it attracted me. From an escapist dream my concept gradually evolved to a spreading network of intentional communities *within* the framework of present-day civilization. Someday, I resolved, I would start such a community myself.

It isn't often that one's boyhood dreams are fulfilled later in life. With God's grace, this dream has been. That tale, however, must await the telling until a later chapter.

I gave much thought also at Kent to the possibility of paranormal phenomena—prophecy, telepathy, and the mental control of objective events—and to the question of what life must be like after death. I wondered whether I might serve my fellow man better if I tried to develop extra-sensory powers myself. But no, I decided, this whole subject was too remote from common experience to be widely meaningful. Instead I would share with others through the written word whatever insights I gained into life's truths. By clear common sense, perhaps, I would inspire in others a loftier vision.

While I was mentally improving the world, however, my own little world was rapidly deteriorating. A few of the older boys evinced a positive dislike for me. Ineptness I suppose they might have excused; not everyone, after all, could hope to match them in their excellence. But while self-admittedly inept in their ways, I had gone on from this recognition of failure to develop other—to them, inadmissible—interests. Was not this implied rejection of their standards an unthinkable presumption? They began threatening openly to make my life "really miserable" next year, when a few of them would be returning to Kent as student body leaders.

I felt I could take no more. In tears that summer I pleaded with Mother to take me home.

Stroking my head tenderly, she said, "I know, dear. I know. You're like your Dad. He's always been shy when people didn't want what he had to give them. Yet he has so much to offer. And so do you. People haven't understood it, but never mind. Stay home now, and live with us who love you. Here you'll be happy."

What relief flooded my heart! I never saw Kent again. Who can say whether I might yet have coaxed a few useful lessons from its dreary walls? But I felt I had taken from them every blessing I possibly could. I was ready now, inwardly as well as outwardly, for a different kind of schooling.

CHAPTER 6

A Paper Rest House: the "Popularity Game"

M OST OF THE young people I met during my adolescence seemed
secure in their values. The 1940s were not like today, when it
is common for young people to question society's values, to seek
Meaning, to ponder its, and their, relationship to the universe and to
God. When I was in high school, as nearly as I could tell I walked
alone in such questing. I knew no guidelines to follow. I wasn't even
sure what it was I was seeking. All I knew definitely was that I wanted *something*, and that that something didn't seem to be what anyone
else wanted.

Others had already planned out their lives more or less confidently. They would get good jobs, make money, get ahead in the
world, marry, settle down in Scarsdale or some other wealthy community, raise children, give cocktail parties, and enjoy the fruits of
a normal, worldly life. But I already knew I didn't want money.
I didn't want to "get ahead" materially. I wasn't interested in mar-
rying and raising a family. I knew well enough a few of the things
I *didn't* want, but had no distinct notion of what it was I *did* want.
And in this uncertainty I sometimes doubted whether my disinclina-
tion for the things others prized wasn't proof of some inadequacy
in myself.

Had others, I wondered, secure as they seemed in their norms,
achieved some insight to which I myself was blind? Certainly my
lifelong inability to adopt a conventional outlook had been for years
a source of intense unhappiness for me.

Now that I had left Kent and was enrolled as a senior in Scarsdale
High School, I determined to overcome what was surely a defect

49

in my own character. This new school year, I decided, I would try a great experiment. I would pretend to myself that I *liked* what everyone else liked, that their values were my values, their norms, mine. I would see whether, by deliberately adopting their outlook, I could not begin at last to feel at home with it. If I succeeded, how easy my life would become! Resolutely I set my sights. This last year of high school would mark my giant step forward into "normalcy."

As a first step toward "swinging with the crowd," I seized energetically on swing music. Every week I listened eagerly to the radio with my brothers to learn which popular songs had made it onto the Hit Parade. I put on crowd-consciousness like a suit, and soon found that it fit snugly enough. In shouting competitions I joined in and shouted. In laughing I bubbled with the best. I dated. I danced. I became the vocalist for a dance band. And as I made all this noise I found, incredibly, that I both liked it and was liked for it.

I began the school year with a major advantage: Both of my brothers were popular. Bob, who was in the tenth grade, was loved by everyone, including upperclassmen. His was not the typical attitude of the Big Man on Campus—more interested in being loved, that is to say, than in loving, and ever careful to associate with only the "right" people. Bob genuinely liked *everybody*. It made no difference to him whether they were looked up to or down upon by others. He was their friend, and they knew it. Unable to tone his voice lower than a gentle boom, he dominated every gathering, but no one seemed to mind. Somehow in his company they felt more generous, more sure of their own goodness.

His enthusiasm for life was boundless. One day, coming home dizzy from playing in a football game, he was found to have a fever of 105°. Ill as he was, he had insisted on finishing the game.

They called him "Bucky," after Bucky Walters, the famous baseball player. Though the nickname remained with him, I myself never used it, for I knew that he also had a deeper side, one that he didn't often reveal to others—a refined sensitivity to music, a deep gentleness, a certain nobility of character, all of which seemed to me rather betrayed by the hail-fellow-well-met implications in that nickname.

From the start it was obvious to everyone that Bob and I were very different specimens. A few of my classmates, besides, had heard from Phil Boote, my ex-roommate at Kent. Phil also lived in Scarsdale, and had shown enough sense of community responsibility to warn them what a social disaster I was. For Bob's sake, however, and because I was so obviously determined to mend my lamentable ways, they gave me the benefit of the doubt, and accepted me kindly enough into their midst.

Scarsdale High was much larger than Kent, a fact which permitted adolescents with a wide variety of interests to mix happily together without the pressure to conform that there had been at Kent. Being Bob's brother automatically threw me into the "in" crowd, a position I boldly accepted as the kind of challenge I needed to bring off my "great experiment" with a maximum of success.

I tried out for the football team. At 136 pounds, I was hardly first-string material. Still, I played hard during practice sessions, and during the games ardently supported our team from the bench. Unfortunately for any dreams of glory I might have harbored, I was a halfback and so also was Charlie Rensenhouse, the team captain. Openings in that position were rare. The only time I actually made it onto the playing field during a game was once when Rensenhouse got hurt.

"Walters!" Coach Buchanan shouted.

My big opportunity? "Yes, Sir!" I cried, leaping eagerly to my feet.

"Walters, get out there and help Rensenhouse off the field."

In track I did better. There hadn't been a track team at Kent, so I had never learned the proper starting techniques, but I was a fast runner, and managed to acquit myself creditably. I actually ran the 100-yard dash in only 10.2 seconds at my first meet. Unfortunately, I pulled a ligament early in the season and was out of the running for the rest of the school year.

Of my classes, my favorite was English. Lucyle Hook, our English teacher, took a keen interest in her subject, loved her students, and obviously wanted with all her heart to share with us what she knew.

She was as much our friend as our teacher. With her encouragement I wrote short stories and poems, some of which appeared in the school magazine. While none of them was particularly consequential, they were good enough at least to gain me a reputation as a budding talent, and fanned my resolution to write for a living.

One of the students in my French class was a girl named Ruth, later voted the most beautiful girl in our senior class. I dated her, and became as infatuated with her as any boy is likely to be with his first girlfriend. But there were potholes on the road to romance.

Dad, for fear of spoiling us boys, gave us a weekly allowance of only fifty cents. I had to save for two weeks merely to take Ruth to the movies. Even then, we usually had to walk the several miles to White Plains and back. This wasn't the ideal setup for making a good impression on a girl.

Worse still, when it came to something so deeply personal as romance, I couldn't put on the extroverted bluff that was carrying me along successfully enough in other departments of my life. Somehow I'd conceived the notion that I was physically unattractive, and that I had nothing really worthwhile to offer anyone. Because I doubted my own worth, moreover, I was afraid to trust myself to another person's feelings about me. When another boy, a large, perennially joking and popular football star, began to date Ruth, I hadn't the self-confidence to compete with him. For that matter, I wouldn't have competed with him even if I'd been bursting with confidence, for I could never see love in the light of self-imposition and conquest.

Singing I found a joy. Mr. Hubbard, our chorus director, tried to persuade me to take it up as a career. "There's money in your voice," he kept insisting, not aware that money was probably the poorest lure he could have offered me.

When I was sixteen, my father offered to buy me a tuxedo. I knew intuitively even then that I had a very different destiny.

"Don't bother, Dad," I said. "I'd never wear it. In fact, I'll never earn enough money to pay income tax." Fanciful as this prediction must have seemed, it was to prove true.

That year I sang in Handel's *Messiah*, and played Sgt. Meryll in Gilbert and Sullivan's *Yeomen of the Guard*. At our Church of St.

James the Less, my brothers and I also sang the roles of the three wise men in the Christmas pageant, an event which, I was surprised to learn many years later, was still remembered by some old-timers in Scarsdale.

Other activities at the church, I must admit, held less appeal for me. Our minister, Father Price, kept threatening us in his sermons that if we didn't toe the straight and narrow we'd soon end up "right in the lap of the Nazis."

Instead, I began bending rather too far in another direction. Doug Burch, a friend of Bob's and mine, introduced me to Nick's, a nightclub in Greenwich Village famous as a hangout for Dixieland jazz enthusiasts. Eddie Condon, Peewee Russell, and other jazz "greats" played here with such consummate skill that I actually found myself growing to like jazz, though later I decided it lacked heart and was too intellectual. Fascinated with this new "scene," I absorbed all its trivia: how the wife of one of the taller players used to beat him up; how the band ate in a nightclub across the street because Nick wouldn't feed them properly; how a little old lady would show up on Saturday

Me at fifteen . . .   . . . and at nineteen.

evenings, take a front table, and clap her hands enthusiastically to the music, shouting, "Yeah! Yeah!" like any teenager. It is amazing that people can make as much as they do out of this kind of "news," merely because celebrities are involved. But they do. And we did.

It was at Nick's that I took my first alcoholic drink. Of all the foolish pastimes to which mankind is given, drinking must surely rank near the top of the list. Few people, I imagine, take up either drinking or smoking for pleasure alone. It seems more a question of not wanting to appear gauche. At any rate, those were my motives. Alcohol I found at least not positively sickening, but smoking was like learning to enjoy rotten food.

I remember clearly the first time I learned to inhale. A girl at a party in Scarsdale showed me the knack. One drag made me so dizzy I almost slipped to the floor. Then, with the kind of twisted idealism that marked most of that year for me, I told myself sternly, "I'm going to *master* this if it kills me!" Little did I realize that *true* mastery would have meant not succumbing to such silliness in the first place. That evening I succeeded in "mastering" smoking, but I'm afraid it wasn't long before smoking mastered me.

The worst thing about drinking, from a spiritual standpoint, is not the temporary stupor it may induce, nor the hangover that can follow an indiscreet "night on the town," nor the illusory "high" one gets even if he drinks only lightly, but rather the long-range effect alcohol has on his personality. In some subtle way it seems to make one more earthy; one's perceptions, less refined. One inclines, even if only slightly, to scoff at things he formerly considered sacred. The ego becomes less sensitively responsive to its environment, and more self-assertive, even aggressive. It is as if one felt a need to grip harder in an effort to compensate for the diminution of one's natural powers. These effects may, as I said, be observed not only during hours of inebriation, but as actual, long-term personality changes.

The explanation may be that things, inert though they seem, actually act as media for various states of consciousness. We may scoff, as I used to do, at "holy Joes" in church who denounce "likker" as a tool of Satan, but laughter has been known to hoot down many a truth. The very inclination, so common in societies where drinking is popular, to tell jokes about drunkenness suggests a subconscious desire to silence the disapproving whisper of conscience. For everyone must know, deep inside, that drunkenness is an insult to man's true nature.

Another "thing" which greatly influences consciousness is music. Looking back, I am astonished to see how quickly, by my willing exposure to swing music, I came to assume attitudes that I had formerly thought quite foreign to my nature. As months passed, it became increasingly second nature to me to see life in terms of sports, romance, and good times, to laugh with the loudest, roam about with the most restless, and give and take in the youthful exuberance of an ego competing more or less insensitively with other egos.

Yet somewhere deep within me there was a watchful friend who remained unimpressed, who questioned my motives, observed my follies with detachment, and demanded of me with a sad smile of reproach, "Is this what you *really* want?" I was honest enough with myself to admit that it wasn't.

Gradually the longing grew within me to stop wasting time. I could see that there was too much in life to learn, too much towards which to grow. For my English source theme at the end of the school year I chose as my subject, "The Different Concepts of the Universe Held by Ancient Civilizations, and the Quality in Each Civilization that Influenced the Development of Its Own Concept." Questions that played no part in my Great Experiment asserted themselves persistently: What is life? Is there meaning in the universe? What is the purpose of life? Such issues could not be laughed away with another evening at Nick's.

One evening a classmate and I visited a local diner, an "in" place with the high school crowd. While we were waiting for seats, my friend began to make an impromptu accompaniment to the music that was playing on the jukebox. Laughingly I encouraged him. All the while, however, my silent inner "friend" demanded of me indignantly, "What is this cacophony, this jerking about, this nodding of the head like an animated puppet, this contortion of the facial muscles? Is not this, too, evidence of a kind of drunkenness?"

My friend wrote in my year book afterwards how much he had enjoyed our "jam session" together. I myself, however, felt merely embarrassed by the memory, as though we had been the playthings of a rhythm-induced hysteria.

At Scarsdale High I learned that I could, if I wanted to, play the Great American Popularity Game and come out, in a sense, a winner. But my success had not made me any happier. If I felt that I now understood something of what other young people wanted from life, I couldn't say that their vision held any gripping attraction for me.

I was back almost at the beginning. The one thing I had learned this year was how to wrap a veil around myself and hide my true feelings from others. Well, perhaps after all this was a useful lesson. There can be little merit in exposing one's highest aspirations to people who don't appreciate them. But it wasn't much of a step towards *fulfilling* my aspirations. My next step, I realized, must be directed more intelligently toward that fulfillment.

CHAPTER 7

To Thine Own Search Be True

I GRADUATED FROM SCARSDALE High School in June 1943, shortly after turning seventeen. The first thing I did after graduation was go to a sort of "peace camp." I no longer remember why I went, or how I'd found out about it, but it turned out to be an indoctrination attempt to interest young people in socialism. I remember a lecture a Swedish woman gave, heavily promoting the socialism in her country. After her talk, I raised my hand.

"You've listed the benefits of socialism," I said. "Surely, if this system were so perfect, it must also be sufficiently convincingly so that there would be no need to *persuade* people to accept it. Are there also reasons why it hasn't been universally accepted? In the name of fairness, it would be helpful if you told us also of its possible drawbacks."

The woman, outraged at my impertinence, fairly spluttered, "Why, there are *no* drawbacks!"

I promptly lost interest in everything she had to say, and in what the camp itself was promoting. I had begun in any case to understand that any outward "perfection" is always diminished, or even nullified, by some opposing imperfection. In fact, I was to learn years later from my Guru that the whole universe is founded on the principle of *dwaita* (duality). For every "up," there is a "down"; for every plus, a minus. Only God is "One, without a second."

An older man from Persia, named (if memory serves) Reza Shashahama, who was also attending the camp, commented to me toward the end of it that my presence had contributed a voice of reason. My attempt to adjust, during the past year, to the norms of others had shown me that no "norm" was fully to be trusted.

After my "peace camp" experience, Bob and I were invited by George Calvert, a school friend of ours, to work with him on his father's farm in upstate New York. There we picked strawberries and pitched hay. The work was vigorous, healthful, and good fun. After six or seven weeks as a farm hand, I decided to take advantage of my vacation to broaden my experience of the world. The change I hit upon was radical: from bucolic pastures to grey skyscrapers and sterile acres of concrete.

New York! I worked there as a messenger boy for the *Herald Tribune*. Every day, dodging determined cars, trucks, and buses, and weaving through impatient hordes of shoppers, my fellow messenger boys and I visited the inner sanctums of well-known department stores, delivered advertising copy to and from countless corporations, and swept pellmell through the rushing bloodstream of big-city life. The myriad sense impressions were stimulating, almost overwhelming. In faces madly bobbing down crowded sidewalks; in the pleading glances of girls from behind drugstore counters; in fleeting smiles, frosty stares, angry gestures, twitching lips, and self-preoccupied frowns, I saw mankind in caricature, exaggerated out of all credible proportion by its sheer multifariousness. Here was a veritable sea of humanity: the youthfully exuberant, the sad and lonely, the stage-struck, the determinedly success-oriented, the hard, the cynical, the fragile, the lost: all, hurrying; all, harassed to desperation by a tumbling surf of conflicting ambitions and desires.

New York! Its surging waves of humanity charm and repel at the same time. They encourage a sense of exaggerated self-importance in those who pride themselves on living in one of the largest, most vital cities in the world. They also drown a person's sense of self-importance in the general indifference. New Yorkers face a perennial conflict between their own boasted self-worth and their crushing, but inevitable, sense of anonymity.

Beneath the frenzied pace of big-city life, God whispers to the soul: "Dance with bubbles if you like, but when you tire of dancing, and the bubbles begin, one by one, to burst, look about you;

see *within* all those bobbing faces their underlying relationship to you. They are your spiritual brothers and sisters, mirrors to your own self! They, O tiny ripple, *are* you! Transcend your littleness. Discover your oneness with all life!"

When autumn came, I began my higher education at Haverford College, a small men's college on the (railway) Main Line to Paoli from Philadelphia. At that time, because of the war, Haverford was smaller than ever.

The students were bright-eyed, enthusiastic, and intelligent; the professors, quiet, sedate, seriously preoccupied with their students' welfare. Haverford is a Quaker college, and conveys the simple, serene dignity that one might expect of any institution run by that pacific sect. I don't mean we students didn't have our normal boyish share of high times, but these were inflicted on a background of gentle disapproval from the discreet greystone-and-ivy buildings, and of restrained dismay from our ever-concerned faculty.

The diminished student body was composed mostly of freshmen, a fact which didn't conduce greatly to the maintenance of certain hallowed traditions, such as freshmen hazing. When a handful of upperclassmen appeared in our dormitory one day to subject us to that ancient rite, we met them with another venerable American institution: the bum's rush. With whoops of joy, flying pillows, energetic shoves, and a solid phalanx of inverted chairs, we drove them down the stairs and out of the building. Thereafter they left us strictly alone, concluding, no doubt, that in wartime there are certain sacrifices that older and wiser heads must make in the name of peace.

We freshman were so dominant numerically that I actually made the football team. One of my problems at Scarsdale High, apart from my light weight, had been the fact that I could never throw the ball properly; my hands were simply too small to get a grip on it. At Haverford our coach, "Pop" Haddleton, solved this problem by making me a running guard. Counting on speed rather than weight, I pulled many a larger lineman off balance while he was still shifting his body into position to block me. I then dashed through the line and often caught a runner before he'd got off to a good start with the ball. The other left guard on our team, a boy named Mason, was as

The pond and some of the buildings at Haverford College, Pennsylvania, where I spent two years.

Our Haverford football team. I am in the front row, third from left.

lightweight as I. Our college newspaper soon began dubbing us "the watch charm guards."

We played the whole game, every game. There was no such thing in those days as offensive and defensive teams. "Sportswise," the season was a success: We were unbeaten, untied, and unscored upon. My big play of the season came near the end of one of the last games. Up to that point, neither team had scored. Our captain decided, in a last, desperate move, to try an end run down half the length of the field. I was to run interference.

We cleared the end safely, and were well on our way into "enemy" territory, when two "big bruisers" rushed up to intercept our runner. I prepared to block the first of them, hoping our runner would succeed in dodging the second. One of my boots, unknown to me, had come untied. Just as I was diving to block the first opponent, I tripped on a dangling shoelace! Sprawling full length on the ground, I made a perfect, though involuntary, double block. Our man went on to make the touchdown, and I was the hero of the hour. I tried to explain what had really happened, but no one wanted to believe me.

As I said, we won every game that season. And so it was that my athletic "career" reached a happy climax, before petering out altogether. For soon afterward, college sports and I came to a rather distant parting of the ways. The separation was due partly to my own increasing preoccupation with the search for meaning, and partly, I'm afraid, to the fact that I was attaching "meaning" to a few wrong things—like sitting in local bars with friends, nursing a variety of poisonous decoctions and talking philosophy into the wee hours.

I began to devote much of my free time also to writing poetry, the themes of which related to questions that had long puzzled me: Why suffering? Why warfare and destruction? How can God countenance hatred, violence, and other forms of human madness? Surely, I thought, suffering can't be His *will* for us? Must it not be a sign, rather, that man is *out of harmony* with His will?

And what of eternal life? Not even matter or energy, I reflected, can be destroyed. Was it not reasonable, then, to suppose that life, too, is eternal? And if so, what about the reality of heaven and hell?

I wrote a poem at this time in which I postulated a world after death that was perceived differently by each individual, seeming to be either beautiful or ugly, happy or sad according to the state of consciousness he brought over from this world. Not so far from the truth, actually! for I have since learned that when people die, they do go to realms that are compatible with whatever state of consciousness they have themselves developed.

At this point in my life I might easily have embraced a religious calling. But I knew too little about religion, and had found no meaningful guidance, rooted in wisdom, from anyone in religion.

Haverford College is a prominent center of Quakerism. In my time there, leading members of this society were on the faculty: Douglas Steere, Rufus Jones, Howard Comfort. I was impressed by their transparent earnestness and goodness. I also liked the Quaker practice of sitting quietly in thoughtful meditation at the Sunday services—"meetings," these were called. Above all, I liked the Quakers for their simplicity. Everything they did seemed to me admirable. At the same time, however, I found no challenge in it. I was seeking a path that would engross me utterly, not one that I could contemplate benignly while puffing on a pipe.

Sunday meetings became, all too frequently, scenes of genteel competition. The Quakers have no ordained ministers; their members sit in silence on Sunday mornings until one of them feels moved "by the Spirit" to rise and share some inspiration with others. Haverford being an intellectual community, our Sunday meetings were more than usually taken up with this kind of spiritual generosity. Hardly a minute passed in silence before someone else was on his feet, sharing with us all. Sometimes two or more simultaneously were "moved by the Spirit"—though in such cases courtesy always prevailed. I myself never felt moved to speak, for I was still questioning the nature of truth.

I'll never forget Douglas Steere rising to his feet one day to inquire brightly, "Is there a little bird in your bosom?" Involuntarily my hand went to my chest. The solemnity of the occasion, and my own respect for him, prevented me from succumbing to hilarity on the spot. Afterward, however, my friends and I made up delightedly for our heroic repression.

Needless to say, I had much still to learn, not the least of it being reverence and humility. It may be that those religious leaders had more to teach me than I knew. Since I didn't know it, however, I had no choice but to follow my own star.

Early during my first semester at Haverford I made friends with Julius Katchen, who later acquired fame in Europe as a concert pianist. I loved his intensity and enthusiasm. And though I was less agreeably impressed by his egotism, loudly affirmed, I found compensation for it in his romantic devotion to every form of art, music, and poetry. Our friendship flourished in the soil of kindred artistic interests. In this relationship, Julius was the musician, and I, the poet. Through our association my feelings for poetry became more musical, artistically more romantic. Julius's mother, too, had been a concert pianist. When I visited the Katchen home in Long Branch, New Jersey, I was caught up in his entire family's devotion to the arts.

At this time, also, I took a course in poetry composition at nearby Bryn Mawr College under the famous poet, W. H. Auden. Auden encouraged me in my poetic efforts. For some time thereafter, poetry became my outward focus of self-expression.

Yet there was another side of me that could not remain satisfied for long with beautiful phraseology, nor with Keats's romantic fiction, "Beauty is truth, truth beauty,—that is all ye know on earth, and all ye need to know." In every question, what mattered most to me was not whether an idea was beautifully stated, nor whether the truths it expressed were themselves beautiful, but whether in some much deeper sense it and they *really were true*. In this concern I found myself increasingly out of tune with the approach our professors took, which was to view any actual commitment with suspicion. Scholarly detachment, not involvement, was their guiding principle.

That's all very well, I would think. I want to be objective, too. But I don't want to spend my life sitting on a fence. Even objectivity ought to lead to conclusions of *some* kind. To my professors, scholarly detachment meant holding a perennial question mark up to life. It meant supporting, "for the sake of discussion," positions to which they didn't really subscribe. It meant showing equal interest in every argument, without endorsing any of them. I was impatient with such indecisiveness.

My need for truths to which I could commit myself had posed a problem for me in our debating society at Kent School. It made me a failure in public speaking classes during my freshman year at Haverford. It made me a bad actor in the plays I occasionally took part in at college and afterward. My firm commitment to truth spoiled my chances, years later, of becoming a radio announcer, when I learned that the job demanded an excited outpouring of lyrical enthusiasm for every product, every issue, the sponsors of which were paying for their block of time. Were I to accept the job, I'd be expected to promote products and ideas about which I knew nothing. A professional announcer told me, "It's very simple: a sort of trick. I just put my mind on automatic pilot, and don't even listen to the words coming out of me." Could I wax poetic over a special brand of soap just because the advertisers raved about the shiny bubbles it produces? If I spoke, I had to mean what I said. Otherwise, my only alternative was silence. I could not be false or hypocritical even about trivial issues—or non-issues.

More and more, my hunger for truth gave me difficulties as a student as well, particularly in such subjects as English literature and philosophy. I *had* to know whether what was being given us for our consideration was true. In reaction against my professors and their insistence on a spirit of polite scholarly inquiry, I gradually developed a rebellious attitude toward college in general.

It was at about this time that I met a student at Haverford whose search for truth coincided more nearly with my own. Rod Brown was two years older than I, very intelligent, and a gifted poet. At first, our relationship was one of learned sage and unlettered bumpkin of a disciple. Rod treated me with a certain amused condescension, as the ingenuous youngster that I certainly was. My poems he read tolerantly, never lavishing higher praise on them than to call them "nice." His own poems I couldn't even understand. He would quote at length from countless books I'd never

My college friend, Rod Brown, and I in Wellesley, Massachusetts.

heard of, and manage to make each quotation sound so important, the listener got the impression that only a confirmed ignoramus would dare to face life without the ability at least to paraphrase that passage.

Rod was a sensitive young man who had learned early in life to fend off others' rejection of him by treating them with disdain. It was purely a defense mechanism, but he carried it off well. I was as intrigued by his superior attitude towards me for my ignorance as I was captivated by his single-minded devotion to philosophical realities. Surely, I thought, if he knew enough to look down on me, it behooved me to learn what the view was from his altitude.

In time we became fast friends. I discovered that, besides his enthusiasm for the truth, he had a delightful sense of humor. He was also eager to share with others his ideas and opinions, always fresh and interesting. Rod only raised a supercilious eyebrow at my theories about God, suffering, and eternal life. Rhetorically he would ask me, "How can anyone know the truth about such issues?" He directed my thinking constructively, however, toward more immediate issues. For the time being, my quest for spiritual truths was, if not abandoned, at least put on a shelf. Where the search is for truth, however, can *true religion* be very far away?

Indeed, Rod's thinking and mine verged constantly on the spiritual. He introduced me to Emerson and Thoreau. I drank eagerly at the fountain of wisdom in Emerson's "The Over-Soul," in "Self-Reliance," and in Thoreau's *Walden*. These writings were the closest I had come so far to the vast panorama of Indian wisdom,* for though I didn't realize it at the time, both authors admired the Indian scriptures, and echoed in their own writings the lofty teachings of the *Upanishads* and the Bhagavad Gita.

Rod urged me to stop concerning myself with abstractions and to face the more concrete problem of how to live sensibly in the present day. One of the principles we discussed night after night was the importance of non-attachment. Another was the courage to reject values that we considered false, even if everyone else believed in them. Amusing as it seems now, we spent hours in intellectual discussion on the uselessness of intellectuality. And, deciding that the uneducated masses were surely more genuine in their simple, earthy interests than we ourselves, we set out with exploratory zeal to frequent the haunts of truck drivers and manual laborers. No deep wisdom ever came of these outings, but then, people who cherish theories rarely feel a need to sustain their mental fare on the coarse diet of facts!

Not everything Rod said or did won my support. He told me approvingly, for instance, of an older French friend of his, named Jean, whose heart was unnaturally small. To both Rod and his friend this fact suggested a wholesome absence of the emotions that distort the intellect's clear perceptions. True insight, they believed, demanded the complete separation of the intellect from feeling of any kind, which would result in non-attachment and true objectivity. I disagreed with their equation, however, for I considered non-attachment and feeling not at all incompatible. I felt the important point, rather, was for one's feelings also to be *impersonal*. Non-attachment releases one from personal identity with things, but

---

* In those days, courses in Indian studies were comparatively rare. The only actual exposure I ever got to them was from Douglas Steere, in his freshman course on the history of philosophy. For the first twenty minutes of his first class Dr. Steere touched lightly on the *Vedas*, giving us the impression, merely, that Indian philosophy existed.

should therefore permit an *expansion*, not an elimination, of feeling. It is *personal* feelings, resulting in emotions, that distort objectivity.

Rod also believed that, armed with a genuine spirit of non-attachment, one could behave in as worldly a manner as he pleased. This argument struck me, however, as too convenient a rationalization for his own worldly tendencies. Rod, despite his disdain for middle-class values and his praise of lower-class simplicity, betrayed a marked fondness for upper-class luxuries. Though he often mocked me for it, I myself considered innocence a truer safeguard of non-attachment.

Rod, like most people, had his shortcomings. He was, among other things, somewhat intolerant of disagreement, proud of his own brilliance, and unabashedly lazy. For all that, however, he was at heart a loving and true friend; deeply concerned about others despite his vaunted indifference to them; more hurt by anyone's rejection of him than honestly disdainful in return; and a great deal more conservative in his values than he would ever have admitted. While others clucked at him disapprovingly, I saw him as someone who could help me to think boldly for myself. For this reason above all, I was grateful for his friendship.

Yet in my association with him I also acquired some of the very traits I didn't approve of in him. Such, indeed, is the power of all human associations. Like Rod, I developed intellectual pride as a defense against rejection and misunderstanding. Worst of all, perhaps, I acquired some of his worldliness, though never so much of it that Rod ceased to twit me for what he called my naiveté.

In those days it was Rod who gave me my real education. My classes formed a mere backdrop; they taught me facts, but in discussions with him I learned what I would do with facts. Night after night we sat discussing life over pots of coffee in our rooms, or over drinks in bars, or over milk shakes in an off-campus restaurant with the engaging name, "The Last Straw." We had few friends, but this fact no longer really mattered to me. I was seeking truth now, not the mere popularity of shared opinions.

CHAPTER 8

Joy Is the Goal

M Y FIRST YEAR at Haverford was spent in joyously welcoming new ideas. My second year, at the age of eighteen, I tried to digest those ideas and make them my own. During the process of absorption I greatly broadened my horizons, deepened my inner search, grounded it, and then sent it soaring up in skies of hopeful expectation.

Rod had confirmed me in my desire to rise above excessive concern over other people's opinions. While he scoffed at my more "mystical" preoccupations, and inspired me to seek solutions that were wholly grounded in human realities, my own nature kept me wanting to break out from even these confining walls. Rod and I met, however, on the question of right attitudes, such as non-attachment, objectivity, and the question of right behavior in this world.

I don't recall that human suffering particularly preoccupied him, but with me it lingered as one of my deepest concerns. Now, however, the problem seemed capable of resolution—not (as most people think) by medicine, money, or sensory excitements, but by a changed attitude, which I realized is basic to true and lasting happiness.

An important question remained for me: Is right attitude based on mere mental resolution, or is it born of higher-than-sensory experience?

One night, in a dream, I found myself flying through the air. "This isn't possible," I thought. "People don't fly about like birds!"

I tried to reason the whole thing out: Was I dreaming, or was I fully awake? Careful logic—dream-logic, however—led me at last to the conclusion that in fact I was awake; I was only doing something unusual.

What was my surprise then, a moment later, to wake up! The whole thing, careful reasoning and all, had been a dream!

Is life itself then, I asked myself, only a dream? If so, what is reality? Can we simply resolve, in this dream-existence of ours, to "dream" better? Can we, by affirmation alone, overcome suffering, achieve good health, and attain happiness? Is suffering, too, only a dream, and if so could it not be overcome by the simple expedient of strong, positive affirmation?

No, I decided, for even if life really is only a dream, the dream logic we use is subject to dream realities.

I am getting ahead of myself a little here, but a few months later, in Mexico, I met an English girl who had embraced Christian Science. Ignorant as I was of its justifications for what it taught, I remember saying to her, "One can't rid himself of life's dream-hypnosis merely by wishful thinking. Somehow we've got to discover *how* to awaken from the dream."

And yet, affirmation did take me a long way toward achieving everything I wanted. As we'll see also, presently, it was an important step in my own progress.

First, I needed to affirm my own worth, a truth I had doubted at Hackley and Kent, then affirmed artificially at Scarsdale High. Now, at Haverford, I found myself beginning to discover in myself a basis for genuine self-acceptance.

The better I succeeded, the more completely I found that I could express once again that most battered of virtues: trust. In the words of Emerson, I now began to feel that the world was my "oyster": that life is basically sunny, right, and beautiful. Even the disapproval of worldly people could no longer dampen my expanding trust in life, and, on a certain level, in those very people. For I felt they merely lacked the courage to live up to a truth which they must know, deep in their own hearts. I longed to share with everyone my consciousness of joy.

Trust! The joyful offering I now made to life was selfless and pure. Yet the wise have ever said that one should trust fully only in God;

that to place faith in earthly accomplishments is like expecting perpetual stability of a ship at sea. Alas, I hadn't that wisdom to guide me. All my faith I now flung with ardent enthusiasm into the fragile basket of this world.

For my sophomore year I was assigned to a suite in Lloyd Hall, which in normal times was reserved for upperclassmen. My roommate, Roberto Pablo Payro, was from Argentina. He has since become a researcher, translator, and editor for the International Labor Office. Roberto was quiet, dignified, and ever courteous: ideal qualities in a roommate. We got along well together, though the goals we pursued were different. Roberto's social life was separate from mine, though he seemed to like serious, sophisticated discussions, mostly on such down-to-earth subjects as politics and sociology. He rather marveled that such abstractions as "life" and "truth" could command from me the intense enthusiasm they did.

My tendency was to seize a thought firmly, wrestle with it for days until I felt I'd mastered it, and then dash out joyfully in search of friends with whom I could celebrate my victory. To Roberto I must have seemed alternately far too intense, and inconsistently frivolous.

But thinking itself was, for me, a joyous adventure. It was only years later, after I met my Guru, that I learned that thinking is only a by-path to truth, whereas the highest perceptions are possible only when the fluctuations of the mind have been stilled.

Rod and I spent much time together, continuing our nocturnal rounds of coffee, drinks, and wee-hour philosophizing. But I was beginning also to spend more time now in the search for truth on my own.

For my college major I selected English literature. I loved reading the great works that comprise our true heritage—a heritage of insights and inspiration, not of mere worldly accomplishments. Reading Shakespeare, Sir Walter Scott, Jane Austen, eighteenth-century French playwrights and modern playwrights like John Millington Synge, as well as numerous others, I pondered a new question: In what ways has great literature served the cause of truth? As an aspiring writer myself, I hoped to make whatever I wrote serve as an instrument of the highest insights.

But there was buoyant good humor, too, in Rod's and my seeking. We could laugh merrily over the gravest of issues. A few somber souls there were who viewed our unconventional levity with dismay. I think they considered it a proof that we were dissolute, drowning our misspent youth in drunkenness and debauchery. We had little patience, however, with people who equated seriousness with an absence of joy. Taking my cue from Rod, I would sometimes delight in pretending we were in league with forces unspeakably dark. (The effort to imagine such forces I left entirely to our critics!)

One of our fellow students, with the appropriate last name of Coffin, used to carry a Bible around with him wherever he went, in order the more sadly to reproach anyone who showed an occasional disposition to kick up his heels. "The wages of sin," Coffin would remind us "sinners" gravely, citing chapter and verse, "is death." As my own reputation for cheerful irreverence spread, he took to bringing me, particularly, the Good News. Entering my room one morning before I'd fairly tested the world to make sure it was still there, he sat on the edge of my bed, the Bible open in his hands, looked at me dolefully, and—sighed.

If only religion weren't made so lugubrious, I think many people might be inspired to seek God who presently equate ministers of religion with undertakers. It was years before I myself learned that religious worship needn't verge on the funereal—that it can be, as Paramhansa Yogananda put it, the funeral of all sorrows. As things stood, I satisfied a natural craving for religious inspiration by laughing at the lack of it in religion as I found it practiced. Had I known better, I might have sincerely worshiped.

During our second year at Haverford someone gave Rod a few guppies in a glass bowl. *Guppy*, we decided, was far too undignified a name for even such nondescript fish as these. We renamed his new pets, accordingly, "The Sacred White Fish." Soon, enlarging on this grand concept, we joyously set out to create an entire religion, complete with ceremonies, dogmas, and ritual responses. I even found a partially completed, abandoned chapel for our rites. Needless to say, our comedy never advanced beyond the playful planning stage, but we had great fun with it.

One day Rod was summoned into the office of Mr. Gibb, dean of our very proper Quaker college. "What's this I hear, Mr. Brown," he began cautiously, "about . . . ah . . . how shall I put it? . . . a new religion? Something about the . . . ah . . . sacred . . . ah . . . white . . . *fish*? Have I heard this incredible tale correctly?" We never learned whom it was we'd shocked into reporting us to the dean, but even the anonymity of this outrage added fresh zest to our game.

Yet I also felt, inexplicably, a deep and almost wistful thrill at the thought of helping to found a new religion. Perhaps it was because the fun we were having over those guppies underscored for me the joy that I missed in church. To me, however, it was more than fun. My search for truth, and for joy as the very essence of truth, held an almost life-or-death earnestness. And I yearned, not only for myself but for others, to discover new insights into truth.

On another matter, I felt less keenly the need to cloak my interest under a guise of playfulness. A continuous aspiration of mine since the age of fifteen had been the founding of a "utopian" community. Utopia literally means "not a place"; the word is generally used to describe any impractical communitarian dream. But I was convinced that an intentional community founded on high ideals could, with down-to-earth realism and foresight, be made viable. During this period at Haverford, and for years thereafter, I devoted considerable time to studying and thinking about the problems connected with such a project; I read everything I could find on the subject. On some deep level of consciousness I believed that it was my duty someday to found such a community.

Among my friends, however, I encountered little sympathy for the idea. When I spoke of it to them they expressed mild interest, only to lose it altogether when they realized I was in earnest. After that, they left me to dream alone.

Undaunted by their lack of interest, I simply broadened my horizons to include the rest of the human race! The more I thought about intentional communities, the more clearly I saw them not as a step backward into primitive simplicity, but as a step *forward* in social evolution, a natural progression from machine technology and the self-defeating complexity of modern life to a new kind of *enlightened* simplicity, one in which technology served human, not merely mechanical or economic ends.

Decentralization seemed to me a growing need, too, in this age. The essentially sterile demands for efficiency that are served by centralizing power in big industry and big government would, I believed, be balanced by the human and idealistic values that would be emphasized in small, spiritually integrated communities.

With my growing enthusiasm for life I also took increasing pleasure in singing. At last I resolved to take singing lessons. Dr. Frederick Schlieder, a noted pianist and organist, recommended to Mother that I study under Marie Zimmerman, a singing teacher in Philadelphia. "She is a real musician," he assured Mother. "Your son is fortunate to be in college so nearby."

One day I took a train into Philadelphia and visited Mrs. Zimmerman in her studio. Seventy-five years old she must have been at the time. A concert singer in her younger days, her voice, now no longer beautiful, was still perfectly placed.

"The voice," she explained to me, "is the one musical instrument which can't be seen. I can't *show* you how to use it, as I could demonstrate how to play the piano. You'll have to listen sensitively as I sing a note, then try to imitate the sound I make. The more perceptively you listen, the more quickly you'll learn."

Next she placed my right hand over her stomach. "I'm going to show you how to breathe properly," she explained. As she inhaled, her diaphragm moved downward, pushing the stomach out. I prepared to listen to a full, operatic tone.

"Moooooooooooo!" came the feeble croak, sounding hardly powerful enough to fill a pantry, let alone a concert hall. I fought to suppress my mirth.

But her voice *was* well placed. Recalling Dr. Schlieder's high recommendations, I decided to study with her.

"You will pay me five dollars a lesson," she announced firmly. "It isn't that I need the money. I don't. But *you* need to pay it. It will help you to take your lessons seriously."

I didn't want to bother Dad for the weekly fees, so I took a job waiting on tables one night a week at The Last Straw. From those earnings I paid for my lessons.

Marie Zimmerman proved an excellent teacher. Unlike most voice teachers, she wouldn't let me sing on my own for the first weeks. Gradually only, as my placement improved, did she allow me to practice a little at home, then a little bit more. The farther I progressed, the more I found myself enjoying these lessons, until at last they became the high point of my week.

Marie Zimmerman was not only an excellent teacher and a fine musician; she was also a remarkable woman. Deeply, calmly spiritual, she was content with only the highest and noblest in everything. She was, in fact, an impressive example of a truth that was becoming increasingly clear to me, that the chief masterpiece of an aspiring artist must be *himself.*

One day at about this time I had what was, to me, a revelation. Sudden, vivid, and intense, it gave me in the space of a few minutes insights into the nature of art, and of art's relationship to truth, that have guided my thinking ever since.

The word *art*, as Rod and I used it, encompassed *all* the creative arts, including music and literature. We had pondered reputed authorities whose claim was that art should be for art's sake alone; that it must capture reality as a camera does, literally; that it ought to reflect a sense of social responsibility; to be a purely personal catharsis; or to express the spirit of the times in which the artist lives.

Suddenly I felt certain of a truth deeper than all of these. Most artistic theories, I realized, emphasize primarily the *forms* of art. But art is essentially a human, not an abstract phenomenon. A man's intrinsic worth is determined not by his physical appearance, but by his spirit, his essential attitudes, his courage or cowardice, his kindness or selfishness, his wisdom or ignorance. With art, similarly, it is the artist's vision of life, not his mode of expression, that determines the validity of his work. Inspiration—or sterility: Either can be expressed as well through realism as through impressionism. The essential question is: *How great does the artist's work reveal HIM to be, as a man?* Only if *he* is great will his work stand a chance of being truly great also. Otherwise it may reveal superlative craftsmanship, but lest plumbers deserve acclaim also as great artists, mere skill cannot serve to define art.*

My first task as a writer, I decided, was no different from my first task as a human being. It was to determine what constitute ideal human qualities, and then to try to develop *myself*, accordingly.

At about this time we were given the assignment in English class of writing an essay on our personal criteria for greatness in literature. Not feeling myself competent as yet to explain some of the subtler nuances of my revelation, I confined myself to one aspect of it—one perhaps subtler than all the rest! I wrote that, after reading Homer's *Iliad*, I had sensed that a blazing white light emanated from it. Later, as I contemplated other great works, I had sensed again in each case a bright light, though in no case so intense as Homer's. Chaucer's light seemed of a duller hue than Milton's, Dante's, or Shakespeare's. From lesser works than these I sensed no light at all; it was as though their authors were spiritually dead.

I admitted that I saw no objective reason for giving Homer the highest marks; his epic seemed to me, on the surface, only a good, rousing war story. But I knew from the light it emanated that it must be a work of superlative greatness.†

My poor professor! Shaking his head in bewilderment, he gave me a flunking grade. Yet even today I consider the criterion of greatness I'd described in that paper to be just and valid.

Rod and I continued our discussions on philosophical matters: intellectual integrity, for example, and living in the *now*, and the importance of non-attachment. Non-attachment, I was coming to realize, is crucial to human happiness. No one can truly enjoy anything that he fears to lose.

One evening my non-attachment was put to an unusual test. I was sitting in my bedroom, studying for a philosophy exam. The textbook was exceedingly dull. Midway through my study, as I was reflecting glumly that this author valued pedantry over clarity,

* I discuss this subject in a book of mine, *Art as a Hidden Message* (Crystal Clarity Publishers, 1997).

† Homer was customarily referred to by ancient Greeks as "*divine* Homer."

I heard footsteps approaching stealthily over the dry leaves on the ground outside my window. I glanced at my watch: Nine-thirty, the hour the library closed. One of my friends must be planning to play a joke on me, on the way back to his room. Smiling, I stepped over to the window to show him that I'd caught him at his little game.

At once, the footsteps fled into the night. Whoever it was would, I assumed smiling, come around through the front door and we'd enjoy a friendly chuckle before he returned to his own room.

To my surprise, no one came.

Smiling at the improbable fancy, I thought, "Maybe someone wanted to shoot me!"

Twenty minutes passed. Again the footsteps, this time even more softly over the dead leaves.

Who could it be? My friends, I reflected, weren't this persistent at *anything*! Perhaps it really *was* someone planning to shoot me. Silently I stepped to the window. Once again, the steps faded away quickly into the darkness.

By this time my curiosity was thoroughly aroused. How would I ever know who this mysterious intruder was, or what he wanted, if I persisted in frightening him away? I decided that if he returned a third time, I would pretend I hadn't heard him.

Another twenty minutes passed. Finally once again: footsteps, this time more stealthy than before. Moments later, a shoe scraped lightly on the ledge below my window. A hand grasped the metal grating over the window.

Suppressing a smile, I kept my eyes glued to the page before me.

Suddenly: an ear-splitting shot! For several seconds I heard nothing but the ringing in my ears; then, gradually, the clock on my dresser resumed its ticking; a car in the nearest parking lot revved its motor and roared off the campus at high speed.

Amazed, I leaned back in my chair and—laughed in sheer delight! It seemed incredible that such a thing could have actually happened. I checked my body: No holes anywhere. No blood. No pain. What? *Nothing* to show for this absurd adventure? I stepped over to examine the window. The screen was intact. What did it all mean?

Days later I learned that that evening had been Halloween—
a day when children in America traditionally play pranks! Evidently
some village boy had decided as a Halloween prank to put the fear
of God into one of the college students. He'd fired a blank cartridge!

I knew one ought to show a greater sense of responsibility toward
one's body than I had. But I was happy at least to have had in this
experience some proof of my non-attachment.

Soon, however, I received another test of my non-attachment, and
this one I didn't pass so easily. It was a test of my developing ability
to offer trust unreservedly.

Haverford boys usually dated Bryn Mawr girls. I did so too,
whenever I had the inclination for it—and the money, which was
seldom. I finally met a girl at Bryn Mawr named Sue, who came to
epitomize for me everything that was good, kind, and holy in life.
Her tastes were simple. Her smile expressed so much sweetness that,
whether blindly or with actual insight, I could not imagine her holding a mean thought. Our joy in each other's company was such that
we never felt the need to go anywhere in particular. A quiet walk
through green fields, a friendly chat, a communion of hearts in precious silence: These were the essence of a relationship more beautiful
than any I had ever known before.

I had no thought of marriage, of long years spent together, or of
anything, really, beyond the present. Sue was for me not so much
a girlfriend as a symbol of my new gift for trust, for giving myself
to life joyously without the slightest thought of receiving in return.
How she felt toward me seemed almost irrelevant. It was enough,
I felt, that my own love for her was true.

And yet there were times, in the happiness of our moments together, when she would gaze at me sadly. She wouldn't say why.
"Never mind," I would think, "I will only give her the more love,
until all her sadness is washed away."

For Christmas vacation I went home. Shortly after the New Year
I received a letter from Sue. Eagerly I tore it open.

"Dear Don," it began, "there is something I've been needing to tell
you. I realize I should have done so early in our friendship, but I enjoyed your company and didn't want to lose it." She went on to say

how deeply she had come to feel about me, and how sad also, that the realities of her life were such that she could never see me again. She was married, she explained, and was even then carrying her husband's baby. Her husband was in the Navy, stationed overseas. She had realized that she would not be allowed to return to college once it became known that she was pregnant; hence her resolution of silence. But she had been feeling increasingly unhappy about this resolution where I was concerned. She realized she should have had the courage to tell me sooner. Now she would not be returning to Bryn Mawr to finish the school year. She hoped I would understand the loneliness that had motivated her to go out with me. She had never wanted to hurt me, and was unhappy in the knowledge that such a hurt now was inevitable.

The effect of her letter was devastating. I didn't blame Sue. Rather, I sympathized with the predicament she'd been in. I reminded myself that I had never asked her to return my love, that in fact I'd never contemplated marriage to anyone. But, oh, the pain! And had I, I asked myself, been wrong to trust so completely? Put differently, was the whole structure of my inner development, in which trust played so vital a role, made of sand?

Much time was to pass before I understood that life, without God, is *never* trustworthy. It is not earthly fulfillment that deserves our faith, but God alone; not outer circumstances, but His inner blessings in the soul. These alone can never fail, never disappoint. For God is our only true love. Until we learn to place ourselves unreservedly in His hands, our trust, wherever else we give it, will be—indeed, *must* be—betrayed again and again.

Can a boat ride calmly in a storm? How can a world in constant flux offer more than delusive security?

For months to come my problem was not disillusionment, for I determined with all my heart to trust life in spite of anything that might come to hurt me. My problem, rather, was how to find a firm base on which to repose my trust.

I blessed Sue when I received her letter. I bless her even more now. For through our friendship, and even more through our parting, I was brought closer to God.

CHAPTER 9

He Gathers Strength for the Climb

A T ABOUT THIS time in my life I had an interesting dream. I was living with many other people in a torture chamber. For generations our families had lived here, knowing no world but this one; the possibility of any other existence simply never occurred to us. One awoke, one was tortured, and, at night, one found brief respite in sleep. What else could there be to life? We didn't particularly mind our lot. Rather, we imagined ourselves reasonably well-off. Oh, to be sure, there were bad days, but then there were also good ones—days together, sometimes, when we were less tortured than usual.

The time came, however, when a handful of us began to think the unthinkable. Might there, we asked ourselves, just possibly be *another*, a better way of life? Moments snatched when our torturers were out of earshot, and we could share our doubts with a few friends, served to kindle our speculations. At last we determined that there simply *had* to be an alternative to being tortured. A small group of us decided to rebel.

We laid our plans carefully. One day, rising together from our tasks, we slipped up behind the torturers, slew them, and escaped. Sneaking cautiously out of the great room, fearing lest armies of torturers be lying in wait for us outside, we encountered no one. The torture chamber itself, it turned out, occupied only the top floor of a large, otherwise empty building. We walked unchallenged down flights of stairs, emerging from the ground floor onto a vast, empty plain. Confined as we'd been our whole lives in the torture chamber, the horizon seemed incredibly distant. Joyfully we inhaled the fresh air. Gazing about us, we all but shouted the previously never-imagined word: "Freedom!"

Before departing the building forever, we glanced up at the top floor, scene of the only life we'd ever known. There, to our astonishment, we saw the very torturers we thought we'd slain. They were going matter-of-factly about their business as though nothing had happened! Amazed, we looked to one another for an explanation.

Suddenly the answer dawned on me. "Don't you see?" I exclaimed. "It's ourselves we have conquered, not the torturers!"

With that realization, I awoke.

I felt that this dream held an important message for me. The torture chamber, located as it was on the top floor of the building, symbolized the human mind. The torturers represented our mental shortcomings. The emptiness of the rest of the building meant that once one has overcome his mental torturers, there are no more enemies left to conquer. All human suffering, in other words, originates in the mind. We cannot slay universal delusion; all we can do is slay our own mental torturers. They will always remain on the scene, inflicting on others their painful lessons.

My dream, I felt, held a divine message for me. Its implication was that the time had come for me to seek a higher way of life. My problem was, *how* to seek it? I knew nothing of great saints who had communed with God. To me, the very word, "saint," connoted only a person of frail goodness, not someone filled with divine love, and certainly not someone soaring in ecstasy. All I knew of religion were the stylized church services I had attended, the uninspired ministers I had heard—insecure men who sought support for their faith in the approval of others, not in the unbribable voice of their own conscience.

Though I didn't realize it at the time, my ignorance concerning the spiritual path was my own chief "torturer"; it hindered me from seeking the good for which my soul longed. Subordinate to ignorance there were other, more evident, failings—doubt, for example. Had I approached truth by love I might have gone straight to the mark. But I was trying to *think* my way to wisdom. God I looked upon as Something to be thought about, not Some*one* with whom I could commune. I wanted desperately to trust, even to love, but I had no idea what or whom, specifically, to trust or to love. I had reached a point where I thought about God almost constantly; but He remained silent, for I never called to Him.

Another of my mental torturers was fear. Certainly I had never considered myself a fearful person, but that was because in most matters I was not attached. In one test of my non-attachment, however, I had shown myself exceedingly vulnerable: I feared disappointment from others.

Peace in this world depends on cheerfully relinquishing attachment to all things, even to ego. As long as I strove to protect my sense of personal worth, I would suffer again and again, ever in essentially the same ways.

I was not yet wise enough to see clearly, but at least my vision was improving. My dream about the torture chamber, conveying as it did a sense of divine guidance, had made me more aware of realities beyond those which could be known through the senses. This awareness, coupled with the trust and affirmation that I had worked on developing earlier, led me now to an interesting discovery.

I hit upon what was, as far as I knew then, a novel theory: To be lucky, *expect* luck. Don't wait passively for it to come to you, but go out and meet it halfway. With strong, positive expectation, combined with equally positive action, success will be assured. With this simple formula I was to achieve some remarkable results.

*   *   *   *   *   *   *

Not long after the New Year our first semester ended. At that time Rod and one or two other friends flunked out of college. It was hardly surprising, considering the disdain all of us felt for "the system." Their departure put me on my own now in my efforts to understand life more deeply. My independence proved a wholesome opportunity.

I visited Sue's dormitory occasionally, hoping in chats with a few of her friends to relive a little of the happiness I had known with her. But the pain of her absence was keen, and after a time I stopped going.

In Sue's dormitory there lived a girl from India, a friend of Sue's named Indira Kirpalani. Indira was perhaps the most beautiful girl I have ever seen. I had no romantic interest in her, but she was part of Sue's scene, which I'd enjoyed. Indira hinted more than once that she wished I would date her.

One day I accepted her invitation to escort her to a Bryn Mawr dance. That evening I allowed myself to enter into her mood. Throwing myself merrily into the occasion, I became "the parfait gentle knight," or, alternatively, a kind of Arthur Murray. To my surprise, at one point everyone in the hall cleared the floor to watch us go whirling around. For me, however, the occasion was only merry-making. I realized that Indira's attraction to me was based on an image that was not at all my true reality. Far from being the dashing young sportsman of her imagination, I was, inwardly, in my almost desperate search for eternal verities, becoming more and more withdrawn from the "normal" social scene.

How often our perception of others is merely a projection of our own concepts, desires, and conditioning! Though I was only eighteen, in comparing myself to Indira's image of the youths she admired I felt positively ancient.

Granted, this was only a subjective impression. One day, when I went to Philadelphia for my weekly singing lesson with Marie Zimmerman, she noticed that I was in low spirits and inquired what was wrong. I related my little tragedy.

"Ah!" she exclaimed impatiently. "Puppy love! I lived with my husband nearly fifty years. In all that time our friendship kept growing deeper. Since his death we are closer than ever. *That* is love!"

Offended, I told myself she simply didn't understand. But her words remained with me, gently reminding me in my deeper self that I probably had much in life yet to learn.

My college classes had lost all appeal for me. I seldom mixed with the other students. To protect myself in my unhappiness, I put on an over-intellectual front, did frequent battle with words, and assumed an air of self-assurance in which there was considerably more affirmation than self-recognition. My heart was vulnerable, but my reason and will were unshaken.

Mainly, however, I spent my days thinking, thinking, thinking, as if to wrest from life insights into its farthest secrets. Why, I asked myself, did the promise of joy so often prove a will-o'-the-wisp? And was it not essential to a well-ordered universe that love given be in some way returned? Again, where lay the pathway to true happiness?

"Relax!" cried Roberto one day, seeing me staring sightlessly out the window. "Can't you ever relax!"

So the semester passed. In recollection it all seems a grey mist.

My draft board called me in for an examination, which I failed owing to weak eyesight. Resolved thereby was the dilemma of whether or not to register as a conscientious objector. I had doubted whether I could register as one in completely good faith, since it wasn't a matter of my religious convictions; I simply knew with perfect certainty that, even if my own life depended on it, I could never take the life of another human being.

In April, Dad was sent to Rumania as petroleum attaché to the U.S. diplomatic mission in Bucharest.

My job at The Last Straw convinced me and everyone else (especially my employer) that, whatever my mission in life, it was not to wait on tables. I kept absent-mindedly sitting down with groups of customers, quite forgetful that there were other tables waiting to be served; then forgetting to change the total on the bill when the customers increased their orders. I'm afraid I came close to being The Last Straw's last straw!

My singing lessons were the only really bright spot in my life. Marie Zimmerman was a demanding teacher. After six months of weekly lessons she stopped me one day in the midst of a song.

"There!" she cried triumphantly. "*That note.* That's how all your notes should sound!"

There were other compensations besides the sheer joy of learning from her how to sing. Once she said to me, "If any singing teacher worthy of the name—I mean a real *musician*—were to hear you now, he would be impressed."

And toward the end of the college year, she told me softly, "I am living for only one thing now: to see you become a *great* singer!" She raised a hand impressively into the air. "It isn't only your voice; others have good voices, too. But you have a mind; you *understand*."

Dear Marie! (May I call you that, now that you've left this world? To call you Mrs. Zimmerman seems too formal when addressing your soul.) How sad I have been that I had to disappoint you. That was our last class together. I *couldn't* go back to you. I knew that to be a singer, even a world-renowned one, was not at all my calling. But maybe you are pleased with the fact that I *have* touched people with my gift—not for money, but for love. And maybe someday, too, if we meet in heaven or in some other lifetime on earth, I can sing for you again. One of my deepest prayers on the spiritual path has been that all the people I have ever loved be blessed with divine peace and joy. May you be even more blessed than most, for those fulfillments were what your own soul was actively seeking.

As the college year began drawing to a close, my prolonged inattention to the daily class routine brought me to a rather awkward predicament. Most of my courses I was confident of at least passing, though barely. Greek, however, was a downright embarrassment. It became a standard joke in class to see whether I would recognize one, or two, Greek words in a paragraph when called upon to translate. (I was a cinch for words like "a" and "the"!) That entire semester I did hardly three Greek assignments. As we prepared for the final exam, Dr. Post, our professor, remarked more than once, "Not everyone in this room need trouble himself to appear for that event." Every time he said this, the other students would glance at me, and laugh.

I determined to show up for the exam, however, and to pass it. It might take a bit of luck not to flunk, but then, I reminded myself, I also had my new theory on how to attract luck: *Expect* to be lucky, then meet luck halfway with a vigorous, positive attitude.

Unfortunately, I felt anything but vigorous and positive towards the one activity that really mattered: study. A week before the day we were to sit for the exam, I finally picked up the textbook and glanced halfheartedly at the first page. It was no use. Giving up, I flung the book aside. "Tomorrow," I assured myself, "I'll study *twice* as long as I would have, today." But the next day my good intentions were again routed ignominiously. For the rest of that week I showed persistence only in my continued willingness to procrastinate.

Almost before I knew it, the last evening loomed menacingly above my head. And I hadn't studied at all! Even now I fully intended to pass, but I can't imagine anyone in his right mind endorsing these roseate expectations.

Necessity, it is said, is the mother of invention. Fortunately for me, my present extremity displayed the right, maternal instinct. Out of the blue an inspiration appeared.

"You are a Greek," I told myself with all the concentration I could muster; I resolutely adjusted myself to this new identity. The results were astonishing.

As an American, I had found the study of Greek difficult. Now, however, as a Greek, "my own" language came to me with surprising ease. Through some subtle channel in the network of consciousness that binds all men together, I felt myself suddenly in tune with Greek ways of thinking and speaking. Approaching this new language as an old friend, moreover, I no longer faced the age-old problem of the student who, while trying to attract knowledge with one half of his mind, pushes it away with the other half by his unwillingness to learn. My entire mental flow was unidirectional. For two hours I absorbed Greek grammar and vocabulary like a dry sponge in water. At last I could hold no more.

The following morning, "Mother Necessity" gave birth to another inspiration. Our class had been studying the New Testament in the original Greek. Dr. Post had told us that we'd be asked to translate a portion of that scripture into English. This morning, then, mindful of my theory on attracting luck, it occurred to me to turn to the King James translation of the Bible. I had time enough only to read one chapter, but, I thought, if my luck held this would be the chapter from which the passage would be selected.

It was! The exam that year, as it turned out, was exceptionally difficult: Only two students passed it. My theory on luck was vindicated, however: I was one of those two.

From this experience I learned several useful lessons: for one, the mind's power for positive accomplishment, once it learns to resist its own "no"-saying tendency, is almost limitless. Much of what people do, indeed, amounts only to pushing simultaneously on opposite sides of a door. Working themselves to exhaustion, they yet accomplish little or nothing. If they would only learn to say "Yes!" to life and to all its challenges, with the full conviction of their being, their capacity for success might be expanded almost to infinity.

This discovery of the latent power within me, and within everyone, was important for me, but even so its interest was secondary to another problem that eluded me still: the secret of happiness.

Is not joy, I asked myself, what all men, in their hearts, are really seeking? Why, then, do so few people experience it? And why is it so common for people to suffer in the very pursuit of happiness?

Toward the end of the semester it occurred to me that perhaps the fault lay with our restless life-style in America. How, I asked myself, could anyone find true happiness while chasing ever-elusive rainbows, satiating himself with sense pleasures?

Years later, on learning that the cow, in India, commands special affection, an amusing comparison occurred to me. The Indian is, himself, in some ways cow-like: slowly ruminative, reflectively chewing the cud of his ideas. By contrast, Americans, who love dogs, seem actually to have a certain affinity with them, as they dash about in mad pursuit of endless and quite unnecessary goals, eagerly wagging their tails in an effort to be liked.

Thoreau's statement in *Walden* impressed me: "Of a life of luxury the fruit is luxury." For the materialist, the heights of inspiration are unimaginable. The worst disease of modern life is, I concluded, its superficiality. True joy is ever creative; it demands fresh, vital, *intense* awareness. How, I thought impatiently, will happiness worthy of the name ever be felt, if one is too superficial to hold an unconventional thought? Material pleasures and acquisitions cannot bring anyone happiness.

It is not unusual for this kind of judgment to be met with indulgent smiles, as though the sheer frequency with which it is made, especially by the young, rendered it invalid. Considering the fact, however, that it is arrived at more or less independently by so many who seek honest values, I think it might be wise to ponder whether it may not hold an element of truth.

At any rate, my own solution that year to the shortcomings I identified with life in America was to travel abroad. I imagined people in less industrialized countries turning to their daily tasks with a song on their lips and inspiration in their hearts. Nearby Mexico, surely, was such a country. I would spend my summer vacation there among simple, happy, spontaneous, *genuine* human beings.

Getting there was my first problem. If I took a job to earn the money for the journey, my vacation might end before I could save enough. How, then—short of robbing a bank—could I "get rich quick"? What my dilemma called for, obviously, was another application of my theory on luck.

Affirming a bright, positive attitude, I cast about hopefully for a solution. Our college yearbook, I remembered, offered cash prizes for a variety of literary contributions. If I won a large enough prize, my problem would be solved! I leafed through the book. Most of the prizes listed were small: ten, fifteen, twenty-five dollars. But then a more promising figure caught my eye: one hundred dollars! This amount would take me far, indeed.

Eagerly I checked to see what I must do to win it. Then my heart sank. The requirement was for an essay on the subject, "The Basic Principles Underlying the Government of the United States." Some law professor, probably, had coughed up this legal tidbit! Why, I thought with a sigh, must educators continually place the highest price on the driest matter? Who would ever write an essay on such a ponderous subject?

I was on the point of passing on to other prospects when the answering thought came: "That's right: Who *would*?" Examining the information more closely, I found no one listed as having won this prize the previous year. I checked several earlier yearbooks: None of them showed a winner. Perhaps there *was* hope after all! Ignorant though I was of the legal or historical points implied in the topic, if mine was the sole entry. . . .

Anyway, I reflected, I wasn't *completely* ignorant. At least I knew America's basic principles as they are popularly defined: *life, liberty, and the pursuit of happiness.* That brief phrase might not make much of an essay, but what if I took a fresh approach to it? Would the judges decide I had skirted the issue if, for example, I examined our present-day society in the light of how truly it was living up to those principles? Here at least I'd be on familiar ground.

Dividing my essay into three chapters — "Life," "Liberty," and, "The Pursuit of *Property*" — I demonstrated how, by our relentless acquisitiveness, we were depriving ourselves of all three of our basic rights: life and liberty, as well as happiness.

My paper was the sole entry, and would therefore have won the prize anyway. But I was told afterward that the faculty had passed it around thoughtfully among themselves.

Another prize offered in the yearbook was of fifteen dollars for the best poem submitted. Though this was hardly "big money," it seemed worth a stab; I already had a few poems completed that I could submit. In this effort, I knew, I faced competition. The campus poetry club had been debating which of its members would walk away with the prize; they'd already made clear their view that I, who wasn't a member, didn't stand a chance. In the past we'd crossed swords on the subject of solitary, versus group, creativity. To me a poetry *club* seemed a contradiction in terms. I saw it as a victory for my own point of view when this prize came to me.

Thus, with $115 in my pocket before the vacation had even started, I decided I had enough money for the journey. If I found later that I needed more, Lady Luck would no doubt provide it. Barely nineteen years old, never before on my own, and with my parents far away in Rumania: I considered myself an adventurer indeed!

Before leaving for Mexico, I took a short trip to Massachusetts in order to visit Rod. Soon thereafter my great odyssey began. Hitchhiking southward, I made use of a return-trip train ticket that I held from New York to Philadelphia. From Philadelphia I planned to continue hitchhiking, armed with my until-now-successful formula for attracting luck, and burdened with nothing but a knapsack.

A young couple seated behind me on the train noticed the knapsack, and engaged me in conversation. Was I a hiker? They themselves were enthusiastic youth hostelers. We chatted pleasantly; soon we were singing folk songs together. By the time we reached Philadelphia we were like old friends. They invited me to spend the night at their family home in Ardmore, the town before Haverford on the Main Line.

This home turned out to be no mere residence, but a veritable mansion. Their hospitality, too, was extraordinary. A member of the family was about to be married; relatives were arriving from distant parts. Food fit for the most educated palate was being served at every meal. Lady Luck, I reflected, seemed particularly well disposed towards me!

The following morning, as I sat in the living room preparatory to leaving, the dowager of the clan entered and took a chair next to mine. Her smiling manner hinted at good news.

"I have a nephew," she began, "who is being sent by his firm to Mexico City. He will be leaving tomorrow by car. As he is traveling alone, I'm sure he would appreciate company. Do you think you might like to go with him?"

A three-thousand-mile ride! Lady Luck was taking a most welcome interest in my case. Bob Watson, the nephew, not only took me along, but appointed me his extra driver, thereby paying all my travel expenses from his expense account. When we reached Mexico City, he put me up in his home. Thus my money, which I found had less purchasing power than I'd imagined, lasted me the entire summer.

Bob, and later his wife Dorothy (who joined us later), were the kindest of friends to me. Our Mexican adventure was as new and fascinating for them as it was for me. Together we shared its daily lessons, rewards, and comic twists as we reported our new experiences to one another in the evenings.

Recalling my impromptu system for learning Greek, I resolved now to learn Spanish the same way. The day we crossed the border at Nuevo Laredo, I told myself with deep concentration, "You're a Mexican." Some hours later, having carefully rehearsed my words, I entered a restaurant and asked for a glass of water to drink, taking pains to get the accent as right as possible. An American tourist lady was standing nearby. Hearing me speak, she promptly boosted my confidence by exclaiming in astonishment, "Why, you're Mexican!"

In one week, by following what was, I realized, a definite principle for self-education, I was speaking Spanish well enough to carry on protracted, if halting, conversations on a wide variety of subjects with people who spoke no English. By the end of two and a half months my Spanish was fairly fluent.

The principle, I discovered, is to put oneself completely in tune with whatever subject one wants to master. Inborn talent, though helpful, is not nearly so important as deep concentration. Anyone can do well if he will attune himself sensitively to his subject, and resolutely exclude from his mind any thought of the task's foreignness.

I have tested this principle many times since then—in learning to write music; to play musical instruments; to paint; to understand some of the deeper aspects of numerous subjects, both abstract and practical; to attract money when I needed it; to found a successful community; and to receive helpful answers to countless questions, whether during meditation or while working or lecturing. Always, the system has taken me far deeper into my subject than intellectual study alone could ever have done. Friends also, to whom I have taught this principle, have had remarkable success with it.

The principle has many ramifications, one of which is my theory on attracting luck. I've learned that a strong, positive affirmation of success is more effective when it is sensitively attuned to one's goal, and protected from the thought of possible failure.

This innocence of the chances of failure is largely responsible, I think, for the phenomenon popularly known as "beginners' luck."

An English girl of my acquaintance in Mexico City (I mentioned her earlier in connection with her Christian Science beliefs) once told me, "A few weeks ago Mummy and I accompanied Daddy to the racetrack. He goes often, but for us it was the first time. He spent most of the afternoon making fun of our 'system' for betting. We'd choose a horse, you see, because we liked the cute white spot on its nose, or because we liked its name. Daddy's system was more scientific. But would you believe it? He usually lost, whereas we won every time!"

If my theory is valid, a beginner's temporary advantage over more seasoned players is that, not knowing the obstacles before him, his expectations are entirely positive. Of course, ignorance of those obstacles also places *limitations* on his success; it takes sensitive awareness of all aspects of a subject, including its difficulties, to achieve genuine mastery.

I had an opportunity during my stay in Mexico to test the mind's power in another direction also. Near the end of summer I succumbed to a debilitating combination of diseases: streptococcal infection, tonsillitis, dysentery. It was several days before I was even strong enough to go see a doctor. When at last I did so, he hurried me off urgently to a hospital. "You'd better reconcile yourself," he told me, "to staying here *at least* two weeks." Worried that I might not be able to afford such a long stay, I made a few discreet inquiries, and found my fears amply justified. To get money from America would have been difficult, though Dad had left emergency funds there for us boys. The most obvious solution was for me to get well at once.

"You're in perfect health," I told myself firmly, saturating my mind with the thought of well-being, and rigidly excluding any slight indulgence in the thought that I was ill. Within two days I left the hospital, fully cured.

Years later a friend corroborated my belief in the mind's healing power. He had once worked as a physiotherapist in a polio sanitarium. While there, he had noticed that the poor patients, who couldn't afford a long stay, were far more likely to recover than the wealthy ones. His conclusion was that the strong desire to get well, based on dire necessity, generated the energy the body needed for healing. In the rich patients, the longer time spent there caused their paralysis to become ingrained.

My Mexican adventure proved on the whole exciting, interesting, and fun—even though, in its innocent exposure to a wide variety of experiences, it bore some resemblance (as Dad put it later) to the travels of Pinocchio. I didn't derive from it, however, what I'd been most keenly seeking: a better way of life. I'd hoped if nothing else to find more laughter there, more human warmth, more inspiration. For a time I imagined I was actually finding these *desiderata*. But then I realized that what I was experiencing was only my own happy sense of adventure. Meanwhile, the people around me were trudging through the same dull round of existence as the people back home. Mexicans differed from Americans only superficially; in essence, both were the same. All of them lived, worked, bred, and died— Solomon Grundies, all! The imaginations of a rare few, anywhere, soared above mundane activities.

Worse still, from my own point of view, I found that I too was basically no different whether in Villa Obregon and Cuernavaca, or in Scarsdale. I experienced the same physical discomforts, the same need to eat and sleep, the same loneliness. I could appreciate more fully, now, Thoreau's statement with which he dismissed the common fancy that a person was wiser for having traveled abroad. "I have traveled a good deal," he wrote, "around the town of Concord." He had, too. He knew more about his home town and its environs than any other man living.

One day he was walking through the fields with a friend. The friend lamented that no trace any longer remained of the indigenous tribes. Thoreau replied, "Why, their traces are everywhere!" Stooping over, he picked up an arrowhead from the ground. His friend had seen it only as a pebble.

The important thing, I realized, is not what lies around us, but the mental attitude with which we look. Answers will not be found merely by transporting our bodies from one clime to another. To those people who expect to find abroad what they have overlooked at home, especially *in themselves*, Emerson's words are a classic re-buke: "Travel is a fool's paradise."

In college that fall I was discussing with a few friends a movie we'd all seen, called *The Razor's Edge*. It is a tale about a Westerner who traveled to India and, with the help of a wise man he met there, found enlightenment.

"Oh, if only I could go to India," cried a girl in our group fervently, "*and get lost!*"

Newly returned as I was from my Mexican adventure, I had few illusions left concerning travel as a solution to the human predicament. "Whom would you lose?" I chuckled. "Certainly not yourself!"

Illness towards the summer's end, and disappointment at not finding what I had hoped for in Mexico, left me a little dispirited for a time. I continued my search for reality, but did so with less than my normal enthusiasm.

It is a striking fact that, until my faith returned in all its former vitality, Lady Luck withheld from me further proofs of her favor.

CHAPTER 10
Intellectual Traps

A N ANCIENT GREEK myth relates that Icarus and his father, Daedalus, escaped from Crete on artificial wings fashioned by Daedalus out of wax and feathers. Icarus, growing overconfident in his joy of flying, ignored his father's advice not to soar too high. As he approached nearer and nearer to the sun, the wax on his wings melted, and Icarus plunged to his death in what has been known ever since as the Icarian Sea.

Many of the old Greek myths contain deep psychological and spiritual truths. In this story we find symbolized one of man's all-too-frequent mistakes: In his joy at discovering within himself some hitherto unsuspected power, he "flies too high," ignoring the advice of those who have learned from experience to value humility.

I had discovered that by will power, faith, and sensitive attunement to certain things I wanted to accomplish, I could turn the tide of events to some degree in my favor. I could learn new languages and speak them adequately in as short a time as a week. (This discovery was one, of course, that I made over a period of time as I traveled around the world.) I could choose to be well, and I was well. I could walk confidently toward certain of life's closed doors, and they opened for me. In all these little successes there had been two key words: *sensitivity*, and *attunement*. In learning Greek, I had tried to attune myself sensitively to the Greek consciousness; the operative principle had been not my mere *resolution* to learn the language, but my inner attempt to *tune in* to it. In the affirmation "I'm a Greek," *Greek*, not *I*, had been the key word.

Now, however, in my youthful exuberance, I fairly flung myself into the breach. Partly, indeed, I was moved to enthusiasm by the sheer grandeur of my new insights. But because my enthusiasm was excessive, sensitivity and attunement often got lost in the dust kicked up by my overly affirmative ego.

I wanted wisdom. Very well, then: I *was* wise! I wanted what I wrote to inspire and guide people; I wanted to be a great writer. Very well, then: I *was* a great writer! (And if they weren't inspired, it was *their* problem.) How very simple! All I had to do was, some fine day, produce the poems, plays, and novels that would demonstrate what was already, as far as I was concerned, a *fait accompli.*

The idea probably had a certain merit, but it was marred by the fact that I was reaching too far beyond my present realities. In the strain involved there was tension; and in the tension, ego.

Faith, if exerted too far beyond a person's actual abilities, becomes presumption. It is best, above all, to submit positive affirmations to the whispered higher guidance of the soul. Knowing nothing of such guidance, however, I supplied my own. That which I decreed to be wisdom *was* wisdom. That which I decreed to be greatness *was* greatness.

It was not that my opinions were foolish. Many of them were, I think, basically sound. But their scope was circumscribed by my pride. There was no room, here, for others' opinions. I had not yet learned to listen sensitively to that "truth which comes out of the mouths of babes." At the same time, I expected ready agreement with my opinions even from those whose age and experience of life gave them some right to consider *me* a babe. I would be no man's disciple. I would blaze my own trails. By vigorous mental affirmation, I would bend destiny itself to my will!

Well, I was not the first young man, nor would I be the last, who imagined the popgun in his hand to be a cannon. At least my developing views on life were such that, in time, they refuted my very arrogance.

For my junior year I transferred to Brown University in Providence, Rhode Island. New perceptions would flourish better, I felt, in a new environment. At Brown I continued my major in

English literature, and took additional courses in art appreciation, philosophy, and (since a science course was required) geology. My attitude toward formal education, however, was becoming increasingly cavalier. I didn't see that a college degree would be of any possible use to me in my chosen career as a writer. Nor did I have much patience with an accumulation of mere facts, when it was the *why* of things that interested me.

Even our philosophy course, which ought to have been at least relatively concerned with the *whys*, was devoted to categorizing the mere *opinions* of those whose works we were studying. When I found I wasn't expected to preoccupy myself with the *validity* of their opinions, I took to reading poetry, in silent protest, in the classroom.

Intent on developing the identity I had selected for myself, I played the role, for all who cared to listen to me, of successful author and philosopher. A few people actually did listen. For hours we sat together, engrossed in the adventure of philosophical thinking. I got my friends to see that joy *has* to be the real purpose of life; that non-attachment is the surest key to joy; and that a person ought to live simply, seeking joy not in things but in an ever-expanding vision of reality. Truth, I insisted, can be found, not in the sordid aspects of life, as so many writers of the day claimed, but in the heights of human aspiration.

Most of the writing of my student days has long since been consigned to fire and blessed oblivion. One piece that escaped the holocaust, however, expresses some of the views I was expounding at that time. It may serve a useful purpose for me to quote it here, unedited, for I still consider its teaching valid.

> My countrymen, having begotten what is in many respects a monstrosity, go about saying what had never before been said so strongly, that we must go with the age if we would create great things. That it is necessary for them to repeat what should normally be too obvious for repetition shows how slight is the hold this century has on our hearts.
>
> They have, moreover, misunderstood the true meaning of democracy, which is not (as they suppose) to debase the noble

man while singing the virtues of the common man, but rather to tell the common man that he, too, can now become noble. The object of democracy is to raise the lowly, and not to praise them for being low. It is only with such a goal that it can have any real merit.

God's law is right and beautiful. No ugliness exists except man's injustice and the symbols of it. It is not life in the raw we see when we pass through the slums, not the naked truth that many "realists" would have us see, but the facts and figures of our injustice, the distortion of life and the corruption of truth. If we would claim to be realistic it is not reality we shall see from the squalid depths of humanity, for our view will be premised on injustice and negation. Goodness and beauty will appear bizarre, whereas misery, hatred and all the sad children of man's misunderstanding will seem normal, and yet strange withal and unfounded, as if one could see the separate leaves and branches of a tree and yet could find no trunk. It is not from the hovel of a pauper that we can see all truth, but from the dwelling place of a saint; for from his mountain, ugliness itself is seen, not as darkness, but as lack of light, and the squalor of cities will be no longer foreign, but a native wrong, understood at the core as a symptom of our own injustice.

The more closely we watch the outside as a means of understanding the inside, the farther off the inside withdraws from our understanding. The same with people as with God.

My ideas were, I think, and as I've already said, basically valid. Ideas alone, however, do not constitute wisdom. Truth must be *lived*. I'm afraid that, in endless discussions about truth, the sweet taste of it still eluded me.

One day a friend and I were crossing campus on our way back from class. Lovingly he turned to me and remarked, "If ever I've met a genius in my life, it is you."

For a moment I felt flattered by his words. But then, as I reflected on them, shame swept over me like a wave. What had I actually done to deserve my friend's praise? I had *talked*! I had been so busy talking that I hadn't even had much time left over for writing. And his compliment had been sincere! It was one thing to have played the part of author and philosopher to convince *myself*. It was quite another for my act to have convinced others. I felt I'd been a hypocrite.

Sick with self-disappointment, I withdrew thenceforth from most of my associates at Brown, and sought to express in writing the truths I had hitherto been treating lightly as coffee shop conversation.

It didn't take me very long to realize that it is much easier to talk hit-or-miss philosophy over a coffee table than to transform basic concepts into meaningful writing or living. There are levels of understanding which come only when one has lived a truth deeply for years. Initial insights may suggest almost the same words, yet the power of those words will be as nothing compared to the conviction that rings through them when their truths have been deeply lived.

St. Anthony, in the early part of the Christian era, was called from his desert retreat by the bishop of Alexandria to speak in defense of the divinity of Jesus Christ. Arguments had been raging through Christendom in consequence of the so-called Arian heresy, which denied Christ's oneness with God. St. Anthony gave no long, carefully reasoned homily in defense of his theme. His words, however, were charged with the fervor of a lifetime spent in prayer and meditation, and conveyed such deep power that, among those who heard him that day, all further argument ceased. What St. Anthony said was, "I have *seen* Him!"

Alas, *I* had *not* seen Him. Nor had I deeply lived a single truth. The words I painted on my verbal canvas were more sketches than finished works. Try as I would to express my ideas in writing, the moment I picked up a pen I found my mind becoming vague and uncertain. Whatever I did write was more to develop my literary technique than to express what was really in my heart to say. I described situations with which I wasn't personally familiar. I wrote about people whose living counterparts I had never met. To master my craft, I imitated the styles of others, hoping to find in their phrasing and choice of words secrets of clarity and beauty that I might later develop into a style of my own.

I had the satisfaction of being praised by certain professors and professional men of letters. Some of them told me they expected me someday to become a front-ranking novelist or playwright. At nineteen, however, I was far from justifying their kindly expectations. Worst of all, in my own opinion, was the fact that I was saying almost nothing really worthwhile.

I worked on the psychological effects, in poetry, of different patterns of rime and rhythm. I studied the emotion-charged rhythms of Irish-English, which the great Irish playwright, John Millington Synge, had captured so beautifully. I wondered why modern English was, by comparison, so lacking in deep feeling. I pondered how, without sounding studied and unnatural, I might bring beauty to dramatic speech.

One of the dogmas I had been taught in English class was that iambic pentameter, the blank verse form of Shakespeare, is the most natural rhythm for poetic speech in the English language. Shakespeare, of course, was trotted out as the ultimate justification for this dogma. But in *modern* English, blank verse sounded to me much too courtly.

Maxwell Anderson, the twentieth-century American playwright, used it in several of his plays, and the best I could say of them was that they were brave attempts. I certainly didn't want to confine myself to the sterile formulae modern writers so often followed in trying to render speech realistically. ("Ya wanna come?" "Yeah, yeah, *sure.*" "Hey look, I'm not beggin' ya. Just take it or leave it." "Okay, okay, smart boy. Who says I don't wanna come?") Shakespeare, even when imitating common speech, idealized it. My problem was how to follow his example without sounding artificial. If literary language couldn't uplift, there seemed little point in calling it literature. And if dramatic writing couldn't inspire, why give back to people a mere echo of the way they spoke already?

For my summer vacation in 1946 I went to Provincetown, on Cape Cod—a haven for artists and writers. There I rented a small room, made an upside-down dresser drawer serve as a desk, and devoted myself to writing a one-act play. To make the few dollars I had stretch as far as possible, I ate the chef's special every day for lunch at a local diner. For forty-five cents I got a greasy beef stew with one or two soggy slices of potato in it, and, if I was lucky, a sagging piece of carrot. After two months of this daily banquet, even that bargain price could no longer tempt me to endure such punishment another day. I went into the diner one afternoon, ordered the chef's special, watched a slice of potato disintegrate as I stabbed at it halfheartedly with a spoon, then got up and walked out again, never to return.

Toward the end of the summer I spent a week on a distant beach, "far from the madding crowd." (How wonderful it would be, I thought, really to be a hermit!) My one-act play, which I finished on those dunes, didn't turn out badly, though I hadn't been able to shake off the hypnotic charm of Synge's English.

The summer itself was pleasant also, despite my penury. But above all what it did was show me that I was as much an outsider in artistic circles as in any other. Increasingly it was becoming clear that I would never find what I was seeking by *becoming* anything. To say, "I'm a writer," or even, "I'm a great writer," wasn't at all the answer. What I needed above all concerned the deeper question of *what I was already*.

CHAPTER 11
By-Paths

L IVING IN PROVIDENCE, a short train ride away from Boston, I often visited Rod and Betty. Rod lived in Wellesley Hills, a Boston suburb. Betty, a dear friend as well as my first cousin, was a student at nearby Wellesley College.

Rod had enrolled at Boston University. He was as good-humored and intense about everything as ever. Together we devoted much time to what might, with some generosity, be described as the Indian spiritual practice of *neti, neti* ("not this, not that").* That is to say, we engaged in a running analysis, complete with droll commentary and merry exaggeration, on some of the follies to which mankind is addicted.

There was the living-to-impress-others dream: "I work on Wall Street. *(Pause)* Of course, you know what *that* means."

There was the "Protestant ethic," the I'm-glad-I'm-not-happy-because-that-means-I'm-good dream: "I wouldn't *think* of telling you what you should do. All I ask is that you *(sigh)* let your conscience be your guide."

A favorite of ours was the if-you-want-to-be-sure-you're-right-just-follow-the-crowd dream: "You'd better march in step, son, if you want the whole column to move."

Rod was a wonderful mimic. He could make even normally reasonable statements sound ridiculous. He attained his height when imitating someone hopelessly inept trying to sound like a big shot.

* By examining every human delusion dispassionately, one abandons each one with the conclusion, "This, too, is unreal (*neti, neti*)." The seeker thereby arrives at last at the perfect understanding of Truth.

My cousin Bet, at Wellesley College, Massachusetts.

We also discussed seriously the fulfillments we both wanted from life. The longer we talked, the longer our list of minuses grew, and the shorter, that of the plusses. For Rod, these narrowing horizons meant the gradual loss of ambition to become a writer. For me, it meant a gradual redirection of ambition from worldly to spiritual attainments: from writing about truth to *living* it.

In those days, as I've mentioned earlier, college students were not so preoccupied as they are today with the search for meaning. For most of them, the ideal was "Get to the top; become wealthy, respected, and important; marry someone suitable; buy a big home and populate it with children; let everyone see you enjoying life; better still, get them to *envy* you for enjoying it." Needless to say, the gradations of worldly ambition are many, by no means all of them crass. Youth, however, in its quest for personal directions, is seldom sensitive to the directions of others. If Rod and I were ungenerous, it was partly because we were still preoccupied with defining our own goals.

Not surprisingly, some of the people whose values we rejected reciprocated to some degree with antagonism. Rod, in fact, almost invited hostility by judging *them*, along with their values. Ever tend-

ing to extremes, he either praised people to the skies as "perfectly wonderful," or condemned them to the depths as "dreadful" or
"ridiculous."

Judgment forms a barrier, however. In excluding others, one's
criticism of them also encloses himself. Rod, by his judgmental attitude, was gradually painting himself psychologically into a corner.
After all, if others didn't measure up to his ideals, it behooved him
to prove that he himself did measure up. The stricter his standards
became for others, the more impossible they became for himself.
I remember a space of two or three months when, though supposedly working on a novel, he never progressed beyond typing "Page
one, Chapter one," on an otherwise blank page. In time I suppose he
had no choice but to abandon writing altogether. It was a pity, for
his was one of the most talented, intelligent, and deeply perceptive
natures I have ever known.

I myself, though not so judgmental as Rod, could be cutting in my
remarks. I justified this tendency by telling myself that I was only
trying to get people to be more discriminating. There is never a *good*
excuse, however, for unkindness. In one important respect, indeed,
my fault was greater than Rod's, for whereas his judgments were directed at people he scarcely knew, my criticisms were reserved for
my friends.

I once wrote a stinging letter to Betty, simply because I felt that
she wasn't trying hard enough to develop her own very real spiritual
potential. Occasionally even my mother came under fire from me. It
was years, and many hurts to myself, before I realized that no one
has a right to impose his will on others. Everyone has a right to his
own level of freedom. Respect for that freedom is, indeed, essential
if one would counsel others wisely. Without due regard for another
person's right to be himself, one's perception of his needs will be
insensitive, and will seldom be wholly accurate. I, certainly, had all
the insensitivity of immature understanding. The hurts I gave to others were never compensated for by any notable acceptance, on their
part, of my advice.

Often on my path I have thought, How can I make amends for
the hurts I have given to so many of my friends and dear ones? And

as often the answer comes back to me: By asking God to bless them with *His* love.

Towards the end of my first year at Brown, Rod, having dropped out of Boston University, came to live with me in a room I had taken off campus. We cooked our own meals with the help of a book I had bought for its reassuring title, *You Can Cook If You Can Read*. I had always looked on cooking as a kind of magic. It delighted me to find in this book such quasi-ritualistic advice as, "To ascertain if the spaghetti is done, throw a piece of it at a wall. If it sticks there, it's ready to eat." (Bad advice, I learned years later in Italy. Spaghetti should be "*al dente*," which means, "somewhat resistant to chewing.")

Rooming with Rod, I got an opportunity to observe on a new level the truth, which I'd discovered during my last semester at Haverford, that subjective attitudes have objective consequences. Rod's tendency to judge others attracted antagonism not only from people he knew, but even, in some strange way, from perfect strangers. In restaurants, people sitting nearby would sometimes scowl at him for no evident reason. One evening a passer-by in a crowded street pulled a gun on him, warning him to mind his own business and leave his girlfriend alone, though Rod hadn't even noticed them until that moment. Another evening, six men with knives chased him down a dark street; Rod eluded them only by hiding in a doorway. Whenever he and I went out together, all was calm and peaceful. But Rod by himself continually, in some obscure way, invited disaster. Fortunately, I think because he really meant no harm, he always got off without injury.

At this time Rod's life and mine were beginning to branch apart. Rod shared some of my interest in spiritual matters, but not to the extent of wanting to get involved in them personally. I, on the other hand, was growing more and more keen to mold my life along spiritual lines. We talked freely on most subjects, but on this one I found it better to keep my thoughts to myself.

One day, as I was reading a book, a sudden inspiration came to me with complete certainty; I felt its truth on some deep level of my consciousness. Stunned at the depth of my conviction, I said to Rod, "I'm going to be a spiritual teacher!"

"Don't be silly!" he snorted, not at all impressed.

Very well, I thought, *I'll say no more. But I know.*

The thought of sharing spiritual truths with others, however, in no way inspired me to spend more time in church, where religion held no appeal for me at all. "Hel-*lo!*" our campus minister simpered sweetly, almost embarrassingly self-conscious in his effort to demonstrate "Christian charity" when he passed us in the hallways. People, I thought, attended church services chiefly because it was the respectable and proper thing to do. Some of them, no doubt, wanted to be good, but how many, I wondered, attended because they *loved God*? Divine yearning seemed somehow incompatible with going to church, carefully ordered as the services were, and devoid of spontaneity. The ministers in their pulpits talked of politics and sin and social ills—and, endlessly, of money. But they didn't talk of God. They didn't tell us to dedicate our lives to Him. No hint passed their lips that the soul's only true Friend and Beloved dwells within, a truth which Jesus stated plainly. Socially inconvenient Biblical teachings, such as Jesus' commandment, "*Leave all*, and follow me," were either omitted from their homilies altogether or hemmed in with cautious qualifications that left us, in the end, exactly where we were already, armed now with a good excuse.

My impression was that the ministers I listened to hesitated to offend their wealthy parishioners, whom they viewed as customers. As for direct, *inner* communion with God, no one ever mentioned it. Communion was something one took at the altar rail with the aid of a priest.

One Sunday I attended a service in Boxford, a little town north of Boston. The sermon title was "Drink to Forget." And what were we supposed to forget? Well, the wicked Japs and their betrayal of us at Pearl Harbor. The brutal Nazis and their atrocities. Nothing, here, about righting our own wrongs, or seeing God in our enemies. Nothing even about forgiving them *their* wrongs. The sacrificial wine served that morning was supposed to help us to forget all the bad things *others* had done to us. I could hardly suppress a smile when that Lethe-inducing nectar turned out to be, not wine, but grape juice!

If there was one subject that roused me to actual bitterness, it was the utterly commonplace character of religion as I found it taught and practiced in the churches. My bitterness was not because the demands this religion made were impossible, but because they were so unspeakably banal; not because its assertions were unbelievable, but because they were carefully preserved (as if in theological formaldehyde) at the safest, most vapid level of common acceptability. Above all I was disturbed because the churches struck me as primarily social institutions, not lighthouses to guide people out of the darkness of spiritual ignorance. It was almost as if the churchmen were trying to *reconcile* themselves to that ignorance. With dances, third-class entertainments, and watered-down messages they tried their best to get people simply to come to church, but they neglected the commandment of Jesus: "Feed my sheep."

Frank Laubach, the great Christian missionary, once launched a campaign to get more ministers simply to *mention* God in their Sunday sermons. His campaign suggests the deepest reason for my own disillusionment. Of all things in life, it was for spiritual wisdom that I longed most urgently. Yet, most notably, it was the churches that withheld wisdom from me. Instead, they offered dead substitutes. For years I sought through other channels the fulfillment I craved, because the "ministers of the Gospel" from their pulpits made a mockery of the very fulfillments promised in the Bible. To paraphrase the words of Jesus, I asked of them the bread of life, and they offered me a stone.[*]

Thus, hungry as I was for spiritual understanding, I saw no choice but to pursue my career as a writer, looking elsewhere for the inspiration which, had I but known it, only God can supply. It was like walking into darkness for lack of any better place to go. A sense of emptiness kept increasing in my heart, and I knew not how to fill it.

My college classes were becoming increasingly burdensome. Intellectualism was bringing me dryness of heart. It seemed to me almost unbearably trivial to be studying the eighteenth-century novel, when it was the meaning of life itself that I was trying desperately to fathom.

[*] Matthew 7:9.

* * * * * * *

My parents had recently returned from Rumania. I sought their permission to take a leave of absence from college. Reluctantly they gave it. Thus, midway through my senior year I left Brown University. I never returned.

Thereafter, for several months, I lived with my parents. I struggled—gamely, perhaps, but without real hope—over the composition of a two-act play. It concerned nothing I wanted to say. But then, the things I did want to say were the last that I felt myself decently qualified to express.

Occasionally I went into New York City, where I spent hours walking about, gazing at the tragedy of people's transition from loneliness to apathy. How bereft of joy they all seemed, in their struggle merely to survive in those desolate concrete canyons!

At other times I would stroll, almost in a kind of ecstasy, through the happier setting of Washington Square, observing mothers with their babies, laughing children playing on the lawns, young people singing with guitars by the fountain, trees waving, the fountain spray colorfully playing in the sunlight. All seemed joined together in a kind of cosmic symphony, their many different lives but one life, their countless ripples of consciousness part of one great sea of joy.

The valleys and the peaks of life! What grand truth could level them, bind everything, and make all of this variety one again in God?

Back home one day I told Mother I wouldn't be going with her to church anymore. This was one of the few times I ever saw her weep. "It pains me so deeply," she cried, "to see you pulling away from God!" I wasn't aware of the promise she'd made to God before my birth, giving me, her first-born child, to God. I would in any case have loved to reassure her, and I was deeply touched by her concern for me. But what could I do? My first duty was to be honest with myself, and I was still too uncertain of my own directions.

A few days later Mother sought me out. Hopefully she quoted a statement she had read somewhere that morning to the effect that atheism sometimes presages a deep spiritual commitment. I said,

"You have understood." I was by no means the atheist she thought me to be; nevertheless, it relieved me to see that she understood my rejection of her church as being part, at least, of a sincere quest for truth. I didn't explain my deep inner feelings to her at the time, however, for fear of diluting the intensity of my own search.

That summer I traveled up to the little town of Putney, Vermont, where my youngest brother Dick was in school. Dick was maturing into a fine young man; I loved him deeply. Something he'd told me had touched me particularly. One day he drove to a house to pick up a group of his friends. As the car rolled slowly to a halt, its bumper lightly touched a dog that was standing complacently before it. The dog wasn't hurt, but its owner, a small, older man and no physical match for Dick, was furious. Rushing up to the car door, he punched Dick in the jaw through the open window.

At that moment Dick's friends emerged from the house. Dick, anxious lest they hurt the man for what he had done, said nothing of the matter either to them or him.

During my stay at Putney, a drama teacher there recommended the Dock Street theater in Charleston, South Carolina, as a good place to study stagecraft. For my twenty-first birthday Dad had given me five hundred dollars. (Dick's comment: "A pleasing precedent has been set!") I decided, albeit rather in a mood of desperation, that if I was going to be a playwright I might as well go to Charleston with this money and seek, at that theater, direct experience in my craft.

CHAPTER 12

"Who Am I? What Is God?"

"Aᴌᴌ ᴛʜᴇ ᴡᴏʀʟᴅ's a stage," says Jaques in Shakespeare's *As You Like It*. Few people realize how little their personalities represent them as they really are. Emerson, in his essay on "The Over-Soul," wrote:

"We know better than we do. We do not yet possess ourselves, and we know at the same time that we are much more. I feel the same truth how often in my trivial conversation with my neighbors, that somewhat higher in each of us overlooks this by-play, and Jove nods to Jove from behind each of us. *Men descend to meet* [italics mine]."

Every man is, in his soul, divine. He merely persuades himself, by concentrating on his outer life, that he is a baker, banker, teacher, or preacher; that he is rude or sensitive, athletic or lazy, genial or solemn. He sees not that all these are only roles, reflections of the likes and dislikes, the desires and aversions he has accumulated over incarnations. What has once been acquired can as surely be shed again. The outer self changes endlessly. Only in his inner Self is the soul changeless and eternal.

Much of my life seems almost, in retrospect, to have been planned for me. Certainly my experiences up to this time had given me, basically, the lessons I had a need to learn. It was perhaps due to this same "suspicious Someone's" plan for me that I spent the better part of the next year working at the Dock Street Theater. The various roles I acted on the stage taught me to stand back mentally from myself, to observe this peculiar specimen, Don Walters, acting out his normal daily role as a young American male of somewhat cheerful disposition, an aspiring playwright, and a more or less perennial innocent abroad.

My associations at the Dock Street Theater helped me, in time, to see the shallowness of *all* role-playing, whether in or out of the theater. For most of the people I met there were always "on stage"; they even based their self-esteem on how well they could pretend. A year spent with them added immeasurably to my yearning for values and attitudes that were *true*.

I arrived in Charleston toward the end of June. The Dock Street Theater, I learned, was closed for the summer months and scheduled to reopen only in September. I took a room in a small boarding house, where I received lodging and three generous meals a day for only ten dollars a week.

The atmosphere there was pleasantly familial. Most of my fellow boarders were students at The Citadel, a nearby college for men. The friendship of congenial companions my own age threatened for a time my intentions of devoting myself to writing. Rationalizing the threat, I told myself that, as a budding writer, I needed to absorb all that I could of local color. Aside from a few scattered poems,* my "accomplishments" now were limited to a succession of parties, outings to the beach, and merry "bull sessions" where everything was discussed from politics to girls to recent gossip.

Gradually I expanded my frontiers to a study of the way people at various levels of Charleston society lived their lives. I went everywhere; met people in widely diverse walks of life; explored some of the dingiest "dives"; was a guest in several prominent homes.

Charleston was a small city then, of some 70,000 people (it is much larger now). I found within its narrow boundaries a representative cross section of America. With the middle and upper social strata, and to a lesser degree with the lower, I was already somewhat familiar. But the lower strata I now encountered were an eye-opener. I'm not referring to the poor, whose simple dignity often gives the lie to that condescending designation, "lower class." Some of the people I met were actually wealthy, but their meanness of heart, their narrow outlook, and their indifference to others' well-being condemned

* One of which is included at the end of this book.

them to lives of criminal greed. Included among them were the own-
ers and operators of sordid speakeasies, which posed as fronts for
still-more-illicit gambling rooms upstairs, and (one suspected) for
other hush-hush activities as well. These people projected an almost
visible aura of dishonesty, cold brutality, and evil. Some of them
were, as I say, wealthy, but their riches had been acquired at the pigs'
trough of human desperation.

Equally sordid were the lives of most of the people who fre-
quented these places. For the customers, too, were out purely for
what they could get for themselves. Their conversation reflected
a hardness; their brittle laughter crackled like ice. Such people were
the perennially homeless, in consciousness if not in fact. They were
men and women who wandered aimlessly from city to city, seeking
transient jobs and still more transient pleasures; individuals whose
character was fast losing distinction in the blur of alcoholic fumes;
couples whose family lives were disintegrating under jackhammer
blows of incessant bickering; lonely people who hoped blindly to find
in this wilderness of human indifference just a glimpse of friendship.

Everywhere, I saw desolation. This was, I reflected, the stuff of
countless modern plays and novels. *Why*, that literary preoccupation
with meanness and desolation? Is great literature something merely
to be endured? Who can possibly gain anything worthwhile by exposure to grey hopelessness?

Yet these too were, undeniably, a part of life. Their effect on me
spiritually, moreover, proved to some extent wholesome. For the
awareness they gave me of man's potential for self-degradation lent
urgency to my own aspiration for a higher potential in myself, and
in others.

Consequently, I took another stab at attending church. I even
joined a church choir. But I soon discovered that this meant only
exchanging one kind of sterility for another. The church atmosphere
was more wholesome, no doubt, but partly for that very reason it
was also more smug, more resistant to any suggestion that some
higher perfection might be attainable.

Civilized man prides himself on how far advanced his present state
is from that of the primitive savage. We look condescendingly on his

tribal way of endowing trees, wind, rain, and heavenly bodies with human personalities. Now that science has explained everything in prosaic terms, modern man considers himself wiser for having lost his sense of awe. But I'm not so sure that he deserves congratulation. It strikes me rather that, dazzled by his own technology, he has only developed a new kind of superstition, one infinitely less interesting. Too pragmatic, now, to worship, he has forgotten how to commune. Instead of relating sensitively to Nature around him, he shuts it out of his life with concrete "jungles," air conditioning, and "muzak"; with self-promotion and noisy entertainments. He is obsessed with problems that are real to him only because he *gives* them reality. He is like a violin string without the wood for a sounding board. Life, when cut off from its broader realities, becomes weak, thin, and meaningless.

Modern technology alienates us from the universe and from one another. Worst of all, it alienates us from ourselves. It directs all our energies toward the mere manipulation of *things*, until we ourselves assume qualities that are almost thing-like. In how many modern plays and novels are men idealized for their ability to act with the precision and unfeeling efficiency of a machine! We are taught to behave in this world like uncivilized guests, rudely consuming our host's plenty without offering him a single word of thanks in return. Such is our approach to nature, to God, to life itself. We make ourselves petty, then imagine that the universe is petty also. We rob our own lives of meaning, then call life itself meaningless. Self-satisfied in our unknowing, we make a dogma of ignorance. And when, in "civilized" smugness, we approach the question of religion, we address God Himself as though He had better watch His manners if He wants a place in our hearts.

After a month or so of paddling in the waters of Charleston's social life, both high and low, I finally decided that I'd exposed myself quite enough to cross-sections of a society whose members seemed at least as blind as I was. None of my new acquaintances had contributed anything positive to my search for meaning. And of "local color," I felt that I had seen altogether too many browns and greys.

My own "purism," of course, held a certain narrowness of its own. Had I been less rigidly critical in my attitudes, I might have attracted more uplifting human associates. Or I might have discovered in the very people I met qualities truer than I dreamed. On the other hand, to do myself justice, it was to a great extent with the very aim of overcoming such rigidity in my own nature that I had made it a practice to mix with so many different types of people.

Toward the end of summer, I moved out of my boarding house to a small apartment at 60 Tradd Street. Here I began to write a one-act comedy titled, *Religion in the Park*. Bitter as well as funny, the play concerned a woman who wanted to live a religious life and eagerly sought instruction from a priest, only to have him discourage her every devotional sentiment by careful emphasis on religious propriety. Meanwhile a passing tramp rekindled her fervor with tales of a saint who, he claimed, had cured him of his lameness. Here at last was what she'd been seeking: religion *lived*, religion *experienced*, not couched in mere social customs and theoretical dogmas!

Alas, in the end the tramp proved to be a fraud also. An alcoholic, he had merely invented his tale in the hope of coaxing a few easy dollars out of her.

This woman's hope and subsequent disillusionment reflected my own spiritual longings, and the skepticism that continued to prevent my actual commitment to a religious life.

An interesting sidelight on that one-act play is that the "saint," according to the tramp's story, lived in California—the very state where I was later to meet my Guru. Could I have been aware, on some deep level of consciousness, that this was where my own destiny lay?

Once, as a child, while crossing the Atlantic, I had met a boy from California. I remember thinking at the time, "*That* is where I must go someday." Years later, when first contemplating my trip to Mexico, I had considered briefly whether I might go to California instead. Then I'd put off the idea with the verdict, "It isn't yet time." Emerson's words come back to me now, more in question than in certainty: "We know better than we do." *Had* I known?

When the Dock Street Theater opened in September, I went to seek affiliation with it. I was told, however, that the only way

I could do so officially was to enroll in its drama school as a student. Counting myself well out of the academic scene, I asked if I might not be given some other status. Finally the director permitted me, partly on the strength of my new play, to affiliate with them as an "unofficial" student. Under this arrangement I was able to study stagecraft in the evenings, and at the same time devote my days to writing.

During the following months I acted in a variety of plays, mingled freely with teachers and students, and served in a number of useful, if more or less nondescript, capacities. These activities gave me some understanding of the business of stagecraft, particularly that of putting on plays in a small community theater. As an actor, however, I'm afraid I was by no means a star. "This isn't *me*!" I kept thinking. "How will I ever learn who I really am, if I keep on playing people I'm not?" The experience was worthwhile, however, from a standpoint of my intended profession as a playwright.

The daylight hours I spent by myself, at first writing, and then, increasingly, thinking, thinking over my old problems: What is the purpose of life? Who am I, really? Hasn't man a higher destiny than (I looked about me desperately)—than *this*? Most important of all: What is true happiness? Can it be found? If so, How?

During the time I spent writing, I threw myself into the task of developing the techniques of my craft. Curiously perhaps for a budding playwright, I wrote no plays at this time; I wanted to keep my mind flexible to pursue new directions in stagecraft—and, more importantly, in myself—as they presented themselves. Instead, I wrote poetry, and tried (still) to develop a sense for poetic speech in drama.

I also pondered the theater's potential for inspiring a far-reaching spiritual renaissance. To this end I studied the plays of the Spanish playwright, Federico García Lorca, to see whether his surrealistic style might be adapted to induce in people a more mystical awareness.

My probing thoughts led me one by one, however, to a dead end. How much, after all, can the theater really accomplish for people, spiritually speaking? Did even Shakespeare, great as he was, effect any deep-seated changes in the lives of individuals? None, surely, at any rate compared to the changes religion has inspired. I shuddered at this comparison, for I loved Shakespeare, and found little to attract me in the churches. But the conclusion, whether I liked it or not, was inescapable: Religion, for all its fashionable mediocrity, its sham, its devotion to the things of this world, remains the most powerfully beneficial influence in the history of mankind. Not art, not music, not literature, not science, politics, conquest, or technology: The one truly uplifting power in history, always, has been religion.

How was this possible? Puzzled, I decided to probe beneath the surface and discover what deep-seated element religion contained that was vital and true.

Avoiding what I considered to be the trap of institutionalized religion, of "churchianity," I took to walking or sitting for hours together by the ocean, pondering its immensity. I watched little fingers of water as they rushed in among the rocks and pebbles on the shore. Did the vastness of God find *personal* expression, similarly, in our own lives?

The juxtaposition of these thoughts with my daily contacts in and out of the theater filled me with distaste. How petty seemed man's desires compared to the impersonal vastness of the ocean, and of infinity! The loftiest aspirations of the people around me seemed mean, their values to an incredible degree selfish and ignoble. Egos pitted themselves against other egos in petty rivalry. My fellow students at the theater insisted that such behavior laid bare the realities of human nature: So, in fact, had declared the modern dramas they admired. Alas, far from bemoaning these "realities," my friends gloried in them. Aspiring actors that they were, they prided themselves on pretending selfishness, "rugged egoism," indifference to the needs of others, and rudeness—until the pretense itself became their reality.

My associates of those days helped me, spiritually, more than I realized at the time, for the more they mocked me with their insistent claim, "This is life!" the more my heart cried out silently, "It isn't! It *just can't* be!" And as my cry increased in urgency, it deepened my own search. More and more I understood that what they termed *life* was only living death.

This isn't to say that sordidness has no objective reality of its own. God was trying to get me to see, rather, the depths to which man, without Him, can sink.

One evening outside my apartment I encountered a fellow student walking in a daze, almost staggering, hardly able to hew a straight line. My first thought was that he must be drunk. Then I noticed dried blood on his forehead. Evidently something more serious was amiss. I led him indoors. Between long pauses of mental confusion he related the following story:

"I was sitting quietly on a park bench, enjoying the evening air. I remember hearing footsteps approach behind me. The next thing I knew I was lying on the grass, returning slowly to consciousness. My coat and trousers were gone. So was my wallet.

"Minutes passed. Confused as I was, I had no idea what to do. Then I saw a police car on the other side of the little park. In relief I staggered over and explained my predicament. My natural assumption was that these policemen would help me.

"Well, can you guess what they did? They arrested me for not being decently clothed! At the police station I was put into a jail cell without so much as a chance to protest against this outrage to justice.

"For some time I tried to get them at least to let me make a phone call. Finally they made that much of a concession. 'Just one call,' the sergeant said. I phoned a couple of friends of ours, who came over with fresh clothing.

"Now—would you believe it?—*our friends* are in jail, and *I'm* out!" Shaking his head unbelievingly, he concluded, "I still don't understand how it all happened."

What had occurred, I learned later, was that these friends, infuriated at this example of police indifference, had cried, "You don't even seem to care that a crime has been committed!"

"You're under arrest!" bellowed the police sergeant.

When our friends resisted this further outrage, they were set upon by every policeman in the room, beaten up, and thrown into jail. My injured friend, meanwhile, was released, presumably because he was now decently dressed, and told to go home and forget the whole thing. It was hardly fifteen minutes later that I met him, wandering about in confusion.

I immediately returned with him to the police station. As we entered, wild screams issued from a back room. Moments later, a couple of policemen emerged, dragging a screaming black woman across the floor by her heels. They dumped her unceremoniously before the sergeant's desk, where she passed out. One of the men, to whom this silence must have seemed disrespectful, brought out a rubber hose and beat her with it on the soles of her bare feet. Some moments later she regained consciousness, and began screaming again. Satisfied, they dragged her into the jail and flung her, still screaming, into a cell. The remainder of the time I was there I heard her moaning quietly.

Throughout this grim episode the rest of the policemen in the room, about fifteen of them, stood around, laughing. "I haven't had this much fun in *years*!" gloated one of them, as he rubbed his hands gleefully together.

Obviously, to reason with such brutes was impossible; I therefore tried to get information out of them. The sergeant finally gave me the name of a judge whose word he required, he said, "before I can release these hoodlums." It was already late, but before the night ended I succeeded in getting the judge out of bed, and our friends out of jail.

From this utter mockery of justice I at least learned a salutary lesson. First, of course, I reacted to such brutality with normal human indignation. Subsequent reflection, however, convinced me that injustice of one kind or another is inevitable in this world. For aren't we all to some extent lost in ignorance? Blind as I myself was, what right had I to blame others simply because their blindness differed from my own? My first thought had been, "We need to change society!" But then I realized that what was needed was a new kind of change: religious or spiritual, not social.

Religion. Again that word! This time I was being pushed toward it by human injustice instead of pulled by my own longing for some higher good. I began now to wonder if evil weren't a conscious will inherent in the universe. How else to account for its prevalence on earth? for man's cruelty to man? for the brutality of the Nazis? for the terrors millions have suffered under communism? How else to explain the appalling twist of fate that causes the good intentions of many who embrace communism to result in human debasement, slavery, and death? What, outside of a renewed, widespread return to God—*a revolution in spirit*—could correct the unnumbered, almost unimaginable wrongs in this world?

I gave much thought at this time to communism as a force for evil. My parents had returned from Rumania with tales of Russian atrocities. Our Rumanian friends there were suffering under the new regime; some of them had been deported to slave labor camps in Siberia. Surely, I thought, the common argument against communism, that it is inefficient, misses the point altogether. What is truly wrong with it is not that its top-heavy bureaucracy results in the production of fewer material conveniences; nor is it even that communism denies people their political rights. What is monstrous about it is that it treats materialism* itself as a virtual religion. Denying the reality of God, communism sets up matter in His place and demands self-abnegation of its adherents much as religions do everywhere.

For committed communists, the shortage of material goods reveals, not the inefficiency of their system, but the measure of their willingness to sacrifice for "the cause." Believing in nothing higher than matter, they see spiritual values—truthfulness, compassion, love—as utterly meaningless. They feel morally justified, rather, in committing any atrocity that will advance their own ideology. Their motto is, "In every circumstance, ask yourself only, What is best for the cause?"

Theirs might be called a religion of unconsciousness, of non-values. It does offer, however, a pseudo-moralistic rationale for the materialistic values of our age. For this reason its teachings will continue to spread, I'm afraid, until mankind everywhere embraces another, a true kind of religion, one that perceives God, not matter, at the heart of reality.

Pursuing these thoughts, I found myself concluding, for reasons both objective and subjective, and for the sake of mankind generally

---

* Materialism, in this context, refers to the philosophical theory that all phenomena, including those of the mind, must be attributed to material agencies.

as well as for my own sake, that what I wanted, what all mankind really needs, is God.

The question returned to me with increasing urgency: *What IS God?*

One evening, taking a long walk into the gathering night, I deeply pondered this question. I dismissed as absurd, to start with, the popular notion of a venerable figure with flowing white beard, piercing eyes, and a terrible brow striking fear into all those who disobey Him. Science has shown us an expansive vastness comprising countless galaxies, each one blazing with innumerable stars. How could any anthropomorphic figure have been responsible for creating all that?

What, then, about fuzzy alternatives that had been proposed to suit the abstract tastes of intellectuals? A "Cosmic Ground of Being," for example: What a sterile evasion—what a non-concept! Such formulas I considered a "cop-out," for they gave one nothing to work with.

No, I thought, God has to be, if nothing else, a *conscious Being*. I had read alternate claims that He is a *dynamic force*. Well, He had to be that, too, of course. But could it be a *blind* force, like electricity? If so, whence came human intelligence? Materialists claim that man's consciousness is produced by "a movement of energy through a pattern of nerve circuits." Well! But intelligence, I realized, is not central to the issue anyway. Intelligence implies reasoning, and reasoning is only one aspect of consciousness; it might almost be called a mechanical aspect, inasmuch as it is conceivable for something electronic to be devised that will do much of his reasoning for him.

René Descartes' famous formula: "I think, therefore I am," is superficial, and false. One can be fully conscious without thinking at all. Consciousness obviously exists apart from ratiocination, and is a precondition for any kind of *thoughtful* awareness.

What about our sense of I-ness: our egos? We don't have to ponder the question objectively. We simply *know* that *we* exist. This knowledge, I have come to understand, is intuitive. Even a newborn baby making its first cry doesn't become self-aware *because of* that cry. It requires self-awareness for it to suffer! Even a worm demonstrates self-awareness: prick it with a pin, and it will try to wriggle away.

Obviously, then, consciousness is at least *latent* everywhere, and in everything. God Himself *must* be conscious, and, having created everything, must also have produced it out of consciousness: not out of *His* consciousness, for consciousness cannot be something He possesses: He *is* consciousness: Essential Consciousness.

What about self-awareness? This, too, must be inherent not only in all life, but in everything. We are not merely His creations: We *manifest* Him! We exist, because He exists.

To "cut to the chase": all of us, as His manifestations, have the capacity to manifest Him more or less perfectly. Surely, then, what we need is to deepen our awareness of Him at the center of our being.

What a staggering concept!

I recalled the days I had spent watching the ocean surf break into long, restless fingers among the rocks and pebbles on the shore. The width of each opening, I reflected, determined the size of the flow. Similarly, if our deepest reality is God, might it not be possible for us to chip away at our granite resistance to Him, and thereby *widen* our channels of receptivity? And would not every aspect of His infinite consciousness flow into us, then, like the ocean, abundantly?

If this was true, then obviously our highest duty is to seek attunement with Him. And the way to do so is to develop that aspect of our nature which we can open to Him. The way to do that, obviously, is to lift our hearts up to Him, and to seek His guidance in every thought and deed. In so doing He *must*—since we are a part of His consciousness—assist us in our efforts to broaden our mental channels.

I realized, now, that true religion is no mere system of beliefs, and is a great deal more than any formalized attempt to wheedle a little pity out of the Lord by offering up pleading, propitiatory rites and prayers. If our link with Him consists in the fact that we are already a part of Him, *then it is up to us to receive Him more completely, and express Him more fully.* *This*, then, is what true religion is all about!

---

* "But as many as *received* him, to them gave he power to become the sons of God." (John 1:12)

What I had seen thus far of religious practices, and eschewed in disappointment, was not *true* religion, but the merest first, toddling steps up a stairway to infinity! One might, I reflected, devote his entire life to this true religion, and never stagnate. What a thrilling prospect!

This, then, would be my calling in life: I would seek God!

Dazed with the grandeur of these reflections, I hardly knew how or at what hour I found my way home again. "Home" at this time was a large, five-room apartment on South Battery which I shared with four of my fellow drama students. On my return there I found them seated, chatting, in the kitchen. I joined them, more or less automatically, for a cup of coffee. My thoughts, however, were far away from that convivial gathering. So overwhelmed was I by my new insights that I could hardly speak.

"Look at Don! What's he got to be so solemn about?" When they found that I couldn't, or wouldn't, participate in their jocularity, the laughter turned to teasing.

"Don keeps trying to solve the riddle of the universe! Yuk! Yuk! Yuk!"

"Ah, sweet mystery of life!" crooned another.

"Why, can't you see?" reasoned the fourth, addressing me solemnly. "It's all so simple! There's no riddle to be solved! Just get drunk when you like, have fun, shack up with a girl whenever you can, and forget all this craziness!"

"Yeah," reiterated the first, heavily. "Forget it."

To my present state of mind, my roommates sounded like yapping puppies. Of what use to me, such friends? I rose and went quietly to my room.

A few days later I was discussing religion with another acquaintance.

"If you want spiritual teachings," he remarked suddenly, "you'll find all your answers in the Bhagavad Gita."

"What's that?" Somehow I found this exotic name deeply appealing, and also, in some unaccountable way, familiar.

"It's a Hindu scripture."

Hindu? And what was *that*? I knew nothing of the Indian teachings. This name, however, the Bhagavad Gita, lingered with me.

If religion was a matter of becoming more receptive to God, it was high time, I decided, that I got busy and worked on making myself receptive. But how? It wasn't that I had no idea how to improve myself. Rather, I saw so much room for improvement that I hardly knew where to begin.

There was the question of my psychological faults: intellectual pride, an overly critical nature. No one, myself included, was happy with these traits in me. But how was I to work on them? And for that matter, were they entirely unmixed evils? Was it wrong, for instance, to *think*? Was it wrong to stand honestly by the fruits of one's thinking, regardless of what others thought? And was it so wrong to be critical of attitudes which one's discrimination declared to be false? People who were more concerned for their own comfort than for my spiritual development condemned these traits in me outright. But to me it seemed that there were aspects to my very faults that must be considered virtues. How was I to sift one from the other?

Contemplating my more socially acceptable virtues, I saw that, here, the very opposite was true: In some ways these "virtues" assumed the nature of faults. My compassion for the sufferings of others, for example, prompted me to try to help them beyond any power I had to give. How else to account for my desire to help them by my writings, when I didn't even know what to write? when I didn't, by personal experience, know truth? Here again: How was I to sift truth from error?

Was there *any* way out of the psychological labyrinth in which I now found myself?

Even on a physical level, the possibilities for self-improvement seemed bewilderingly complex. I read in a magazine advertisement the names of several famous people who had been vegetarians. *Vegetarians?* Was it really desirable, or even possible, to live without eating meat? Again, I read somewhere else that white flour is harmful to the health. *White flour?* Heretofore, my idea of a balanced meal had been hamburger on a white bun, decorated with a thin sliver of tomato and a limp wisp of lettuce. It seemed now that there were all sorts of points to consider on even so basic a subject as diet.

Finally, bewildered by the sheer number of choices before me, I decided that there could be but one way out of my imperfections: God. I must let *Him* guide my life. I must leave off seeking human solutions, and give up defining my search in terms of human effort.

And what of my plans to be a playwright? Well, what had I been writing, anyway? Could I, who knew nothing, say anything meaningful to others? I had deluded myself for a time with the thought that perhaps, by vague allusions to the truth, I might write works with cryptic messages that others would understand even if I myself had no idea what those messages were. But now I realized that in this way out, common as it is among writers, I had not been honest. No, I must give up writing altogether. I must give up even thinking about flooding the world with my ignorance. Surely, out of very compassion for others, I must leave off trying to help them. I must renounce their world, their interests, their attachments, their pursuits. I must seek God in the wilderness, on a mountaintop, in complete solitude.

I would become a hermit.

And what was it I hoped to find, once I made such a complete renunciation? Peace of mind? Inner strength, perhaps? A little happiness?

Wistfully I thought: happiness! I recalled the pure happiness I had known as a child, lost now in the pseudosophistication of my intellectual youth. Would I ever find happiness again? Only, I thought, if I became once again simple, like a child. Only if I forsook my over-intellectuality and opened myself completely to God's love.

I pursued this line of thinking for a time. Then a new doubt seized me: Was I losing my mind? Whoever had heard of anyone actually seeking God? Whoever had heard of anyone communing with Him? Was I a complete lunatic to be dreaming of blazing trails where no man—so far as I knew—had ever ventured before?

For I knew nothing, as yet, about the lives of true saints. Vaguely I'd heard them described as people who lived close to God, but the mental image I had formed of them was of no more than ordinarily good people, going about smiling at children, doing kind deeds, and perhaps murmuring benignly, "*Pax vobiscum,*" or some such pious formula, to anybody who got in their way. What demon of presumption possessed me that caused me to dream of actually *finding* God? Surely, I *must* be going mad!

Yet, if this *were* madness, was it not a more solacing condition than the world's vaunted "sanity"? For it was a madness that promised hope, in a world bereft of hope. It was a madness that promised peace, in a world of conflict and warfare. It was a madness that promised happiness, in a world of suffering, cynicism, and broken dreams.

I knew not how to take even my first steps toward God, but my longing for Him had by now become an obsession.

Where could I turn? To whom could I look for guidance? The religious people I had met, the monks, priests, and ministers of the Gospel, had seemed quite as lost in ignorance as I was.

It occurred to me that I might find in the scriptures a wisdom that those monks, priests, and others had overlooked. At least I must give scripture a *try*.

And what of my plans to become a hermit? This path, surely, I must follow also. Ah! but where? how? with what money to buy the essentials of life? with what practical knowledge to build a shelter, plant food, and otherwise care for myself? Was I not, after all, a complete fool, lost in wild-eyed, impractical dreams? Surely, if practical steps had to be taken, there must be a more pragmatic solution to my dilemma than drifting off to an existence for which I was utterly untrained.

At this point, Reason stepped onto the scene briskly to offer me a resolution for my dilemma.

"There's nothing wrong with you," it asserted, "that vigorous, healthful country living can't cure. You've been spending too much time with jaded city people. Get out among simple, genuine, *good* country folk if you want to find peace of mind. Don't waste your life on impossible dreams. Get back to the land! It isn't God you want; it's a more natural way of life, in Nature's harmony and simplicity." Shades of my Mexican fiasco!

Ease, in fact, not simplicity, was at the heart of this message. For God poses so mighty a challenge to the ego that man will grasp at almost anything rather than heed the call to complete self-surrender.

And, weakling that I was, I relented. I would, I decided, heed Reason's counsel. I would go off to the country, commune with Nature, and live there among more *natural* human beings.

CHAPTER 13

A Search for Guide-Maps

M Y DECISION TO seek peace of mind in an environment of bucolic simplicity coincided with the end of the school year and the
summer closing of the Dock Street Theater. I returned to New York.

Dad had recently been posted to Cairo, Egypt, as Esso's exploration manager there. Our home in Scarsdale was let, and mother had
taken a house temporarily in White Plains preparatory to departing
for Cairo at the end of August to join Dad. I stayed with her two or
three weeks.

My plans for the summer were already set. I said nothing of them,
however, giving out only that I was going upstate New York; my
spiritual longings I kept a carefully guarded secret. But I put immediately into effect my plan to study the scriptures. Borrowing Mother's
copy of the Holy Bible, I began to read it from the beginning.

"In the beginning God created the heaven and the earth. . . . And
God said, Let there be light: and there was light." Who is not familiar
with these wonderful lines?

"And the LORD God planted a garden eastward in Eden; and
there he put the man whom he had formed. . . . And the LORD God
commanded the man, saying, Of every tree of the garden thou mayest freely eat: But of the tree of the knowledge of good and evil, thou
shalt not eat of it: for in the day that thou eatest thereof thou shalt
surely die."

But—what was this? How could God possibly want man to *remain* ignorant?

And so man ate the fruit, became wise, and in consequence was
forced to live like a witless serf. What kind of teaching was this?

Chapter Five: Here I learned that Adam lived nine hundred and thirty years; his son, Seth, nine hundred and twelve years, and Seth's son, Enos, nine hundred and five years. Cainan, Enos's son, "lived seventy years, and begat Mahalaleel: and Cainan lived after he begat Mahalaleel eight hundred and forty years, and begat sons and daughters: And all the days of Cainan were nine hundred and ten years: and he died. And Mahalaleel lived sixty and five years, and begat Jared. . . . And Jared lived an hundred sixty and two years, and he begat Enoch. . . . And Enoch lived sixty and five years, and begat Methuselah. . . . And all the days of Methuselah were nine hundred sixty and nine years: and he died."

What in heaven's name did it all mean? Was some deep symbolism involved?* All this said nothing whatever to my present needs. Disappointed, I laid the book down.

Over the years since then, a number of well-meaning Christians have sought to persuade me that God's truth can be found only in the Bible. If this were true, I cannot imagine that one who sought as ardently as I did could have been turned away at the very threshold by what he read in the Good Book itself. It wasn't until I met my Guru, and learned from *him* the deep meanings in the teachings of the Bible, that I was able to return to it with a sense of real appreciation. For the time being, I'm afraid I simply bogged down in the "begats."

In Mother's library I found another book that captured my interest. This one, called, *A Short World Bible*, contained brief excerpts from the major religions of the world. Perhaps here I would find the guidance I was seeking.

The selections from the Bible in this book proved more meaningful to me. Even so, though, they seemed too anthropomorphic for my tastes, steeped as I was in a more modern, scientific view of reality. The Judaic, the Muslim, the Taoist, the Buddhist, the Zoroastrian: I found poetic beauty and inspiration in all of these sacred works, but for me, still, something was lacking. I was being asked to believe, but so far, and as nearly as I could tell, none of these scriptures was

---

* Later, when I read my Guru's explanation of the story of Adam and Eve, I found its inner meaning profound, and deeply inspiring.

asking me to *experience*. Without actual experience of God, what was the good of mere beliefs? The farther I read, the more all of these scriptures impressed me as—well, great, no doubt, but at last hopelessly beyond me. Perhaps it was simply a question of style. The standard language of scripture, I reflected, was cryptic to the point of incomprehensibility.

At last, then, I came upon excerpts from the Hindu teachings— a few pages only, but what a revelation! Here the emphasis was on cosmic realities. God was described as an Infinite Consciousness; man, as a manifestation of that consciousness. Why, this was the very concept I myself had worked out during my long evening walk in Charleston! Man's highest duty, I read, is to attune himself with the divine consciousness: Again, this was what I, too, had worked out! Man's ultimate goal is—I found the thought echoed back to me— to experience that divine reality *as his true Self*. But, how scientific! What infinite promise!

Poetic symbolism abounded here, too, as in the other scriptures. Here, however, I found also explanations, presented with crystal clarity and logic. Best of all, I found the counsel I had been seeking: not only on how to live a religious life generally, but, more specifi- cally, on *how to seek God*.

I was astounded! This was exactly what I'd been seeking! I felt like a poor man who has just been given great riches. Hastily I skimmed through these few excerpts from the book; then, realizing the awesome importance this all held for me, I put the book aside, and resolved to wait for a later time when I would be free to read these selections slowly, digesting them. Casually I asked Mother if I might take the book upstate with me for the summer. "Of course," she replied, never suspecting the depth of my interest.

My Aunt Alleen, Mother's half-sister, visited us in White Plains during my stay there. Sensing the turmoil seething within me, she remarked to Mother one day, "I bet Don ends up in a theological seminary."

"Oh, not *Don!*" Mother's tone implied the thought, "Almost anyone else." The change in my life, when it came, caught her com- pletely by surprise.

Two or three times during my stay in White Plains I took the train into New York City. There I contemplated the rushing throngs of tense, worried faces. How many human tragedies were written there in lines of desperation, of bitterness, of hidden grief! More keenly than ever I felt with them our common bond of humanity. The worst criminal, I reflected, lived a life that might have been mine, had my mistakes taken me in his direction. Who, indeed, was safe from ignorance? Doubtless the very worst drug addict felt a certain justification in attitudes that had drawn him, like a fly, into his spider's web of confusion. What, then, of my own attitudes? Did I dare to trust them? How could anyone, at any given hour in his life, know *for a certainty* whether his best-intentioned behavior would advance him toward freedom, or, instead, enmesh him more helplessly in bondage? My growing conviction that everything is a part of one Reality, though it gave me a deep sense of kinship with others, awakened in me also a terrifying sense of my own vulnerability. I was drifting on a sea of ignorance, where my potential to sink or to rise was equally great.

It was high time, surely, that I took myself in hand. Too long had I been drifting haphazardly on heaving seas of uncertainty, hoping vaguely that my general direction would be toward the shores of truth, but with no certainty of anything. Now I must begin to direct my life more deliberately.

One afternoon I was walking down Fifth Avenue. The heat was oppressive. A bar, cool and inviting, stood before me on a street corner. I stepped in and had a couple of refreshing beers. Though by no means intoxicated, I realized that my reflexes were a little less keen than they had been on entering. I'd never considered drinking to be a personal problem, nor had I seen anything wrong with it in moderation. It occurred to me now, however, that if anything could lessen my self-control, even to this slight degree, I would be wise to avoid it. On leaving that barroom I resolved never again to take another drink. Nor have I ever done so.

My trip to upstate New York had been intended originally to help me find peace effortlessly amid the beauties of Nature. By the time I left White Plains, however, my resolution to work on myself, encouraged by the brief excerpts I had read from the Indian scriptures, had stiffened markedly. Having given up drinking—and also, two or three months earlier, smoking—I was beginning to feel keenly enthusiastic for self-discipline.

My thought now, however, was to find what I was seeking in some more "balanced" way than by seeking God. I still hoped that more natural surroundings would contribute something to my peace of mind, but I had no illusions that all my answers would be found in a random assortment of hills and trees. God saw to it, as I shall soon explain, that I found *none* of my answers there.

As a start toward transformation, I decided on vigorous physical discipline. My initial enthusiasm, of course, made me overdo it.

I set out from White Plains on a one-speed bicycle, taking with me a knapsack that held only Mother's book of scriptural excerpts, a few clothes, and a poncho. I had no sleeping bag; absurd as it may seem, I knew nothing of camping procedures, and wasn't even aware that sleeping bags existed.

My first night I spent in an open field, the poncho spread out under me as protection against the damp earth. At three in the morning I awoke, freezing cold, to find myself sloshing about in a puddle of water collected by my poncho from the heavy dew. Further sleep was impossible. Finally, I got up resignedly and set out on my bicycle again. Mile followed weary mile through deserted mountain terrain, scarcely a village in sight anywhere. Toward afternoon the seat of my bicycle had become so hard that, though I tried to soften it with a folded towel, I could hardly bear to sit on it. After ten or twelve hours of ceaseless pedaling, my legs, unaccustomed to this strenuous effort, felt with every upgrade that they must soon give out altogether.

Towards late afternoon I began to watch hopefully for signs of a village with an inn, for on one point I was resolved: I would not, if I could possibly help it, sleep in another field. Alas, I came upon not a house. Sixteen hours I pedaled that day, mostly uphill, on my one-speed bicycle, covering well over a hundred miles.

The sun was low in the west when I met a hiker who informed me that there was a village two miles or so off the road I was on, and that the village had a guest house. With very nearly my last ounce of strength I pedaled there. In the center of the village I found a house, in the front yard of which stood the reassuring sign, "Rooms for Rent." Literally staggering indoors, I collapsed into a chair by the front door.

"May I please have a room?"

"Oh, I'm *so* sorry. We've been meaning to take that sign down. We no longer rent rooms."

I was seized by despair. "Is there no place nearby where I can spend the night?"

"Well, there's an inn down the road about a mile. I'm sure they'd have a room for you."

A whole mile! Even that short distance seemed beyond my powers, in this state of exhaustion; I hardly had strength enough left to stand. "Please, do you think you might phone and ask them to come fetch me in their car?"

A ride was arranged. Lying in bed that night I actually thought I might die. I didn't realize it at the time, but since early childhood I'd had a minor heart condition. That entire night my heart pounded on the walls of my chest as if trying to break them. I slept around the clock. Mercifully, by mid-morning my heartbeat had returned to normal. Feeling refreshed, though sore in every muscle, I was eager to continue my journey.

An important passage in the Bhagavad Gita, which unfortunately I had not yet read, counsels moderation in all things.* I had discovered the merits of this precept quite on my own! From now on, I decided, I'd better proceed on the pathway to perfection at

---

* But for earthly needs
Religion is not his who too much fasts
Or too much feasts, nor his who sleeps away
An idle mind; nor his who wears to waste
His strength in vigils. Nay, Arjuna! call
That the true piety which most removes
Earth-aches and ills, where one is moderate
In eating and in resting, and in sport;
Measured in wish and act; sleeping betimes,
Waking betimes for duty.
     —Bhagavad Gita in Sir Edwin Arnold's poetic translation, *The Song Celestial*

a more measured pace. I must, so to speak, tighten the screw carefully, lest it split the wood.

And so I proceeded, this time more slowly, to the small mountain town of Indian Lake, where I rented a room and settled down eagerly to my reward: a careful study of the excerpts I possessed from the Indian scriptures.

CHAPTER 14

Joy Is Inside!

"Perfect bliss
Grows only in the bosom tranquillised,
The spirit passionless, purged from offense,
Vowed to the Infinite. He who thus vows
His soul to the Supreme Soul, quitting sin,
Passes unhindered to the endless bliss
Of unity with Brahma."

READING THESE WORDS from the Bhagavad Gita (as translated by Sir Edwin Arnold), my imagination was deeply stirred. The task I faced, I was now learning from the excerpts before me, was to calm my thoughts and feelings, thereby making myself an open and empty receptacle to be filled by God's grace. If I did offer myself thus, so these teachings averred, God would enter my life and fill it with "endless bliss."

How different, these simple precepts, from the meandering theology I had heard proclaimed from pulpits on Sunday mornings! Here I found no beggarly self-abasement—the weak man's masquerade of humility; no talk of the importance of seeking a religious institution as a doorway to heaven; no effort, by the diplomatic address of formal prayer, to hold God at a distance; no hint at compromising one's spiritual commitment by concern over its social acceptability. What I read here was fresh, honest, and convincing. It gave me extraordinary hope.

One thing that had disturbed me about all the churches I had visited was their sectarianism. "Ours is the one, the only true way" was a dogma implied even when it wasn't stated. Invariably suggested also was that all other ways were false, that even if other groups loved the same God, *their* message in some indiscernible manner was inadequate, and perhaps even "of the devil."

How different were the teachings I read now! All paths, they assured me, lead to the same, infinite goal. "As a mother," one stated, "in nursing her sick children, gives rice and curry to one, sago and arrowroot to another, and bread and butter to a third, so the Lord has laid out different paths for different men, suitable to their natures."

How beautiful! How persuasive in its utter fairness!

Another point that had always troubled me about the usual minister of religion was his tendency to discourage questioning. "Have faith," he would tell me. But what sort of "faith" is it that refuses to submit itself to honest questioning? Could the motive behind such refusals be anything but what it seems on the surface: a lack of clarity in one's own convictions? The motive might be fear, even, lest one's entire belief system turn out to be like a house built on sand. Even in their efforts to be reasonable, these men seemed to be wearing blinders. They quoted scripture in support of their beliefs, but never admitted the possibility that their very quotations might contain other and deeper meanings than those they ascribed to them.

Jesus often scolded even his closest disciples for mistaking his true meanings. Is it wise and humble for us, then, who live so distant from him in time, to insist that *we* understand him perfectly? Scriptures are written to expand our understanding, not to suppress and suffocate it.

But then, as my Guru was later to point out to me, one difference between scriptural writings and a living teacher is that the mere pages of a book cannot point out the seeker's misunderstandings, whereas a man of living wisdom can do so, sharply or softly as the occasion demands.

The Indian teachings, unlike any minister of the Gospel I had ever met, stressed the need for testing every scriptural claim. Direct, personal experience of the truth, not dogmatic or uncritical belief in it, was the "litmus paper" they proposed. They also suggested intermediate tests by which the veriest beginner could know whether he was headed in the right direction, or slipping off onto one of the innumerable detours from the path.

One such test was to see whether one is finding greater, unfluctuating happiness in himself. Another: whether life itself now seemed more consistently beautiful. For, as Yogananda was later to teach me, meditation enlivens all the senses.

Another test lay in other people's reactions to oneself. For a person might think he was developing non-attachment to outwardness, when in fact he was only growing dull-minded. If others find increasing inspiration in association with him, he might take their reaction as an outward confirmation of his inward progress.

I had already realized from personal experience that the differences between right and wrong decisions can be subtle. I was impressed, therefore, with teachings that could be verified not only after death, but here on earth, in this lifetime.*

These were the teachings for which I had been longing. Yes, I vowed again, I would dedicate my life to the search for God! Too long had I delayed, too long vacillated with doubt, too long sought earthly, not spiritual, solutions to life's deepest problems. Art? Science? Social systems? What could any of these accomplish significantly, or for very long? Without inner transformation, outer improvements in the human lot were like attempts to reinforce a termite-ridden building with a fresh coat of paint.

One parable in the reading I was doing affected me especially. It was from the sayings of a great saint of the nineteenth century, Sri Ramakrishna. Not knowing who he was, I assumed the saying was taken from some ancient text.

"How," Sri Ramakrishna asked, "does a man come to have dispassion? A wife once said to her husband, 'Dear, I am very anxious about my brother. For the past one week he has been thinking of becoming an ascetic, and is making preparations for it. He is trying to reduce gradually all his desires and needs.' The husband replied, 'Dear, be not at all anxious about your brother. He will never become

---

* The Bible, too, stresses verification by actual experience. "Test the spirits," wrote St. John in his first epistle. Religionists who emphasize blind belief until death generally haven't themselves tasted the fruits of the religious life, having never practiced it.

a *sannyasin* [renunciate]. No one can become a *sannyasin* in that way.'
'How does one become a *sannyasin*, then?' asked the wife. 'It is done
in this way!' the husband exclaimed. So saying, he tore into pieces
his flowing garment, took a piece out of it, tied it round his loins,
and told his wife that she and all others of her sex were thenceforth
mothers to him. He left the house and never more returned."*

The courage of this man's renunciation stirred me to my depths.
By contrast, how I myself had been vacillating in my doubts!

These excerpts were all saying essentially the same thing: Perfection
can be found only within the self, not in the outer world. Of the
truth of this teaching God evidently had it in mind to supply me with
abundant proof that summer.

Indian Lake is a beautiful place of pine trees and cool forest glades,
of rolling hills and gently rippling water. "If I'm to relate more deeply to higher realities," I thought, "I could begin in no better place
than right here." Indeed, the very scenery invited communion.

I tried consciously to *feel* the thrill of a raindrop quivering on
a pine needle; the exquisite freshness of the morning dew; a burst of
sunlight through the clouds at sunset. Always I had loved Nature,
and had felt deeply drawn to her beauty in woods, lakes, flowers, and
starry skies. But now, as I endeavored to intensify my sensitivity by
entering directly into the life of Nature all around me, I discovered
with a pang what an utter prisoner I was, locked in my little ego.
I could see; I could not *feel*. Or, to the extent that I *could* feel, I could
do so with only a small part of me, not with my whole being. I was
like an eight-cylinder motor hitting on only one cylinder. Surely if
even here, in these perfect surroundings, I could not rise out of myself and attune myself to greater realities, no mere *place* would ever
accomplish such a transformation for me. Obviously it was I, myself,
who needed changing. Whether my outer environment was beauti-

---

* This story must be understood in its cultural context. Marital fidelity is highly regarded in India. The Hindu scriptures state, however, that what is otherwise
a duty ceases to be such when it conflicts with a higher duty. Man's highest duty is
to seek God. It is understood in India that one's spouse can and should be supportive in one's search. Only if the desire for God is intense, and one's spouse poses an
obstacle to that search by his or her worldliness, is it permissible to break the marital
bond without mutual consent.

ful or ugly was not particularly significant. What mattered was what I made of my own inner "environment": my thoughts, feelings, attitudes, and reactions.

I was now spending some time every day in a brave attempt at meditation. I didn't know how to go about it, but I believed that, if I could only calm my mind a little bit, I would at least be heading in the right direction. I prayed daily, too: something I had never had faith enough to do, previously.

For my outer life God was saying to me, I suspect with a friendly chuckle, "You expected to find better human beings in the country? Take a good look around you! Man is not better for *where* he lives. Dreams of outer perfection are a delusion. Happiness must be sought inside; otherwise, it will remain elusive!"

My first plan for a job at Indian Lake had been to work as a lumberjack. I asked my landlady what she thought of my chances of finding such employment.

"What!" she cried. "And get knifed in a drunken brawl? Those men aren't your type at all."

Well, I had to admit her description left something to be desired. But I wasn't to be put off so easily. For two days I trudged about in the woods, looking for a logging camp that was said to be in the vicinity. Perhaps it was God's will that I missed it. At any rate, all I encountered were swarms of deer flies. On the third day, covered with stings, I found myself more receptive to my landlady's warnings. I decided I would seek elsewhere for employment.

That morning a local farmer agreed to hire me as a handyman. I'd had a little experience with farm work after my graduation from high school, and had enjoyed it then. Never before, however, had I worked for anyone like this.

My intention had been to work quietly, thinking of God. My employer, however, had other, and to him infinitely better, ideas: He wanted me to play the fool in his little court. "What else is a handyman for?" he demanded of me rhetorically when I remonstrated at being made the constant butt of his rustic jokes. Humor I didn't mind, but I drew the line at *witless* humor. There are few things so exasperating as meeting a gibe with a clever thrust, only to have it soar yards above the other fellow's head. When, after a few clever (but ignored) sallies on my part, I lapsed resignedly into silence, the farmer persisted, "C'mon, flannelmouth! I hired you to *work*. Don't stand there jabbering all day." And that, as I recall, was the high point in his comedy routine. My image of the genuine, innocent, *good* rustic was growing grey around the edges.

I soon left this worthy's employ. Putting peaceful Indian Lake resolutely behind me, I set off down the road on my bicycle in search of other work. Hours later I came to a mine owned by the Union Carbide Corporation. There the hiring clerk looked at me dubiously.

"We have work, all right," she said, "but it isn't your kind of work."

"What do you mean, not my kind of work? I can do anything!"

"Well, you won't like this job. You'll see. You won't last a week." With that encouragement I was hired.

The atmosphere of the sintering plant, where I was put to work, was so thick with the dust of the ore they were mining that one couldn't even see across the room. At the end of every day my face and hands were completely black. Some idea was beginning to form in my mind of what that woman had meant.

But it wasn't the work itself that finally got me. It was another of those simple, genuine, innocent, *good* rustics—a complete fool who, finding me too polite to tell him, as everyone else did, to go to hell, mistook me for an even greater fool than he. All day, every day, he regaled me with lies about his heroic feats before, during, and after World War II. Then, taking my silence for credulity, he began to preen himself on his own superiority. Finally he informed me disdainfully that I was too stupid to be worthy to associate with one of his own incomparable brilliance.

The hiring clerk didn't even trouble to remind me of her prediction when, after a week, I appeared for my severance pay.

How, I wondered, would I ever become a hermit? I'd need money for food. Probably I'd have to find employment from time to time simply to stay alive. But if these were samples of the kind of work I'd find out in the country, I wasn't so sure that my spiritual losses wouldn't outweigh the gains. Perhaps, I thought, if I could find some place where the money I earned could be stretched farther. . . .

That was it! I would go to some part of the world where the cost of living was low: yes, South America beckoned as offering such places. I would work first in this country, and save up. It wouldn't cost much, surely, to get to South America; perhaps I could even work my way down there on a ship. And there I'd be able to live on my savings for months, perhaps years, meditating in some secluded spot in a jungle or on a mountaintop. My problem, now, was how to earn as much money as possible, as quickly as possible.

One of my co-workers at the mine had entertained me after work with tales of the huge earnings he'd accumulated one summer in tips as a bellhop at a resort hotel. The thought of milking people of their money by doing them favors was odious to me, but perhaps, I thought, if I kept my goal firmly in mind, I would find it possible to suppress that distaste.

My next stop was the resort town of Lake George. Stopping at a hotel, I approached the owner and asked if he needed a bellhop.

"Got one already." He replied, then eyed me speculatively. "Where you from?"

"Scarsdale."

"Scarsdale, eh?" His eyes flickered with interest. "Wouldn't hurt to have someone from Scarsdale working here." He paused a moment. "Okay, you're on."

Well, by no stretch of the imagination could *this* worthy be called a rustic! He was first, last, and forever a devotee of turning little fortunes into big ones. His guests received as little as possible in return for everything he could squeeze out of them. The janitor and cleaning woman were first cousins of his, emigrants from Europe, but he treated them like serfs. When I saw him for what he was, it shamed me to be working for him. And it shamed me almost more to accept tips from the guests, whom it was my pleasure to serve. When one couple tried to tip me a second time for fetching something else from their car, I simply refused to accept their offer.

I found a copy of Tolstoy's *War and Peace*, from which I emerged with slow dignity when the hotel owner cried, "Front, boy!" (He never tried that one again.)

Hardly a week passed before I was off down the road again. It was time in any case for me to return to White Plains and help Mother prepare for her long ocean voyage to Egypt.

My trip south held for me a measure of hope, also. A co-worker at the mine had suggested that I might get a job in the merchant marine, where the veriest beginner earned as much as $300 a month. In those days, this was good pay. Better still, since I would be sailing the high seas on free board and lodging, I'd be able to save quite a lot of money quickly. I decided to try my luck "before the mast."

That summer had proved, so far, a mixed bag: uplifting in the truths I'd learned, but, materially speaking, a fiasco. More and more I was beginning to wonder if I hadn't somehow landed on the wrong planet. None of my experiences over these past months had helped me to feel that this world was my home.

Yet my desire to "drop out" seemed, from every practical standpoint, wildly unrealistic. I could not but admit to myself that my plans for becoming a hermit rested on the shakiest possible ground. I knew nothing of the practical skills I'd need to live alone in the wilderness. I had no idea how much money I'd actually need, to remain a long time in South America. Worst of all, I knew so little of the spiritual path that I had no idea how to walk it alone. I didn't know how to meditate. I didn't know how to pray. I didn't know what to think about when I wasn't meditating or praying. It was becoming clear to me that, without proper guidance, I was as good as lost.

Yet I knew of no one to whom I could go for guidance out of the swamp of institutional religion into the clean air of universal truths. The path I was contemplating seemed, from every practical viewpoint, utter folly. I was contemplating it, however, because I had ruled out every conceivable alternative.

The thought of living a so-called "normal," worldly life filled me with dread, the more so because I was so alone in my rejection of it. Most of my friends were getting married and settling down to good jobs. The pressure on me from all sides to do likewise was, in a sense, unceasing. To my mind, however, even a lifetime of starvation and suffering would be worth it, if only by so living I could find God.

And what did I hope to gain from finding Him? There, my notions remained vague, though certainly I would have considered even peace of mind an incomparable blessing. What mattered to me most, however, was that to know Him would be to know Truth, and that not to know Him meant wallowing in falsehood and delusion. Wherever my path led, I knew that I had only one valid choice: to offer my life to Him. It would be up to Him, thereafter, to lead me where He willed.

CHAPTER 15

A Map Discovered

Aₛ soon as possible after my return to White Plains I went to
Bowling Green, in New York City, to apply for a merchant
mariner's card. I received the card on August 24 with the classifica-
tion, "Ordinary seaman, messman, wiper." I was told it was now
only a question of waiting for a ship that would give me a berth.
I hoped to ship out as soon as possible.

Meanwhile I helped Mother to pack. On her sailing date, I accompanied her to the dock in New York and saw her safely off on
her journey. Next I went down to Bowling Green to see if any ship
had come in. No luck: "Come back in a few days." With most of the
afternoon still before me, I went uptown to browse at Brentano's,
a famous bookstore on Fifth Avenue.

At Brentano's I got into a discussion on spiritual matters with
a sales clerk, who showed me a few books by Thomas Merton,
the young Protestant Christian who had converted to Roman
Catholicism and had then become a Trappist monk. I was intrigued,
though I didn't feel personally attracted. It was the catholicity—
which is to say, the *universality*—of India's teachings that had won
my devotion.

From Brentano's I went further up Fifth Avenue to another bookstore: Doubleday-Doran (as it was named then). Here, I found
an entire section of books on Indian philosophy—the first I had
ever encountered. Hungrily I feasted my gaze on the wide variety
of titles: The *Upanishads*, the Bhagavad Gita, the *Ramayana*, the
Mahabharata, books on yoga. I finished scanning these shelves, then
stood up to go over them again. This time, to my surprise, the first

book I saw, standing face outward on the shelf, was one I hadn't noticed at first. The author's photograph on the cover affected me strangely. Never had I seen any face radiate back to me so much goodness, humility, and love.

Eagerly I picked up the book and glanced again at its title: *Autobiography of a Yogi*, by Paramhansa Yogananda. The author, I saw, lived in America—in California! Was this someone at last who could *help* me in my search? As I leafed through the first pages of the book, the first words to catch my attention were: "Dedicated to the memory of Luther Burbank, an American saint."

An American *saint*? But, how preposterous! How could anyone become a saint in this land of the "almighty dollar"? this materialistic desert? this. . . . I closed the book in dismay, and returned it to its place on the shelf.

That day I bought my first book of Indian philosophy—not *Autobiography of a Yogi*, but Sir Edwin Arnold's beautiful translation of the Bhagavad Gita. Eagerly I took this treasure home with me to Scarsdale, where I had temporarily rented a private room. For the next couple of days I fairly devoured what I read, feeling myself to be soaring through vast skies of wisdom.

> By this sign is [the sage] known
> Being of equal grace to comrades, friends,
> Chance-comers, strangers, lovers, enemies,
> Aliens and kinsmen; loving all alike,
> Evil or good.

What wonderful words! Thrilled, I read on:

> Yea, knowing Me the source of all, by Me all creatures wrought,
> The wise in spirit cleave to Me, into My being brought. . . .
> And unto these—thus serving well, thus loving ceaselessly—
> I give a mind of perfect mood, whereby they draw to Me;
> And, all for love of them, within their darkened souls I dwell,
> And, with bright rays of wisdom's lamp, their ignorance dispell.

These marvelous teachings were dispelling all my doubts. I knew now, with complete certainty, that this was the right path for me.

The day after I finished my first reading of the Bhagavad Gita, I returned to New York, intending to visit Bowling Green and see if

Luther Burbank and Paramhansa Yogananda, at the
garden in Santa Rosa, CA.

any ship had come in. I was walking down Seventh Avenue toward
the subway, the entrance to which was on the far side of the next
cross street, when I recalled the book I'd rejected so summarily on
my last visit to the city: *Autobiography of a Yogi*. As I remembered
that beautiful face on the cover, I felt a strong inner prompting to go
buy it. I thrust the thought firmly out of my mind.

"That isn't what I'm looking for," I told myself. Chuckling,
I added, "An American saint, indeed!" Resolutely I continued to
walk toward the subway.

The thought returned: "How can you know what the book is
really like, if you won't even read it?"

"No!" I repeated. I then offered reasons: "I've got to stop read-ing books; I'm too intellectual as it is. Besides, if I'm ever to become a hermit, I'm going to have to *save* money, not continue to spend it!"

I reached the corner, and was proceeding toward the curb ahead of me, when I felt that an actual force was turning me left, toward Fifth Avenue. I'd never experienced anything like this before. Amazed, I asked myself, "Is there something in this book that I'm *meant* to read?" Unresisting now, I hastened forward, eager to reach Doubleday-Doran.

On entering the store, I made straight for the shelves of Indian books and bought *Autobiography of a Yogi*. As I turned to leave, I bumped into Doug Burch, that friend from Scarsdale High School who had introduced me to Nick's and to Dixieland jazz. We ex-changed news briefly. Doug began to describe in glowing terms his plans for a career in radio and advertising. The more he talked, the more closely I hugged to my heart this increasingly precious acquisition.

Imperceptibly, my doubts about it had vanished. I felt as though Yogananda shared my dismay at the shining prospects Doug was describing—a way of life that, to me, spelled desolation. My new book in hand, I felt suddenly as though this Indian yogi and I were old friends. The world and I were strangers, but here was one human being—the very first!—who knew and understood me. And I hadn't yet even met him, physically!

The reprint of the original unaltered 1946 first edition of the *Autobiography of a Yogi*, published by Crystal Clarity Publishers, Nevada City, California.

I waited until I'd reached my room in Scarsdale before opening the book. And then began the most thrilling literary adventure of my life.

Autobiography of a Yogi is the story of a young Bengali Indian's intense search for God. It describes a number of living saints he met on his journey, especially his own great guru, Swami Sri Yukteswar. It also describes, more clearly than any other mystical work I have ever read since, the author's experiences with God, including the highest one possible, *samadhi*: mystical union. In chapter after chapter I found moving testimony to God's *living* reality, not only in infinity, but in the hearts and lives of living human beings. I read of how Yogananda's prayers, even for little things, had been answered, and of how, by placing himself unreservedly in God's hands, his unanticipated needs had been met unfailingly. I read of intense love for

God such as I myself yearned to possess; of a relationship with Him more intimate, more dear than I had dared to imagine possible.

Until now, I had supposed that a life of meditation might give me, at best, a little peace of mind. But here I discovered, all at once, that the fruit of the spiritual life is a love and bliss "beyond imagination of expectancy"!

Until recently I had doubted the value of prayer, except perhaps as a means of uplifting *oneself*. But now I learned, and could not for a moment doubt, that God relates individually, *lovingly*, to each and every seeker.

Miracles abound in this book. Many of them, I confess, were quite beyond my powers of acceptance at the time. Instead of dismissing them, however, as I would certainly have done had I read about them in almost any other book, I suspended my incredulity. For the spirit of this story was so deeply honest, so transparently innocent of pride or impure motive that it was impossible for me to doubt that its author believed implicitly every word he wrote. Never before had I encountered a spirit so clearly truthful, so filled with goodness and joy. Every page seemed radiant with light. As I read *Autobiography of a Yogi*, I alternated between tears and laughter: tears of pure joy; laughter of even greater joy! For three days I scarcely ate or slept. When I walked it was almost atiptoe, as if in an ecstatic dream.

What this book described, finally, was the highest of sciences, Kriya Yoga, a technique that enables the seeker to advance rapidly on the path of meditation. I, who wanted so desperately to learn how to meditate, felt all the excitement of one who has found a treasure map, the treasure in this case being a divine one, buried deep within my own being!

Autobiography of a Yogi remains the greatest book I have ever read. One perusal of it was enough to change my whole life. From that time on, my break with the past was complete. I resolved in the smallest detail to follow Paramhansa Yogananda's teaching.

Finding that he recommended a vegetarian diet, I immediately renounced meat, fish, and fowl. He could have recommended a diet of bread and water, and I'd have adopted that diet without a qualm.

For, more than anything else, what this book gave me was the conviction that in Yogananda I had found my guru, my spiritual teacher for all time to come. Only a few days earlier I hadn't even known this strange word, *guru*. I hadn't known anything about yoga, or reincarnation, or karma, or almost any of the basic precepts and terminology of Indian philosophy. Now, incredibly, I felt such deep and utter trust in another human being that, ignorant of his philosophy though I was, I was willing to follow him to the end of life. And while I had yet to meet him, I felt, as I had on seeing his face on the cover of the book, that he was the truest friend I had ever known.

The day after becoming a vegetarian I was invited by friends of my family, Mr. and Mrs. Lloyd Gibson, to lunch at their home. To my combined amusement and dismay, the main dish consisted of chicken à la king. Not wanting to hurt my friends' feelings, I compromised by pushing the chicken bits to one side and eating the vegetables in their chicken sauce.

George Calvert, on whose father's farm Bob and I had worked after my graduation from high school, had invited me the following day to lunch at his parents' home, and to a polo game afterwards. This time I had no choice but to refuse the thick, juicy hamburger sandwich that his mother offered me. To make matters still more awkward, George had considerately provided me with a date! I must have seemed strange company indeed, eating hardly anything, and paying as little attention to the girl as politely possible, from the opposite end of the room. (Yogananda was a monk: I, too, would be a monk.) The polo game gave me an opportunity for a little surreptitious meditation, so I didn't view the game as a total loss.

Later that day I met my brother Bob and Dean Bassett, a friend of ours, at Nielson's, an ice cream parlor in Scarsdale village. Dean had been voted the "biggest wolf" in my senior high school class. He and Bob were discussing Dean's favorite subject: girls.

I listened in silence for a time. At last I protested, "Don't you see? Desire only enslaves one to the very things he desires!"

Bob and Dean gazed at each other quizzically. "What's wrong with him?" Dean asked.

It was years before I realized that comprehension, like a flower, must unfold at its own pace. Until a person is ready to embrace a truth, even the clearest logic will not make it acceptable to him.

As soon as I finished reading *Autobiography of a Yogi*, my impulse was to jump onto the next California-bound bus. But I didn't want to be impulsive, so I waited a whole day! I even debated for several hours whether it might not be wiser for me to go to sea, as I'd first planned, and there meditate a few months before making such an important decision. But of course I knew already that it *was* the right decision. The following day I packed my bag and took an early train into New York City.

My godfather, Dr. Winthrop Haynes, had been sympathetically concerned for my future. He and his wife were like second parents to me; I didn't feel I could leave New York without bidding him farewell. On my way to the bus station, therefore, I stopped by his office at Rockefeller Center. Finding him out of his office, I left a note on his desk with the message, "I'm going to California to join a group of people who, I believe, can teach me what I want to know about God and about religion." This was the first intimation I had given anyone that God was my true goal in life.

I took the next available westbound bus. Thereafter, for four days and four nights, my home was a succession of long-distance buses.

My break with the past was so sudden, so complete that I sometimes ask myself whether some very special grace had not been needed to make it possible. I wonder what I'd have done, for example, if Mother had still been in America. Would I have had the courage to take such a drastic step? Who knows? She would almost surely have opposed my directions, unprecedented as they were. After all, what did I know of the Indian teachings? Nothing! And here I was, planning to devote my entire life to them.

Had Mother been there, would she have succeeded in deflecting me from my purpose? The question has become academic, but even so, wasn't it remarkable that it was the very day I put Mother on her ship to Cairo that I discovered the book that was to change my life?

Strange indeed are God's ways! I was to see much of them in the years that followed. Never have they ceased to make me marvel.

CHAPTER 16

The Pilgrim Meets His Guide

I ARRIVED IN LOS Angeles on the morning of Saturday, September 11, 1948, exhausted from my long journey. There I took advantage of the first opportunity I'd had in four days to shave and shower. I then continued south by bus, one hundred miles to Encinitas, the little coastal town where, as I'd read, Yogananda had his hermitage. In the fervor of first reading, it had somehow escaped my notice that he'd founded an organization. Perhaps I had subconsciously "tuned out" this information, because of my long-standing resistance to religious institutionalism. In my mind, his little seaside hermitage was all that existed of his work. It was to him I was coming, not to his organization.

I arrived in Encinitas late that afternoon, too tired to proceed at once to the hermitage. I booked into a hotel and fairly collapsed onto my bed, sleeping around the clock. The next morning I set out for the Self-Realization Fellowship hermitage, walking perhaps a mile through a neighborhood of picturesque gardens, colorful with ice plant and bougainvillea. Many of the flowers I saw here were new to me. Their vivid hues made a gay contrast to the more conservative flowers in the East—a contrast, I was to discover, that extends to numerous other aspects of life on the two coasts.

I approached the hermitage with bated breath. Yogananda, I recalled from his book, had once visited a saint without sending prior notice of his arrival. He had yet to reach the saint's village when the saint himself came out to welcome him. Did Yogananda, too, I asked myself, know I was coming? And would he, too, come out and greet me?

To the second question, anyway, the answer I received was: No such luck. I entered the grounds through an attractive gate. On either side of me were large, beautifully kept gardens—trees on the left, beyond a small house; on the right, a pleasant lawn. At the end of the driveway stood a lovely white stucco building with a red tile roof. I imagined disciples going quietly about their simple chores inside, faces shining with inner peace. (Did *they* know I was coming?)

I rang the front doorbell. Minutes later a gentle-looking, elderly lady appeared.

"May I help you?" she inquired politely.

"Is Paramhansa Yogananda in?"

My pronunciation of this unfamiliar name must have left something to be desired. Moreover, the white palm beach suit I wore didn't mark me as the normal visitor. I'd assumed, mistakenly, that palm beach was the accepted attire in Southern California, as it was in Miami and Havana. My unusual appearance, together with my obvious unfamiliarity with Yogananda's name, must have given the impression that I was a utility man of some sort.

"Oh, you've come to check the water?"

"No!" Gulping, I repeated, "Is Paramhansa Yogananda in?"

"Who? Oh, yes, oh, I see. No, I'm afraid he's away for the weekend. Is there something I can do for you?"

"Well, yes. No. I mean, I wanted to see *him*."

"He's lecturing today at the Hollywood church."

"You have a *church* there?" I let my astonishment show. I'd always imagined Hollywood as containing only movie studios. My astonishment must have struck my elderly hostess as unseemly. After all, why *shouldn't* they have a church in a big city like Hollywood? Soon it became clear to me that I wasn't making the best possible impression.

Well, I thought, perhaps it *did* seem a bit strange, my bursting in here and asking to speak to the head of whatever organization there was here, and—worse still—not even realizing that he had an organization. My companion drew herself up a little stiffly.

"I want to join his work," I explained. "I want to live here."

"Have you studied his printed lessons?" she inquired, a trifle coolly, I thought.

"Lessons?" I echoed blankly. "I didn't know he had lessons to be studied." My position was getting murkier by the minute.

"There's a full course of them. I'm afraid you couldn't join," she continued firmly, "until you'd completed the lot."

"How long does that take?" My heart was sinking.

"About four years."

Four years! Why, this was out of the question! As I look back now on that meeting, I think she was probably only trying to temper what must have seemed, to her, my absurd presumption in assuming I had merely to appear on the scene for me to be welcomed with joyous cries of, "You've arrived!" In fact, the requirements for acceptance were not so strict as she'd made out. It is usual, however, and also quite proper for the spiritual aspirant's sincerity to be carefully tested.

It looked less than proper to me at the time, however. Only later did I learn that this first person to greet me had been Sister Gyanamata,

Paramhansa Yogananda's most advanced woman disciple. She herself, as it happened, having been married, had had to wait years before she could enter the hermitage. The mere *prospect* of a wait must have seemed to her completely normal, and not very much of a test.

Well, I reflected rebelliously, this was not *Yogananda's* verdict. Swallowing my disappointment, I inquired how I might get to the Hollywood church. She gave me the address, and a telephone number. Soon I was on my way back to Los Angeles.

Sister Gyanamata,
Yogananda's foremost female disciple.

On the way there I alternated between bouts of indignation (at *her* presumption!) and desperate prayers to be accepted. This was the first time in my life I had wanted anything so desperately. I couldn't, I simply *mustn't* be refused.

At one point, thinking again of my elderly informant, my mind was once again waxing indignant when, suddenly, I remembered her eyes. They had been very calm—even, I reflected with some astonishment, wise. Certainly there was far more to her than I'd noticed in the urgency of my desire. "Forgive me for my misjudgment," I prayed, mentally. "It was in any case wrong of me to think unkindly of her. She was only doing her duty. I sense now, however, that she is a great soul. Forgive me."

A cloud seemed suddenly to lift within me. I knew in my heart that I'd been accepted.

Arrived in Los Angeles, I checked my bag at the bus depot and proceeded at once to 4860 Sunset Boulevard, the address of the church I was seeking. It was about three o'clock in the afternoon. The morning service had ended long since, and the building, apart from a small scattering of people, was empty. A lady greeted me from behind a long table at the back of the room.

"May I help you?"

I explained my mission.

"Oh, I'm afraid you couldn't possibly see him today. His time is completely filled."

I was growing more desperate by the minute. "When *can* I see him?"

She consulted a small book on the table before her. "His appointments are fully booked for the next two and a half months," she informed me.

Two and a half months! First I'd been told I couldn't join for four years. Now I was told I couldn't even *see* him for. . . .

"But I've come all the way from New York just for this!"

"Have you?" She smiled sympathetically. "How did you hear about him?"

"I read his autobiography a few days ago."

"So recently! And you came . . . just . . . like that?" She cooled a little. "Usually people write first. Didn't you write?"

Bleakly I confessed I hadn't even thought of doing so.

"Well, I'm sorry, but you can't see him for another two and a half months. In the meantime," she continued, brightening a little, "you can study his lessons, and attend the services here."

Morosely I wandered about the church, studying the furnishings, the architecture, the stained-glass windows. It was an attractive chapel, large enough to seat well over one hundred people, and invitingly peaceful. An excellent place, I thought, for quiet meditation. But my own mind was hardly quiet or meditative. It was in turmoil.

"You *must* take me!" I prayed. "You *must*! This means everything to me. It means my whole life!"

Two or three of the people sitting in the church were monks, whose residence was at the headquarters of Self-Realization Fellowship on Mt. Washington, in the Highland Park section of Los Angeles. I spoke to one of them. Norman his name was. Tall and well-built, his eyes were yet kind and gentle. He talked a little about their way of life at Mt. Washington, and their relation, as disciples, to Paramhansa Yogananda. "We call him 'Master,'" he told me. From *Autobiography of a Yogi* I already knew that this appellation, which Yogananda used also in reference to his own guru, denoted reverence, not menial subservience.

How deeply Norman's description of Mt. Washington attracted me! I simply *had* to become a part of this wonderful way of life. It was where I belonged. It was my home.

Norman pointed out two young men seated quietly, farther back in the church.

"They want to join the monastery, too," he remarked.

"How long have they been waiting?"

"Oh, not long. A few months."

Disconsolately I wandered about awhile longer. Finally it occurred to me—novel thought!—that perhaps I simply wasn't ready, and that this was why the doors weren't opening for me. If this were true, I decided, I'd just go out and live in the hills near Hollywood, come to the services regularly, study the lessons, and—I sighed—

wait. When I was ready, the Master would surely know it, and would summon me.

With this resolution in mind, and with no small disappointment in my heart, I made for the front door.

No doubt I'd needed this lesson in humility. Perhaps things had always gone too easily for me. Maybe I was too confident. At any rate, the moment I accepted the thought of my possibly not being ready spiritually, the situation changed dramatically. I had reached the door when the secretary—Mary Hammond, I later learned her name was—came up behind me.

"Since you've come such a long way," she said, "I'll just ask Master if he'd be willing to see you today."

She returned a few minutes later.

"Master will see you next."

Shortly thereafter I was ushered into a small sitting room. The Master was standing there, speaking to a disciple in a white robe. As the young man was about to leave, he knelt to touch the Master's feet. This was, as I'd learned from Yogananda's book, a traditional gesture of reverence among Indians; it is bestowed on parents and other elders as well as, and particularly, on one's guru. A moment later, the Master and I were alone.

What large, lustrous eyes now greeted me! What compassionate sweetness in his smile! Never before had I seen such divine beauty in a human face. The Master seated himself on a chair, and motioned me to a sofa beside him.

"What may I do for you?" For the third time that day these same, gentle words. But this time, how fraught with meaning!

"I want to be your disciple!" The reply welled up from my heart irresistibly. Never had I expected to utter such words to another human being.

The Master smiled gently. There ensued a long discussion, interspersed by long silences, during which he held his eyes half open, half closed—"reading" me, as I well knew.

Over and over again I prayed desperately in my heart, "You *must* take me! I know that you know my thoughts. I can't say it outwardly; I'd only burst into tears. But you must accept me. You *must*!"

Early in the conversation he told me, "I agreed to see you only because Divine Mother told me to. I want you to know that. It isn't because you've come such a distance. Two weeks ago a lady flew here all the way from Sweden after reading my book, but I wouldn't see her. I do only what God tells me to do." He reiterated, "Divine Mother told me to see you."

"Divine Mother," as I already knew from reading his book, was the way he often referred to God, who, he said, embraces both the male and the female principles.

There followed some discussion of my past. He appeared to be pleased with my replies, and with my truthfulness. "I knew that already," he once remarked, indicating that he was only testing me to see if I would answer him truthfully. Again a long silence, while I prayed ardently for acceptance.

"I am taking fewer people now," he said.

I gulped. Was this remark intended to prepare me for a letdown?

I told him I simply could see nothing for myself in marriage or a worldly life. "I'm sure it's fine for many people," I said, "but for myself I don't want it."

He shook his head. "It isn't so fine for *anybody* as people make out. God, for everyone, is the *only* answer. Anything less is a compromise." He went on to tell me a few stories of the disillusionments he had witnessed. Then again, silence.

At one point in our discussion he asked me how I had liked his book.

"Oh, it was wonderful!"

"That," he replied simply, "is because it has my vibrations in it."

Vibrations? I'd never before thought of books as having "vibrations." Clearly, however, I had found his book almost alive in its power to convey not merely ideas, but a new state of awareness.

Incongruously, even absurdly, it now occurred to me that he might be more willing to take me if he felt I could be of some practical use to his work. And what did I know? Only writing. But that, surely, was better than nothing. Perhaps he was in need of people with writing skills. To demonstrate this ability, I said:

"Sir, I found several split infinitives in your book." Twenty-two years old, literarily untried, but already a budding editor! I've never lived down this *faux pas*! But Master took it with a surprised, then a good-humored, smile. The motive for my remark was transparent to him.

More silence.

More prayers.

"All right," he said at last. "You have good karma. You may join us."

"Oh, but I can wait!" I blurted out, hoping he wasn't taking me only because I hadn't yet found any other place to live.

"No," he smiled. "You have good karma, otherwise I wouldn't accept you."

Gazing at me now with deep love, he said, "I give you my unconditional love."

Immortal promise! I couldn't begin to fathom the depth of meaning in those words.

"Will you give me your unconditional love?"

"Yes!"

"And will you also give me your unconditional obedience?"

Desperately though I desired acceptance, I had to be utterly honest. "Suppose, sometime," I asked, "I think you're wrong?"

"I will never ask anything of you," he solemnly replied, "that God does not tell me to ask."

He continued, "When I met my master, Sri Yukteswar, he said to me, 'Allow me to discipline you.' 'Why, Sir?' I inquired. 'Because,' he replied, 'in the beginning of the spiritual path one's will is guided by whims and fancies. Mine was, too,' Sri Yukteswar continued, 'until I met *my* guru, Lahiri Mahasaya. It was only by attuning my haphazard will to his wisdom-guided will that I found true freedom.' In the same way, if you attune your will to mine, you too will find freedom. To act only on the inspiration of whims and fancies is not freedom, but bondage. Only by doing God's will can you find what you are seeking."

"I see," I replied thoughtfully. Then from my heart I said, "I give you my unconditional obedience!"

My guru continued: "When I met my master, he gave me his unconditional love, as I have given you mine. He then asked me to love him the same way, unconditionally. But I replied, 'Sir, what if I should ever find you less than a Christlike master? Could I still love you the same way?' My master looked at me sternly. 'I don't want your love,' he said. 'It stinks!'"

"I understand, Sir," I assured him. He'd struck at the heart of my greatest weakness: intellectual doubt. With deep feeling I said to him, "I give you my unconditional love!"

He went on to give me various instructions.

"Now, then, come kneel before me."

I did so. He made me repeat, in the name of God, Jesus Christ, and the rest of our line of gurus the vows of discipleship and of renunciation. Next he placed the forefinger of his right hand on my chest over the heart. For at least two minutes his arm vibrated almost violently. Incredibly, from that moment on, my consciousness in some all-penetrating manner was transformed.

I left his interview room in a daze. Norman, on hearing that I'd been accepted, embraced me lovingly. It was unusual, to say the least, for anyone to be accepted so quickly. A few moments later, Master came out from behind the open curtain on the lecture platform. Smiling at us quietly, he said:

"We have a new brother."

PART II

CHAPTER 17

Mt. Washington Estates

Mt. Washington, in the Highland Park district of Los Angeles, rises above that vast city like a guardian angel. Located not far from downtown, the mountain yet stands remote behind its succession of foothills. At the mountaintop the sound of traffic in the busy streets below is hushed to a quiet hum. In this tranquil spot, the problems of mankind appear more susceptible of harmonious solution. Though *in* the world, the very place seems to be not wholly *of* the world.

It is atop Mt. Washington, at 3880 San Rafael Avenue, that the determined visitor, after braving the steep, winding access road, arrives at the international headquarters of Self-Realization Fellowship.

At the turn of the twentieth century, Mt. Washington Estates, as this property is also known, was a fashionable hotel. Wealthy people desirous of escaping the strain and bustle of city life went there to relax, or to attend gala social events. Tournaments were held on the tennis courts; banquets and colorful balls in the spacious lobby. Guests were brought up the steep mountainside to the hotel by cable car from Marmion Way, a thousand feet below, where connection was made with a railroad from downtown Los Angeles.

The "city of angels" was much smaller then: some 100,000 inhabitants. In time, the increasing popularity of the automobile, and the city's inexorable engulfment of its surrounding orchards and farmlands, induced Mt. Washington's fashionable clientele to seek their recreation farther afield. Mt. Washington Estates fell on hard times. The hotel closed its doors at last. Weeds began to grow out of widening cracks on the once famous tennis courts. The hotel, like an indigent but still-proud aristocrat, continued to survey the world with smug condescension from its twelve-acre domain. Its lofty mood, however, became increasingly difficult for it to sustain as, with the passing years, paint began peeling off the walls of the main building, the grounds lost their carefully tailored elegance, and on every side there appeared unmistakable signs of neglect. Alas, to such universal indifference are all brought who too pridefully oppose Time's all-leveling scythe. The busy world paid court to Mt. Washington no longer.

Mt. Washington Estates, headquarters of Self-Realization Fellowship.

Unlike most once-fashionable resorts, however, pathetic in their memories of a heyday forever vanished, Mt. Washington's erstwhile glory was but the prelude to a far more glorious role.

Around the turn of the century, at the time when Mt. Washington Estates had attained the height of their popularity as a resort, there was a young boy in India who, during periods of ecstatic meditation, caught glimpses of a mysterious mountaintop monastery in a distant land. The message conveyed by his enigmatic visions concerned the mission that, he knew, he was meant someday to fulfill.

Mukunda Lal Ghosh, age 6.

Mukunda Lal Ghosh, later known to the world as Paramhansa Yogananda, was the son of a senior executive in the Bengal-Nagpur Railway; as such, he faced the prospect of wealth and high worldly position upon growing up. But it was not this world that attracted him. From earliest childhood he had longed for God as intensely as others long for human love or for worldly recognition. Mukunda's favorite pastime was visiting saints.

"*Chhoto Mahasaya*" they often called him—"Little Sir," or, literally, "Little Great-Minded One." Treating him not as a child, but as their spiritual equal, many (as he was to tell me, with an amused smile, during his last years) posed him deep questions, or sought his advice on spiritual matters.

Clearly this was no ordinary child, though in his autobiography Yogananda presents himself so unassumingly that the reader, unfamiliar with the intense preparation required for high yogic attainments, might draw the conclusion that anyone similarly placed might have reached the young yogi's spiritual attainments.

Soon after graduation from high school, Mukunda met his guru,* the great Swami Sri Yukteswar of Serampore, Bengal. At the feet of this great master he attained, in the amazingly short period of six months, the high state of *samadhi*,† or unconditioned oneness with

---

* Spiritual teacher. The word *guru* is often applied, broadly, to any venerated teacher. On the spiritual path, however, it refers to the *sadguru* or *true* teacher—that enlightened sage who has been commissioned by God to lead the spiritually fit seeker out of darkness, and into the experience of Supreme Truth. While the seeker may have many lesser teachers, he can have only one such divinely appointed *guru*.

† See footnote, p. 240.

God. His guru kept him in the *ashram** another nine and a half years while training him for his mission: the dissemination of yoga in the West. "The West," Sri Yukteswar explained, "is high in material attainments, but lacking in spiritual understanding. It is God's will that you play a role in teaching mankind the value of balancing the material with an inner, spiritual life."

In 1917, Mukunda, now a monk with the name Swami Yogananda,† took the first outward step toward the fulfillment of his mission by founding a small school for boys in the village of Dihika, Bengal. In 1918 the Maharaja of Kasimbazar graciously gave him permission to transfer this fast-growing school to the Kasimbazar palace in Ranchi, Bihar, where the school flourished. An institution offering education in the divine art of living, along with the standard curriculum, made an instant appeal to parents and children alike. In the first year, enrollment applications reached two thousand—far more than the existing facilities could absorb. By the end of two years, the young yogi-headmaster's educational theories were already beginning to have a marked impact on other educators.

Dear as Yogananda's Ranchi school was to him, however, there was another, broader mission for which the Lord was even now

---

* A place of retirement from worldly life for the purpose of pursuing spiritual practices.

† *Swami*: literally, *lord*—that is to say, one who has achieved mastery of himself. *Swami* is the title commonly given to *sannyasis* (renunciates), in affirmation of the truth that he alone is a true ruler in this world who rules himself. Renunciates, for the same reason, are often called *Maharaj* (Great King).

Ananda (divine bliss) usually forms part of the *sannyasi*'s monastic name. Thus the name *Yogananda* means "Divine bliss through union (yoga) with God," or, also, "Divine bliss through the practice of yoga techniques for achieving union."

The custom of adding *ananda* to a *sannyasi*'s name derives from the time of Swami Shankara, known also as Swami Shankaracharya, ancient reorganizer of the renunciate order in India. Shankaracharya rescued India from the atheistic misconstruction that the Buddha's followers had come to place upon the sublime teachings of their founder. Shankaracharya explained that, while Truth (as taught by Lord Buddha, who consistently refused to speak of God) is indeed beyond human conception, it nevertheless exists and can be experienced.

The highest state of divine ecstasy is revealed as ineffable bliss—"beyond imagination of expectancy," as Yogananda described it. Swami Shankara's definition of God was *Satchidananda*—"existence, consciousness, bliss." Paramhansa Yogananda translated this definition as "ever-existing, ever-conscious, *ever-new* Bliss."

preparing him. In 1920 the youthful yogi was meditating one day when he had a vision: Thousands of Americans passed before him, gazing at him intently. It was, he knew, a divine message. The time had come for him to begin his life work in the West.

The very next day he received an invitation to speak as India's delegate to an International Congress of Religious Liberals, being held that year in Boston, Massachusetts, under the auspices of the American Unitarian Association. "All doors are open for you," Sri Yukteswar told him, when he applied to his guru for instruction. "Your words on yoga shall be heard in the West." Thus commanded, Yogananda accepted the invitation.

In America he found many people hungry for India's spiritual teachings, and for the liberating techniques of yoga. Accordingly, he stayed on in Boston, where for three years he taught and lectured. Gradually he accustomed himself to the American culture, and studied how he might reach past his listeners' preconceptions to their very hearts.

In 1923 he began a series of lectures and classes in major American cities. His success everywhere was extraordinary. Crowds flocked to him in unprecedented numbers, sometimes queuing up for blocks to get in. Unlike most other teachers from India, he never tried to impose his own country's cultural modes on Americans, but sought rather to show Americans how to spiritualize *their own* culture. Dynamically, and with contagious joy, he set out to persuade minds that were steeped in the virtues of "down-to-earth practicality" that the most practical course of all is to seek God.

His magnetism was irresistible. On January 25, 1927, in Washington, D.C., after a lecture attended by 5,000 people, the *Washington Post* reported, "The Swami has broken all records for sustained interest." For some time a famous photographer kept a life-size photograph of the Master on the street outside his shop. President Calvin Coolidge received the swami at the White House. In New York's famous Carnegie Hall, on April 18, 1926, the Master held a crowd of three thousand spellbound for an hour and a half, repeating with him the simple chant "O God Beautiful!" which he had translated from the original Hindi of Guru Nanak. That night

Master's usual everyday wear was a business suit. His desire was not to "Indianize" Americans, but to help them spiritualize their own culture.

many in his audience found themselves transported to a state of divine ecstasy.

In 1924 Swami Yogananda toured westward across the continent. As he taught and lectured, countless thousands found their lives transformed—not by his words alone, but by his magnetic love and the sheer radiance of his inner joy.

Louise Royston, an elderly disciple who first met him during those early years, described him to me as a man so alive with divine joy that he sometimes actually came running out onto the lecture platform, his long hair streaming out behind him, his orange robe flapping about his body as if with kindred enthusiasm.

"How is everybody?" he would cry.

"Awake and ready!" came the eager response, in which he led them.

"How *feels* everybody?"

Again the shout: "Awake and ready!"

Only in such a charged atmosphere was he willing to talk about God, whom he described as the most dynamic, joy-inspiring reality in the universe. Dry, theoretical lectures were not for him. He had not come to America to philosophize, but to awaken in people an ardent love for God, and an urgent longing to *know* Him. The forceful, inspiring personality of this teacher from India utterly captivated his audiences.

Louise Royston told me a charming little story from Yogananda's 1927 visit to Washington, D.C. There Mme. Amelita Galli-Curci, the world-renowned opera singer, became his disciple. At this time Galli-Curci had reached the pinnacle of her own extraordinary fame. One evening, while singing before a packed concert hall, she spotted her guru seated in the balcony. Interrupting the performance, she pulled out a handkerchief and waved it eagerly in his direction. The Swami in his turn rose and waved back at her. The audience, finally, seeing whose presence it was that had interrupted the program, broke into enthusiastic cheers and applause, sustaining the acclamation for several minutes.

One reason for the almost overwhelming response the Master received everywhere was that, unlike most public speakers, he never

Mme. Amelita Galli-Curci, opera singer and
disciple of Yogananda.

looked upon his audiences as nameless crowds, even when they numbered many thousands. He was amazingly sensitive to each listener *as an individual*. Often he would address himself to the specific needs of a single member of his audience. I myself sometimes had the experience of hearing him, during the course of a public lecture, address briefly some private difficulty of my own. When I thanked him mentally, he glanced smilingly at me before continuing his discourse.

Mr. Oliver Rogers (later, Brother Devananda), an older man who entered Mt. Washington as a monk a year or two after me, once told the Master in my presence:

"I heard you lecture twenty-five years ago at Symphony Hall, in Boston. Through the years since then I often wondered where you were. I suppose it was my karma that I had to seek God first in other ways, but the compelling inspiration behind my search was always that evening with you in Symphony Hall.

"It was strange, too," Mr. Rogers continued reflectively. "That huge hall was completely packed, yet through your entire lecture you kept your eyes fixed on me!"

"I remember," replied the Master with a quiet smile.

Above all, during every public lecture, Swami Yogananda sought souls who were spiritually ready to devote their lives to God. As he often put it, "I prefer a soul to a crowd, though I love crowds of souls."

During his transcontinental tour in 1924, many would have been thrilled for Swami Yogananda to make his home in their cities. To every such invitation, however, he replied, "My soul calls me to Los Angeles." Years later, a guest at Mt. Washington asked him, "Which do you consider the most spiritual place in America?" "I have always considered Los Angeles the Benares* of America," the Master replied.

---

* Benares, or Varanasi as it is now named officially, is the holiest city of the Hindus. Thousands of years old—indeed, quite possibly the oldest continuously inhabited city in the world—Varanasi possesses an aura of timelessness and world detachment. Numerous ashrams and temples exist here. Devout pilgrims from all over India come to bathe in the sacred river Ganges, which at that point flows northward toward its source in the Himalayas, a direction of flow which bestows on the city its spiritual appellation, Kashi.

Paramhansa Yogananda lecturing to thousands of yoga students in Washington, D.C., in the 1920s.

To Los Angeles he came. People flocked to his lectures in unprecedented numbers even for that city, noted as it is for its interest in matters spiritual. Weeks passed in unceasing public service. And then he informed his delighted students that he planned to establish his headquarters in their city.

Numerous properties were shown him. None corresponded to the visions he had received in India, however. He continued his search.

In January 1925, he was out driving one day with two or three students, including Arthur Cometer, a young man who, with Ralph, another student, had chauffeured the Master across America. They drove up winding Mt. Washington Drive. As they passed Mt. Washington Estates the Master cried out, "Stop the car!"

"You can't go in there," his companions protested. "That's private property!"

The aged and the infirm flock here, convinced that to die in Benares is a guarantee of salvation. Indeed their faith is founded, albeit symbolically, on a divine truth. For Hindus who take their mythology literally, Benares is considered the earthly abode of God in the form of Sri Viswanath, "Lord of the Universe." And truly, one who lives and dies in the *inner* abode of God, which is to say in His consciousness, is assured of salvation.

But Yogananda was not to be dissuaded. He entered the spacious grounds, and strolled about in silence. At last, holding onto the railing above the tennis courts, he exclaimed quietly, "This place feels like home!"

As it turned out, the property had recently been put up for sale; there were other people already who wanted to buy it. But Yogananda knew it was destined to be his. So certain was he, in fact, that he invited all his students in southern California to a dedication ceremony on the still-unpurchased land. During a speech that day he informed them, "This place is yours."

The price of the property was $65,000. The Master was on the very point of signing the purchase agreement when his hand froze into immobility. "God held my hand from signing," he told me years later, "because He wanted me to have the property for less money." A few days afterwards another real estate agent was found who agreed to negotiate terms. The seller consented to come down to $45,000, provided that the sum was paid in full at the time of purchase, and that the date be set no later than three months from the day Yogananda signed the agreement. The price, though excellent, represented a lot of money, particularly in those days when the dollar had a much higher value than it has today.

When Yogananda's students learned that he had only three months to raise the entire sum, their interest waned noticeably. One lady exclaimed in dismay, "Why, it would take you twenty years to raise that much money!"

"Twenty years," replied the Master, "for those who *think* twenty years. Twenty months for those who think twenty months. And *three* months for those who think three months!"

He did, in fact, acquire the money in three months. The story of how he did it illustrates wonderfully the power of faith.

There was a student of the Swami's, a Mrs. Ross Clark, whose husband some months previously had contracted double pneumonia. The man's doctors had said he couldn't live. "Oh yes he will live," declared the Master when Mrs. Clark turned to him for help. Going to her husband's bedside, he had sat there and prayed deeply. The man was cured. Thus it was that when Mrs. Clark learned of the Master's dilemma, she told him, "You saved my husband's life. I want to help you. Would you accept a loan of $25,000 without interest for three years?" *Would* he!

"Other money," he told me, "began pouring in from our centers around the country. Soon we had another $15,000, making $40,000 in all. But the final purchase date was approaching, and we still lacked $5,000 of the total price. I wrote Mrs. Clark again to see if she could help us with this amount. Regretfully she answered, 'I've done all I can.' I thanked her once again for the enormous help she had given already. But where was that help going to come from?

"At last just one day remained! The situation was desperate. If we didn't get those five thousand dollars by noon the next day, we would forfeit our option."

Master chuckled, "I think Divine Mother likes to keep my life interesting!

"I happened to be staying in the home of someone who was rich, but insincere. He could easily have helped us had he been so inclined, but he made no move to do so. I was battling with God, 'How do You plan to give me that money before noon tomorrow?'

"'Everything will be all right,' my host said, soothingly.

"'Why do you say that?' I demanded. I knew the money would come, but God needs human instruments, and this man had shown no interest in serving the work in this capacity. The man left the room.

"Just then a gust of wind* turned my face toward the telephone. There I saw the face of Miss Trask, a lady who had come to me twice for interviews. A voice said, 'Call her.' I did so at once, and explained my predicament to her.

---

* As I understood this story from Master, this was a spiritual, not a physical, manifestation. Wind is one of the manifestations of *AUM*, the Holy Ghost. We find a reference to it in Acts of the Apostles: "And when the day of Pentecost was fully come, they were all with one accord in one place. And suddenly there came a sound from heaven as of a rushing mighty wind, and it filled all the house where they were sitting. . . . And they were all filled with the Holy Ghost." (Acts 2:1,2,4) The visions that St. Bernadette Soubirous received of the Virgin Mary at Lourdes were also preceded by a gust of wind. Others couldn't feel it.

"After a pause she said, 'Somebody just the other day returned a loan I made him years ago. I never expected to get it back. It was for $5,000! Yes, you may have it.'

"Silently I offered a prayer of thanks. 'Please,' I urged her, 'be at Mt. Washington Estates tomorrow before noon.'

"She promised to come. But by noon the next day she hadn't yet arrived! Several prospective buyers were waiting like wolves! One of them was telling everyone that he planned to turn the place into a movie school. But the seller announced, 'We will wait the rest of the day.'

"Minutes later Miss Trask arrived. The drama was over. We paid the full purchase price, and Mt. Washington was ours!"

Thus was founded the international headquarters of Self-Realization Fellowship, the institution through which Paramhansa Yogananda disseminated his yoga teachings throughout the world.

When I came to the Master in 1948, Mt. Washington Estates was a monastery. At first, however, he had planned to make it a "how-to-live" school similar to his well-known institution in India, because his hopes for spiritualizing the West included an all-round education for the young. He soon realized, however, that his educational dreams for this country would have to wait until enough grown-ups were converted to his ideals; only then could there be properly trained teachers, and enough parents willing to send their children to his schools. Soon, therefore, Mt. Washington became a residential center for adults desirous of devoting their lives to God.

In 1925, though many Americans derived inspiration from Yogananda's message, relatively few were ready to give their entire lives to the spiritual search. Even in India, so Lord Krishna stated in the Bhagavad Gita, "Out of a thousand, one seeks Me; and out of a thousand who seek, one fully knows Me."[*] Swami Shankaracharya (also known simply as Swami Shankara; *acharya* means "teacher") once remarked, "Childhood is busy with playthings; youth is busy with romance and family; old age is busy with sickness and worries: Where is the man who is busy with God?" Here, in the materialistic West, few indeed were willing to spare the time for deep meditation. By ones they came. Many left; few remained.

---

[*] The Bhagavad Gita, VII:3.

Yogananda might have compromised his high standards and made it easier for many more to stay, but he never would do so. And by ones they *did* come, among whom were a growing number of deeply seeking souls. Slowly, a monastic order developed, in time to achieve

such a high spiritual caliber as I have seen nowhere else, not even in India.

For some years Swami Yogananda continued to tour the country, lecturing, teaching, and attracting to his work a gradually growing band of dedicated disciples. At last he felt guided by God to end his spiritual "campaigns," as he called them, and return to Mt. Washington to devote his time to training the souls he had sent there.

There now began for him and his little band a period of severe testing. During his previous years of public teaching, all the money he had sent home had, as things turned out, been spent, often not wisely. No doubt those in charge had imagined the supply would never run out. To replenish the depleted bank account the Master might have gone out campaigning again, but he felt that God now wanted him at Mt. Washington, and he obeyed the divine summons unflinchingly. He and his little group planted tomatoes on the hillside. For months their diet consisted of raw tomatoes, stewed tomatoes, fried tomatoes, baked tomatoes, tomato soup. They found that with a little culinary imagination, even this drastically limited fare could be pleasantly varied.

With the passing years, more and more students around the country realized that what the Master had brought them was far more than an adjunct to the church teachings with which they had grown up: It was a complete spiritual path in itself. He always encouraged

Paramhansa Yogananda in the 1920s.

his students to remain loyal to their own churches, if they so desired. Increasing numbers of them, however, as they practiced his teachings, began to feel that *his* work was all the church they needed. Thus his work developed, not by missionary tactics of conversion, but by his students' own, personal experience of the efficacy of his teachings. More and more, those whose worldly responsibilities prevented them from entering his monastery began to unite together in their own towns to form Self-Realization Fellowship centers. Lessons were compiled at Mt. Washington from his teachings and writings,* and sent to devoted students around the country, eventually reaching students throughout the world. By 1935 the work was firmly established and flourishing.

This was the year that Yogananda's guru, Swami Sri Yukteswar, summoned him back to India. The now-famous disciple spent a year there traveling about the country, addressing large audiences.

A visitor to Sri Yukteswar's Serampore ashram compared Swami Yogananda one day to a certain other well-known swami, famous in both India and America. The great guru, though rarely one to bestow even the mildest praise, replied now with quiet pride, "Don't mention them in the same breath. Yogananda is *much* greater."

Swami Yogananda, during his "campaign" days, had sometimes asked his audiences to clasp their hands together. Then he'd tell them, "Those who are in tune with me will not be able to separate their hands until I tell them they are free." When he returned

Paramhansa Yogananda with his guru Swami Sri Yukteswar, during Yogananda's visit to India during the 1930s.

---

* Louise Royston, the disciple mentioned earlier in this chapter, was chiefly responsible for this labor of love.

to India he performed this demonstration sometimes, just to show the power of the mind. When I went to India in 1958, someone who had been there told me that, one evening, Motilal Thakur, an advanced disciple of Sri Yukteswar, had gone around the hall, blowing on the tips of his fingers, then flicking them toward people in an attempt to release them from Yogananda's power. He failed to break the swami's spiritual influence.

During that year Sri Yukteswar bestowed on his beloved disciple the highest of India's spiritual titles, *Paramhansa.** It was hoped by many Indians that Yogananda would remain in India now. But God was already inwardly calling him back to America. His guru's death was a further, outward sign that God was releasing him to go back. Accordingly, in 1936, he returned to Mt. Washington. And now a new phase of his mission began.

In conjunction with his early visions of Mt. Washington, Yogananda had always seen two other buildings. The first was the main hall of his Ranchi school. The other had yet to be brought into outward manifestation. It was a beautiful hermitage somewhere by the sea.

---

* Literally, "Supreme Swan." The swan has been since ancient times a symbol of divine enlightenment. The reason is threefold. First, like the swan, which is equally at home on land and on water, the enlightened yogi is at home both in this world and in the ocean of Spirit. Second, the swan is believed to have the ability, when it sips a mixture of milk and water, to swallow only the milk; presumably what it does is curdle it. Similarly, the *hansa*, or enlightened yogi, can discriminate clearly between the "milk" of divine truth and the "water" of delusion. Third, *hansa* (swan) in Sanskrit means also *han sa* ("I am He"): words expressive of the blissful realization of a true master. Supreme among such "*hansas*" is the *parama* (supreme) *hansa*. Already liberated, the *paramahansa* no longer *needs* to combat earthly delusions with the sword of discrimination, for he sees the Divine at all times effortlessly, everywhere.

Yogananda wrote his title *Paramhansa*, without the additional *a* in the middle. This is how the word is pronounced in India. According to Sanskrit scholars, "paramhansa" is more properly written *paramahansa*, with an extra *a* in the middle. Scholarly precision, however, doesn't always coincide with unscholarly comprehension.

In English, that middle *a* increases the problem of pronunciation to the point where people pause there, thus giving emphasis to a letter that, in India, is not even pronounced. The average American or Englishman, in other words, and very likely the average non-Indian, pronounces the word thus: "param*a*ahansa." The correct pronunciation, however, is *paramhansa*.

For Westerners who want simply to know, with some degree of accuracy, how to pronounce this (to us) difficult word, Sanskrit scholars accept the spelling *paramhansa*.

Several times, while driving down the California coast to San Diego, he had felt attracted to a certain spot in the little town of Encinitas. Each time that the attraction had awakened in him, he had received the inner message: "Wait. Not yet." Obedient to his inner guidance, he had never pursued the matter further. After his return from India, however, a surprise awaited him. On the very spot that had interested him on those drives, James J. Lynn, a wealthy disciple and highly advanced spiritually, had purchased and built for him the hermitage of his visions! Here it was that Paramhansaji,* as many people now began calling him, over the next several years spent most of his time writing books, among them his spiritual classic, *Autobiography of a Yogi.*

His days now were an idyll of divine tranquillity. After years of traveling, spiritual "campaigning," and courageously meeting a never-ending series of challenges to his mission, he was able to enjoy for a time some of the fruits of his labors. The challenges he met now were in the more congenial realm of spiritual ideas.

In order to share this idyll with devoted students, he constructed a small, beautiful place of worship in 1938 on the grounds in Encinitas. "The Golden Lotus Temple," he named this new building. Situated in the garden, fairly close to the main hermitage, it overlooked the Pacific Ocean. Here the Master led group meditations, with the ocean "backdrop" as a visible reminder of the vastness of Spirit. He shared with devotees some of the deep inspirations that were pouring daily through his pen. The Golden Lotus Temple attracted widespread public interest. Visitors sometimes compared it to the Taj Mahal. One person said of it, "It is like seeing paradise without dying!"

But the Master's idyll didn't last long. In 1939 World War II started in Europe. Its disruptive vibrations could not but affect the tranquillity of a work as attuned as Yogananda's was to serving the needs of mankind everywhere. In 1942, not long after America's entry into the war, The Golden Lotus Temple slipped into the sea. Its foundations had been undermined by soil erosion caused by water

* *Ji* is a suffix commonly added to names in India as a mark of respect.

Master meditating on the beach in Encinitas, California.

seepage from the road outside the hermitage property. The loss of this famous structure received front-page Associated Press coverage in hundreds of newspapers across the nation. To Paramhansaji, however, the loss was not a tragedy, but a sign of God's will. The time had come for the next stage in his mission.

God's true lovers seem to attract more than their share of trials. Perhaps the reason is to give the rest of us a lesson from their example, that adversity, if met with divine faith, proves invariably a blessing in the end. Hardship is but a shortcut—tunneled, so to speak, through mountains so as the more quickly to reach the fertile meadows beyond them. Paramhansaji declared that from the destruction of his Golden Lotus Temple many other places of worship would arise. To him, then, its loss meant that the time had come to expand his work, reaching out more actively to the world through the medium of his organization, which by this time was firmly established.

Within a year and two months of the loss of the Encinitas temple, two new places of worship were established. The first was in Hollywood, at 4860 Sunset Boulevard, dedicated in August 1942. The second was in San Diego, at 3072 First Avenue, dedicated in September 1943. The Master now began lecturing in these churches on alternate Sundays.

This increase in his public activities attracted an ever-larger number of lay disciples to the churches, in addition to those coming to live as renunciates at his Mt. Washington and Encinitas ashrams. It was now that an old dream, one that he had often described in lectures and in magazine articles, began to take definite shape.

One of the primary aims of his work had been, from the beginning, "to spread a spirit of brotherhood," as he put it, "among all people, and to aid in establishing, in many countries, self-sustaining colonies for plain living and high thinking." It was to the establishment of such a "world brotherhood colony"—his designation for this new style of living—that he now turned most of his energies.

The problem to which he addressed himself was similar to the one that had first inspired his interest in child education. "Environment," he used to say, "is stronger than will power." The environment in which a child lives determines to a great extent his attitudes and behavior after he grows up. The environment in which an adult lives can make all the difference, similarly, between success and failure in his or her efforts to transform old, unwanted habits.

Paramhansaji urged people if possible to live in harmonious environments. For single persons with a deep desire for God, he often suggested the monastic life. But although for students with worldly commitments he recommended regular attendance at Self-Realization Fellowship church or center services, he was sadly aware of the obstacles these people faced. Most modern environments, alas, even when they are outwardly harmonious, are not spiritually uplifting.

The solution he arrived at was to provide places in which *all* devotees, whether married or single, could live among divine influences: places where family, friends, job, and general environment would all conduce to spiritual development—in short, a spiritual village, or "world brotherhood colony." In the early 1940s he set himself to found the first such community.

Encinitas was the site he chose for this project. Here he began to accept families. In lecture after lecture in the churches he urged people to combine their meditative efforts with the simpler, freer life-style of a spiritual community.

The Hermitage at Encinitas.

A number of the projects that he undertook during his lifetime must be considered guidelines for the future, inasmuch as their fulfillment depended on the preparedness of society as a whole, and not only on his own far-seeing vision and vigorous power of will. Society was not yet ready for them. Thus, although he had dreamed of founding "how-to-live" schools in America, and actually tried to start one in 1925 at Mt. Washington, America simply wasn't yet spiritually developed enough to permit the fulfillment of this dream.

Everything he did, however, was done for a good reason. Indeed, what better way to indicate his wishes for the work in years or even generations to come than by making a serious effort to carry those wishes out during his own lifetime?

Great men cannot hope to materialize all the inspirations of their genius during the short time allotted to them on earth. How much clearer a demonstration of their intentions, then, for those who come afterward, if they can start something tangible, however inchoately, instead of merely talking about it. Such was Yogananda's "how-to-live" school at Mt. Washington. Such also was a Yoga University that he founded there in 1941 with a California State charter, which had to be abandoned later owing to public indifference. Such, too, was his "world brotherhood colony" in Encinitas.

It was not possible, alas, for him to complete this project during his lifetime. America simply wasn't ready for it. Perhaps also certain of the renunciate disciples weren't ready, either. The fact that he dropped it, however, cannot be viewed as a change of heart, considering the lifelong importance he attached to this concept. Rather, this practical demonstration of his interest in it can only have been intended to inspire others, or even some *one* other. I say this because I myself seem to have been selected for that one, taking up the plan in later years, when the timing for its fulfillment was right.

*   *   *   *   *   *   *

In 1946, his best-known book, *Autobiography of a Yogi*, was published. Its appearance marked the beginning of the last chapter of his life: the completion of his major literary works, and the arrival of a veritable flood of new disciples.

In the summer of 1948 he experienced a supreme state of ecstasy, or *samadhi*. God, in the form of the Divine Mother of the Universe, showed him the secrets of cosmic creation. It was as though, in lifting these last veils, She wanted to prepare him for his own departure from this outward stage of manifestation.

"I sent you a few bad ones in the beginning," She told him during that ecstasy, "to test your love for Me. But now I am sending you angels. Whoever smites them, I shall smite."

Indeed, it was within this period—from approximately 1946 onwards—that the majority of his destined disciples came. We may

Moments before this picture was taken, Master was asked if he would let himself be photographed. "Just a moment," he replied, "let me first go into *samadhi*." Two or three seconds later he said, "All right." So perfect was his control over his mental processes!

suppose that God had wanted his life, during his earlier years, to stand out more brilliantly than it might have done, had all his energies been spent in the personal training of hordes of followers.

In the life of the great Sri Ramakrishna, too, most of his disciples came during the last years of his life. Thus, now, in the closing chapters of Paramhansa Yogananda's life, a swelling throng of dedicated souls began arriving. They helped to ensure the continuance of his work after he had departed from this earth.

Within this period of time, too, he acquired several new properties: a retreat in the desert at Twenty-Nine Palms, California, where he went for periods of seclusion to work on completing his writings; a new church in Long Beach, California; another one in Phoenix, Arizona; and a lake and temple in Pacific Palisades, California. He also developed the already-existing church property in Hollywood, adding an auditorium and an excellent vegetarian restaurant.

The lake and temple in Pacific Palisades were dedicated by him in 1950. This was his last and most beautiful property. SRF Lake

Shrine, he called it. The Lake Shrine is formed by a natural bowl in a steep hillside that almost surrounds a charming jewel of a lake. The property contains a church, an outdoor temple, tiny shrines to each of the major world religions, and beautiful flower gardens. The place is enjoyed by thousands of visitors every year.

Increasingly, during these last years of his life, he spent his time working on his writings. One of the major assignments that his guru had given him was to demonstrate the intrinsic compatibility of the Indian scriptures, particularly the Bhagavad Gita, with the Old and New Testaments. At Twenty-Nine Palms he wrote commentaries on the Bhagavad Gita, Genesis, and Revelation. (The teachings of Revelation, he said, are "pure yoga.") He had already completed detailed commentaries on the four Gospels of the Bible.

On March 7, 1952, he left his body. It had been an incredibly fruitful life. By the time it ended, SRF centers flourished in many countries. Yogananda's disciples around the world numbered many tens of thousands. He had opened the West to India's teachings in a way that no other teacher has ever been able to do. This was the first time that a great master from India spent the greater part of his life in the West. It is largely as a result of his teaching and radiant personal example that there has been, in recent decades, such a widespread and growing interest in India's spiritual teachings.

The headquarters for this vast movement was Mt. Washington Estates. Here it was that my own life of discipleship began.

CHAPTER 18

First Impressions

Rev. Bernard, the disciple I'd seen briefly in Master's interview room at the Hollywood church, drove Norman and me to Mt. Washington. On our way we stopped by the bus terminal to pick up my bag. My first glimpse of Mt. Washington Estates as we entered was of tall palm trees along both sides of the entrance driveway, waving gently in the slight breeze as if to extend a kindly greeting: "Welcome!" they seemed to murmur. "Welcome home!"

Norman showed me about the spacious grounds. We then went and stood quietly above the two tennis courts, which, Norman said, were now used for gentler, more *yogic* forms of exercise. In silence we gazed out over the city far below us.

Yes, I reflected, this *was* home! For how many years had I wandered: Rumania, Switzerland, England, America, and so many countries fleetingly in between. Always my feelings, if not my nationality, had stamped me, "a foreigner." I had begun to wonder if I belonged *anywhere*. But now, suddenly, I knew that I did belong: *right here* in this ashram; *here* with my Guru; *here*, with his spiritual family! (Yes, I decided happily, all of these people here were my true family, too.) Gazing about me, I breathed deeply the peace that permeated this holy place.

Norman stood by my side, wordlessly sharing my elation. After a time we both faced the opposite direction, and looked up across an attractive lawn towards the large main building. Calmly self-contained, it seemed to suggest an almost patrician benignity.

"Master's rooms are those on the top floor, to the right of us," Norman said, pointing to a series of third-storey windows at the eastern end of the building. "And that," he indicated a room that protruded outward above the main entrance, "is the sitting room, where he receives guests.

"Women disciples live on the second floor," he continued, "and also on the third floor, to the left of Master's apartment. In addition, there's a sort of second-floor annex at the back, where a few nuns live. Because we're renunciates, the men and women aren't allowed to mix with one another, so I can't take you up there. But come, I'll show you around the first floor. That part is more or less public."

He led me into a spacious lobby, simply and tastefully furnished. We passed through a door at the eastern end into three rooms that had been converted into a print shop. Proceeding towards the back of the building, we crossed over a narrow bridge that overlooked a small interior garden, and entered the main office which, this being Sunday, was empty of workers. From here, Norman explained to me, books, printed lessons, and a continuous stream of correspondence went out to yoga students around the world.

We re-entered the lobby at the western end. Here, large, sliding doors opened into a chapel, where we found two nuns seated together at an organ, one of them playing selections from Handel's *Messiah*, the other one listening. They looked so relaxed and happy that I forgot the rule, for a moment, and greeted them. The dignified, yet kindly, way they acknowledged my greeting, without in the least encouraging further conversation, impressed me.

I was impressed also by the tasteful simplicity of my new home. Everything looked restful, modest, and harmonious. Leaving the chapel, I turned eagerly to Norman. "Where do the men live?"

"In the basement, most of them," he replied laconically.

"The basement!" I stared at him incredulously. Then suddenly we were both laughing. After all, I told myself, what did it matter? If humility was a virtue, anything that encouraged it must be considered a blessing.

We went downstairs to the men's dining room, which, Norman explained, had once served as a storeroom. Without windows, it stood at the dark end of a dim hallway. The only light in the room came from a single light bulb. In a small adjoining room all the monks showered, brushed their teeth, and washed the dishes. Meals were brought down three times daily from the main kitchen upstairs.

"Come," said Norman, "let me show you our rooms. You've been assigned the one next to mine."

We left by a basement exit and, proceeding down the front driveway, arrived at a cottage in front of and about fifty feet from the main building, set picturesquely amid spreading trees, fragrant flowers, and succulents. I was charmed by the unassuming simplicity of this little outbuilding. Here, decades earlier (Norman explained), the hotel guests had waited to take the cable car down to Marmion Way. Recently, he went on, smiling, the waiting room had been "renovated, after a manner of speaking," and divided into sleeping quarters for two. His was the larger of the new rooms; mine was the smaller. Why, I marveled, had we, young neophytes as we were, been assigned such delightful quarters?

Understanding came moments later, as we entered the building. I tried to suppress a smile. Here, set so idyllically amid stately grounds, was a scene incongruously reminiscent of the hasty reconstruction that must have followed bombing raids during the war. Schoolboys, Norman explained, had done all the work. As I examined the consequences, I wondered whether the boys hadn't considered the windows and the window frames separate projects altogether. At any rate, the windows hung at odd angles, as though disdaining to have anything to do with mere *frames*. Months later, as if to atone for their stern aloofness, they extended a friendly welcome to the winds of winter to come in and make merry.

The walls, made of plasterboard, had been cut more or less according to whim. They did manage to touch the ceiling—shyly, I thought—here and there, but the gap between them and the floor was in no place less than two inches. The resulting periphery made a lair, conveniently dark, for spiders and insects of other kinds.

It was the floor, however, that provided the *pièce de résistance*. It appeared to be composed of a cross between pumice and cement. This substance, I later learned, was the proud invention of Dr. Lloyd Kennell, the alternate minister at our church in San Diego. Dr. Kennell had boasted that his product would "outlast the Taj Mahal," but in fact it was already doing its best to prove the Biblical dictum "Dust thou art." Every footstep displaced a part of this miracle substance, which rose in little clouds to settle everywhere: on clothes, books, bedding, furniture. . . .

Not that the room held any furniture, except for a hard wooden bed which, Norman assured me, improved one's posture. The small closet had no door to protect clothes against the ubiquitous dust. With Norman's help I found an old, discarded quilt in the basement storeroom. Folded double, it made a more-or-less adequate mattress. I also located an old dresser, wobbly on its legs, but steady enough when propped into a corner. Next I found a small table, which acquitted itself adequately when leaned against the wall. For a chair, an orange crate was pressed into service. And a few days later I came upon a large, threadbare carpet in the storeroom. Though the pattern was so worn as to be barely discernible, it proved an important addition, for it helped to hold down the dust from the fast-disintegrating floor. In place of a closet door, further search through the storeroom yielded a strip of monk's cloth, two feet wide, which I used to cover part of the opening. (Now at least I didn't have to *see* the dust as it settled on my clothes!) A light bulb dangled precariously at the end of a long, rather frayed wire in the center of the room. The house had no bathroom, but there was one in the main building, which, however, was kept locked at night.

It wasn't until a year later that I was given curtains for the windows.*

It no longer mystified me why the older monks preferred to live in the basement. But as for me, I didn't mind at all. Quite the contrary, the disadvantages of my ramshackle quarters only added fuel to my soaring happiness. I was so utterly thrilled to be here, in the ashram of my Guru, that every fresh inconvenience only made me laugh the more delightedly.

---

* My way of getting them showed a slight touch of rebellion. After my several requests for them had gone unanswered, I stripped down to my undershorts one evening and, with the light on, lay face down on my bed and read Shakespeare. After a while, one of the nuns passed my window on her way to the main building from the garage, which was attached to our "outhouse" bedroom. The next day word came down to me: I would be getting my curtains.

I laughed often now. The pent-up agony of recent years found re-lease in wave after fresh wave of happiness. Everything I had always longed for seemed mine now in my new way of life.

"There must be many good people here," I remarked to Norman on my first day there.

He was astonished. "Why, they're *all* good!"

It was my turn for astonishment. Could it really be, I wondered, that in this mixed bag of a world a place existed where *everyone* was good? Then I concluded that Norman must be right: This *had* to be such a place. For hadn't everyone come here to find God? And what higher virtue could there be than the desire to commune with the very Source of all virtue?

Thrilled though I was to be at Mt. Washington, my mind importuned me with innumerable questions, many of which I inflicted day after day on my poor brother disciples. (Surely another demonstration of their goodness was the unfailing patience with which they answered me!) My heart and soul had been converted indeed, but my intellect lagged far behind. Reincarnation, karma, superconsciousness, divine ecstasy, the astral world, masters, gurus, breathing exercises, vegetarianism, health foods, *sabikalpa* and *nirbikalpa samadhi*, Christ consciousness— huff! puff! For me all these were new and overwhelming concepts; a week or two before I hadn't even known any of them existed.

It was part of the excitement of those early days for me to dive into these strange waters and play in them joyfully. But confusion often assailed me also, and doubt—doubt not about the reason I was here, but about some puzzling point in the teachings. At such times I would sit down wherever I happened to be, and try to calm my mind. For I knew that soul-intuition, not the intellect, was the key to real understanding.

My greatest help at this time, apart from Master himself, was Rev. Bernard. Bernard was the alternate minister at our Hollywood church. He had a brilliant mind, and a clear understanding of the teachings. Fortunately for me, he seemed to enjoy answering my questions. Less fortunately, I hadn't as many opportunities to be with him as my searching mind would have liked. I sought answers, alternatively, wherever I could find them.

One of the monks, a young man with the improbable name of Daniel Boone, was friendly, loquacious, and willing to share with me not only the teachings he had received from Master, but anything else he might have stumbled upon during years of metaphysical reading. In fact, he suffered from what Master described as "metaphysical indigestion." I was too new on the path to realize that Boone's seeming strength was actually his greatest weakness. But the more I pondered his answers, the more I began to suspect some of them of fallibility.

"Did *Master* say that?" I would challenge him. Only if he said, "Yes," would I accept without question whatever he told me.

A more reliable, if less erudite, aid was Norman. A veritable giant, Norman had a heart almost as big as his body. It inspired me to see the intensity of his love for God. Not at all interested in the theoretical aspects of the path, he understood everything in terms of devotion. God was to him, simply, his Divine Friend. He required no intellectual explanations to clarify his perception of God's love for him, and of his for God.

"I don't know any of those things!" he would exclaim with a gentle smile whenever I posed him some philosophical conundrum. "I just know that I love God." How I envied him his childlike devotion! (Even Master was touched by it.) And how I longed to be able to still my own questioning mind, which from habit demanded answers that it already knew full well were not the wisdom I craved. For I knew that love was the answer—not knowledge; not intellectual acumen. Love was the highest wisdom. More and more I struggled to progress on the fragrant pathway of devotion.

Another aid to me in those days was an older man named Jean Haupt. Jean, true to his Germanic heritage, had extraordinary will power. He was determined to find God in the shortest time possible. Whenever he wasn't working, he meditated. One weekend his meditation lasted forty hours without a break. "It seemed more like forty minutes," he told me with a quiet smile.

I worked on the grounds with Jean and Norman, gardening, plastering, and doing whatever odd jobs were required. Jean, though fifty-five years old and little more than half Norman's size, could do more work than Norman and I combined. If he saw Norman struggling too long at some heavy job—one time it was carrying a refrigerator up the stairs—Jean would mutter impatiently, "Here, let me do it!" Moments later the job would be done. I was as deeply impressed by his will power, and as anxious to emulate it, as by Norman's devotion.

The most attractive feature of my new quarters was a small basement, reached by a set of narrow steps at the far end of the room from the door. This basement had once housed the motor which pulled cable cars up the steep mountainside. It seemed ideal for a meditation room. I carted out piles of rubble that had accumulated over decades of neglect; constructed a trap door for the opening to ensure virtual silence; and soon was devoting all my free time to meditating in this, my "Himalayan cave" (as I thought of it). Over the ensuing months I put in a ceiling, painted the room a soothing dark blue, and found everything here that a young yogi could possibly desire in the way of silence, remoteness from the demands of daily life, and divine tranquillity.

My first evening at Mt. Washington, Rev. Bernard visited me in my room. "Master wants me to give you instruction in the art of meditation," he said. He taught me an ancient yoga technique of concentration, and added some general counsel.

"When you aren't practicing this concentration technique, try to keep your mind focused at the point between the eyebrows. This is called the Christ center, because when Christ consciousness is attained one's awareness becomes centered here."

"Would it help," I asked, "to keep my mind focused there all day long as well?"

"Very much! When Master lived in his guru's ashram he practiced keeping his mind fixed there all the time.

"And another thing," Bernard added, "this is also the seat of the spiritual eye. The more deeply you concentrate your gaze at this point, the more you'll become aware of a round light forming there: a blue field with a bright, golden ring around it and a silvery white, five-pointed star in the center."

"This isn't just a subjective experience?" I inquired. "Does *everybody* see it?"

"Everybody," he assured me, "provided his mind is calm enough. It's a universal reality, like the fact that we all have brains. Actually, the spiritual eye is the astral reflection of the medulla oblongata, at the base of the brain. I'll tell you more about that some other time.

"For now, suffice it to say that energy enters the body through the medulla, and that by the sensitive application of will power one can actually *increase* this energy-inflow. The Christ center is the body's seat of will power, and also of concentration. Notice how, whenever you concentrate deeply, or strongly will something to happen, your mind is drawn automatically to this point. You may even tend inadvertently to frown a little in the process. By concentration on the Christ center, your will power will increase. Consequently, the amount of energy flowing in through the medulla oblongata increases also. And with this greater flow, the spiritual eye forms naturally in the forehead.

"Through concentration on the spiritual eye, the consciousness gradually becomes attuned to the subtle rate of vibration of this light. At last one's consciousness, too, takes on the quality of light. That is what Jesus meant when he said, 'If thine eye be single, thy whole body shall be full of light.'* It is in this purified state of awareness that ecstasy comes."

After Bernard left me, I sat awhile practicing the techniques he had taught me. Later on I went out of doors and stood above the tennis courts again, this time gazing out over a vast carpet of twinkling lights. How lovely, in the evening, was this huge, bustling city! I reflected that those myriad lights were manifestations of the same divine light which I would someday behold in deep meditation, within myself. But electricity, I told myself, provides light only for the pathways of this world. The divine luminescence lights pathways to the Infinite.

---

* Matthew 6:22. Modern translators, unaware of the hidden significance of this passage, have changed the word *single* in the King James version to read "sound," or "clear." *The New English Bible* even changes *eye* to "eyes," thus: "If your eyes are sound." One wonders how often the scriptures have been tampered with by scholars who, though intellectually learned, are steeped in spiritual ignorance.

"Lord," I prayed, "though I stumble countless times, I will never stop seeking Thee. Lead my footsteps ever onward toward Thy infinite light!"

CHAPTER **19**

The First Days of a Neophyte

THE DAILY ROUTINE at Mt. Washington was fairly individual. Freedom was given us, as it is in most Indian ashrams, for private spiritual practice. We met regularly for work and for meals, and held occasional evening classes in the SRF printed lessons, following the classes with group meditation. Paramhansaji had expressed the wish that we meditate together more often. We lacked a leader, however, and group initiative that has no one to stimulate it seldom travels in a straight line. Rev. Bernard, whom Master had placed in charge of our daily activities, wouldn't assume responsibility for our spiritual life, which he viewed as Master's exclusive domain.

Indeed, I suspect Master himself didn't greatly mind our lack of organization. For while daily group meditations might have kept a few of the less dedicated monks more firmly on the path, it would also have interfered with the free time the rest of us could devote to longer, private meditations. Master wanted our spiritual endeavors to spring from the depths of a sincere yearning for God, and not merely to follow mechanically the well-worn paths of established habit. To be sure, he stressed the importance of *regular* practice, but I think the clockwork regularity of Western monastic discipline must have struck him as rather too mechanical, and too much a part of that most far-reaching of Western delusions: the belief that perfection can be achieved through outward, not inward, reforms. At any rate, Master himself often lifted us out of any groove of routine into which we'd become too firmly settled. In his company, there was little danger that our mental grooves would become ruts!

I myself was glad for the opportunity to develop a meditative routine of my own. Soon I was rising at four o'clock every morning—staggering out of bed, admittedly, with the indispensable aid of an alarm clock. After practicing Master's exercises for recharging the body with energy, I would meditate two or three hours. At seven o'clock I would enter the main building, where I showered and breakfasted before going out into the garden for work. At noon I would put food aside for myself in the men's dining room, then meditate half an hour in the main chapel upstairs. Evenings I would eat lightly (a heavy meal in the stomach, I discovered, makes it difficult to meditate deeply), study a little, then go down to my "cave" and meditate two or three more hours before bed.

Soon I was looking forward to my meditation times as eagerly as the worldly man looks forward to an evening's partying—indeed, much more eagerly. Never had I dreamed there could be such a wealth of enjoyment within my own self!

The monks energizing on the tennis courts at Mt. Washington.

In addition to techniques of meditation, Paramhansa Yogananda taught, as I've indicated, a series of energization exercises. He based these exercises on a little-known truth, which Rev. Bernard explained to me on my first evening at Mt. Washington. Cosmic energy is drawn into the body by the agency of the will through the medulla oblongata. "The greater the will," Master said, "the greater the flow of energy." Practicing these exercises gratefully every morning and evening, I found them marvelously effective for banishing fatigue and developing a radiant, lasting sense of well-being.

Saturdays, no work was scheduled. This gave us time for personal chores, and for longer private meditations. Usually I meditated late into the morning, then kept silence the rest of the day. Sometimes I fasted. In the evening I meditated again for several hours.

Sundays we attended morning and evening services at our church in Hollywood. There being only a pickup truck to get us there, we younger monks piled happily into the back of it for the trip, which took fifteen or twenty minutes. In winter, to harden ourselves against the cold and to develop *titiksha* (endurance), we sometimes bared our bodies from the waist up, joyously welcoming the invigorating air and laughing with youthful good spirits as we bounced along. ("You should learn *tumo*," Boone shouted to me one day as the wind whistled around us. "What's that?" "It's a Tibetan technique for overcoming cold." From then on, if ever Boone looked a little chilly, I would shout to him to "do mo' *tumo*!")

The Hollywood church was charming in its simplicity. Its color scheme, both inside and out, was blue, white, and gold—"Master's colors," Boone informed me. Little niches on either side of the sanctuary contained figurines depicting various leaders in the great world religions. Paramhansa Yogananda had named this a "Church of All Religions." His teachings stressed the underlying oneness of all faiths. Seats for about 115 people faced the small stage from which services were conducted. Before and after services, curtains were usually drawn shut across this stage. When they were parted, there stood revealed along the back wall an altar containing five niches, each with a picture of one of our line of gurus: Babaji, Lahiri Mahasaya, Swami Sri Yukteswar, Paramhansa Yogananda, and Jesus Christ.

Bernard, who was to conduct the service in the church the first Sunday after my arrival, showed me around beforehand. "Why," I asked him, "is the picture of Jesus Christ on our altar, too? Surely

Self-Realization Fellowship Church in Hollywood, California, where Paramhansa Yogananda spoke regularly. I gave regular classes and services here from 1949 onwards. From 1955–1958 I served as the main minister of the church.

Interior of the Hollywood church. Master built two pulpits in the church, one on either side of the stage. The left pulpit, as seen from the audience, was originally planned for our own ministers, and the right one, for guest speakers. It was his plan to invite ministers from other churches to speak there, in keeping with his universal ideals, as expressed in the name "Church of All Religions." Although the pulpits were never used in the way Master planned, the concept is worthy of preservation.

he isn't in our line of gurus. Do we include him just to avoid criticism from the Christian denominations?"

Bernard smiled. "Master has told us it was Jesus himself who appeared to Babaji, and asked him to send this teaching of Self-Realization to the West. 'My followers,' Jesus asserted at that meeting, 'have forgotten the art of divine, *inner* communion. Outwardly they do good works, but they have lost sight of the most important of my teachings, to "seek the kingdom of God first."'*

"The work he sent to the West through Master is helping people to commune inwardly with God," continued Bernard. "Jesus, too, through people's practice of meditation, is becoming a living reality for them—a being with whom they can commune, rather than merely read about in the Bible. This was what Jesus meant when he said that he would come again. Master often speaks of this work as the Second Coming of Christ, for it teaches people how to fulfill the true promise of Jesus—not to return again outwardly, but in the souls of those who loved him and communed with him."

"That isn't what most Christians believe." I smiled wryly.

"True! But you may recall several Biblical accounts in which Jesus rebuked the apostles themselves for taking words literally that he had meant metaphorically. 'I have meat to eat that ye know not of,'† he said, and they thought he must have food hidden about his person! Jesus himself, moreover, placed his Second Coming *within the present lifetimes* of his listeners. 'Verily I say unto you,' he told them, 'This generation shall not pass, till all these things be fulfilled.'‡ In those days, and many times since then, he *has* fulfilled his promise to appear—not to fanatical adventists, some of whom have waited for him on hilltops in flowing, white gowns, but to true devotees who sought him humbly and ardently in their own souls."

"Tell me," I said, hesitating before taking this philosophical plunge, "why do we have pictures on our altar at all? If the state

* Matthew 6:33.

† John 4:32.

‡ Matthew 24:34.

of consciousness we're seeking is formless and omnipresent, something we're supposed to commune with in our own selves, doesn't it hinder our development to have our attention diverted outwardly toward individuals?"

"No," Bernard replied. "You see, our masters *have* that state of consciousness. For us, it is difficult even to visualize such a state! By attuning ourselves to them, we begin to intuit what it is that they have, and to develop the same consciousness in ourselves. This is what is meant in the Bible by the words, 'As many as received him, to them gave he power to become the sons of God.'"*

"Then is it more important to try to tune in to Master's consciousness in meditation, than to concentrate on what he says and does outwardly?"

"Very much so! I don't mean, of course, that his outward teachings don't hold vital lessons for us also. But the very gist of those teachings is to guide us into inner attunement. One might say that *attunement* is the essence of discipleship."

I wondered whether such an intensely personal relationship to one's guru might not cause emotional attachment to him, thereby limiting the disciple's consciousness instead of freeing it. Most important of all, I wondered, would attunement with Master threaten my attunement with God? Would it externalize my attention, instead of interiorizing it?

As time passed, and I got to know Master better, it became obvious to me that the attunement he encouraged in his disciples was impersonal. It was his practice to turn people's devotion resolutely away from himself as a human being, and toward the omnipresent Divinity that was the sole object of his own devotion. Attunement with him, I found then, meant attunement, not with his human personality, but with his universal state of awareness. Indeed, in the deeper sense there was no personality there for us to attune ourselves to. As he often put it, "I killed Yogananda long ago. No one dwells in this temple now but God."

At first, unaware as yet of how deeply impersonal his consciousness was, I saw him rather as a great and wise man. He sought to help

* John 1:12.

me expand my mental horizons. Looking deeply into my eyes one day, he said, "If you *knew* my consciousness!"

If anyone betrayed toward him the slightest attachment, or presumption as a result of some favor received, Master invariably became more than usually impersonal toward that disciple. Those who were closest to him were, without exception, disciples whose relationship with him was a relationship primarily in God.

*   *   *   *   *   *   *

The day of our first meeting on September 12, Master returned to Encinitas. I didn't see him until two weeks later, when he was scheduled to preach again at Hollywood Church.

The church that day was divinely peaceful. As we entered, music sounded on the organ. The organist, Jane Brush (later, Sahaja Mata), was playing her own arrangements of devotional chants that Master had written. I found her arrangements so sweet, so devotionally inspiring, that my heart soared up in longing for God. Of all the renditions I have ever heard of Master's chants, none have moved me so deeply as hers.

After some twenty minutes, it was time for the service to begin. The curtains parted; and there stood Master, a deep, penetrating gaze in his eyes that seemed to bestow on each person present a special blessing. Then suddenly he was smiling, radiant with divine joy. We rose spontaneously to our feet. As had been his practice during his early "campaign" days, he demanded, "How is everybody?"

"Awake and ready!" we all shouted.

"How *feels* everybody?"

"Awake and ready!"

We sat down, inspired by his dynamic power. He led us in chanting and meditation, then gave a brief interpretation of selected passages from the Bible and the Bhagavad Gita. His sermon followed — an altogether delightful blend of wit, devotional inspiration, and wisdom. I had always supposed that deep truths must be spoken portentously, in measured cadences, rather in the style of Emerson's essays. Rev. Bernard had addressed us rather that way the Sunday before (indeed, his very conversation had a certain ring of gravity to it!), and I had been suitably impressed. But Master now lectured in a manner so totally natural that, for several minutes, I was quite taken aback. Was *this* the way to convince people of the importance of divine truths? He made no attempt to impress us with the depth of his insight. Frequently, rather, he sent us into gales of laughter. Only gradually did I observe that his flashes of humor invariably preceded some profound spiritual advice. Yogananda wore his wisdom without the slightest affectation, like a comfortable old jacket one has been wearing for years.

"Behind every rosebush of pleasure," he cautioned us, "hides a rattlesnake of pain." He went on to urge us to seek our "pleasures" in God, and to ignore the fickle promises of this world.

"There are two kinds of poor people," he remarked—"those who wear rags of cloth, and those who, though traveling in limousines, wear spiritual rags of selfishness and indifference to truth and to God. It is better to be materially poor and have God in your heart, than to be materially wealthy without Him.

In front of my cottage at Mt. Washington, in the autumn of 1949.

"Never say that you are a sinner," he went on to advise us. "You are a child of God! Gold, though covered for centuries with mud, remains gold. Even so, the pure gold of the soul, though covered for eons of time with the mud of delusion, remains pure 'gold' forever. To call yourself a sinner is to identify yourself with your sins instead of trying to rid yourself of them. It is to affirm sinfulness. To call yourself a sinner is the greatest sin before God!"

He proceeded to discuss different levels of spiritual development: "I slept and dreamed life was beauty. I woke up, and found life was duty. But even in this, my dutiful ego, I dreamed myself separate from God. And then I awoke in Him, to realize that life truly *is* beauty! For the beauties we seek in this world can never be found except in Him. To experience them, we must first be dutiful to His will. Only then can we rise above self. We have not been sent down to earth to create here a pleasure garden. This world is a battlefield! Our highest duty is to seek the Lord. 'Seek ye the kingdom of God first,' Jesus said, 'and all these things shall be added unto you' — 'neither be ye of doubtful mind!'"

Finally, Master gave us this invaluable suggestion: "Never go to bed at night until you have convinced your mind that this world is God's dream."

Following the sermon, Bernard made a few announcements. He concluded by recommending *Autobiography of a Yogi* to newcomers. At this point Master interrupted him to say, "Many are coming from afar after reading the book. One man recently read it in New York, and—Walter, please stand up."

I glanced around to see this "Walter" who, like me, had read the book recently in New York. No one had stood up. Turning back to Master, I found him smiling at me! *Walter?!* "Ah, well," I thought philosophically, "a rose by any other name. . . ." Self-consciously I rose to my feet.

"Walter," Master continued affectionately, "read the book in New York, and left everything to come here. Now he has become one of us."

Members, lay and renunciate alike, smiled at me in blessing.

"Walter" was the name Master called me ever thereafter. No one else used this name, until, after Master's earthly passing, I longed for every possible reminder of those precious years with him. I then asked my brothers and sisters on the path to call me by that name.

Master spent the next few days at Mt. Washington. During this period I saw him several times, though not privately. Indeed, such was my inner turmoil, caused by this drastic change in my life, that I doubt whether another private interview with him at this time would have helped me very much. For Master's part, he probably was waiting for me to assimilate the instructions he had given me at our first meeting.

A few days before Master's return to Mt. Washington, Norman had talked me into joining him in what is known to health-faddists as the "Grape Cure," a diet of only grapes and grape juice. A few weeks of this cure would, Norman assured me, purify my body, and help me to make rapid progress in the spiritual life. Master saw us that Monday morning.

"Devotion is the greatest purifier," he remarked, smiling.

"Is it your wish then, Sir, that we break this fast?" I asked him.

"Well, I don't want you to break your will, now that you have set it this way. But your time would be better spent in working to develop devotion. A pure heart is the way to God, not a pure stomach!"

Heeding his counsel, I soon lost "heart" for the grape cure, though I continued it another day or two so as, in his words, not to "break" my will. It wasn't long, however, before I took up the infinitely more rewarding, though also far more demanding, task of deepening my love for God by chanting and holding constantly to the thought of God's presence in my heart.

Mental habits, alas, are not so easy to change as to think about changing. Months passed before I felt that I had made substantial progress against my years-old tendency to over-intellectualize. Master, seeing my desire, helped me from the start with constant encouragement and advice.

"Get devotion!" he would tell me. "You *must* have devotion. Remember what Jesus said"—here he paraphrased the words of the Gospel—"'Thou dost not reveal Thyself unto the prudent and the wise, but unto babes.'"

Swami Sri Yukteswar, a saint of wisdom if such ever existed, and one therefore (so people might think) more likely than most to endorse intellectual attitudes, said that love alone fits a person for the spiritual path. In his book, *The Holy Science*, he wrote, "This heart's natural love is the principal thing to attain a holy life. . . . It is impossible for man to advance a step towards [salvation] without it." The present age, alas, perhaps even more than most, affords all too little encouragement for developing the all-surrendering love which saints have ever praised. "Mawkish sentimentalism" is the common judgment on deep, positive feelings of any kind.

Indeed, an unfeeling heart is often taken as evidence of a "scientific outlook." In truth, however, without love no one can penetrate deeply to the center of things, which is often described, with unconscious wisdom, as their "heart." For whereas emotions can, and sometimes do, cloud the mind, calm, pure love clarifies it and makes possible the subtlest intuitions.

A certain visitor once requested a private interview with Master. On the appointed day he arrived armed with a long list of what he considered "profound" questions.

"Love God," Master said in answer to the first of them.

The man paused a moment uncomprehendingly, then shrugged and posed his second question.

"Love God!" Master persisted.

Nonplussed, the visitor proceeded to the third "deep" question on his list.

"*Love God!*" came the Master's reply once more, this time sternly. Without another word he rose, concluding the interview, and left the room. The intellectual guest never did grasp the relevance of Master's counsel to his questions. Years later, in fact, he became a sort of spiritual teacher in Chicago, and often cited this episode to illustrate, as he put it, that even great masters have their human failings. Paramhansaji was telling him, however, that until he developed love, the doors to true wisdom would remain closed to him.

Stern discipline from an all-compassionate master sometimes puzzles devotees. The neophyte, when first his guru "treats" him to a good scolding, may even ask himself, "Has he lost his temper?" A true master, however, lives on a plane far above such corrosive emotions. Sometimes he may indeed make a *show* of anger, but if he does so it is only to emphasize some counsel which, if delivered gently, might not sink in deeply enough. A mother may be obliged, similarly, to scold her child if he won't heed her gentle admonishments. Which of two mothers, indeed, shows the more genuine love: the one who, if her little child steps off the curb into heavy traffic, admonishes him gently, "I wouldn't do that, Johnny, if I were you"—or the one who snatches him back, scolds him, and maybe spanks him lightly to reinforce her counsel?

Jean Haupt told me of one occasion when Master was upbraiding one of the nuns in his presence. "You'd have thought the roof would fly off!" said Jean, chuckling. "Master was pacing the floor, shouting. I was seated at one end of the room; the nun was at the other end. Each time Master faced her, he emphasized his meaning by a stern look. When he turned his back to her, however, his face relaxed into an amused smile. He didn't stop shouting, but he winked at me before turning back toward her fiercely."

Master disciplined only those who accepted his discipline. Otherwise he was the soul of consideration. I remember him sometimes inquiring gently of a new disciple, to whom he'd offered mild correction, "You don't mind my saying that, do you?"

One of the traits that impressed me most deeply about him was his quality of universal respect. It was a respect born of the deepest concern for other people's welfare. The veriest stranger was, I am convinced, as dear to him as his own closest disciples.

Debi Mukerjee, a young monk from India, told me of an example he had seen of the universality of Master's love. Master had invited him out one afternoon for a drive. They were on their way home, near sundown.

"Stop the car!" Master ordered suddenly. They parked by the curb. He got out and walked back several doors to a small, rather shoddy-looking variety shop. There, to Debi's astonishment, he selected a number of items, none of them useful. "What on earth can he want with all that junk?" Debi marveled. At the front counter the owner, an elderly woman, added up the price. When Master paid it, she burst into tears.

"I very badly needed just this sum of money today!" she cried. "It's near closing time, and I'd almost given up hope of getting it. Bless you, Sir. God Himself must have sent you to me in my hour of need!"

Master's quiet smile alone betrayed his knowledge of her difficulty. He offered no explanation. The purchases, as Debi had suspected, served no practical purpose thereafter.

At first I found it a bit awkward living with someone who was, as I soon discovered, conscious of my innermost thoughts and feelings. Nor was space any barrier to his telepathic insight. Wherever his disciples happened to be, he read them like a headline.

Boone and Norman told me of an occasion, a few weeks before my arrival, when they had traveled by bus together to Encinitas. Their conversation had apparently been somewhat less than edifying.

"Master met us at the gate," Norman told me. "He looked stern. After quoting to us several of our more colorful remarks on the bus, he gave us a good scolding. 'You've come here to forget worldly things,' he said. 'Spend your time, when possible, by yourselves, talking to God. When you mix with others, talk more of Him.' He ended up telling us not to mix with each other!"

James Coller, another disciple, visited us at about this time from Phoenix, Arizona; Master had appointed him to be the minister of our church there. James, though deeply devoted to God and Guru, had a tendency to be a little casual about hermitage discipline.

"I was driving from Phoenix to Encinitas recently," James told us, "to see Master. It was late at night, and I was getting hungry. After some time I came to a restaurant that was still open, and eagerly went in. As bad luck would have it, all they had to serve was hamburgers. What was I to do? I

James Coller, fellow disciple, minister of the SRF Phoenix, Arizona church.

knew Master wanted us to be vegetarians, but still. . . . I mean, I was *really* hungry! 'Oh, well,' I decided finally, 'he won't know!' So I ate two hamburgers. After I reached Encinitas, I spoke with Master. At the end of our conversation, he remarked gently:

"'By the way, James, when you're on the highway late at night, and you come to a place that serves nothing but hamburgers—

better not eat anything.'" It may comfort those who have similar problems with self-discipline that Master said James would be spiritually free in this life. His saving grace was deep love for God.

Disconcerting though it might have been to live in the company of someone who had free access to the hidden recesses of my mind, I was increasingly grateful for his insight. For here at last, I realized, was one human being whose misunderstanding I never need fear. Master was my friend, ever firmly and quietly on my side, concerned only with helping me through every error toward the highest understanding. Almost incredibly, moreover, he was exactly the same, inwardly, to all, no matter what they did nor how they treated him. His concern was entirely with giving to them, never with receiving from them.

He once scolded Rev. Stanley, the minister at the SRF Lake Shrine.

"But please, Sir," Stanley pleaded, "you will forgive me, won't you?"

"Well," Master replied, astonished, "what else can I do?"

I never knew him to hold a grudge.

There was a man who for years, out of intense jealousy, had slandered Master. One day, a few days before the end of Master's life, the two of them met at a formal gathering.

"Remember," Master said, gazing into the man's eyes with deep forgiveness, "I will always love you!" I saw the man later, gazing at Master with deep love and admiration. A photograph of that encounter appears in the published story of Master's *mahasamadhi*, or final conscious exit from his body.

Master's counsel to people, born as it was of divine love, was always particular to their needs. Seeing me one day on the grounds, he advised me, "Do not get excited or impatient, Walter. Go with slow speed." Only he, who knew my private thoughts in meditation, could have perceived the galloping zeal with which I'd embarked on the spiritual path. It was not an attitude that I displayed outwardly.

Toward the end of September he invited me to Encinitas, where he said he would be spending the next week or so. There a small group of us meditated with him one evening in the peaceful salon of the hermitage, overlooking the Pacific Ocean. Sitting in his presence, I felt as though some powerful magnet were uplifting my entire being and concentrating it at the point between the eyebrows. The thought came to me, No wonder the Indian scriptures praise above all else the uplifting influence of a true guru! Never, by my unaided efforts alone, could I have plunged into meditation so suddenly, or so deeply.

Soon thereafter Master invited me to Twenty-Nine Palms, where he said he was planning to go for a period of seclusion. Here it was, over the years, that I accumulated my most precious memories of him.

CHAPTER 20

Twenty-Nine Palms

"Y OU MUST KEEP this place a secret," Bernard warned me as we
drove into Twenty-Nine Palms. "With the rapid growth of the
work, Master needs a place where he can go to concentrate on his
writings. Otherwise it's telephone calls and interviews all day long.
He's even bought the property in his family name, Ghosh, to safeguard his privacy."

This was the first time I'd ever seen a desert. The vast wasteland of
sand, sagebrush, Joshua trees, and tumbleweed held a strange fascination for me. It seemed a different dimension, as though time here
had slipped imperceptibly into timelessness. The sky, pastel hues
of blue, pink, and orange-yellow in the waning afternoon sunlight,
looked almost ethereal. I gazed about me in wonder.

Bernard noted my expression. "I see the desert's magic is working
on you already!" He added, "Master says the light here resembles
the astral light."

The monks' retreat, at which we arrived soon afterward, was
a small cottage on some fifteen acres of land. It was without electricity. A tall windmill creaked and clanked complainingly with every
breeze as it pumped water up from a well. A grove of blue-green
smoke trees hid the cottage from the seldom-traveled sand road.
Even with the windmill, which seemed determined to go public with
news of how hard it was made to work, this seemed a perfect spot
for seclusion and meditation. Over the coming years I was to spend
many months in these tranquil surroundings.

Master's place was five miles up the road. Located in a more developed area, it had city water, and electricity, which he needed since he

did much of his writing at night. His property nestled near the base of a range of low hills which, because of their barrenness, looked almost like a more distant mountain range. Master's house had pale stucco walls, in the Spanish style typical of southern California. Surrounding it were a profusion of plants and delicate Chinese elms. The entire property, enclosed by a low wire fence, was one or two acres in size.

My first visit to Twenty-Nine Palms was for a weekend. We visited Master at his place. My first recollection of him on that occasion isn't so much of the things he *said*, as of what he *didn't* say. I didn't know it at the time, but he placed great importance on silence. Disciples working around him were permitted to speak only when necessary. "Silence," he said, "is the altar of Spirit."

Master was seated out of doors by the garage; Bernard and I were standing nearby. Master asked Bernard to go into the house and fetch something. Suddenly, for the first time since my acceptance as a disciple, I found myself alone with my Guru. It seemed an opportunity not to be missed: a chance to learn something—*anything!* Master, evidently, didn't see it in the same light. He made no move to speak. Finally I decided I'd better "break the ice."

I had learned from Bernard how to commune inwardly with AUM, the Cosmic Sound, which manifests itself to the yogi in deep meditation. "Sir," I inquired, "what does AUM sound like?"

Master gave a prolonged "Mmmmmmmmmmm." He then reverted comfortably to silence. To me, alas, his silence was anything but comfortable.

"How does one hear it?" I persisted, though I already knew the technique.

This time Master didn't even bother to answer, but simply assumed the prescribed position. After holding it briefly, he returned his hands silently to his lap.

Some months later I told him I was having trouble calming my breath in meditation. "That," he replied, "is because you used to talk a lot. The influence has carried over. Well," he added consolingly, "you were happy in that."

Silence is the altar of Spirit. As I grew into my new way of life, I began to value this maxim.

The monks' retreat at Twenty-Nine Palms.

The swimming pool at Master's retreat, Twenty-Nine Palms, built mostly by Norman and me.

Soon after our first visit to Twenty-Nine Palms, Bernard drove Norman and me out there again. Master had devised a project for the two of us to work on, probably to give us an excuse to be near him while he concentrated on his writings. He asked us to build him a small swimming pool behind the house, near his bedroom. It was not that he particularly *wanted* a pool; in fact, once it was finished he never used it. But it did give Norman and me the opportunity to be with him for weeks at a time.

Soon we were busy shoveling out a deep hole in the sand. Master, taking an occasional break from his writing, would come out and work with us for fifteen minutes or so. Whenever he did so, I felt a deep blessing. But I hadn't yet adjusted to his habitual silence. One warm, sunny afternoon I noticed that he was panting slightly with the physical exertion, and remarked conversationally, "It's hot work, isn't it?"

"It is *good* work." Master gazed at me a moment as if with reproach, then returned in silence to his digging.

Gradually, inspired by his example, I learned to speak less, and to listen more to the soundless whispers in my soul.

Late one afternoon we were sitting with Master on a little porch outside the sitting room where he dictated his writings. After several minutes of silence, Master posed me an unexpected question.

"What keeps the earth from shooting out into space, away from the sun?"

Surprised, and not as yet familiar with the cryptic way he often taught us, I assumed he simply wanted a lesson in astronomy. "It's the sun's gravitational pull, Sir," I explained.

"Then what keeps the earth from being drawn back into the sun?"

"That's the earth's centrifugal force, pulling it constantly outward. If the sun's gravity weren't as strong as it is, we'd shoot off into space, out of the solar system altogether."

Master smiled significantly. Had he intended more than I realized? Some months later I recalled this conversation, and understood that he had been speaking metaphorically of God as the sun, drawing all things back to Himself, and of man as the earth, resisting with desires and self-interest the pull of divine love.

One hot day at noon Norman and I stood up from our digging and stretched, grateful that lunchtime had arrived at last. We enjoyed our work, but there was no denying that it was also tiring. Besides, we were famished. Briefly we surveyed the yawning pit at our feet.

"God, what a hole!" exclaimed Norman. We gazed out over the mounds of sand we'd deposited about the grounds with the wheelbarrow. The very sight of them, lumped about in mute testimony to our exertions, only reinforced our fatigue.

At that moment Master came out and joined us.

"Those mounds don't look very attractive," he remarked. "I wonder if they couldn't be leveled out. Would one of you mind fetching a two-by-four?"

Armed with the board, we stood before him a little apprehensively, awaiting further instructions.

"Each of you take the two-by-four at one end," Master said. "Then—just come over to this mound here. Pull the sand back toward you by pressing down hard on the board, and moving it slowly back and forth between you."

Probably even this meager description suffices to convey some idea of how difficult the job was. By the time we'd leveled one mound, Norman and I were panting heavily. Well, we reflected, at least we'd demonstrated that it could be done. Master, his curiosity satisfied, would no doubt tell us to go now and have our lunch.

"Very good," he commented approvingly. "I *thought* that method would work. Now then, why don't we try it just once more—on that mound over there?"

Adjusting our expectations accordingly, we started in a second time.

"Very good!" Master commented once again. Evidently not wishing to place obstacles in the way of the momentum we'd built up, he said, "Let's do just one more—this one over here."

And after that: "One more."

And then again: "Just one more."

I don't know how many mounds we leveled, but Norman, strong as he was, was beginning to moan softly under his breath. "Just one more," Master said again.

Suddenly, getting the joke at last, I stood up and laughed. Master smiled back at me.

"I was playing with you! Now—go have your lunch."

Often, in his training of us, he would push our equanimity to the limit to see which way we would break. If we rebelled, or if, under the strain, we grew upset, it meant we had failed the test. But if we responded with an extra spurt of energy, and affirmed a bright, positive attitude, we found his tests immeasurably strengthening.

In the foregoing test, Master helped Norman and me to learn to resist the thought of fatigue. Curiously, I found I was actually *less* tired after leveling those mounds than I had been beforehand. "The greater the will," as Master often said, "the greater the flow of energy."

One day Norman and I sat down to lunch, ravenous as usual. We reached for the tray that had been set before us, and gasped. It was practically empty! Two cups of tepid water, faintly flavored with chocolate, and a couple of dry sandwiches that had perhaps been waved in the general vicinity of an open jar of peanut butter. That was all.

"What a banquet!" Norman cried in dismay. We paused a moment. Then suddenly we were both laughing. "What comes of itself," Master often said, "let it come." One of the keys he gave us to unshakable inner peace was an ability to accept life as it is. Our meager fare that day gave us adequate food for meditation, if not for our bodies!

Shortly after the test of the two-by-four, Master began inviting us indoors after hours to listen to him while he dictated his writings. The truths I learned during those sessions were invaluable. So also were a few of the lessons I received, some of them less weighty, during periods of relaxation when he wasn't dictating.

As I've indicated earlier, the concept I had formed of a sage during my college years was of one to whom everything was a Serious Matter. I myself had laughed frequently, but it was more often *at* folly than in innocent joy. Like most college-trained intellectuals, my notion of wisdom tended to be rather dry. But until the intellect has been softened by heart qualities, it is like earth without water: weighty but infertile. Master was anxious to wean me from this addiction to an arid mental diet, even as I myself was anxious to be weaned.

One evening Norman and I were sitting with him in the kitchen. Master summoned one of the sisters and asked her to fetch a brown paper bag with something in it from his bedroom. When she returned, he switched off the lights. I heard him remove something from the bag, then chuckle playfully. Suddenly there was a metallic buzzing sound as sparks came leaping out of a toy pistol. Laughing with childlike glee, Master turned the lights back on. Next, from another toy pistol out of the bag, he shot a tiny parachute into the air. We watched together gravely as it descended to the floor. I was utterly astonished.

Master glanced at me merrily, though with a covert gaze of calm understanding. "How do you like them, Walter?"

I laughed, trying earnestly to enter into the spirit of the occasion. "They're fine, Sir!" My comment was almost an affirmation.

Looking at me deeply now, but with love, he quoted the words of Jesus: "Suffer little children to come unto me, for of such is the kingdom of God."*

One of the most amazing things about Master was his complete inner freedom. In the deepest matters he maintained the simplicity and light-hearted innocence of a child. In severe trials he could find cause for joy. Yet even when he laughed he retained the calm, detached outlook of one who beheld God alone everywhere. Often in the veriest trifles he saw some deep truth illustrated.

There was a dog at Twenty-Nine Palms named Bojo, who belonged to a neighbor. Bojo had decided, since Master's retreat was untenanted much of the time, that it belonged within his rightful domain. On our first arrival Bojo objected fiercely to Norman and me, growling and barking at us continually as we worked on the pool. It was Norman finally who won him over, with a combination of roughhouse and love: Whenever Bojo barked, Norman would tumble him onto his back, then pat him and throw sticks for him to fetch. Soon our canine neighbor began visiting us as a friend.

One day Master joined us out of doors for lunch. Bojo smelled the food and approached, sniffing hopefully.

* Luke 18:16.

"Look at that dog," Master remarked chuckling. He gave Bojo a little food from his plate. "Do you see how his forehead is wrinkled up? Though his thought is only for the food, in his earnest concentration his mind is focused at the spiritual eye!"

During dictation one evening, Master touched on the subject of reincarnation.

"Sir," I inquired, "have I been a yogi before?"

"Many times," he replied. "You would have to have been, to be here."

At this time Master began also revising his printed lessons. He was not able to get very far with them, unfortunately; the task proved simply too big, considering the many new writings he had in mind to complete. The first evening he worked on this project, Dorothy Taylor, his secretary, read to him from the old first lesson. She arrived at a passage where Master had said one can't get answers to scientific questions by merely praying for them; the appropriate experiments must be conducted also. Spiritual truths, similarly, so the lesson stated, require verification in the "laboratory" of yoga practice and of direct, inner contact with God.

"Mm-mmm," Master interrupted her, shaking his head. "That's not completely true. If one prayed deeply enough he *would* get answers, even to intricate scientific questions." He pondered the problem awhile.

"No," he concluded, "the point here concerns the need for verification by *appropriate* methods. In this sense, what has been written is valid, since prayer is effective in such matters only for those who already have some contact with God. I think I'll let it stand the way it is."

In this way, paragraph by paragraph, he would analyze what had been written before, clarify certain portions, and deepen the import of others. The insights I received from him thereby were priceless. Impressive to me also was his *manner* of teaching. Universal in outlook, never self-assertive, conscious of the relationship to the broadest realities of whatever he was considering, he was, I realized more and more, a true guide to the Infinite.

I was struck also by the sheer, dynamic courage of his teaching. Many a teacher would, I knew, be tempted to tone down what he said or wrote, as if hoping, by making them bland, to make them more popularly acceptable. But the hallmark of greatness is extraordinary energy, and such energy always poses a challenge to "one-horsepower" minds.

I was amused, some months later, by an example of the tendency to try to level every peak of energy. I have mentioned how Master, in his early years in America, would sometimes actually run out onto the lecture platform, challenging his audiences to come up to his own level of divine enthusiasm. Even now, long since those "campaign" days, he began his Sunday worship services with the joyous demand, "How is everybody?" He then led his congregation in the vibrant response: "Awake and ready!"

Dr. Lloyd Kennell, his alternate minister in San Diego, a sincere and good man, couldn't match Master's high energy-level. "I like to keep things on a moderate level," he explained to me before commencing his service one Sunday morning. He went out onto the stage. "Good morning," he began. "I trust that everyone present this morning is feeling awake and ready?" (No shouted response, of course.)

Master, more than any other teacher I have ever known, could stir people, shake them with the unexpected, charm them suddenly with a funny story, or startle them into alertness with some novel piece of information. Like Jesus, the words he uttered had the ring of truth. The veriest newcomer found his conviction irresistible.

No one else would have dared it, but for the first lesson of his correspondence course Master dictated a passage in support of his claim that a close karmic bond exists between our own direct line of gurus and the great master Jesus.

"Babaji, Lahiri Mahasaya, and Sri Yukteswar," he dictated, "were the three wise men who came to visit the Christ child in the manger. When Jesus became old enough, he returned their visit. The account of his trip to India was removed from the New Testament centuries later by sectarian prelates, who feared that its inclusion might lessen his stature in the eyes of the world."*

Master often talked to us of our line of gurus, and their special mission in this age. For he was the last in a direct line of spiritual succession. What he taught represented no radical new theory, no Eastern counterpart to our own interminable "scientific break-throughs" in the West, but the purest, highest, and indeed oldest spiritual tradition in the world.

Babaji is the first in this direct line of gurus. A master of great antiquity, he still lives in the Badrinarayan section of the Himalayas, where he remains accessible to a few highly advanced souls. In the latter half of the nineteenth century, Babaji, feeling that in the present scientific age mankind was better prepared to receive higher knowledge, directed his disciple, Shyama Charan Lahiri, to reintroduce to the world the long-hidden, most central science of yoga. Lahiri Mahasaya, as his disciples called him, named this exalted science *Kriya Yoga*, which means simply, "divine union through a certain technique, or spiritual act." Other yoga techniques bear the same name, but according to our own line of gurus the Kriya Yoga of Lahiri Mahasaya is the most ancient and central of all yoga techniques.

Babaji explained that it was to this technique that Lord Krishna, India's greatest ancient prophet, was referring in the Bhagavad Gita when he said, "I related this imperishable yoga to Bibaswat; Bibaswat taught it to Manu [the ancient Hindu law-giver]; Manu gave it to Ikshvaku [the renowned founder of the Solar dynasty]. In this way it was handed down in orderly succession to great sages until, after long stretches of time, knowledge of that yoga deteriorated in

---

* The fact that the Bible *says nothing at all* about those missing eighteen years offers the strongest possible evidence that the account of them was later deleted. For it is simply not credible that all four of the apostles would have omitted all mention of so large a segment of their Master's brief life span on earth. Even granting the possibility, which seems doubtful, that those eighteen years were too uneventful to record, any conscientious biographer—not to mention a *disciple*—would never on any account have left out altogether even a bridging sentence. At the very least he would have said something like, "And Jesus grew up, and worked in his father's carpentry shop." The fact that nothing at all is said suggests the later work of priests, whose religious convictions inspired them to delete, but prevented them from being so brazen as to add words of their own.

the world [because the generality of mankind had lost touch with spiritual realities]."

Lahiri Mahasaya, like Babaji, was a great master of yoga—a "*yogavatar*," Master called him, or "incarnation of yoga"—though at the same time a householder with worldly responsibilities. Of the many disciples that he initiated, the chief was Swami Sri Yukteswar—modern India's *gyanavatar*,* or "incarnation of wisdom," as Yogananda designated him. Thus it was, through Sri Yukteswar, that Paramhansa Yogananda was sent to America with the high technique which, our Gurus said, would give wise direction to the hitherto scattered, and potentially dangerous, development of modern Western civilization.

"In the divine plan," Yogananda stated on another occasion, "Jesus Christ was responsible for the evolution of the West, and Krishna (later, Babaji), for that of the East. It was intended that the West specialize in developing objectively, through logic and reason, and that the East specialize in inner, intuitive development. Now, the time has come in the cosmic plan to combine these two halves of a circle. East and West must unite."

During these evening dictations Master reviewed also the lessons on Kriya Yoga, and made certain changes in the way he had taught them previously. "This doesn't alter the technique itself," he explained, "but it will make it easier to understand."

---

* *Gyana* (wisdom) is often spelled *Jnana* in books. Master once commented to me on the problems of transliteration from Sanskrit to Roman characters. He was going over some of his writings with me at Twenty-Nine Palms, after I'd been with him about a year, when we came upon this word, *gyana*. "*Jnana* is how scholars like to spell it," Master scoffed. "It isn't *pronounced J-nana*. And how else are you going to pronounce it if you find it spelled that way? This is just an example of scholars' pedantry. *Gyana* is the correct pronunciation. The *g-y* in English doesn't show it exactly [pronounced rightly, there is a slight nasal touch to the sound], but at least it's much closer to the right way of saying it.

"Another transliteration that scholars prefer," Master continued, "is *v* in place of *b*. Instead of *Bibaswat*, they write *Vivaswat*. Instead of *Bishnu* they write *Vishnu*. Why? The way *v* is pronounced in English makes this Sanskrit pronunciation wrong. Again, *b* isn't exact, but it's closer."

In his native Bengali the sound is distinctly *B*. Pure Sanskrit resembles the *b* in the Spanish word *hablado*, where it is between a *b* and a *v*. (In Spanish, incidentally, the *d* is more like the *th* in our word, *the*.)

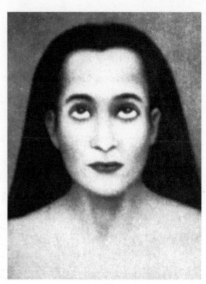

Jesus Christ   Babaji-Krishna

Our Line of Gurus

"In the divine plan," Paramhansa Yogananda stated, "Jesus Christ was responsible for the evolution of the West, and Krishna (later Babaji), for that of the East. It was intended that the West specialize in developing objectively, through logic and reason, and that the East specialize in inner, intuitive develpment. But in the cosmic plan the time has come to combine these two lines into one. East and West must unite."

JESUS CHRIST *(above left)*. Master said to me once, at Twenty-Nine Palms, "What a pity that none of the pictures of Jesus Christ really look like him." This painting by Hofmann was the one he preferred, because it resembled the Galilean master better than most.

BABAJI-KRISHNA *(above right)*. Babaji is known as *Mahavatar*, or Great Incarnation.

LAHIRI MAHASAYA *(opposite page, upper left)*. Disciple of Babaji. Paramhansa Yogananda described him as a *Yogavatar*, or Incarnation of Yoga.

SWAMI SRI YUKTESWAR *(opposite page, upper right)*. Disciple of Lahiri Mahasaya. Paramhansa Yogananda described him as a *Gyanavatar*, or Incarnation of Wisdom.

PARAMHANSA YOGANANDA *(opposite page, bottom)*. Disciple of Sri Yukteswar. Rajarshi Janakananda, Yogananda's foremost disciple, bestowed on his guru the title *Premavatar*, or Incarnation of Love. My title would be Bliss Avatar.

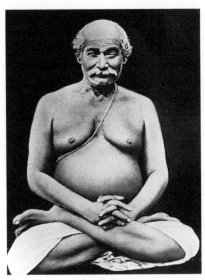

Lahiri Mahasaya

Swami Sri Yukteswar

Paramhansa Yogananda

I was avidly absorbing Master's every word: I hadn't yet been initiated into Kriya Yoga! Master paused suddenly.

"Say—Walter!" he exclaimed, "you haven't had Kriya initiation!"

"No, Sir." I was smiling smugly. He had already dictated enough for me to understand the technique.

"Well, in that case I shall have to initiate you right now." Interrupting his dictation, Master told us all to sit upright in meditative posture. "I am sending the divine light through your brain, baptizing you," he said from where he sat across the room. I immediately felt a divine current irradiating my brain from the Christ center between the eyebrows. He went on to guide me in the practice of the technique.

"Don't practice it yet, however," he concluded. "I shall be giving a formal initiation at Christmas time. Wait until then."

Gradually, as weeks passed, I found my heart opening like a flower under the sunrays of Master's love. More and more I was coming to appreciate what a blessing it was to have him for my guru.

During his dictation one evening he explained a method for attuning oneself to the Guru's subtle spiritual vibrations.

"Visualize the Guru," he said, "at the point between the eyebrows, the Christ center. This is the 'broadcasting station' in the body. Call to him deeply at this point. Then try to feel his response in your heart, which is the body's 'receiving set.' When that response comes, it will be here that you feel it intuitively. When it comes, pray deeply, 'Introduce me to God.'"

Sometimes also I visualized Master seated in diminutive form on the top of my head. Either way, as I meditated on him, I often felt a wave of peace or love descend over me, suffusing my entire being. Sometimes answers to questions would come, and a clearer understanding of qualities that I was trying to develop, or to overcome. Sometimes, in a single meditation on Master, I would find myself freed of some delusion that had plagued me for months, perhaps even for years. On one such occasion, as I approached him afterward and knelt for his blessing, he commented softly, "Very good!"

Master occasionally came over to the monks' retreat at Twenty-Nine Palms. At such times he would walk about the grounds with us, or sit with us and talk. Sometimes we meditated together. After one such meditation I recorded his words:

"This is the kingdom of AUM. Listen! It is not enough just to hear it. You must *merge* yourself in that sound. AUM *is* the Divine Mother." He paused a few minutes. "Om Kali, Om Kali, Om Kali. Listen. . . ." He paused again. "Oh, how beautiful it is! Om Kali, Om Kali, Om Kali!"*

On another occasion I was sleeping at the monks' retreat. It was late at night. Suddenly I awakened with the feeling that a divine presence was in the room. The impression was overwhelming. I sat up to meditate, then caught a glimpse of Master walking outside the house in the moonlight. Inexpressibly grateful to him, I went out and silently touched his feet.

Later he joked, "I thought you were a ghost!"

Master had the amazing gift of universal friendship. Each of us felt in some way uniquely loved by him. At the same time, it was a completely impersonal relationship, one in which outward favors counted for little. Such always, as I have come to understand, is divine friendship. Yet I have been in ashrams where human personalities were so much the focus of attention that, almost within minutes of one's arrival, one knew who the important disciples were, what they did, what the Guru said about them. By contrast, during my first few months as a monk in SRF I doubt whether I would have recognized more than one or two names in a "Who's Who" of Master's closest or oldest disciples. We received simply no encouragement to be curious about them.

---

* *Om* is a common transliteration for *Aum*, especially in English, where the vowel consists of two sounds. I have written it thus here to indicate how it should sound when chanted in English, though, technically, *Aum* is the more correct spelling because those three letters indicate the three distinct vibrations of cosmic manifestation: creation, preservation, and destruction. For pronunciation, this spelling can be misleading, for the *a* is not pronounced long, as in *car*, but short, as in the word "afar," where the first *a* is short; the second, long. The resulting diphthong sounds rather like the letter *o* in English.

In Hindu mythology the three vibrations of cosmic manifestation are represented by Brahma, Vishnu, and Shiva. *Aum* is the vibration by which the Supreme Spirit brings all things into manifestation. It is the Holy Ghost of the Christian Trinity.

Thus it was that, when word came that fall that Faye Wright (now Daya Mata, the third president of Self-Realization Fellowship) had been taken seriously ill, her name, though high on the list of Master's close disciples, meant nothing to me. I learned of her illness itself only as the explanation for why Master had suddenly departed Twenty-Nine Palms for Los Angeles.

"It would be a serious loss to the work if she died," Bernard assured me gravely.

"She was already gone," Master announced on his return from Los Angeles. "Just see how karma works. The doctor, though summoned in plenty of time, diagnosed her case wrongly. When he discovered his mistake, it was too late. She would certainly have died. But God wanted her life spared for the work."

Master counseled us not to be preoccupied over matters that didn't directly concern us. "Always remain in the Self," he counseled me once. "Come down only to eat or talk a little bit, if necessary. Then withdraw into the Self again." I didn't meet, or even see, Daya Mata until I had been with Master almost a year.

My immediate concern at Twenty-Nine Palms was our job. We'd dug the hole for the swimming pool. Other monks then came out to help construct the wood forms. Bernard informed us that the pouring of the concrete would have to be done continuously, to prevent seaming. We did the whole job by hand, mixing and pouring with the aid of a small cement mixer. I shoveled the sand; someone else added the gravel; others maneuvered wheelbarrows to the pouring sites. Twenty-three hours we labored, pausing only occasionally to refresh ourselves with sandwiches and hot drinks. Inwardly, however, as we worked, we chanted constantly to God, and the hours passed joyously. At the end of it all I think we actually had more energy than at the day's start. We were all smiling happily.

All of us, that is, but one. This man, after an hour or two of half-hearted labor, had grumbled, "I didn't come here to shovel *cement!*" Sitting down, he watched us for the remainder of the day, reminding us occasionally that this wasn't what the spiritual path was all about. Interestingly, at the end of that long day he alone felt exhausted.

The subject of this particular disciple's unwillingness came up a few months later in a discussion with Master. "He told me, Sir," I remarked, "that he feels he can't obey you implicitly, because he wants to develop his own free will."

"But his will is not free!" Master replied wonderingly. "How can it be free, as long as he is bound by moods and desires? I don't *ask* anyone to follow me, but those who have done so have found true freedom.

"Sister," he continued, using the name by which he always referred to Sister Gyanamata, the elderly disciple whom I'd met on my first visit to Encinitas—"Sister used to run up and down all the time doing my bidding. One day a few of the others said to her, 'Why are you always doing what *he* says? You have your own will!' She answered, 'Well, but don't you think it's too late to change? And I must say, I have never been so happy in my life as I have been since coming here.'"

Master chuckled. "They never bothered her again!"

Already I could endorse in my own little way Sister Gyanamata's reply to those reluctant disciples. For the more I tuned my will to Master's, the happier I found myself becoming.

"My will," Master often said, "is only to do God's will." The proof of his statement lay in the fact that the more perfectly we followed his will, the freer we ourselves felt, in God.

As Christmas approached, my heart was singing with a happiness I had never before even dreamed existed. Christmas was an important holiday at Mt. Washington, the most sacred of the entire year. Master had divided it into its two basic aspects: "spiritual Christmas," which we celebrated on Christmas Eve, and "social Christmas," celebrated the following day with traditional present-opening and a banquet. (Master later shifted our "spiritual Christmas" back to the twenty-third, so that devotees wouldn't have to stay up all night afterwards, preparing food for the large Christmas Day banquet.)

On the twenty-fourth we gathered in the chapel at ten in the morning for an all-day meditation, inviting the infinite Christ to be born anew in the "mangers" of our hearts. I don't know how many have approached their first experience of this long meditation with-

Christmas at Mt. Washington, 1949. St. Lynn (Rajarshi Janakananda), Master, and Dr. Lewis are seated at the table. Mrs. Lewis is standing behind St. Lynn. I am standing in the background.

out trepidation. Few, I suspect, and among them certainly I don't include myself.

We took our seats, Master at the front of the room facing us. The doors were closed. From that moment on, save for a short break in the middle, no one was supposed to enter or leave the room except in an emergency.

We began with a prayer to Jesus Christ, our other masters, and "the saints of all religions" to bless us on this holy occasion. There followed some fifteen or twenty minutes of chanting.

Paramhansa Yogananda's "Cosmic Chants" consist of simple sentences repeated over and over again, each time with deeper concentration and devotion. I had been raised on the intricacies of Western classical music. It had taken me some time, as Master's disciple, to adjust fully to this rather stark form of musical expression. By now, however, I had come to love the chants. In their very simplicity I found beauty, and a power that surpassed that of most, if not all, the music I had ever heard. For these were "spiritualized" chants: Master had infused subtle blessings into them by singing each one until it elicited a divine response. As buildings and places develop vibrations according to the consciousness of the people who frequent them, so music also develops vibrations beyond those of the actual sound. Chants that have been spiritualized, particularly by great saints, have a heightened power to inspire whoever sings them.

One chant we sang that day was "Cloud-colored Christ, come! O my Christ, O my Christ, Jesus Christ, come!" I found it marvelously effective for taking me deep into meditation. Sessions of chanting alternated with increasingly long periods of meditation. Sometimes, to alleviate any physical tension we might be feeling, Master had us stand while chanting; for some of the more rhythmic chants he had us clap our hands. A couple of times he requested Jane Brush to play devotionally inspiring pieces on the organ, while we listened meditatively.

At some time during that afternoon Master had a vision of the Divine Mother. In an ecstatic state he related Her wishes to many of those present. Some he told to give themselves unreservedly to God. Others he informed that the Cosmic Mother had blessed them specially. And then he spoke to Her directly, out loud, that we might hear at least one side of this blissful dialogue.

"Oh, You are so beautiful!" he repeated over and over. "Don't go!" he cried at last. "You say the material desires of these people are driving you away? Oh, come back! Please don't go!"

The meditation that day was so deep that the customary ten-minute recess halfway through it was omitted. The apprehension I had felt at the outset proved a delusion. "The soul loves to meditate," Master used to tell us. It is the ego, in its attachment to body-consciousness, that resists entering the inner vastness.

On Christmas Day we exchanged gifts in the traditional manner. Included with a more serious present that I gave Master was a "Slinky" toy, in memory of that incident of the toy pistols at Twenty-Nine Palms. In return, I received from him a four-color pencil—"To split infinitives with!" he told me with a smile.

This day had, for its main feature, an afternoon banquet at which Master presided. I helped to serve the curry dinner. Afterwards Master addressed us. The sweetness of his speech so uplifted me that, to me, it was as though I were living in heaven. Never had I thought such divine inspiration possible on this prosaic earth.

The following day Master gave Kriya Yoga initiation—primarily, if not entirely, to the renunciates. As I approached him for his blessing, I prayed mentally for his help in developing divine love. After I'd been touched by him at the Christ center, I opened my eyes to find him smiling at me blissfully.

Toward the end of the initiation ceremony, Master said, "Lots of angels have passed through this room today." And then these thrilling words of promise: "Of those present, there will be a few *siddhas*, and quite a few *jivan muktas*."*

On New Year's Eve we gathered in the main chapel for a midnight meditation, again led by Master. At one point during the proceedings he beat a large gong, softly, then with gradually increasing volume, alternately decreasing and increasing the volume in waves. "Imagine this as the sound of AUM," he told us, "spreading outward to infinity."

At the same instant, one hundred miles south in Encinitas, another group of disciples was meditating in the main room of the hermitage. They, too, heard the gong as Master was striking it. One of the monks later told me, "It was as though it were being struck in the hallway just outside the room we were in."

The meditation that followed at Mt. Washington was enthralling.

Midnight came: Suddenly, waves of noise sweeping up from the city below, and inward from the surrounding neighborhood—factory whistles, car horns, shouts as countless celebrants ushered in the New Year. The door of a neighboring house opened, and a voice with a tone almost of desperation shouted into the night: "Happy New Year!"

What a contrast, between the frantic, emotional, almost febrile excitement in the sounds that were being unleashed by the thousands of celebrants around us, and the calm, expanding soul-joy we experienced in ourselves, in the sublime peace of our little chapel! And how blessed, I reflected, how wonderful it was to be in this holy place, at the feet of my divine guru!

I prayed that the New Year would bring me an ever deepening awareness of God's love.

---

* A *jivan mukta* is one who has become freed of delusion, but still has some past karma to overcome. A *siddha* has been freed from all traces of past karma.

CHAPTER 21

Paramhansa Yogananda

ON JANUARY 5, THE disciples gathered at Mt. Washington to celebrate Paramhansa Yogananda's birthday. As the function began, we went up to him individually and knelt for his blessing. After a banquet, later, he spoke of his longing to see an awakening of divine love throughout the world. In a more personal vein he continued:

"I never dreamt, during my first years of teaching in this country, that such a fellow-feeling in God's love would be possible here. It exists only because you have lived up to the ideals that I have cherished, and for which I lived in the company of my great guru."

Friendship in God, surely, was the key to our relationship with him. It implied no easy-going relationship such as worldly people enjoy with one another, but demanded of us, rather, the utmost that we had to give. The friendship our Guru extended to us was to our souls. To reciprocate in kind meant to strive unceasingly to meet him on that divine level. Those who clung to the desire for ego-gratification could not coax from him a compromise in the pure quality of his friendship. If a disciple flattered him, Master would gaze at him quietly as if to say, "I will not desecrate the love I bear you by accepting this level of communication." Always he held out to us the highest ideal to which each of us might aspire. Such perfect love imposes the most demanding of all disciplines, for ultimately it asks nothing less of the disciple than the total gift to God of himself.

I used to pray to Master, "Teach me to love you as you love me." Chatting with a group of us one day after hours in the main office, he looked at me penetratingly and said, "How can the little cup expect to hold the whole ocean of love? First it has to expand and become as big as the ocean!"

The Indian scriptures state that when the soul has released its hold on egoic individuality, it merges into the ocean of Spirit, becoming one with it. While most of us loved Master from varying degrees of ego-identification, his love for us was without limit—indeed, cosmic. To ordinary human beings, such love is inconceivable. "I killed Yogananda long ago," he used to say. "No one dwells in this temple now but God." His love for us was God's love, manifested through his human form.

"Whenever I look at you," Norman once wrote Master in a note, "I see only the Divine Mother."

"Then behave accordingly," Master replied with impersonal calmness when next they met. This was no modest disclaimer, but only an objective acceptance of things as they were. Yogananda was the humblest man I ever knew, yet it was humility only in the sense that there was no ego there at all, not in the sense that his manner was self-deprecating. Indeed, when someone once praised him for his humility, I recall the simple answer he gave: "How can there be humility, when there is no consciousness of ego?"

In essence, our relationship with him was not only a friendship *in* God, but *with* God, whose love alone he expressed to us. Always, with firm resolution, he turned toward the Divine all the love we gave him. Whenever we touched his feet in the manner customary among Indian disciples to their guru, he held his right hand reverently at his forehead, extending the fingers upward, to indicate that he directed our devotion to God. And if anyone's affection for him displayed the slightest attachment, he often became distant and reserved until that person had understood it was God's love alone that he extended to us.

Daya Mata tells a story dating back to when she was a teenager and new on the path. At first, in her association with him, he had treated her lovingly, like a daughter (which indeed she had been to him in a former incarnation). Once her feet were planted firmly on the path, however, he began to teach her the superior merits of impersonal love. To her now, feeling for him as she did the affection of a devoted daughter, he seemed all at once aloof, even stern.

One evening in Encinitas he addressed her that way. She went out onto the bluff above the ocean behind the hermitage, and prayed deeply for understanding. At last she reached a firm resolution. "Divine Mother," she vowed, "from now on I will love only Thee. In beholding him, I will see Thee alone in him."

Suddenly she felt as though a great weight had been lifted from her. Later she went indoors and knelt before Master for his blessing, as she always did before retiring

Paramhansa Yogananda

for the night. This time he greeted her gently, saying, "Very good!"

From then on he showed himself once more affectionate toward her. Now, however, their relationship was on a deeper level, for the disciple saw him at last in that impersonal light in which he beheld himself.

For us who came to him years later, it was an inspiration to see between Faye and Master a friendship truly divine. Such, too, was the friendship he extended to each of us, although few—alas—ever came to appreciate so fully the extraordinary sensitivity of his gift. Each of us struggled in his own way to reconcile the apparent contradiction between this kindest, most considerate of friends, as he so often showed himself to be, and on the other hand one who was willing to subject us to painful lessons. For though we knew the lessons were for our good, often it was a good that awaited us beyond our present ability to understand. Yet the contradiction lay, in fact, in ourselves: between the petty demands of our egos for comfort and reassurance, and the uncompromising call to inner perfection of our souls.

Master himself was completely self-integrated. Living in the impersonal Spirit made him in no way indifferent to human pain. Both levels, the human and the divine, were to him parts of a single reality—the human part being merely its limited, outward manifestation.

He didn't want us to ignore the human aspect, for it was this which drew us toward the divine. I remember one occasion, when he was standing with a small group of us, about two yards away from me. The thought came, "He isn't really standing here with us: He is inside me. In essence, he is infinite."

Just then Master walked over to me with a quiet smile, and gave me an apple! He was implying, "Don't be so sternly philosophical that you reject the human aspect of our relationship."

He once said to me, "I prefer to work with love. I just wilt when I have to work in other ways." I myself noted, whenever he scolded me, a deep regret in his eyes at the lack of understanding on my part that had made his reprimand necessary. He reassured us, however, "I scold only those who listen. I won't scold those who don't." It wasn't that he *couldn't* relate to us on a human level. Rather it was that, for those who wanted the most precious gift that he had to bestow—the knowledge of God—he knew he had to destroy our every egoic attachment.

With other people—and with us, too, when he chose to relax his discipline—he was, I think, as charming, warm-hearted, and utterly delightful a human being as ever lived. In the truest and best sense of the word he was a *noble* man. Because his self-integration was flawless, divine perfection expressed itself even in his casual behavior. To some of the disciples, also, he showed complete approval and acceptance: to those who were able to relate to him truly in God.

To hear him talk informally with such disciples was deeply inspiring. I think what struck me most about his relationship with them was its quiet dignity, its foundation in the fullest mutual respect. When they laughed together, it was as though they shared some deep, inner joy of which laughter was merely an outward expression, and by no means a necessary one. Manifestly, their deepest communion together was in silence.

The more I attuned myself to Master, the more deeply I came to appreciate the transcendent beauty of his inner friendship. It was a communion that needed no outward proximity for confirmation. Blessed with it, one even rejoiced when others endeavored to set themselves higher than oneself in the Guru's esteem. For one knew that egoic approval had nothing to do with that inner attunement.

In some ways I think it was his utter respect for others that impressed me the most deeply about Master. It always amazed me that someone whose wisdom and power inspired so much awe in others could be at the same time so humbly respectful to all. I had always considered respect something one gave only where it was due. And in a sense, of course, Master gave it in that spirit, too, but what it meant in his case was a demonstration of deep respect because he saw God in everyone. As Master said once to Dr. Lewis, his first disciple in America, "Remember, God loves you just as much as He loves me. He is our common Father."

Sometime during my second year at Mt. Washington a man came from India with a letter of introduction to Master. He asked permission to stay two or three days in the ashram. To everyone's

Paramhansa Yogananda with Dr. Lewis, his first American disciple.

inconvenience, those "two or three days" extended to many weeks. He had already extended his expected visit by more than a week when, one day, he sent Master a complaining letter. The food, it seemed, was too Western for his tastes; would Paramhansaji kindly rectify the matter? Master quietly arranged for Indian-style food to be sent to him from his own kitchen.

I once saw Master chat with a group of Indians after a public performance in Pasadena. One man in the group was, as the saying goes, "feeling no pain." Affecting great familiarity in his drunkenness, he threw an arm around Master's shoulders and shouted playfully, as though considering the two of them old drinking buddies. Debi, who was standing nearby, made some deprecating remark in Bengali.

"Don't," Master replied in English, shaking his head a little sternly. In his eyes this man, regardless of his temporary condition, deserved the respect due him as a child of God.

A certain religious teacher in Los Angeles, a woman of considerable worldly means, once helped the Master's work financially, and behaved in consequence as if she owned him. Master, as unbuyable a person as ever lived, continued to act only as God guided him from within. Gradually the woman developed toward him a sense of possessive jealousy, and on several occasions spoke to him venomously, hurling such insults as would have made any ordinary person her enemy. Master, however, remained unalterably calm and respectful toward her. Never sharp in his replies, always kind, he was like a fruit tree in full bloom which, when an axe is laid to its roots, showers its malefactor with sweet-smelling blossoms. The lady gradually developed high regard for him, praised him to others, and often took her friends and students to visit his centers. All her anger and jealousy became converted into ungrudging esteem.

In Ranchi, India, I was told a touching story dating back to Master's return there in 1935. It seems that an anniversary banquet was planned at his school. Someone was needed to preside over the function and give it official standing. The name of Gurudas Bannerji, a prominent judge, was recommended. Widely esteemed, this man was, everyone agreed, the best possible choice. Master went to invite him.

What was Master's surprise, then, when the judge coldly refused to come. He knew all about India's so-called "holy men," he said; he was looking at a typical example of them right before him. They were insincere, after people's money, a drain on the community. He had no patience with them, nor time to speak for their worthless causes.

Master, though astonished by this reception, was unruffled by it. As he often told us, "Praise cannot make me any better, nor blame any worse. I am what I am before my conscience and God." After hearing the judge out, he replied in a friendly tone, "Well, perhaps you'll reconsider. We should be greatly honored if you would come."

The principal of a local school, meanwhile, agreed to preside in the judge's stead. When everyone had assembled for the banquet that evening, and the affair was about to begin, a car drove up. Out stepped the caustic judge. Since Gurudas Bannerji was such a prominent figure in those parts, the school principal readily offered his own place to him.

After the banquet there were several preliminary reports. One dealt with the school's growth, and with the number of students who had gone on after graduation to become monks and religious teachers. "If the present trend continues," the report read, "soon all of India will be covered with our graduates spreading the ancient wisdom of our land."

Then came the judge's turn to speak. Rising, he said: "Today is one of the happiest days of my life. This morning your Swami Yogananda came to visit me. I felt great joy on beholding him, but I decided to test him and see whether he was really as good a man as he looked. I spoke to him as rudely as I knew how. Yet he remained so calm, and answered me so kindly, that I tell you in all sincerity he passed my test better than I would have imagined possible. And I will tell you something more: Never mind the numbers of your graduates who are becoming monks. India has many monks. But if you can produce even one such man as this, not your school only, nor only our city, but our whole country will be glorified!"

One of my brother disciples, acting under the spell of a violent delusion, once wrote Master a long letter filled with scathing criticism for what he imagined to be Master's faults. The letter announced his intention of leaving the ashram immediately. He must subsequently have seen his error, for he remained. One day, shortly after writing that letter, he was standing with a group of us when Master came downstairs. Seeing him, Master remarked, "You should take up writing. That was the best letter Satan ever wrote me." Master's voice, free of any resentment, held a note of genuine admiration.

His humility didn't prevent him, however, from giving a strong reply sometimes, if he felt that one might prove helpful. An orthodox minister once, incensed at the presence of an orange-robed "heathen" in this, our most Christian land, and perturbed especially because the Master wouldn't endorse certain of his more narrow dogmas, shouted at him one day on a train, "You will go to hell!"

Master, seeing the anger etched on the man's face, replied affably, "Well I may get there by and by, but my friend, *you* are there already!" The passengers in the carriage had been following this dialogue with interest. At this answer, there came a general wave of laughter.

Wonderful as was Master's quality of universal respect, it might be supposed that it entailed at least one disadvantage: an inability to see the funny side of what is often called the human comedy. The supposition would not be valid. In truth, I have never known anyone with a keener sense of the ridiculous. Master's capacity for amusement, as we see from the foregoing story, was lively enough to remain undaunted even when faced with what might be termed the "ultimate denunciation." Under similar circumstances, most people would have been reduced to humorless anger, or at least to indignation.

In the case of that fanatical minister, Master had a lesson to impart to him. He never made fun of others, however, if he thought that doing so might inflict unnecessary pain on them. Herein, indeed, lay a fundamental difference between his sense of humor and that of most people.

For that performance at Pasadena, which I touched on a few paragraphs back, his presumptuous guest from India had somehow managed to grab star billing as a Hindu dancer. As far as I know, the only actual "dancing" he'd ever done was in the boxing ring, where he'd achieved some success. His large physique, however, was impressive. When he announced that he intended to dance, it was understood by everyone that he meant business.

His performance that evening was planned to portray a deer being stalked by a hunter. Assuming both roles to himself, he alternately lumbered through his representation of the deer gamboling playfully in forest glades, and stalked ferociously through tall grasses as the hunter. Presently it became clear that he wasn't keeping in time with the music. This realization finally dawned on him, too, and of course only one explanation would do: It had to be the orchestra; it wasn't following *him*. Indignantly he instructed the players to suspend their playing, then strode down to the footlights and apologized for the musicians' lack of musicianship.

"They aren't professionals," he explained gravely. Thereafter, every time his playful gamboling took him past where they sat ranged against the back of the stage, he waved his arms and hands, urging them in a fierce undertone to keep the time.

Master and I, seated together, were in paroxysms of mirth. Tears streamed down our cheeks, though we managed fairly well to keep from laughing out loud. "Don't!" squeaked Master unsteadily when I let slip a muffled guffaw.

Well, the hunter finally shot his deer. Was this—finally—the end? By no means! The poor creature had now to be portrayed writhing about the stage in agony. After many minutes the deer gasped its last, and sprawled full length on the "forest floor." There followed a little scattered applause—less, I think, from a desire to congratulate the dancer than out of relief. The relief was premature, however. The hunter still lived!

Leaping up now in his alternate role, our boxer flung the deer over his shoulders and began a sort of victory cakewalk. Already we knew he had no sense of timing. Now it appeared that he also had no sense of *time*, for his performance gave evidence of reaching out to embrace eternity. Through tears of laughter we finally saw one of the musicians glance offstage and make a lowering motion with his hand. The curtain began to fall. The hunter, poised in yet another victory

stance, saw it coming and shot a furious glance offstage. Immediately
he began to move in that direction. The last we saw of him was his
legs from the knees downward, striding offstage with grim purpose
to give the hapless stagehand a piece of his mind.

Master had laughed as heartily this evening as I ever saw him laugh.
Yet he showed no inclination, afterward, to discomfit his guest. Such
indeed is the nature of pure joy; though good-humored, it is always
kindly. When the man complained later at his mistreatment, Master's
mood was gently consoling. "I understand," he said. And he did,
too. He understood all aspects of the matter. He could feel the man's
indignation and sympathize with it on its own level, though he knew
it was founded on a delusion. Master described divine consciousness
as, "center everywhere, circumference nowhere." His sympathy for
the "performer" was completely sincere.

But then, it was his sympathy for all of us, in our multifarious delusions, that inspired his lifelong labor of teaching, counseling, and
self-sacrifice on our behalf. He once said, "Divine Mother has a good
sense of humor."

One day, in Chicago, a drunken stranger staggered up and
embraced him affectionately.

"Hello there, Jeshush Chrisht!"

Master smiled. Then, to give the man a taste of the infinitely better
"spirits" he himself enjoyed, he looked deeply into the man's eyes
and gave him a taste of divine joy.

"Shay," the fellow cried thickly, "whad're *you* drink'n'?"

Master replied, his eyes twinkling, "Let's just say, it has a lot of
kick in it!" The man was sobered by this glance. "I left him," Master
told us later, "wondering what had happened!"

Is it not particularly interesting that this man should have addressed Master as Jesus Christ? The Master's olive-colored skin,
black hair, and brown eyes didn't at all correspond to the popular
Nordic image of a blue-eyed, blond Jesus. Master, moreover, kept
no beard.

A woman whom I once met at an SRF center meeting in New York
described a reaction similar to that man's. "I bought a painting," she
told me, "in a dusty old second-hand store. It was a portrait, but

I didn't know who the subject was; I just knew his eyes inspired me. I used to think of him as Jesus Christ. Placing the painting on my mantelpiece, I prayed daily in front of it. Years later I came upon *Autobiography of a Yogi*. The moment I saw Master's photograph on the cover, I recognized him as the very man in that painting!"

Another woman, a member of our Hollywood congregation, told me, "I used to pray deeply to God to draw me closer to Him. One day I had a vision of someone I'd never seen before. A voice said, 'Christ is coming!' Shortly thereafter, a friend brought me to this church for the first time. Master was conducting the service. The moment I saw him, I said to my friend, 'Why, that's the very face I saw in my vision!'"

Another member of our Hollywood church told me, "Years before I knew anything about Master, my husband and I happened to catch a glimpse of him through a restaurant window. 'Look at that man!' I exclaimed. 'He must be the most spiritual human being I've ever seen!' Years later I met Master, and knew him immediately for that very man."

Even as a boy, the Master's magnetism was extraordinary. Dr. Nagendra Nath Das, a Calcutta physician and lifelong friend, visited Mt. Washington in July 1950. He told us, "Wherever Paramhansaji went, even as a boy, he attracted people. His father, a high railway official, often gave us travel passes. No matter where we traveled, within minutes after we'd descended from the train a group of boys would gather around us."

Part of the basis for Master's amazing charisma was the fact that, seeing his infinite Beloved in everyone, he awakened them to an inchoate belief in their own goodness. With the impersonality of true greatness, he never accepted the thought others projected onto him that he was essentially different from them.

Bernard, upon whom Master had been urging some difficult undertaking, remonstrated one day, "Well, Sir, *you* can do it. You're a *master*."

"And what do you think *made* me a master?" the Guru demanded. "It was by *doing*! Don't cling to the thought of weakness, if your desire is to become strong."

"There was a devotee," Master once told us, "who was sitting be-fore the image of his guru, chanting and casting flowers onto it as an expression of his devotion. His concentration became so deep that suddenly he beheld the whole universe contained within his own consciousness. 'Oh!' he cried, 'I have been placing flowers on an-other's image, and now I see that I, untouched by this body, am the Sustainer of the universe. I bow to myself!' And he began to throw the flowers onto his own head.

"Oh! when Master [Sri Yukteswar] told me that story I was so thrilled I went into *samadhi*.* That devotee wasn't speaking from ego. Rather, he was rejoicing in the *death* of his ego."

This was the relationship Master sought ever to establish with us: a relationship wherein we realized with our entire being that we, too, were That.

Leo Cocks, one of the younger monks, used to take photographs of Master whenever he could. The walls of his room became papered over with them.

"Why do you keep on taking photographs of this physical form?" Master demanded of him one day. "What is it but flesh and bones? Get to know me in meditation if you want to know who I really am!"

And once, when we were serving him, he remarked, "You all are so kind to me with your many attentions." Karle Frost, one of the disciples present, exclaimed, "Oh, no, Master. It is *you* who are kind to us!"

"God is helping God," Master replied with a sweet smile. "That is the nature of His cosmic drama."

The closer we drew to him spiritually, the less he sought to teach us by words. "I prefer to speak with the eyes," he once told me. He never wanted to *impose* his instructions on us from without. His method of teaching was, rather, to help us dig wells of intuitive in-sight within ourselves. The closer we felt to him, the closer we came to knowing our own true Self: the God within us.

---

* *Samadhi* (cosmic consciousness) is the state of infinite awareness that comes to the yogi once the hypnosis of ego has been broken. Christian saints have sometimes described this state as "mystical marriage," for in it the soul merges into God, be-coming one with Him.

CHAPTER 22
Renunciation

M<small>Y SUDDEN CONVERSION</small> to this totally unexpected life had the effect on my earthly family of a grenade hurled unexpectedly into one's dining room during a leisurely Sunday breakfast. My parents believed strongly in giving us children the freedom to follow our own lights, but even so, their concern for my happiness made them anything but indifferent to what struck them as a sudden plunge into insanity. Nor did I help matters much when, in my zeal of conversion, I endeavored to persuade them that my choice was the only sane one.

Some weeks after my arrival at Mt. Washington, I received a letter from Father Kernan, the associate minister at our Church of St. James the Less, in Scarsdale. Was I, he inquired sympathetically, in some emotional or spiritual difficulty? And was there anything I might like from him in the way of help or advice? Though I was touched by his considerateness, I replied that, if he really wanted to understand why I'd left the church, he might read *Autobiography of a Yogi*. Some months later he remarked to Mother, "We don't ask enough of people like Donald."

Next, some military officer came out (I don't recall his connection with my family), offered to help if he could, decided he couldn't, and left—presumably to report that at least I wasn't starving to death. Some time after that, Sue and Bud Clewell, relatives in Westwood Village (a suburb of Los Angeles; my mother and Sue were first cousins), visited me with pleas that I not estrange myself from the family. My brother Bob wrote from New York to ask if I wouldn't join him in some housing-development scheme; he wanted me to write the brochures for it. Dick, my youngest brother, wrote from Williams College, "Couldn't you have found what you wanted in one of the monastic orders of your own church?"

Bernard told me one day of his own experience—not with relatives in his case, but with erstwhile companions. "Shortly after I moved to Encinitas," he said, "a group of my old friends arrived, determined to kidnap and hold me forcibly until I agreed to give up this 'wild-eyed fanaticism'—in other words, to become, like them, a devotee of the dollar! Fortunately I wasn't around to receive them: Master had sent me that morning on some urgent errand to Mt. Washington. My friends, thwarted, soon abandoned their plan."

Whether by coercion or by love, it is not unusual for people who dedicate their lives to high ideals to encounter opposition from well-meaning friends and relatives. For between selfless idealism and worldliness there exists a fundamental incompatibility. Worldliness lives in the constant expectation of personal rewards and benefits, of desires satisfied, of value *received*. Idealism scorns personal benefit, renounces selfish desires, and views life rather in terms of value *given*. It finds its highest benefit in the very act of sacrifice, and considers that a true gain which worldliness views only as a loss. "Fanaticism," is the verdict commonly pronounced by worldly people on any but the most pallid expressions of idealism.

And if that verdict isn't forthcoming, "ulterior motives" is the back-up charge. All the while, however, worldliness feels vaguely uneasy in the presence of selfless dedication, as though sensing in it some hidden threat to all that it holds dear. For the soul of every human being knows that its true home is not in this world, but in infinity.

Perfect representatives of either side are rare, of course. Worldliness and renunciation are qualities that people *manifest* to varying degrees, but no single human quality ever suffices to define an individual. Worldly people may even, in one part of their natures, applaud heroic self-sacrifice in others. And many, of course, are no strangers to self-sacrifice themselves; in fact, they sacrifice much for their own families and their more worldly ideals. Moreover—strange twist of human nature!—it is frequently the worldly man who most sternly censures the renunciate who falls from his ideals. And of course the renunciate, for his part, must do constant battle in himself against worldly self-interest.

But the fact remains that between worldliness and renunciation, considered as abstractions, there is not and can never be the slightest compatibility. As the Bible puts it, "Whosoever will be a friend of the world is the enemy of God."*

The renunciate's worldly friends and relatives would always prefer to see him keep his feet in both boats. Indeed, he may legitimately show them love as children of God. But if he dwells *pleasurably* on the thought, "These are *my* people," or if he looks on their worldliness with sympathetic favor, he places himself in real danger of losing his vocation. For one who keeps his feet in two boats may fall in between and drown. Many a renunciate has abandoned his high ideals because he tried to reconcile in his own mind these two conflicting worlds.

In the Biblical story of the Jews' exodus from Egypt lies a deep spiritual allegory. Only those who had been born out of captivity, in the wilderness, were permitted to enter the Promised Land. With man, similarly, only those mental qualities which are born in the "wilderness" of meditative silence—qualities such as humility, devotion, and soul-joy: gifts, all, of divine grace—can be brought over into the "Promised Land" of divine union. Pride, anger, greed, lust—the offspring, in short, of man's ego-bondage—must die, before God-consciousness can be attained. ("Blessed are the pure in heart," Jesus said, "for they *shall see God*."†) Even a wise, discriminating ego—symbolized in this story by Moses‡—though capable of leading one out of worldly captivity and of shepherding him through the long process of spiritual purification, must eventually offer itself up into the infinite light. Moses was permitted to behold the Promised Land from afar, but he had to die before his people could enter and live there. As Jesus put it, "He who will lose his life [who will, in other words, offer it completely to God] for my sake shall save it."§

* James 4:4.

† Matthew 5:8.

‡ Symbolism apart, Paramhansa Yogananda once told me that Moses was a true master.

§ Luke 9:24.

The worldly person asks first of life, "What do *I* want?" The devotee is indifferent to questions of personal, egoic fulfillment, and asks only, "What does God want?" Renunciation is an inner state of consciousness, not an outward act. All men, whether married or single, who love God and want to know Him must reconcile themselves to living for Him alone. The pathway of the heart is too narrow for the ego and God to walk it together; one of them must step aside and make way for the other.

"Living for God," Yogananda said, "is martyrdom": martyrdom of the ego; martyrdom of self-will and selfishness; martyrdom of all that worldliness clings to so desperately. But the true devotee comes in time to see that this isn't martyrdom at all, since its end is blissful freedom in the only *true* Self: God. We are sons of the Infinite! Anything that binds us to a limited existence desecrates this divine image within ourselves. Renunciation is no abject self-deprivation, but a glorious affirmation of the universe of joy that is our birthright.

As St. John of the Cross put it:

> In order to arrive at having pleasure in everything,
>   Desire pleasure in nothing.
> In order to arrive at possessing everything,
>   Desire to possess nothing.
> In order to arrive at being everything,
>   Desire to be nothing.
> In order to arrive at the knowledge of everything,
>   Desire to know nothing.*

The essence of renunciation is to relinquish the poverty-consciousness of a beggar, and the clutching attitude of a miser towards things, places, people, experiences—in short, the limitations of this world—and to offer oneself constantly at the feet of Infinity.

Especially in the beginning of the spiritual life, Yogananda told us, it is better to mix little or not at all with worldly people. For it is essential that one's heart be strengthened to prepare it for making

---

* This poem, incidentally, shows also the close correlation that exists between the mystical experiences of the great Christian saints and those of great yogis. St. John's expressions—"possessing everything, being everything," etc.—are no mere metaphors. He is describing, quite literally, the state known to yogis as *samadhi,* or cosmic consciousness. In Chapter 33 many more such Christian corroborations of the ancient yogic teachings are presented.

this heroic gift to God of every desire, every thought, every emotion. No weakling could even possibly make so total a self-offering. Cowards quickly fall by the wayside. None who enter the spiritual path for its superficial glamour alone can survive tests that have no other purpose than to assault the devotee's every natural inclination. The more completely one can identify himself with an attitude of complete self-surrender, the more likely he is to succeed in his spiritual search.

This is as true for householders as for monks and nuns. Outward renunciation merely helps to affirm the inner resolve, necessary for all devotees, to seek God alone.

In the Self-Realization Fellowship monasteries, Paramhansa Yogananda taught us boldly to claim our new identity as sons of God, and to reject all consciousness of worldly ties.

"Sir," I began one day, "my father. . . ."

"You have no father!" Master peremptorily reminded me. "God is your Father."*

"I'm sorry, Sir. I meant, my *earthly* father."

"That's better," the Master replied, approvingly.

"Milk will not float on water," he often reminded us, "but mingles with it. Similarly, as long as your devotion is still 'liquid'—that is to say, untried—it may be diluted by worldly influences. You should avoid such influences, therefore, as much as possible. Only when the 'milk' of your consciousness has been churned into the 'butter' of divine realization will it float easily on the 'water' of this world, and remain unaffected by it."

"The mind of the worldly man," he once said, "is like a bucket riddled with holes of desires, distractions, and worries. It is impossible for a person in such a state of mind to gather and hold the milk of peace."

---

* "While he yet talked to the people, behold, his mother and his brethren stood without, desiring to speak with him. Then one said unto him, Behold, thy mother and thy brethren stand without, desiring to speak with thee. But he answered and said unto him that told him, Who is my mother? and who are my brethren? And he stretched forth his hand toward his disciples, and said, Behold my mother and my brethren! For whosoever shall do the will of my Father which is in heaven, the same is my brother, and sister, and mother." (Matthew 12:46–50)

Master was compassionate toward those who were weak; he never sought to impose on them ideals that were beyond their reach. Rather, he took each person as he was, and guided him from that point onward. Thus, even in the monasteries, disciples sometimes mistook his kindness and encouragement for leniency, and never realized how drastic was the inner revolution to which he was actually calling us. He would be satisfied with nothing less than the total destruction of our mental limitations. The more of ourselves we gave to God, the more he, encouraged by our willingness, demanded of us.

I've always smiled when I've met people who defined his love for them in terms of the little things he had given them or done for them, outwardly. "Master got me a new job. Master found a new apartment for me." The real definition of his love for us lay not in what he gave to us, except spiritually, but in what he took away. His real purpose was not to tidy up our little mud puddles of delusion and make them more comfortable to play in: It was to take us out of our mud puddles altogether. If this meant subjecting us, in the process, to temporary pain, he flinched no more from that task than a conscientious doctor would in trying to cure his patients of serious physical ailments.

On this subject, a worthwhile lesson springs to mind: When I was a child, as I wrote earlier, I was taken off all dairy products. As a result, my teeth suffered. I remember going to a dentist in Bucharest who, out of "compassion" for my pain (or possibly to spare himself having to listen to me react to it!) stopped drilling, and filled my teeth before the infection had been completely removed. As a result, my teeth eventually suffered a great deal more.

On the subject of renunciation, especially, there was often in Master's manner a certain sternness, as though to impress on us that the staunchness of our dedication to God was, for each of us, a matter of spiritual life or death.

Daya Mata tells the story of how, while still young, she once asked Master whether he thought she ought to go out and find work to support her needy mother. Instead of the sympathetic reply she was expecting, Master cried, "Leave! Go on! Get out this minute! I don't want you here!"

"Master," she begged him tearfully, "I don't want to leave here. This is my entire life!"

"That's better," he replied, gently. "You have given your life to God, and renounced all worldly ties. The responsibility for your mother is now His alone."

On Yogananda's invitation, the mother came to live at Mt. Washington, and remained there until her death some forty years later.

Soon after that scolding, Master began referring to Daya Mata affectionately as his "nest egg." For it was from her arrival that he dated the beginning of his monastic order.

Nothing won Master's approval so much as the willingness to renounce all for God. Renunciation meant to him, however, an inner act of the heart; outward symbols he viewed more tentatively, as potential distractions to sincerity. In Phoenix, Arizona, a raggedly dressed, unkempt man once explained his appearance to him by boasting, "I'm a renunciate." Yogananda replied, "But you are bound again—by your attachment to disorder!"

For this present age, prejudiced as it is against many aspects of the spiritual life, he counseled only moderate adoption of the outward symbols of renunciation, such as monastic robes. Perhaps he felt that these symbols might attract too much attention to oneself, and thus feed the very ego which the renunciate was striving to overcome. Much as he loved St. Francis of Assisi, for example, and referred to him affectionately as his "patron saint," he often said, "St. Francis loved Lady Poverty, but I prefer Lady Simplicity." Renunciation, to him, was not a matter of where one's body is, nor of how it is clothed, but of one's inner, mental purity. "Make your heart a hermitage," he advised everyone. It was not so much that he rejected outward forms; some of the traditional forms, indeed, he favored. His primary concern, however, was that we use them to *internalize* our devotion.

Monasteries, like all human institutions, have a tendency to involve their members outwardly in communal affairs. To some extent, of course, this is necessary, but Yogananda urged us even in our monastic life to remain somewhat apart.

"Don't mix with others too closely," he recommended to us one evening. "The desire for outward companionship is a reflection of the soul's inward desire for companionship with God. But the more you seek to satisfy that desire outwardly, the more you will lose touch with the inner, divine Companion, and the more restless and dissatisfied you will become."

He told me a story in connection with this point: "When I was young, I met someone who was married. He said to me, 'I used to have many friends, and enjoyed their company. After I got married, however, I seldom saw them again. I then realized that my need for their company had actually been a suppressed need for a mate.' 'Thank you very much!' I said to him. 'You've taught me something important.'"

Frequently Master held up to us examples of saints who had remained withdrawn even from their fellow devotees. "Seclusion," he often told us, "is the price of greatness." Though mental withdrawal may not make one popular with less dedicated devotees (Daya Mata, who lived that way through her years of early training, soon found herself dubbed by fellow devotees as "the half-baked saint"), it is a shortcut to God.

Disciples seeking Master's help in overcoming delusion received loving encouragement from him in return, and sympathetic counsel.

"If the sex drive were taken away from you," he told a group of monks one evening, "you would see that you had lost your greatest friend. You would lose all interest in life. Sex was given to make you strong. If a boxer were to fight only weaklings, he too would grow weak in time. It is by fighting strong men that he develops strength. The same is true in your struggle with the sex instinct. The more you master it, the more you will find yourself becoming a lion of happiness."

The three greatest human delusions, he used to say, are sex, wine (by which he meant intoxicants of all kinds), and money. I once asked him to help me overcome attachment to good food. He smiled.

"Don't worry about those little things. When ecstasy comes, everything goes!"

But where the principal delusions were concerned, he was very serious, and worked with infinite patience to help us overcome them.

The desire for money he contrasted to the joys of non-attachment and simple living. "Renounce attachment to all things," he told us, "even to the fruits of your action. Don't work with the thought of what you might get out of it. What comes of itself, let it come. Work to serve God, and for the supreme satisfaction of pleasing Him."

Related to the desire for money is the ambition for worldly power and recognition. "Realize," Master said, "that God's is the only power in the universe. In all your actions, see Him as the true Doer; seek to please only Him." He added, "Worldly power, fame, and riches are like prostitutes: loyal to no one. Only God will stand loyally by you forever."

The desire for "wine" Master related to the soul's deep-seated longing to escape pain and suffering, and to reclaim its lost inheritance of bliss in God. "Pseudo-ecstasy," he labeled intoxicants of all kinds—even the "intoxicant" of too much sleep. He urged his students to escape the delusions of worldly life not by dulling their minds to its sorrows, but by rising above them in the higher "intoxication" of soul-joy. "Meditate," he urged us. "The more you taste God's joy within you, the less taste you will have for those mere masquerades of ecstasy."

In fact, I knew a disciple who at one time had been an alcoholic. He took Kriya Yoga initiation from Master, and thereafter practiced the technique—quite literally!—with a bottle of whiskey in one hand and his prayer beads in the other. In time he found so much enjoyment in Kriya Yoga practice that one day, halfway through his meditation, he disdainfully set the bottle aside, and never touched it again.

In sex-desire Master saw not merely the physical, procreative instinct, but the soul's longing for union with God manifested in the need for a human mate. It was to this unitive urge that he usually addressed himself when referring to the sex instinct. Romanticists in his audiences sometimes objected to the cheerful irreverence with which he tended to treat the "tender passion." But Yogananda was particularly averse to feeding people's illusions: It was his goal to demolish them.

"Marriage," he once told a church congregation, "is seldom the beautiful thing it is so commonly made out to be. I smile when

I think of the usual movie plot. The hero is so handsome, and the heroine so lovely, and after all kinds of troubles they finally get married and (so we are supposed to believe) live 'happily ever after.' And I think, 'Yes, with rolling pins and black eyes!' But of course, the producers end the story hastily before it gets to that part!"

"Remember," he advised me once, "it is the Divine Mother who tests you through sex. And it is She also who blesses, when you pass Her test." He counseled his male disciples to look upon women as living embodiments of the Divine Mother. "They are disarmed," he said, "when you view them in that light." I was never present when he counseled his women disciples in these matters, and have never steeled myself to consult any woman on the subject. I think, however, that his suggestions must have been based on encouraging in them similar attitudes of respect. For only by deep, divine respect for one another can men and women win final release from the magnetic attraction that draws them to seek fulfillment in outer, rather than in inner, *divine* union. The point comes, I have found, when complete respect leads to complete inner freedom. In desire, there is a wish to possess, and in perfect respect that wish ceases to exist.

Another helpful practice is, as much as possible, to avoid hugging others. Hugging is usually, in any case, a very superficial way of showing affection. I tell people truthfully that I feel much closer to them when I embrace them inwardly than when I grapple them in my arms, as if possessively. The touch sensation, so much a part of sexual desire, is a physical cul-de-sac on the way to the feeling of bliss in every atom of creation.

In the monastery, as I mentioned earlier, Master permitted no social contact between the monks and nuns. When necessities of the work demanded communication between them, he counseled them not to look at one another, and especially to avoid looking into the eyes; also, to keep their conversation as brief and impersonal as possible.

So strict was he that he even discouraged many of the normally accepted courtesies that men and women extend to one another. I remember one day, when Master and I were standing out of doors near the entrance to his Twenty-Nine Palms retreat, a young nun came to the door of the house, laden with packages. Observing that she was having difficulty in opening the door, I went over and opened it for her.

"You should not have done that," Master told me, after she had gone inside. "Keep your distance," he added, "and they will always respect you."

It is only when one strives to *overcome* delusion that one discovers its primal power. "As soon as the first thought of sex arises," Master said, "that is the time to catch it." Worldly people scoff at what they consider such exaggerated precautions. "It's absurd," I've heard them exclaim, "to suggest that every time I look at a member of the opposite sex I'm going to feel tempted!" Basic attraction, however, may find an outward expression one day toward "the one, right" man or woman. In any case, the germs of that attraction can distract the heart from one-pointed devotion to God; the process of infection begins long before the stirrings of any noticeable attraction to one human being. The root of attraction lies in an instinctive pleasure at the mere abstraction, "man," or, "woman."

A woman once told me that her little daughter, while still a toddler, had a special giggle that she affected only in the presence of little boys. It was to this deep, instinctive, and generally not specifically directed response that Yogananda was most particularly referring when he spoke of tracing temptation to its "first thought." Years of introspection have shown me that if one can catch this subtle first response—so rarely even noticed by most people—and immediately impersonalize it, the thought of attraction virtually vanishes from the mind. Even then, however, one must be careful. "One is not safe from delusion," Yogananda said, "until he has attained the highest, *nirbikalpa, samadhi.*"

Rejection of the world is only the negative side of renunciation. Master's usual emphasis was positive. "Nothing can touch you," he told us, "if you inwardly love God." Nevertheless, there is a beauty in the act of utter self-offering to God that makes renunciation, even in its more limited, negative aspect, one of the most heroic and noble callings available to man.

Bernard told me of one occasion when a visitor from India came to see Paramhansa Yogananda. The man was received by Sister

Gyanamata, and had the poor grace to treat her condescendingly—
as though, in serving her guru, she were only Master's servant. Later,
inspired by his interview with Master, he apologized to her.

"In India," he said, "we are taught to respect all women as wives
and mothers. Forgive me, please, that I failed to pay you that respect
earlier." Smilingly he concluded, "I offer it to you now."

Sister Gyanamata, in her usual impersonal manner, replied, "At
least half the people in the world are women. Most of them sooner
or later become mothers. There is nothing in either fact that merits
special respect. But you may, if you wish, respect the fact that, in this
life, I have become a renunciate."

The visitor could only bow. For renunciation of egoic desires and
attachments is, ultimately, a necessary steppingstone for everyone,
whether married or single, toward his rediscovery of that divine
image within him which alone gives him importance in the greater
scheme of things.

A final word: Dispassion does not mean indifference to the feelings of others. Concern for them is an important way of expanding
beyond the confines of ego-consciousness, for it helps one in any
effort to eliminate the ego altogether as a focus of one's awareness.

In the hindsight of sixty years on the path, I realize that I received,
during my earlier years of discipleship, a few teachings from senior
disciples that, at the time, I questioned mentally and therefore never
fully accepted. Now I see that my hesitation in accepting them was
that I realized those teachings were valid only in certain respects, but
invalid in others.

Faye, for example, indicated to me several times that she considered it a virtue not to care what anyone thought about anything. Her
aloofness was a virtue to the extent that it affirmed the integrity of
her conscience. It also locked her into her own opinions, however,
and thereby made her less sympathetic than she might have been, not
only to others' opinions, but to their actual needs.

She once received a letter containing a number of criticisms, including (for reasons that I forget) a criticism of her. Would not true
impartiality have made her willing to consider those criticisms, and
to consider them equally? Instead, she addressed only the one that

concerned herself, remarking, "As for what he says about me, he is welcome to his opinions."

These are subtle points, but true renunciation of ego includes not thrusting oneself forward. Her reaction to the opinions voiced in that letter were confined, instead, to those which concerned herself. If all of the opinions expressed had been equally unimportant to her, would she have expressed her reaction only to this one? Dispassion means disinterest in any benefits to oneself, but it doesn't mean lack of concern for the well-being of others, which must include also an interest in their opinions.

CHAPTER 23

God Protects His Devotees

NORMAN ENTERED THE dining room one day at lunchtime looking stunned.

"This morning," he announced shakily, "I was driving the big flat-bed truck down Mt. Washington. As I came to the steepest part of that hill, I stepped on the brake to slow down for the hairpin turn at the bottom, but my foot went right to the floor! I pumped frantically; nothing happened. By this time the truck was going so fast I couldn't shift to a lower gear. In moments I knew I'd be hurtling to my death over the edge of that steep embankment. Desperately I prayed to Master: 'Is this what you want?'

"Suddenly the truck slowed to a complete stop! The brakes still weren't working, but I was able to park safely in gear and curb the front wheel.

"What a blessing," Norman concluded, "to have a God-realized master for a guru!"

As disciples of a great yogi, we often found that we had only to call Master mentally for misfortune to be speedily averted.

A year before Norman's miraculous escape, Jerry Torgerson, another disciple, hitchhiked into Los Angeles. This mode of travel went against Master's advice, but Jerry, like many other young Americans, had been practically raised on hitchhiking; he needed more than Master's casual proscription, evidently, to change his habits.

"Three guys picked me up," he told us. "We were riding along, when suddenly—how, I couldn't say—I *knew* they were criminals. 'I want to get out right here,' I told them. But they wouldn't stop. After some distance we left the main road, and drove through open countryside to a secluded house. One of the men got out; the other two stayed with me in the car. I didn't know what they had in mind, but I can tell you I was plenty scared. I started praying to Master for help.

"Well, the first guy went and knocked at the front door. No answer. He went around the house, knocking and calling at every door and window. Still no answer. By this time the two men in the car were getting worried. 'Let's get outa here!' they called out nervously. The first fellow came back, as nervous as they were. We all drove back to the main road, and there they let me out. The moment I'd slammed the door behind me, they rushed off at high speed.

"I never did find out what they'd had in mind, but I had the strong impression that they were planning to use me in a crime.

"I said nothing to anyone about all this. After church the following Sunday, I went up to Master for his blessing. The moment he saw me, he scolded, 'You see, Jerry? I *told* you not to hitchhike! I had to close the ears of everyone in that house so no one would hear that man when he called to them.'"

Some months later, Joe Carbone and Henry Schaufelberger (now Brothers Bimalananda and Anandamoy) were plastering the lotus tower that forms the archway entrance to the SRF church grounds in Hollywood. Joe was mixing and carrying the plaster. Henry, at a height of about twenty feet, was troweling it onto the wall. The ladder Joe was using was set at a steep angle. On one climb, as he reached up to grasp the top rung, he missed it. The heavy hod of plaster on his shoulder began pulling him backward; now he was unable to grasp the rung with either hand. A twenty-foot drop, with all that weight on his shoulder, might very well have killed him. Realizing that it was too late to save himself, Joe thought urgently of Master and chanted out loud, "Om!"

Both men later testified as to what happened next. As Joe was chanting, some invisible force pushed him slowly back upright. A moment later he was able to grasp the rung again. Gasping with relief, he completed his climb.

Andy Anderson, the foreman on this job, was a professional carpenter and builder who had been hired from outside to oversee our work. He knew nothing of our philosophy, and often chuckled at the thought of working with "all these yogis!" But there was no doubt in his voice when he told me of how he had witnessed an uncanny instance of protection:

"Why you guys don't all get killed on this job beats me. You just aren't careful enough. I was standing right over there one day, when someone on a scaffold dropped a long two-by-four—without even looking below him! Another of you yogis was standing underneath, for all I could tell not even minding his *own* business! The two-by-four struck the ground at such an angle that it couldn't possibly have missed him in falling over. It might've killed him.

"'Look out!' I hollered. Just then that two-by-four—leaning in *his* direction, mind you—stood back upright and, so help me, *fell over in the opposite direction*! I *know* I wasn't just seeing things."

Andy ended up by becoming a lay disciple himself.

James Coller told us of another hitchhiking incident, one in which he and another monk gave a man a lift. The two monks were in the front seat. "When we picked this man up," James said, "there was no room for him in front, so he sat in the back. Some minutes later, as we were driving along, I suddenly heard a voice in my inner ear: 'Look out! He has a knife!' I turned around quickly. The man was leaning forward, a fiendish expression on his face. His hand was upraised, holding a knife; he was on the very point of striking the boy beside me, who was gazing ahead unsuspectingly.

"'Put that knife down!' I commanded sternly. The man was so astonished that he obeyed me. I stopped the car, and he got out without a word."

In the sixty years, now, that I have been on this path, I cannot recall to mind a single instance where a disciple of Paramhansa Yogananda has failed to find protection in time of real need. Considering the length of time involved, and the thousands of disciples I have known during this period, this is quite an amazing record.

The most striking of these cases occurred among those who had placed their lives unreservedly in the Guru's care. Dr. Lewis told of an episode similar to Norman's, when, on a cold winter night in Massachusetts, he had been out driving to a meditation meeting.

With him were two fellow disciples, Mrs. Laura Elliott and Mrs. Alice Hasey (Sister Yogmata). Suddenly, as they approached a narrow bridge, they found their way blocked by another car that had skidded sidewise across the icy road. A crash seemed inevitable.

"At that moment," Dr. Lewis said, "we felt as if a giant hand were being pressed down on the hood of the car. We slowed instantly to a stop, our car still safely on the road."

Señor J. M. Cuaron, the leader of the SRF center in Mexico City, related the following incident to me.

"I was badly in need of a job, but for a long time could find no work anywhere. Then one day an excellent offer came from a company in Matamoros. Taking that job would mean moving away from Mexico City; I therefore wrote Master to request his permission to put the SRF center in someone else's charge. My letter was, to me, a mere formality; I was sure Master would congratulate me on my good luck. Imagine my surprise, then, when he replied *by telegram*: 'No. Absolutely not. Under no circumstances whatever accept that job.' I admit I was a bit upset. But even so, I obeyed him.

"One month later the news came out in the papers: The company that had offered me that job was exposed for fraud. Its officers, including the man who had taken the post I'd been offered, were sent to prison. He hadn't been aware of the firm's dishonesty, just as I would not have been. Because of the position he held, however, he was imprisoned with the rest. It was only by Master's grace that I was spared that calamity!"

Tests there must be in life, of course. They come especially on the spiritual path, for if devotees are to escape the coils of *maya* (delusion), they must learn the lessons they need to develop in wisdom. Master didn't shrink from giving us whatever lessons we needed, to grow. For example, although on that occasion he saved Señor Cuaron from ignominious arrest, he never helped him to find the employment he so badly wanted. Señor Cuaron in fact had enough money to live on simply, as became a world-renouncing yogi. Master evidently saw no good reason to help him return to his former levels of opulence.

But our tests were always blessings; outright misfortune Master spared us. And where a test was not required for a disciple's spiritual growth, Master often removed it from his path altogether.

I remember how he "de-jinxed" a student (not a close disciple) who was having trouble earning money. It was Jean Haupt's brother, Richard. Not long after Master's intercession, the man became quite well-to-do.

In 1955 I went to Switzerland on a lecture tour. There I met a lady from Czechoslovakia who told me a story concerning Professor Novicky, the late leader of a small SRF group in Prague.

"One day," she said, "after Yogananda's passing, a stranger came to Professor Novicky and requested instruction in yoga. The professor didn't know what to do. Normally he kept his spiritual activities a secret so as not to expose himself to persecution. If this man was a genuine seeker, the professor would want to help him. But if he was a communist government spy, any admission of interest in yoga might result in a prison sentence for him. Our friend prayed for guidance. Suddenly, standing behind that self-proclaimed 'devotee,' Paramhansa Yogananda appeared. Slowly the Master shook his head, then vanished. Professor Novicky told the man he had come to the wrong place for information. Sometime later, he learned that the man was indeed a government spy.

"I am free to tell this story now," my informant continued, "for the good professor died recently, of natural causes."

On January 5, 1959, my own life was spared in a remarkable manner. The incident took place in India. I was preparing for a religious gathering in Dakshineswar, outside Calcutta, for which event Daya Mata was to be the principal speaker. Part of my task was to set up the loud-speaker equipment. With both hands I grasped the microphone boom to move it. Suddenly 230 volts of electricity shot through my body, lifting me right off the ground. Involuntarily I cried out. Such high voltage tightens the muscles, making it impossible to release anything one is holding. Unable as I'd have been to let go of the metal boom, I would have been killed instantly. Just at that moment, inexplicably, the fuse blew. The function was delayed half an hour till another fuse was located, but my life was spared.

The only ill effect I suffered was a slight tremor of the heart that lasted two or three days.

Other occasions there have been. One was at the men's retreat at Twenty-Nine Palms. I was out walking one day, when all of a sudden a flock of crows began circling around me. I thought, "This surely is a bad omen." Two days later I unmade my bed—I had been sleeping out on the patio—preparatory to leaving. Between the sheets I found a squashed black widow spider—the sting of which is often fatal.

Death must, of course, come to everyone sooner or later. But I have been struck by its beauty and dignity when it has visited disciples of this path.

A member of our Hollywood church congregation died of a stroke. His wife later told me, "In his final moments, my husband whispered to me lovingly, 'Don't feel badly, dear. I am so happy! And I see a bright, bright light all around me.'"

Another church member, who had known the Master since his early years in America, exclaimed at the end of her life, "Swamiji is here!" Her face was radiant; it wore a blissful smile.

And Sister Gyanamata's last words were, "Such joy! Too much joy! Oh, too much joy!"

Disciples who have died of cancer or other painful diseases have left their bodies peacefully, with a smile on their lips.

People often point to the sufferings of humanity as proof either that God doesn't exist, or that He doesn't care for His human children. Paramhansa Yogananda's answer to that charge was that people don't care enough about God to tune in to His help. Indeed, by their indifference they create the very problems which, later, they lay accusingly at His door. If, in daylight, a person moves about a room with closed eyes, he may bump against a piece of furniture and hurt himself. By closing one's eyes to light, one creates his own darkness. By closing one's heart to love, one creates his own fear, hatred, or apathy. By closing one's soul to joy, one creates his own misery.

In case after case I have seen fulfilled Yogananda's promise that faithful devotees of his path would be protected. "For those who stay in tune to the end," he added, "I, or one of the other masters, will be there to usher them into the divine kingdom." Truly, the words of the great Swami Shankaracharya have found justification in Paramhansa Yogananda's life: "No known comparison exists in the three worlds for a true guru."

It is perhaps the greatest sign of God's aid to His devotees that, when the soul yearns deeply for Him, He sends to that soul the supreme blessing of a God-awakened master to guide it along the highway to Infinity.

CHAPTER 24

True Teaching Is Individual

ONE SOMETIMES HEARS the lament, "There are too many denominations in Christendom." Yet I dare say that even if there were only one, there would still be as many different forms of Christianity as there are Christians. For every man's understanding is conditioned by his own special experiences, his aspirations, his outlook on life—in short, by what he *is*. He might recite the Nicene Creed in church every Sunday, yet attach meanings to it that would surprise some of his fellow worshipers. In reciting the Lord's Prayer, children have been heard to say, "Give us this day our jelly bread," and, "Lead us not into Penn Station." We smile at their innocence. But are we so sure that we ourselves really *know* all that is intended in the Lord's Prayer, or in the Credo?

The same problem confronts us in our efforts to understand one another. Even those people to whom we feel nearest are closed books to us in certain parts of their being, as I had been to my mother in the urgency of my desire for truth, and for God. (And in that case she might have been more open, for before my birth she had deliberately given me to God.) What, then, of a God-realized master? Is it worthwhile even *trying* to comprehend the vastness of his nature?

Whenever fellow disciples spoke to me—as they sometimes did—of trying to "understand" Master, I would marvel. It struck me as rather like trying to understand the universe! The task that Infinity places squarely on the shoulders of every human being is just this: "Understand thyself—*know* thyself." To study the life of a master with the purpose, not of understanding *him*, but of obtaining deeper insight into *one's own* true nature, and into *one's own* potential for divine unfoldment: this is the wise use of discrimination.

Master himself was, to each of us, like a flawless, highly polished mirror. What came back to us from him was not his opinions of us, but our own higher Self's reaction to any lower attitude we projected. His perfect self-transcendence never ceased to amaze me. In another person's company he actually, in a sense, *became* that person. I don't mean that in our company he assumed our weaknesses, our pettiness, our moods of anger or despondency. What he showed us, rather, was the silent watcher at the center of our own selves.

An amazing feature of my own relationship with him was that I could never clearly remember what he looked like. I needed a photograph of him to bring his image clearly to mind. Even among such photographs, I have never seen any two of them exactly alike. When he is shown posing with someone else, in some subtle way he actually looks like that person. Shown with the imposing and slightly portly Señor Portes Gil, the President of Mexico, he somehow *looks* imposing and portly like Señor Gil. Posed with small, fragile-looking Amelita Galli-Curci, the great opera singer, he looks unaccountably like her. Photographed with Goodwin J. Knight, Lieutenant Governor of California, he appears almost to be Mr. Knight's alter ego.* Standing with any disciple, he seems to *become* that disciple. One wonders how a single face could display such a wide variety of expressions. But of course it was not his face that changed: it was the consciousness behind it. Master went a step beyond seeing the god in each of us: He *became* that god, in order that we might see for ourselves our own divine potential, and understand better how the Lord wanted to express Himself through us.

Ah, Master! If only I had comprehended as clearly then as I do now the miracle of your gift to us! But had I done so, I suppose by this time I would be making the same lament, on a deeper level. For evolution never ceases, until at last time itself becomes timelessness, and the ends we seek end in endlessness.

---

* These three photographs may be seen in two publications of Self-Realization Fellowship: the Golden Anniversary booklet, and *Paramahansa Yogananda, in Memoriam* (p. 81).

In his training of us, Master's teaching was individual also. It was not that he *altered* his basic teachings to suit our personal needs. Rather, it was his emphasis that varied. To some he stressed attitudes of service; to others, deep inwardness. To one he emphasized the need for greater joy; to another, for less levity. His emphasis was to a great extent too subtle to be phrased in words. He conveyed it by some intonation of the voice, by an expression in the eyes, or by a tilt of the head. What he said to one person he might never say to anyone else. In a very real sense he was, to each of us, our very own, very *personal*, divine friend.

In the work we did, one might have expected him to honor that basic principle of every well-run institution: "Make the best use of individual talent." To Master, however, this practice would have meant *using* us. His true concern, always, was for our spiritual needs. Sometimes he would actually take us away from some important assignment—one, perhaps, for which no one else could be found—simply to meet some spiritual need of our own. Sometimes, too, he placed people in positions for which they weren't qualified, with a view to prompting them, in their struggle to meet his expectations, to develop needed spiritual qualities. At other times he gave us work we disliked—not particularly because we would be good for that work (I recall a job of carpentry he once put me on: For every time my hammer hit the nail, there must have been nine others that I missed it), but because the work would be good for *us*. Perhaps it was that we needed to learn some spiritual quality—for example, to overcome a natural unwillingness, which I myself had for carpentry.

Sometimes he would not place people in positions for which they were eminently qualified, simply because they no longer needed those particular experiences in order to grow spiritually. One might have thought, for instance, that he would have called upon his most advanced disciples to help him with the ministry. In fact he did say that he appointed only those as ministers who, in former lives, had developed the requisite spiritual qualifications. Along with those qualifications, however, was the still-more-pressing question of what we ourselves needed, to grow spiritually.

Master exemplified the androgynous balance of the perfect
human being. He had the compassion and love of a mother,
and the wisdom and will power of a father. In this picture we
see exemplified the mother aspect of his nature.

Speaking to me once of Saint Lynn, his most highly advanced disciple, he said, "He was leading a center in Kansas City years ago,
but I asked him to give it up. Service in that capacity was no longer
necessary to him for his spiritual development."

Sister Gyanamata, his most advanced woman disciple, and deeply
wise, could have rendered enormous assistance by giving lectures,
teaching classes, and writing articles for the SRF magazine. But Master
never asked her to serve in any such role. That kind of work simply
wasn't necessary to her for her spiritual growth. In fact, in the spring

of 1949 I tried to get her, along with several other senior disciples, to write articles for *Self-Realization Magazine*, which Master had asked me to "spruce up" and make more helpful and attractive to the general reader. "Fill it," he told me, "with short, practical articles on the techniques and principles of right living—articles that will help people on every level: physical, mental, and spiritual."

I wanted to enlist as many disciples as possible in this worthy project, and naturally thought that, the more spiritually developed a writer, the better his or her article would be. To my surprise, however, neither Sister Gyanamata nor any of the others I'd hoped most to hear from responded to my appeal.

Indeed, this was my first confrontation with the truth that a master's training is individual. My first, instinctive response ("Don't they *want* to do Master's will?") conflicted with my awareness that they must know a great deal more than I about his will. I was forced at last to conclude that, while Master wanted the magazine improved, he didn't necessarily want every hand on deck to improve it. It was not only a question of *what* he wanted, but of *whom* he wanted it from. In fact, I now realize that he was focused on helping *me*, specifically, to understand better how to reach out to people in their needs.

My own deep-seated desire had always been to share joy with others. Having perhaps suffered spiritually, myself, I felt deeply the spiritual sufferings of others, and longed to do all I could to assuage those sufferings. Master responded to this deep inner longing in me, and trained me from the beginning for public service.

In January 1949 he put me into office work, answering letters. I typed them in my room, since at that time there was no separate office for the monks. At first my letters tended to be too long.

"I once knew a lady novelist," Master told me one day by way of advice, "who ended her letters, 'If I'd had more time, this letter would have been shorter.'" He corrected me at other times, too, on the best ways of presenting his teachings to others.

Not long after he'd made me a letter writer, he asked me to study the complete set of the SRF lessons. His stated reason for doing so amused me: "I want your suggestions for their improvement." His real purpose, I knew, was to get me to study the lessons deeply.

Soon thereafter he also made me the official examiner for students of the printed lessons. This job meant reviewing and grading students' answers to the tests which, in those days, were sent out at the end of each step.

By these means Master sought to give me a thorough grounding in his teachings.

In March 1949 he asked me also to write articles for our magazine. I began to write under the pen name, Robert Ford. My first endeavor, "You Can Change Your Personality," was featured in the May-June issue of that year.

One evening Master sent for two or three of us, and talked at length about his work in India. A strong intuition awakened within me that Master would someday send me to that country. Eagerly I jotted down everything he said. A few days later I saw him as he stood on his private upstairs porch.

"I have plans for you, Walter," he remarked with a quiet smile.

Certain as to his meaning, I was delighted. But after I'd left him, the thought came, "To go to India would mean leaving Master!" The enormity of this threatened loss threw me into a deep depression. "Master is my India!" I cried silently. "What could I possibly find there that I haven't already, right here?"

Gradually my dark mood left me. As I became calmer, I reflected that Master surely would want nothing of me but what was spiritually for my best. Two days later I saw him again. By this time my depression had vanished.

"No more moods, now," Master said gently when we met. "Otherwise, how will you be able to help people?"

Every year for the next three years he made plans to go to India, and to take me with him. Each time the trip was postponed. It was his death, finally, which canceled the trip for the third time. I did get sent to India eventually, in 1958, and spent the better part of four years there. Many years later, having completed the founding of seven communities in America and Italy, I decided, as I was approaching the end of my life, to found an eighth community near Pune, India.

Sometime in February or March 1949, Master instructed me to stand outside the Hollywood church after the Sunday morning services and shake hands with people as they left. In his lessons he states that people exchange magnetism when they shake hands. Thus, what Master wanted me to do was not merely greet people, but act as his channel of blessings to others. The first time I tried it, I felt so drained of energy afterward that I actually became dizzy. I suppose what happened was that people unconsciously drew from me, in the thought that I was there as Master's representative.

"Master," I said later, "I don't believe I'm ready for this job." I explained what had happened.

"That is because you are thinking of yourself," he replied. "Think of God, and you will find *His* energy flowing through you."

His suggestion worked. By holding to the thought of God, I discovered that I actually felt more uplifted, after shaking hands with congregation members, than beforehand.

"When this 'I' shall die," Master once wrote in a rhymed couplet, "then shall I know who am I."

One of my office jobs was to send weekly announcements to the newspapers to let people know which minister would be speaking at which church the next Sunday, and what his sermon topic would be. Master had been lecturing fortnightly in our San Diego church, alternating weekly between there and Hollywood. During recent months, however, he had taken to going to San Diego only occasionally. The church members there, who naturally wanted to see him, were told to check the church page of the *San Diego Union* every Saturday. Whenever Master's coming was announced, the church was filled to overflowing.

One week in May I was instructed to send in the announcement that Master would appear there the following Sunday. It had been at least two months since his last appearance there. I smiled to think how delighted the congregation members would be.

Saturday morning, Bernard came to my room with horrifying news. "Master can't go to San Diego after all. He wants you to speak in his stead."

"*Me!* But . . . but I've never lectured before in my life!"

"He also wants you," Bernard continued with appalling insouciance, "to give a Kriya Yoga initiation afterwards."

"What! But my goodness, I've only attended one initiation!"

"Two," Bernard corrected me. "Master also initiated you last October at Twenty-Nine Palms—remember?"

"All right, two. What difference does that make? I mean—well, of course I'll obey, but. . . . Oh, those poor people!"

"You'll only have to initiate one of them," Bernard consoled me. "Here's money for the bus. You'd better leave immediately."

In Encinitas, several hours later, Rev. Michael (later, Brother Bhaktananda) reviewed for me the outlines of the Kriya initiation ceremony. I worked hard on my sermon also. With sinking heart I drove down the next morning to San Diego. In a little room behind the church I prayed desperately for help and guidance. As the time arrived for the service to begin, I went out and sat in the chair at the center of the stage, as was the custom in those days. Through the closed curtains I could clearly hear the murmur of a large and eagerly waiting crowd.

The dreaded moment arrived. I stood up. The curtains parted. My worst fears were realized: The church was completely packed. People were standing in the aisles. Others were craning their heads in through the windows. I could feel the wave of shock as something almost physical. Instead of their long-awaited guru, here before them was an unknown and rather lost-looking boy of twenty-two, asking them if they were—still?—awake and ready. I felt so sorry for them in their disappointment that I overlooked the awkwardness of my own position. If everyone there had walked out, I would have understood. But regular meditation, evidently, had made them gracious. No one left.

The Kriya initiation that afternoon frightened me even more than the service. Michelle Evans, the lady I initiated, looked as terrified as I was—infected, as she later admitted to me, by my own insecurity. Master's blessings, however, powerfully present, soon dispelled all my anxiety. The ceremony went smoothly. I returned to Mt. Washington that afternoon, bowed, perhaps, but unbloodied.

Later, Master received compliments on my lecture. "Most of all," he reported, pleased, "they liked your humility." Humility, I reflected, under the circumstances had been virtually unavoidable!

In case anyone wonders at Master's willingness to disappoint so many people, I can only point out that, if his reason for doing so had been some special need of his own, there were other experienced teacher-disciples whom he could have called upon. Since he chose me, he can only have had in mind some reason concerning myself. Over the succeeding months, he made it increasingly clear to me that he was counting on me to spread his message far afield. My youth and inexperience were not, for him, the issue that they were quite naturally for me. He saw us, as he often indicated, in terms of the past lives we had spent with him, and not only of the present life.

He didn't place the same importance on *length* of discipleship in this lifetime that others—notably, often, the disciples themselves—did. Often I heard him quote the words of Jesus Christ, "The last shall be first." His meaning was also, "those who last until the end." What mattered to him most of all, however, as he made clear to us also, was that our relationship with him was "from of old, yea, from everlasting." Those who came to him late in this life might also have done so because they had a role to play long after he had left his body.

From the time of my San Diego church experience onward, Master had me lecture regularly there and in the Hollywood church. He also began referring to me publicly as "Reverend Walter," though the actual formalities of ordination weren't completed until a year later.

"Your desire to be happy," he often told us, "must include others' happiness." I had long known in my heart that I would be called upon someday to serve others through teaching and lecturing. But whether out of the humility that Master sometimes praised in me, or from darker motives of unwillingness, it was several years, I'm afraid, before I could bring myself to believe that my lectures really did anyone any good.

Master made it clear, however, that he expected me to take this responsibility seriously. "Sir," I once pleaded with him, "I don't want to be a lecturer!"

"You'd better learn to like it," he replied pleasantly. "That is what you will have to do."

At informal gatherings of the monks he would usually direct his conversation to me, as if to get me to absorb his philosophy to my depths. At such times I would think, "It must be because I'm so superficial that he won't let me close my eyes and meditate in his presence." For such was the inspiration I felt in his presence that my desire was to deepen the experience of it, inwardly. Master was responding, however, to more deep-seated tendencies in my nature—and was subtly emphasizing that the work of absorbing his teachings, and of sharing them with others, was what I myself needed, to grow.

Master in the Garden at Encinitas.

CHAPTER 25

Work vs. Meditation

"Master once taught me a good lesson on the attitude we should hold toward our work." Mrs. Vera Brown (later, Meera Mata), an advanced older disciple whom Master had made responsible for training some of the newer ones, was sharing with me a few of her experiences with our Guru.

"'You work too hard,' Master told me one day. 'You *must* work less. If you don't, you will ruin your health.'

"'Very well,' I thought, 'I'll try not doing so much.'

"Two or three days later, to my surprise, Master gave me *more* work to do!"

Mrs. Brown's eyes twinkled. "'Okay, Master,' I thought, 'you must know what you're doing.' I took on my new duties. But all the time I kept wondering, 'How am I going to reconcile all this extra work with his instructions to me to work *less*?'

"Well, a couple of days after that, Master again told me, more sternly this time, 'You *must not* work so hard. In this lifetime you've done enough work for several incarnations.'

"What was I to do? Again I tried cutting down my activities, only to find Master, after two or three days, giving me more work than ever!

"We repeated this little comedy several times. Every time Master told me to work *less*, he soon thereafter added duties that forced me to work *more*. I figured he must know what he was doing, and that it was up to me to try and understand what that was.

271

"Well, finally one day I looked at Master. 'Sir,' I said, 'instead of using the word *work* in our life here, why don't we substitute the word *service*?'

"Master laughed. 'It has been a good show,' he said. 'All your life you've been thinking, *work! work! work!* That very thought was exhausting you. But just see how differently you feel when you think of work as a divine service! When you act to please God, you can do *twice* as much and never feel tired!'"

Mrs. Brown, whose frail body never seemed to run out of energy no matter how much she did, laughed merrily. "You see, the very thought of pleasing God fills us with *His* energy. Master tells us it's our unwillingness that cuts off the flow of energy."

"True," I replied thoughtfully, "as often as I've put that principle to practice, I've found it works marvelously. But," I continued, "there's another obstacle I run into: that of being *too* willing. What can one do about that?"

"How can one be too willing!"

"Well, what I mean is, I become over-enthusiastic about what I'm doing. As a result, I lose my inner peace and fall into the old consciousness of hard work, which ends in exhaustion."

"I see." Mrs. Brown nodded sympathetically. "That's right. Without inner peace we lose the consciousness of God's presence. And if we can't feel Him within us, we can't really feel His energy." Again she laughed merrily. "Master taught me a good lesson on that subject, too.

"He was cooking one day in his kitchen. I was there in the room with him. For lack of anything better to do, I decided I'd clean up after him. The moment he emptied one pan, I'd wash it. Whenever he spilled anything, I cleaned up the mess.

"Well, he began dirtying pans and more pans, spilling food and more food. I was working faster and faster to keep up with him. In my whole life I'd *never* seen such sloppy cooking! At last I just gave up. It occurred to me that I might as well wait till he was finished before I did any more.

"As I sat down to watch him, I noticed a little smile on his face, though he said nothing. Presently, I saw he wasn't messing things up anymore. Finally it dawned on me that he'd only been teaching me the difference between calm, God-reminding activity, and the sort of restlessness that one indulges in just for activity's sake. I'd been working in a spirit of busy-ness. Master's way of showing me my mistake was to lead me to its own logical conclusion!"

I myself learned in time to make inner peace my "bottom line." No matter how many calls I have had on my energies, I have never allowed them to bring me to the point where my inner peace became threatened.

The spiritual path would, one suspects, be relatively easy to understand if it involved only meditation, ecstatic visions, and a blissful expansion of consciousness. Why, one asks, must it be complicated by mundane activities like ditch digging and letter writing and cleaning up kitchens? One may sympathize, on one level at least, with that reluctant disciple, on the day we completed the swimming pool at Twenty-Nine Palms, who grumbled, "I didn't come here to pour *cement!*" Many a sincere devotee, too, has probably wondered what pouring cement (or digging ditches, or writing letters, or cleaning up kitchens) has to do with finding God.

The answer is, quite simply: *nothing!* Not in itself, anyway. Master once told the story of a man who placed a hundred-dollar bill in the collection plate at church, then was upset because God didn't answer his prayer. Laughingly Master commented, "God already *was* that hundred-dollar bill—whether in or out of the collection plate! Why should He care where it was placed?" The realm of *maya* (cosmic delusion) is like the surface of an ocean: No matter how high the waves are whipped by the storm, the over-all ocean level remains the same. God doesn't *need* anything that we can give Him. He already *is* everything! The one thing He wants from us, Master said, is our love.

The purpose of spiritual work, then, is not really to do things for God, but rather to do the most important thing of all for ourselves: to purify our own hearts. No work for God is more or less important than any other. The Bhagavad Gita states that He accepts even a flower or a leaf as an offering, if it is tendered with devotion. The important thing is to reach the point where *all* our love, *all* our energy flow naturally toward Him.

Meditation, too, is a kind of work. True, it differs from such labor as digging ditches, but then, so also does mental planning, and who will say that planning is less truly work than the physical execution of plans? Even in the animal kingdom, mental ability is often more highly regarded than brute force. (Witness a group of dogs playing together. Usually it's the brightest one, not the largest, that the others follow.) Meditation is the most refined and exalted of all mental activities. From it have come the greatest inspirations. If one could meditate deeply all day there would be no need for a person seeking divine communion to dig ditches or to do any other work, whether physical or mental.

Monks sitting in meditation around the old pepper tree in the Temple of Leaves at Mt. Washington. In the early days, Master taught classes here.

The criterion, of course, is that word, "deeply."

When Mrinalini Mata, already a disciple when she was still a young schoolgirl, met Master at the breakfast table one day, he remarked to her, "You didn't meditate this morning."

"Sir," she protested, "I meditated a whole hour!"

Master, quite unimpressed, replied, "You should have meditated half an hour." He had seen that in sitting longer, when not in a mood that day to meditate with intensity, she had actually done less *effective* meditation.

Intensity is everything: intensity of *awareness*. Superconsciousness cannot be attained by halfhearted efforts. "You must be calmly active, and actively calm," Master said. "Be intensely aware of everything you are doing." Work, on the spiritual path, is a means of helping one to channel his energies constantly, *dynamically*, toward God.

"Make every minute count," Master said. "The minutes are more important than the years." People who put their whole concentration into working for God find they can also meditate more deeply.

"When you work for God, not self," Master told us one day, "that is just as good as meditation. Then work helps your meditation, and meditation helps your work. You need the balance. With only meditation you become lazy, and the senses become strong. With only work, the mind becomes restless, and you forget God."

Master taught us to consider any work holy that we did to please God. To keep his minister-disciples from imagining that their work of teaching and counseling was more spiritual than that of other disciples who served in the gardens, he gave them manual labor to do also. On that weekend when Master first sent me to San Diego to lecture, I got a valuable lesson from Carl Swenson (later, Brother Sarolananda), a fellow disciple in Encinitas. "Look at my hands!" I lamented. "They're all seamed with cement. People will think I didn't bother to wash them."

"What do you mean?" protested Carl. "They are your badge of honor."

Master taught us not only to offer our work moment by moment to God, but also to see God acting through us as the real Doer. "I slept," he said once, "and dreamt I was working. I woke up, and saw God was working." Action in this spirit wasn't intended to make us automatons. I remember thinking halfway through a sermon one Sunday morning, "If God really *is* the Doer, why not mentally remove myself from the scene altogether, and wait for *Him* to speak through me?" There ensued two minutes of silence! Friends in the audience thought I must have frozen from nervousness. But to me this pause was simply an interesting experiment. I concluded at last that God had no intention of speaking for me. His was simply the inspiration for my words. My job was to draw on that inspiration.

To see God as the Doer, then, means recognizing that it is by *His* energy and inspiration that we live. It means not taking personal credit for anything we do. This attitude keeps one humble, and also vastly increases one's powers of accomplishment.

Master instructed me to pray to God and our Gurus before every lecture, and ask them to use me as their instrument, that I might express what *they* wanted me to say. Humility, alas, is not easy to acquire. After working some months on developing it, I awoke one morning to the realization that I was becoming proud of my humility! In working to develop devotion, too, I discovered that I was becoming pleased with myself for feeling it. (Master's comment: "If you love yourself, how can you love God?") The real secret of humility, I came gradually to realize, is self-honesty. To see everything in its right proportion to everything else reduces the chances of one's taking oneself, or anything else, too seriously.

As Sister Gyanamata once remarked to Bernard, after he'd thanked her for the spiritual help she had lovingly given him over the years: "It is the nature of a fig tree to bear figs." Her words revealed the humility of perfect detachment—that is to say, again, complete self-honesty.

Master, in his effort to break us of halfhearted willingness—what he called "one-horsepower energy"—urged us always to keep a positive outlook, and to affirm possibilities rather than weaken them with too many so-called "reasonable" objections.

I remember his greeting to me one day: "How are you, Walter?"

"Well," I began. . . .

"That's good!" he interposed promptly, nipping in the bud what he saw was only a mild case of "vapors."

Never supportive of us in our moods, he urged us to banish them firmly with vigorous, positive affirmations. "I suffer when you have moods," he said once, "for then I see that Satan gets ahold of you."

Faye, when she was seventeen, was inclined to be somewhat moody. "If you want to be unhappy," Master once said to her, "no one in the world can make you happy. And if you determine to be happy, no one in the world will be able to make you unhappy." She once told me, "Master wouldn't even allow us to be around him when we had moods."

Moods weren't often my specific problem, but I remember one that ambushed me one day, and the helpful method I discovered for combatting it.

It was in February or March, 1949. Master had been away from Mt. Washington several weeks, and I hadn't seen him in all that time. I was beginning to feel his absence keenly. Finally he returned. The next day word came down to me to get someone to carry a five-gallon bottle of drinking water up to his kitchen. Eagerly I appropriated the job to myself. Arriving upstairs with the bottle, I could hear Master dictating a letter in his sitting room. Hoping to attract his attention, I rattled the bottle and made as much noise as I felt I decently could for a job that called for a minimum of tumult. Master paid no attention.

"He doesn't care that I miss him!" I thought, plunging suddenly into a violent depression. "I'm just a worker to him, not a disciple!" I rushed on to brood over the unfeeling nature of this world, where nobody really cares for anyone else. Moments later I made an abrupt about-face: "No, Master cares, but he sees I'm such a hopeless case that he figures he might as well give up pouring water into this bottomless pit!" On and on my mind churned. I tried reasoning with myself: "Look here, he's obviously busy. Why should he drop everything just for you?"

"Yeah?" retorted my recalcitrant mind. "I imagine he said, 'Look out, here comes that worthless disciple, Walter! Quick, let me dictate a letter as an excuse not to have to call him in here.'"

Clearly, reason wasn't going to pull me out of my mental whirlpool. Indeed, reason's tendency is to support any feeling that happens to be uppermost in the mind.

"Do you *like* being moody?" I demanded of my mental citizens.

"No!" came the chorus—unanimously, except for one or two grumblers in the background.

"Very well, then, boys, if reason won't do it, let's see if changing our level of consciousness will do the trick."

I went down to my meditation "cave," and there plunged my mind deeply at the Christ center between the eyebrows. Five minutes was all it took. By the end of that time my mood was so uplifted and positive that I no longer needed to affirm anything. "But *of course* he's busy!" I thought. "Hasn't he told us often that our real communion with him is *inside*, in meditation? And what if all his disciples tried selfishly to take up his time? He wouldn't have any time left over to complete his writings, which will help thousands."

In *Autobiography of a Yogi* Master wrote, "Thoughts are universally and not individually rooted." We don't create them. We only receive them, depending on our level of consciousness.

"Sir," someone once asked Master, "what causes moods?"

"Moods," he replied, "are caused by past overindulgence in sense pleasures, and consequent over-satiety and disgust. If you indulge your moods," he added warningly, "you will reinforce the mind's swing back again toward sense pleasures. For that is how the law of duality works: it moves constantly back and forth, like a pendulum, between opposite states of awareness. If, by not giving in to moods, you remove energy from one end of the pendulum's swing, you will find the hold that the senses have on you at the opposite end will weaken as well."

I learned in another way, too, how important it is not to indulge one's mental tendencies too freely. For some time during my first year at Mt. Washington I was disturbed by periods of almost obsessive sleepiness during meditation. I no sooner sat for meditation than my head began to nod. One day I felt particularly joyful inside, and was eagerly looking forward to that evening's meditation. To my immense disgust, however, the moment I sat to meditate drowsiness descended on me once again like a dense fog. I was furious with myself.

"Since you insist so much on sleeping," I scolded my mind, "I'm not going to let you sleep at all!"

I stayed up all that night—typing letters, walking about the grounds, drinking tea—*anything* to beat down my insistent craving for sleep. When daylight came, I went outdoors and worked hard in the garden. By the following evening my mind had become so submissive—terrified, I imagine, lest I abuse it with sleeplessness a second night!—that my meditative drowsiness ceased completely, and didn't return again for many months.

I worked as hard at meditation as I did during the day at my various jobs. ("*Too* hard," Master once told me. "In meditation, you should place more emphasis on relaxation.") I soon learned that the adage, "Don't put all your eggs in one basket" is as true for spiritual as for mundane expectations.

During my Saturday meditations I had been going deeper and deeper into inner stillness. "Just a *little* more effort," I began to think, "and surely I'll slip into full superconsciousness." One Saturday morning I entered my cave with the determination not to stop meditating until this goal had been achieved. For nine hours I sat, continuously applying every ounce of will power I could summon. In the end, exhausted, I had no choice but to admit defeat. If I had stopped short of exhaustion, I might have avoided discouragement and salvaged enough confidence to keep on trying over successive Saturdays. As it was, however, though I continued to meditate regularly, months passed before I was able again to make a really deep effort. It was from this very failure, in fact, that my obsession with drowsiness began.

Yet even now there were compensations: at times, deep joy during moments of inner stillness, and increasing devotion, and blissful inner sounds—one, particularly, that resembled wind in the trees. Master urged us not to talk about our meditative experiences, so I prefer to keep the most precious of them locked in my heart.

I worked hard to develop devotion, chanting and praying daily for the grace of intense love for God. Master one day smiled at me lovingly. "Keep on with your devotion," he said. "See how dry your life is when you depend on intellect."

His help was available to anyone who called to him mentally in meditation. Here he was the guide, ever subtly inspiring us, according to the measure of our receptivity, to make the right kind of spiritual effort. Sometimes, too, when we met him during the day, he would admonish us on some point concerning our meditations. Indeed, he watched over us in all ways. It never ceased to amaze me that, with so many disciples to look after, he could be so perfectly aware of the needs of each one.

"I go through your souls every day," he told us. "If I see something in you that needs correcting, I tell you about it. Otherwise, I say nothing." On another occasion he said, "I have lived the lives of each one of you. Many times I go so deep into a person at night that when I wake up in the morning I think I *am* that person! It can be a terrible experience, if he is someone full of moods and desires."

Mrs. Michelle Evans, that lady I initiated into Kriya Yoga in San Diego, told me, "I used to drink—not much, but the way most people do—you know, to be sociable. When I met Master, he told me to give it up, so for a while I took nothing alcoholic at all. But then I got to thinking, 'Surely beer doesn't count, does it? or wine? I mean, they really aren't in the same class with whiskey, rum, and brandy are they?' So I went back to drinking beer or wine occasionally. It gave me less explaining to do when we had guests.

"Well, the next time I saw Master at the San Diego church, he looked at me sorta penetratingly and said, 'I meant *all* alcoholic beverages!' Well! Since then, what choice have I got? Any time I slipped, he'd know about it!"

Jan Savage, a young boy of nine who had come to Mt. Washington with his mother, was meditating one day with Daniel Boone when he had a vision of Jesus Christ. Thrilled, he told Boone about it afterwards.

"It could be your imagination," Boone said. "Better say nothing more till you ask Master about it."

Master, who was away at that time, returned to give the service the following Sunday. Afterwards Jan joined the line of devotees that always waited to come forward for Master's blessings. As he approached, Master reached out and tousled his hair affectionately.

"So!" he cried. "Little Jan had a vision of Jesus Christ. That's very good. That was a true vision!"

Boone told me in February of an experience he too had had after keeping his mind steadfastly on Master for two days. He was given a kind of ecstasy in which he was quite unable to feel his body, even while he moved about, performing his daily duties in the print shop.

"I had to pray, finally, that I'd be able to feel my body again," he said. "I was afraid I might harm it in the machinery."

Well, I thought, *that* was for me! More eager for the experience itself, I'm afraid, than for humble attunement with my Guru, I kept my mind on Master one-pointedly. He was in Encinitas at the time. Two or three days later, he returned to Mt. Washington; I met him by the front porch as he arrived.

"What sort of mischief are you up to, Walter?" He smiled significantly.

"None, Sir." Mischief? It didn't seem like mischief to me.

"Are you *sure* you aren't up to some kind of mischief?"

I began to understand what he meant, but was reluctant to accept his definition of what I'd been doing. As he was going indoors, he smiled lovingly, saying, "Goodbye, Walter." Thinking the matter over, I had to admit to myself that, while my practice had been right, my intentions had been wrong.

"Don't seek experiences in meditation," Master told us. "The path to God is not a circus."

More touching was the experience of another disciple, Rev. Michael, who, feeling deep love for Master, would often repeat the words mentally, "I love you, Guru."

One day Master responded to his silent offering. The two of them happened to meet in the hermitage garden at Encinitas. With a gaze of deep tenderness, the Guru said, "I love you, too."

Master responded instantly to sincere love. One day, missing him intensely, I went down to see him in Encinitas where he was staying at the time. Shortly after my arrival he passed a group of us on his way back from a drive. Seeing me, he invited me to ride up with him to the hermitage. "I have missed you," he told me lovingly. How rare is it, I thought, for one's unexpressed feelings to be intuited so sensitively.

Master's help was with us not only in our inner, spiritual struggles, but in our work as well. One day Norman and I were replastering the wall of a garage by the main entrance to the Mt. Washington grounds. The plaster was old, and was setting up fast. Though we kept on adding water, we had all we could do to complete each batch before it hardened completely.

Halfway through the job, Master, on his way out for a drive, saw us and stopped the car. Calling us over to him, he chatted with us for about half an hour. We were delighted, of course. Yet at the back of our minds there lurked a slight apprehension: What about that plaster? I'd just mixed a fresh batch and poured it onto the board. And there it was, getting harder by the second.

By the time Master left us, both Norman and I were certain it would take a sledgehammer to break up the plaster. To our amazement, however, we found it as soft and pliable as it had been when I poured it. For the rest of that day the plaster gave us no trouble at all.

Hard work was as important to our way of life as regular meditation. "You must be intensely active for God," Master said, "before you can attain the actionless state of union with Him." More than either work or meditation, however, was the stress he placed on the importance of devotion. "Without love for God," he told us, "no one can find Him."

Nightly I chanted Master's translation of a song by the great Bengali saint, Ram Proshad: "Will that day come to me when saying, 'Mother! Mother!' my eyes will flow with tears?" Gradually I found myself becoming transformed inwardly. I began to feel I had some cause for self-congratulation, when one day word came to me that Master had been talking with a group of the monks in Encinitas. During the course of the conversation he had remarked lovingly:

"Look how I have changed Walter!"

CHAPTER 26

The Ministry

"YOU MIGHT LIKE to know something of the history of our Hollywood church," Master remarked to me one day, "now that you are lecturing there regularly."

"Naturally, Sir," I replied, "I'm eager to learn everything I can about our work."

"We built the church during the war. New construction wasn't allowed at that time, but we were able to build legally anyway, by renovating an old structure. We bought an old church, and had it moved onto our property. The building was a mere shell," Master chuckled. "How the neighbors howled! But we fixed it up— stuccoing the walls, fixing the roof, painting everything beautifully, and putting in valuable stained-glass windows. At last the building acquired a completely new look." Master paused reminiscently.

"Finding those windows was a real blessing from God. I wanted stained glass, but everyone insisted, 'You can't get that now. There's a war on!' Still, I knew we would get it.

"One morning God showed me in a vision where our windows were sitting, just waiting for us. They were in an old junkyard. I went there. 'I'm sorry,' said the owner, 'we have no stained glass here.' But I knew better.

"'Just look once,' I pleaded.

"'I told you,' he said, losing patience, 'we haven't any!' Growling, he stalked away.

"I went over to an assistant who was standing nearby, and asked him if *he* knew of any stained glass in the place.

"'Boss say no,' he replied, his body stooped with lifelong unwillingness. 'Muss be no.'

"'Here are five dollars,' I told him. 'I'll give them to you if you take me where I want to go.' At this he agreed. Together we went out into the backyard. There, gathering dust against a far wall, was an assortment of old doors and a miscellany of other items. But no sign of any stained-glass windows.

"'You see?' the man said, lifting his head in an attitude of vindication. 'Boss say no. Muss be no!'

"'Just pull those things away,' I requested. 'Let's have a look at what's behind them.'

"'Boss say . . .' he began a third time. Then he remembered those five dollars I'd offered him. Willingness may not have been his strong point, but finally, moaning and groaning, he moved everything out into the yard. And there at last, right up against the wall, were our stained-glass windows!

"In their present condition they looked like nothing but junk. The glass panes were in place, but all were hanging loosely, and covered with filth. The owner let me have the lot of them for next to nothing. We fixed them up carefully, however. Miss Darling* saved us thousands of dollars by framing and gold-leafing them herself. And now—well, you can see how beautiful they are. I am told they are valuable."

"One would never suspect the church of having such a grey past!" I remarked, smiling. It now looked like a charming jewel, immaculate in its white, blue, and gold colors. Set well back from the road, it was fronted by a pleasant garden. Unquestionably, it was now an asset to the neighborhood.

Master continued, "The church carpet came from God, also." This carpet, a soothing, dark blue, covered the entire floor of the church. I had long admired it. Master went on to explain, "I had wanted a beautiful carpet, because I think that if theaters can be designed beautifully to remind one of the beauties of this world, then God's places should be designed even more beautifully, to remind one that He is the Source of all beauty. My wish was for a rich

* Later, Durga Mata.

blue carpet like the one we used to have in our Encinitas temple. I sent people scouting everywhere. But no one found anything that resembled it.

"I myself then telephoned the company that had sold us that first carpet. 'Oh, I'm sorry,' a voice said, 'the man from whom you bought that one went out of business.'

"'Who is this speaking?' I inquired. It proved to be that man's former business partner. He was just about to hang up, when he paused.

"'Say' he exclaimed, 'I've just remembered that we still have a piece of that very carpet you bought left in our warehouse. How much did you say you needed?'

"'A hundred and one yards,' I replied.

"He went and measured his remnant. It came to exactly one hundred and *two* yards!

"I have often said," Master concluded, "that out of the loss of our Encinitas temple came two more temples—this one in Hollywood, and our church in San Diego. Just the other day a visitor remarked to me, 'What a pity that you lost your Encinitas temple!' I answered, 'It was the best thing that ever happened to me!' You see, it forced me to bring these teachings out more widely into the world. And look, even the carpet in our new church came out of the very carpet that had been in the old one!"

By June 1949 I was conducting midweek services more or less regularly in the Hollywood church. Soon afterward I also gave occasional Sunday services, both there and in San Diego.

A problem for any new speaker is how to avoid a feeling of nervousness in front of an audience. I never really had any problem that way, but the fact that I was so young, and looked even younger, was certainly no advantage to me. The average age of my listeners was about forty. I could count on their knowing a great deal more about most things than I. My concern was more for them, I think, stuck as they were with having to listen to me.

Abie George, a disciple in Hollywood of whom we were all particularly fond, suggested a solution. Deeply devoted ("a beautiful soul," Master called him), Abie also had a colorful sense of humor, and an unusual way of expressing it. "It's very simple," he explained

Here, I am conducting a service in Hollywood Church.

with mock earnestness. "No, hey, I mean it," he persisted, laughingly to forestall my anticipated objections, "it really *is* simple. All as you gotta do is picture to yourself alla them there people in fronta you as a buncha cabbage heads. That's all! Just say to yourself, 'You uns out there are nothin' but a buncha cabbage heads!' Like that." I thanked him doubtfully.

James Coller, the minister of our church in Phoenix, offered another suggestion. "I was so nervous when I first started lecturing," he said, "that Master suggested I take a hot bath before my talks, to relax. One evening I was supposed to give an introductory lecture to a series of public classes. The announced subject was, 'What Yoga Can Do for You.'

"Well, I took a long, hot bath beforehand! *Too* long," James added, chuckling, "and *too* hot. It sapped all my energy. I arrived for that lecture so limp that I felt more like a steam-heated towel than a human being! After five minutes of speaking I found I'd covered everything I could think of to say on the subject. It was probably the shortest talk those people had ever listened to!

"Next, Horace took up a collection. He's spastic, you know. After my five-minute lecture on what yoga can do for you, my only assistant went staggering from row to row with the collection plate, clutching at the backs of chairs for support."

This story, told with much laughter, left us holding our sides in merriment. It hadn't seemed quite so funny to his audience, however. They got up and left without uttering a word. Fortunately, the episode had a more gratifying sequel. One man, after leaving the room, returned to it, moved by James's obvious goodness and sincerity. This man later became a devoted follower of Master's work.

"Well, anyway," James concluded, addressing me, "you might try soaking yourself in hot water before your lectures." His story, I confessed, had left me somewhat less than reassured.

The solution I myself found to whatever problem I might have had with nervousness was to imagine the worst audience response possible, and then accept it—in short, to be *willing* to appear a fool. "This is all God's dream anyway," I reminded myself before a lecture, "so what does it matter whether people accept me or reject me?"

Indifference to the fruits of my efforts proved a solution to any possible problem of nervousness, but it didn't help me in the far more important matter of communicating with my listeners. For, in telling myself it was all a dream,* I ended up not really caring whether I spoke well or not.

Only gradually did I become a conscientious speaker, as I began to see the people I was speaking to as manifestations of God; it was *through* them, rather than by appearing before them, that I was being asked to serve Master. This thought cured me also of a temptation that is common to public speakers: to be satisfied if the points they make are convincing to *themselves*. In seeing God manifested in the forms of my listeners, and in the realization that what I had to say

* The Hindu teaching that life is a dream is intended to inspire non-attachment, not irresponsibility. Even in a dream, after all, it is preferable to dream wisely. In the cosmic dream-delusion, man must act as a willing instrument of God, the Divine Dreamer, before he can win the right to eternal wakefulness in Him.

was a service to Him *through* them, it became important to me to express myself in a way that would *reach* His consciousness, in them.

At first I used to pray before every lecture, "Lord, inspire me to say what *You* want said." Later I learned to ask Him also, "Help me to sense what this particular audience needs to hear, through me." Often, sensing needs different from those I had come prepared to address, I would give a completely different talk from the one I'd intended. Indeed, I learned in time to prepare only minimally, if at all, for my lectures, for I found that an open mind enabled me to respond more sensitively to the unvoiced needs of my listeners. The results of this approach were gratifying. Many people thanked me after my lectures for answering some specific question of theirs, or for dealing with problems that had been weighing on their minds. I always shared with them the real secret of my success: "God is the Doer." For it was in this thought above all that Master trained us.*

When I was first learning to lecture, Master gave me the following words of advice: "Before lecturing, meditate deeply. Then, holding onto that meditative calmness, think about what you intend to say. Write down your ideas. Include one or two funny stories, because people are more receptive if they can enjoy a good laugh. Then finish with a story from the SRF lessons. After that, put the subject out of your mind. While speaking, keep mentally before you the salient points of your outline, but above all ask the Spirit to flow through you. In that way you will draw inspiration from that inner Source, and will not speak from ego."

Most important of all to Master was the question of our attunement while we lectured, in order that we might share with our listeners not only our ideas, but our vibrations. Late one Thursday afternoon he spied Dr. Lewis out on the grounds in Encinitas, enjoying a stroll.

"Doctor," he called out, "aren't you giving the service this evening?"

---

* "Take no thought how or what ye shall speak: for it shall be given you in that same hour what ye shall speak. For it is not ye that speak, but the Spirit of your Father which speaketh in you." (Matthew 10:19,20)

"Yes, Sir," Dr. Lewis called back.

"Then what are you doing roaming about? You should be meditating!"

In time, I was able actually to *feel* a power flowing outward from my attunement with Master, filling any room or auditorium in which I might be lecturing. If the hall was large, I could feel his vibrations reach all the way to the back.

If anything I said touched my listeners, the credit, I knew, was due to this power, far more than to whatever actual words I uttered.

During Master's early years in the West, thousands came to his public lectures. When he built churches, however, he made them small, sweet in their simplicity. Smallness, he felt, is more conducive to worship; it permits a sense of inwardness, of closeness to God.

Master told us of a visit he had once paid to a large, well-known cathedral in the American Midwest. "I was admiring it," he said, "when I heard God's voice asking, 'Would you rather have all this, without Me? Or'—here a vision appeared in which I saw myself seated on the ground under a tree, a handful of disciples gathered about me—'this, with Me?'

"'Lord,' I prayed, 'only where Thou art do I want to be!'"

The Master often remarked that an emphasis on large, expensive places of worship, and on crowds of worshipers, necessitates too much concentration on money, and too little on humble, inward communion with God. "The church system has to be revised," he told us. "Outward pomp must be replaced by simplicity, and huge cathedrals, by small temples where sincere devotees gather for meditation. The well-educated minister of a large, modern congregation may lecture eloquently, but if he never meditates, and has no inward realization of God's presence, what is the use of his eloquence? His D.D. degree in this case stands for nothing but 'Doctor of Delusion'!

"If I went to a restaurant that had a good name, but that didn't have the kind of food I wanted, what good would it do me? I'd come away as hungry as I had entered. So what is the use of a famous church, if it is spiritually dead? What is the good of a beehive without honey?"

He then told us, "You are on the eve of a great change. You will see the entire church movement undergo a revolution. Churches will become places where real souls will go to commune with God."

Sometimes, with great merriment, he paraphrased a story from the novel *Heavenly Discourse*, by Charles E. Wood. His version of the tale went something like this: "When Billy Sunday, the famous evangelist, died and went to heaven, St. Peter wouldn't let him enter the Pearly Gates, demanding instead, 'What did you do on earth to deserve admission here?' 'Why,' Billy Sunday protested, 'what about all those thousands I sent up here from my revival meetings?' 'You may have sent them,' St. Peter retorted, 'but they never arrived!'"

"In Milwaukee," Master told us, "I was once taken to a church where a choir sang especially for me. Afterwards one of the singers asked me, 'How did you like our singing?'

"'It was all right,' I said.

"'You mean you *didn't* like it?'

"'I didn't say that,' I replied. 'But please don't press me further.' Well, he kept on insisting, so at last I explained, 'As far as technique went, you were perfect. But you weren't thinking of the One for whom that sacred music was written. You were thinking of pleasing *me*. Next time you sing devotional music, think of God; don't sing to impress others.'"

Master's own services were rich with inspiration. They conveyed none of the orphaned feeling one encounters in many churches of a God living far off in some unimaginable heaven, or of a Jesus Christ who left no more vital testimony to his continuing reality than the printed words in the Bible. In Master's presence, divine truths came thrillingly alive, made vibrant with the immediacy of his own God-realization.

"You are a good salesman!" an American businessman once exclaimed to him after one of his lectures. "That," Master replied, "is because I have first sold myself!"

Some of my most impressive memories of Master are of his public lectures. While they lacked the sweet intimacy of his talks with the disciples, they rang with the spirit of a mission destined, he told us, to bring spiritual regeneration to the world: a new path in the sense of a teaching geared to the attitudes and understanding of this new age of energy.

I remember especially how stirred I was by a talk he gave at a garden party in Beverly Hills on July 31, 1949. Never had I imagined that the power of human speech could be so overwhelming; it was the most moving talk I have ever heard.

"This day," he thundered, punctuating every word, "marks the birth of a new era. My spoken words are registered in the ether, in the Spirit of God, and they shall move the West. . . . Self-Realization has come to unite all religions. . . . We must go on—not only those who are here, but thousands of youths must go North, South, East, and West to cover the earth with little colonies, demonstrating that simplicity of living plus high thinking lead to the greatest happiness!"*

I was stirred to my very core; it would not have surprised me had the heavens opened up and a host of angels come streaming out, eyes ablaze, to do his bidding. Deeply I vowed that day to do my utmost to make his words a reality. Twenty years later, with his inner help and by the grace of God, I was able to start the first of what have since become several thriving communities.

Often during the years I was with Master he exhorted his audiences to fulfill his cherished dream: to found "world brotherhood colonies," or spiritual cooperative communities—not monasteries, merely, but places where people in every walk of life could devote themselves to living for God.

"Environment is stronger than will power," he often told us. He saw "world brotherhood colonies" as environments for fostering right spiritual attitudes such as humility, trust, devotion, respect for others, and friendly cooperation. For people with worldly responsibilities who want a better way of life, small cooperative communities offer the best hope of fulfilling that desire, and also of demonstrating to society at large that people can, indeed, achieve heights so scornfully repudiated in this age of spiritual underachievers. Such communities, Master said, would emphasize cooperative attitudes,

* *Self-Realization Magazine*, November-December 1949, p. 36.

Master chanting "AUM" with his hands raised, registered his thoughts in the ether. After a lecture in Beverly Hills, California, in 1950 he said: "We must go on—not only those who are here, but thousands of youths must go North, South, East, and West to cover the earth with little colonies, demonstrating that simplicity of living plus high thinking lead to the greatest happiness!"

rather than egoic social and political "rights," and present-day norms of cutthroat competition.

"Take the best advice I can give you," he said. "Gather together, those of you who share high ideals. Pool your resources. Buy land out in the country. A simple life will bring you inner freedom. Harmony with nature will bring you a happiness known to few city dwellers. In the company of other truth seekers you will find it easier to meditate and think of God.

"What is the need for all the luxuries with which people surround themselves? Most of what they have they are paying for on the installment plan! Their debts are a source of unending worry to them. Even people whose luxuries have been paid off are not free; attachment makes them slaves. They consider themselves freer for their possessions, and don't see how, in turn, their possessions now possess them!"

He added: "The day will come when this colony idea will spread through the world like wildfire."

In the over-all plan for his work, Paramhansa Yogananda saw individual students first receiving the SRF lessons, and practicing Kriya Yoga in their own homes; then, in time, forming spiritual centers where they could meet once or twice weekly for group study and meditation. In areas where there was enough interest to warrant it, he wanted SRF churches to be built, perhaps with full- or part-time ministers. And where there were enough sincere devotees to justify it, his dream was that they would buy land and live cooperatively, serving God and sharing the spiritual life together on a full-time basis.

As I mentioned in Chapter 17, Master had wanted to start a model world brotherhood colony in Encinitas. He felt so deeply the importance of this communitarian dream that for some years it was the nucleus of his every plan for the work. Indeed, ruler though he was of his mental processes, even he on one occasion became caught up in a whirlwind of enthusiasm for this project. He told a congregation one Sunday morning, "I got so involved last night in thinking about world brotherhood colonies that my mind got away from me. But," he added, "I chanted a little, and it came back."

Another measure of his interest may be seen in the fact that the first edition of *Autobiography of a Yogi* ended with a ringing statement of his hopes to found such a colony. "Brotherhood," he wrote in that edition, quoting a discussion he had had with Dr. Lewis in Encinitas, "is an ideal better understood by example than precept! A small harmonious group here may inspire other ideal communities over the earth." He concluded, "Far into the night my dear friend—the first *Kriya Yogi* in America—discussed with me the need for world colonies founded on a spiritual basis."

Alas, he encountered an obstacle that has stood in the way of every spiritual reformer since the Buddha: human nature. Marriage has always tended to be a somewhat closed corporation. The economic depression of the 1930s had had the effect on a whole generation of Americans of heightening this tendency, by increasing their desire for family security. "Us four and no more" was the way Yogananda described their attitude. America in general wasn't yet ready for world brotherhood colonies.

A further difficulty lay in the fact that his work was already in the grip of monastic disciples who set the tone for all the colonies. Householders couldn't match their spirit of self-abnegation and service. Families were, so to speak, crowded out of the communal garden by the more exuberant growth of plants of renunciation. And Yogananda was too near the end of his life-mission to fulfill elsewhere his "world brotherhood colony" dream.

"Encinitas is gone!" he lamented toward the end of his life. It was not that the ashram was lost. What he meant was that his plans for founding a world brotherhood colony on those sacred grounds would not be fulfilled, at least not during his lifetime. He stopped accepting families into the ashrams, which he now turned into full-fledged monasteries. It was in his renunciate disciples that he had found that spirit of selfless dedication which his mission needed for its ultimate success.

Nevertheless, the idea of world brotherhood colonies remained important to him. It was, as he had put it during that stirring speech in Beverly Hills, "in the ether, in the Spirit of God." Kamala Silva in her autobiography, *The Flawless Mirror*,* reports that as late as five months before he left his body he spoke to her glowingly of this dream. He knew that his dream must, in time, be fulfilled.

Even with regard to so basic a part of his mission as world brotherhood colonies, however, Master was completely free from anxiety. He never saw the world as most people see it. To him this is all God's play—a seemingly endless show of shadows and light in a divine motion picture.

I remember the evening that he recorded some of his chants for public release. Partway through that recording session I was obliged to leave for a class I was giving at the Hollywood Church. On my return, I found Master standing outside on the lawn, listening to one of the chants being played back to him: "What lightning flash glimmers in Thy face, Mother! Seeing Thee I am thrilled through and through." Again and again he had the recording played over. Presently he began almost to dance, swaying to and fro ecstatically, his arms stretched sidewise, waving to the rhythm of the music. He was blissfully engrossed in the beauty of Divine Mother, whom he perceived as wondrous Light spreading out to infinity. I was deeply moved.

Afterwards, as he was taking leave of our little group, he said quietly, "I see all of you as images of light. Everything—these trees, bushes, the grass you are standing on—all are made of that light. You have no idea how beautiful everything is!"

* p. 183. Unfortunately, however, this beautiful book is currently out of print.

CHAPTER 27

Attunement

MASTER WAS TO speak one Sunday morning at Hollywood Church, when Sue and Bud Clewell, my relatives in Westwood Village, came to visit me. After the service, Master graciously invited the three of us to join him for lunch.

A small group of us were served on the stage behind the closed curtains, there being no room in the church large enough to accommodate us. This afternoon was my first opportunity to observe Master in the role of host. I found it a charming experience. His total lack of affectation, delightful wit, gentle courtesy, and warm, kindly laughter which included everyone in his joy would, I think, have enchanted any audience.

Among those present were Dr. and Mrs. Lewis. A lady who had recently become a member, glancing at them, inquired, "Master, Dr. Lewis was your first disciple in this country, wasn't he?"

Master's response was unexpectedly reserved. "That's what they say," he replied quietly. His tone of voice, even more than his words, made such a marked contrast to the affability he had been displaying that the lady seemed taken aback. Noticing her surprise, Master explained more kindly, "I never speak of people as my disciples. God is the Guru: They are *His* disciples."

To Master, discipleship was too sacred a subject to be treated lightly even in casual conversation.

Later, Sue and Bud confessed they had found Master charming. "But," Sue then challenged me a little belligerently, "why do you have to call him 'Master'?" Warming to her subject, she continued,

"This is a free country! Americans aren't slaves. And anyway, no one has a right to be called the master of any other human being!"

"Sue," I remonstrated, "it isn't our freedom we've given him. It's our bondage! I've never known anyone so respectful of the freedoms of others as Yogananda is. We call him 'Master' in the sense of teacher. He is a true master of the practices in which we ourselves are struggling to excel. You might say that he is our teacher in the art of achieving *true* freedom."

"*True* freedom! How can you say that? You can vote, can't you? You can travel anywhere you want to, can't you? Isn't our American way of life proof enough that you're free already?"

"*Is* it?" I smiled. "Think how bound people are by their attachments and desires. They want a thousand things, most of which they'll never get, in the belief that, through them, they'll find happiness. In conditioning their happiness by material objects, they enslave themselves! Happiness isn't *things*, Sue. It's a state of mind."

Sue pondered my words a few moments. "Well," she concluded, unwilling to surrender her point completely, "I still think I'll be happier when we can afford a new sofa!"

(Poor Sue, *were* you happier? In the years after that, I wish I could say that I ever saw happiness in your eyes.)

Sue's objection to our loving appellation for our Guru was by no means unusual. Perhaps if a master were to appear on the stage of life like some Nietzschean Zarathustra, making grand pronouncements on obscure themes that no one in his right mind would ever think on his own, people, mistaking bewilderment for awe, might cry, "Ah, here indeed is a *master*!" But masters usually live more or less prosaically. They get born in mangers. They teach familiar truths in simple ways. One might say they almost flaunt their ordinariness. Human nature doesn't take kindly to greatness in mere *people*. And it is in their perfect humanity that masters most truly reveal their greatness, not in their rejection of all that it means to be a human being.

In this ideal they are both a challenge to us and a reproach. Most people don't want challenges. Still less do they want reproaches. One who isn't willing to face the need for self-transformation cannot view gladly the accomplished fact of such transformation in others. "I'm as good as anyone else," is the common declaration. A true statement it would be, too, if it referred to the eternal, divine image within them. But people who talk like that are not thinking of their souls. Who, in his egoic humanity, can say honestly, "I'm as virtuous as anyone else, as intelligent, as artistic, as wise, as gifted a businessman, as good a leader"? The over-emphasized egalitarianism of our age blinds people to the single most obvious fact of human nature—its vast variety. Belief in complete outward equality is a kind of democratic myth, a preference for pleasing sentiments over the clear vision of reality that comes from winning hard struggles on the battlefield of life. Only when we have banished from our consciousness the delusions that keep us bound to this phenomenal world can we know ourselves truly equal, in God, to the very angels.

"My thoughts are not your thoughts, neither are your ways my ways, saith the Lord. For as the heavens are higher than the earth, so are my ways higher than your ways, and my thoughts than your thoughts."* People rarely see that the greatness of God's ways, as expressed through the lives of His awakened sons, lies in a transcendent view of mundane realities, and not in a rigid denial of those realities. From the thought, "Nothing is divine," man must grow to the realization, "Everything is divine."

Our "bondage" to Master was a bond purely of love. He, far more than we, appreciated the sacredness of this relationship, and treated it with the deepest dignity and respect. Where love was missing on a disciple's part, however, the bond broke, or was never formed. And then even disciples were known to lose sight of what it meant to call their guru "Master."

"I didn't come here," they complained, "to pour *cement!*" No? Why, then, did you come?

"Why, to meditate, of course, to attain *samadhi*."

And did you imagine that *samadhi* would come in any other way than by attunement with your guru?

"Well, no. After all that's why I came here. But what has attunement got to do with pouring cement? It's in my meditations that I need his help."

* Isaiah 55:8,9.

O blind ones, can't you see that self-transformation is a *total* process? that what the Master gives us spiritually must be perceived on *every* level of our being? that no real difference exists between God in the form of cement and God in the form of blissful visions? God is equally present in everything!

Rare, alas, is that disciple who feels no inner resistance, born of ego-consciousness, to complete acceptance of his guru. "I want to express my own creativity!" is a complaint frequently thought, less frequently expressed. Or, "I know Master has the greatest thing of all to give me, but I have something worthwhile to give him, too. I'm a good organizer!" O foolish devotee, don't you see that man has *nothing* to express that he can truly call his own? that his ideas, his opinions, his so-called "inspirations"—all these reflect only currents of consciousness, available equally to everyone? Only by attunement to God's will can we fully express *ourselves*. Everything else is borrowed. And yet, the Divine has a unique song to sing through each of us. It isn't that we shouldn't *try* to be creative. Indeed, unless we exert ourselves to act, God cannot act through us. (The whole of the Bhagavad Gita is an exhortation to selfless activity.) But we must learn to *listen*, to accept, to absorb: herein lies the true and deepest secret of creativity.

For disciples, the surest way to express themselves creatively is to attune themselves to their guru's consciousness and to his wishes for them. His entire task is to speed his disciples on the path of self-unfoldment. *Are* you a good organizer? Then seek inwardly, from your guru, the inspiration needed for any organizational work you do. If you say, "This, at least, is something I know better than he," you close the door to the infinite source of all true inspiration within yourself, which he has been so painstakingly prising open for you.

It is folly in any case, and a sure invitation to vainglory, to dwell on the thought that the guru's understanding is imperfect even in trivial matters. For therein lies the seed of pride; it begins with the thought, "Wise as he is—look! In this particular matter *I* am wiser than he!"

As a matter of fact, our own Master often demonstrated an undreamed-of proficiency in subjects that were far outside the realm of his own human experience. For example, though he had never studied medicine, Master won the respect of many doctors for his familiarity with the esoterica of their profession.

In India once, not satisfied with the work of a certain well-known artist whom he had commissioned to do a portrait of Lahiri Mahasaya, he painted a better portrait of that master himself. And this was his first attempt at painting!

The wife of Señor Cuaron, our center leader in Mexico City, told me in Spanish when I visited them in 1954, "I once had a private interview with Master. I knew he spoke no Spanish, and as you can see, I don't speak English. Yet we conversed for an hour, and I understood him perfectly." My own assumption has always been that, for that one hour, he spoke with her in Spanish.

There were times when I myself felt that Master had erred in some matter, or had not sufficiently grasped some point. There was even a time, as you will see in a later chapter, when my questioning took the form of more serious doubts. But always I found, in time, that it was he who was right. His actions, unusual though they sometimes were and not always reasonable in appearance, were based on sure intuitions that, incredibly, always worked out for the best. Whenever his plans went awry, it was, I think, because of our own want of attunement in carrying them out.

A small example may suffice. Brought up as I had been to the importance of esthetic values, I was mildly disappointed by the Gothic arches on our church altars, which, I was told, Master had designed himself. To my eyes they looked somewhat stark and uninspired, though by no means offensively so. One day, however, I got to see his original sketch: It was exquisite. The subtle oriental sweep of his arches had been missed altogether by the carpenters.

Had we listened more sensitively to the subtle nuances of his guidance, and not run about—"like chickens with their heads cut off" as he himself put it—trying so frenziedly to do his will, nor tried so *reasonably* to obstruct it, I almost think we could have changed the world. Certainly we would all have radically transformed ourselves.

*   *   *   *   *   *   *

Now that Master had, reluctantly, abandoned his dream of founding a world brotherhood colony in Encinitas, and had turned his mind to organizing the existing communities along more strictly monastic lines, the thought was in the air: "Organize!" I don't recall that Master himself said much about organizing at this time. At least, he never did so in my presence. Anyway, for whatever reason, many disciples got caught up in this thought.

There were several monks who, instead of saying merely, "*Now* we must organize," waxed critical of the fact that things hadn't been organized long before. New as I was in the work, I looked up to these men as my superiors on the path. It didn't occur to me that they were actually being negative. When they referred darkly to the ways in which things were, according to them, being mismanaged, my reaction was to feel distress that Master should have been so badly served by the "mismanagers."

Master's way was, if possible, to let the disciples play out their fantasies, and learn from them. I was never really brought fully into the present picture, but one day Boone came charging into my room and announced grandly, "Master has appointed a committee. He wants you and me to be on it."

"A committee? What does he want us to do?"

"We're to organize the work," Boone replied, straightening up self-importantly.

"What aspects of it?"

"All aspects of it—everything!" Boone swept an arm outward in an expansive gesture.

"Well," I said dubiously, "if Master says so. But I don't really know much about the work. I can't imagine how he expects me to help organize it!"

"Oh, you won't have to do much. Just lend a hand whenever we ask for it."

It turned out I didn't really have to do anything. For some weeks various members of the committee met by twos and threes, informally, to discuss everything they felt needed changing. There was much talk, some complaining, and little action. Gradually, complaints assumed the dominant role. The main office, Boone informed me indignantly, was obstructing the committee's work, and thereby, of course, Master's will. I felt incompetent to offer positive suggestions, but shared my fellow members' indignation. It amazed me that disciples should so stubbornly refuse to cooperate with their guru's wishes.

One day Boone dashed into my room in a burst of anger. "Miss Sahly completely refuses to obey the committee's latest directive!"

Why, this was unthinkable! I rose to my feet. "We must go speak to her!" Together we strode over to the main office. I told Miss Sahly (later, Shraddha Mata) that in refusing to cooperate with the committee she was disobeying Master, that the matter in question was a committee decision, and that, for the welfare of the work, she must absolutely accept it.

"You young hotheads!" Master cried when he learned about the episode. "What do you mean by bursting in there and shouting like that?" He proceeded to give me, particularly, the best tongue-lashing I ever heard him give anyone.

I was aghast. I had pictured myself bravely striking blows in his cause, only to find myself fighting on the wrong side! Miss Sahly, it turned out, was a highly respected disciple of many years' standing, and a member of the board of directors. Master, moreover, had never told her, nor anyone else, that our committee had any special powers. (Nor, I suddenly realized, had I ever heard from him directly that we had any!)

Running out of things to say about our office invasion, but finding himself still in fine voice, Master started in on the committee itself. He called it "do-nothing, negative, a complete farce." Most of the monks, including the other committee members, were present. Master's entire tirade, however, was directed at me.

But Master, I thought, *I took hardly any part in the committee's activities!* Outwardly, however, I said nothing; after all, I *was* at least nominally a committee member. But I couldn't help feeling a little resentment at what I considered my undeserved humiliation. Later, I reflected that my reaction only proved all the more my need for correction.

"Sir," I pleaded earnestly that evening, "please scold me more often."

"I understand." He looked at me keenly. "But what you need is more devotion."

It was true. In heeding the negative criticisms of my older brother disciples I had fallen—from what had seemed to me good motives—into judgmental attitudes, forever inimical to love.

Soon thereafter I approached Master. "I'm sorry, Sir," I said.

"That's the way!" Master smiled lovingly. From then on the incident was closed between us.

Master always discouraged negativity, even in a good cause. A couple of years later a certain man tried by trickery to hurt the work in one of our churches. Mr. Jacot, a loyal and devoted member, uncovered the man's scheme and denounced him publicly. Master expressed his gratitude to Mr. Jacot afterward for having saved us in a perilous situation. After thanking him, however, Master gently scolded him for the means he had employed. "It is not good," he said, "regardless of one's intentions, to create wrong vibrations through anger and harsh words. The good that you have accomplished would have been greater had you employed peaceful means."

Negativity, from whatever motive, creates its own momentum. Unfortunately Mr. Jacot failed, even after Master's admonishment, to see the need for curbing righteous anger in defense of a good cause. Thus he gradually developed a judgmental attitude that ultimately took him out of the work.

On another occasion, perhaps a year after our committee episode, I was invited by a certain Masonic lodge (to which one of our members belonged) to appear in a tableau that was to be presented on the occasion of their installation of officers. What caused them to invite me was that they wanted a tableau of Christ at Gethsemane, and I was perhaps the only one around in those days with a beard. Anyway, they asked me to play that part. (All I had to do was look up in silence occasionally, and sigh!)

Master told me to go. The affair went smoothly enough until the time came for the installation ceremony itself. And then smoldering rivalries burst into flame. Half the lodge members walked out in angry protest. The ceremony ended in emotional ashes.

Master commented the next day that he'd heard I looked convincingly Christlike.

"I'd rather *be* like Christ than look like him, Sir," I said.

"That will come," he replied casually. He saw all of us in terms of our spiritual potential.

"How did it go?" Master then inquired of me.

"Not too well," I replied.

"It was a fiasco, wasn't it?"

"Completely, Sir, I'm afraid!"

"Well," he concluded, "don't say anything about it."

His wish that I say nothing at first surprised, and then impressed me. It surprised me because, no matter what I might say, the Masons would never get wind of my remarks. Nor did their internal problems at all affect us. But then I realized, and I was impressed by the fact, that what Master was warning me about was the power of negativity itself.

"Avoid speaking negative things," he said to us one evening. "Why look at the drains, when there is beauty all around? You could take me into the most perfect room in the world, and still I would be able, if I wanted to, to find faults in it. But why should I want to? Why not enjoy its beauty?"

Again he told us, "Don't speak of the faults of the organization. If I wanted to list them, I could start now and never stop! But if we concentrate on the bad side, we lose sight of the good. Doctors say that millions of terrible germs pass through our bodies. But because we aren't aware of them they are far less likely to affect us than if we sensed their presence, and worried about it. So should it be here. For there is a great deal of good in this organization. But when we look at the negative side long enough, we ourselves take on negative qualities. When we concentrate on the good, we take on goodness."

It was several days after the committee episode that I first met Daya Mata (then Faye Wright). I had entered the main office after working-hours to deliver something. A youthful-looking woman of radiant countenance entered the room, her firm step suggestive of boundless energy. I had no idea who she was, but sensed in her a closeness to Master. Seeing me, she paused, then addressed me pleasantly.

"You're Donald, aren't you? I'm Faye. I've heard about you." She smiled. "My, that was quite a stir you boys created with that committee of yours!"

I felt acutely embarrassed. As far as I was concerned, that committee was a dead issue. But she, not knowing how I stood on the matter, decided to help me understand it better. As we conversed, I found myself thinking, "So this is an example of those disciples who were supposed to be 'obstructing' Master's wishes. I'd a thousand times rather be like her than like any of those complainers!" Her calm self-possession, kindliness, and transparent devotion to Master impressed me deeply. From now on, I resolved, I would take her as my model in the ideal spirit of discipleship that I was striving to develop.

"We must learn to give up self-will if we want to please Master. And that," she added significantly, "is what we are trying to do."

Simple teaching, simply expressed! But it rang true. What, I thought, reflecting on her words, was the use of building this, of organizing that, of doing even the most laudable work, if *Master* was not pleased? For his job was to express God's will for each of us. To please him was, quite simply, to please God.

Let others do the important, outward things, I decided. For me only one thing would matter from now on: to do Master's will, *to please him*. I was immeasurably grateful to this senior disciple for her advice.

Ironically, it was very soon afterward—almost as if in response to my determination to court obscurity—that Master singled me out for responsibility. He put me in charge of the monks at Mt. Washington. By this time I had been with him one year—not long enough surely, I thought, for such a heavy responsibility. "He's testing me," I decided. But he must have meant the appointment seriously, for I held this position for the remainder of my years at Mt. Washington.

Several weeks passed. Then one day I was standing with Herbert Freed, one of the ministers, outside the entrance to the basement. We were talking with Master, who was on the point of going out for a drive. Herbert was to leave that afternoon to become the minister of our church in Phoenix, Arizona, and Master was giving him last-minute instructions. After a pause, Master said quietly:

"You have a great work to do."

Turning to Herbert, I smiled my felicitations.

"It is you I'm talking to, Walter," Master corrected me. He said no more on the subject; moments later his car drove away. To what sort of work had he been referring?

Thereafter, in one context or another, he often repeated this prediction. "You must do so-and-so, Walter," he would say, "because you have a great work to do." Or, "You have a great work to do, therefore. . . ." Two years after Master's *mahasamadhi*, Rajarshi Janakananda, his chief disciple, was blessing a group of us one evening in Encinitas. He paused when I came up to him, then said softly, "Master has a great work to do through you, Walter. And he will give you the strength to do it." I was struck by how softly he had spoken—as if not wanting the others to hear him. Was it a secret? And if so, why? Master, too, I had noticed, chose moments when we were alone to speak to me of my life's work.

What was this "great work" to which both of them referred? Neither Master nor Rajarshi ever told me. But Master's words were,

Master with St. Lynn just after the disciple's initiation into *sannyas*, or monkhood. On this occasion Master gave him the name Rajarshi Janakananda.

in their cumulative effect at least, the most insistent he ever addressed to me. They returned often to my mind through the ensuing years, demanding comprehension. Clearly, I reflected, they had been meant as a command, not as a compliment. They seemed intended to invest me with a sense of personal responsibility for some aspect of his mission, and also, perhaps, to inspire me to take that responsibility seriously.

Clearly, too, in the context of his remarks on several of those occasions, mine was to be a public work, one in which I would have to stand, perhaps independently, on my own feet, and one therefore perhaps not closely connected with the institution's activities.

Instinctively I feared such responsibility. I wanted to be in tune with Master, and not to dance the wild jig of outward success and acclaim, fraught as it is with temptations. We are here, Faye had said, to please Master. Couldn't I, I prayed, just please him from the background—the *safe* ground—where no lure of outward importance could intrude?

"I don't *want* to do a great work!" I wrote to Rajarshi the day after he had spoken those words to me. "I just want to serve Master unnoticed." (Rajarshi's reply was to come and bless me again, smiling quietly.)

But when, one time, I resisted Master's efforts to draw me into teaching activities, his response was brusque.

"Living for God," he told me sternly, "is martyrdom!"

CHAPTER 28

Reincarnation

A BOATLOAD OF FISHERMEN in Encinitas had had a bad day. After hours of work and very little to show for it, they were ready to go home. Paramhansa Yogananda happened to be strolling on the beach when they brought their boat in.

"You are giving up?" he inquired.

"Yeah," they replied, despondently. "No fish."

"Why don't you try just once more?" the Master suggested.

Something in the tone of his voice made them heed his advice. Going out once more, they got a large haul.

And thus was added another puzzling item to the growing legend in the local community of Encinitas about the strange, kindly Swami around whom things seemed somehow always to happen for the best.

To me this story, which I heard indirectly from some of the townsfolk there, illustrates a basic truth of human life, one that Master often emphasized: No matter how many times a person fails, he need never accept failure as Destiny's final judgment on him. We have a right as children of the Infinite, he said, to God's infinite bounty. Failure is *never* God's will for us. It is a merely temporary condition we impose on ourselves through some flaw in our attunement with cosmic law. By repeated efforts to succeed, we gradually refine that attunement. "Try just once more," Master said. If our basic intentions are spiritually lawful, failure simply means we haven't yet succeeded. Life, in other words, gives us our failures as steppingstones to success.

In the case of those fishermen, Master's blessings proved a necessary aid, in the sense that they helped attune those men's efforts more quickly to what they were already on the way to accomplishing. Had the men themselves not been ready for such a blessing, he would not have given it, which is another way of saying they would not have attracted it. The *sensitivity* with which one "tries just once more," rather than the mere act of repetition, is the real key to success. There are some people who succeed quickly, whereas others struggle unsuccessfully for years. *Attunement* is the secret. Genius depends far more on attunement than on hard work or intellectual brilliance. And of all existing sorts of attunement, the highest is to be aware of God's power acting through us.

There is another aspect to attunement, however, and it, too, relates to what Master told those fishermen: "Try just once more."

I had this experience when I tried to give up smoking. It was in Charleston, a year and a half before I came to Master. My attempt recalled Mark Twain's rueful comment, "Smoking's the easiest habit in the world to give up: I've done it a thousand times!" Often I would quit in the morning, but with my coffee after lunch I'd think, "A smoke, now, would be very pleasant!" And there I'd find myself, back into regular smoking. I had one thing going for me, however: Never did I say despairingly to myself: "I've failed." Always I said, instead, "I haven't yet succeeded!" Thus, each failure became an affirmation of eventual success.

One evening, after nearly a year of this, I told one of my roommates in Charleston firmly, "I've now given up smoking."

"Yeah, yeah, *sure!*" he scoffed, then sang a line from a popular song: "It seems to me I've heard that song before."

But I knew. The next morning I was just as certain. I kept half a pack of cigarettes in my breast pocket and shared them with friends as long as the cigarettes lasted. Never again, from that day to this, have I ever felt even the slightest desire to smoke. All those affirmations had finally added force to my resolution, making it absolute.

In the episode I related in the last chapter about the famous artist whose portrait of Lahiri Mahasaya failed to win Yogananda's approval, the Master asked him, "How long did it take you to master your art?"

"Twenty years," the man replied.

"Twenty years," Master exclaimed, "to convince yourself you could paint?"

This wasn't at all the comment the artist had expected. Taken aback, he spluttered angrily, "I'd like to see you do as well in twice that length of time!"

"Give me one week," the Master replied calmly. The artist, considering himself insulted, left the room.

The Master then, taking a paintbrush in hand, made several false starts, each time attuning himself more sensitively to the Source of all true inspiration. By the end of a week he had completed a portrait which, the artist himself conceded, was better than his own.

The important thing in life is to keep on trying, and never to say, "I have failed." Rather, after every setback one should tell himself firmly, "I haven't yet succeeded!" As Master put it in his lessons, "The season of failure is the best time for planting the seeds of success."

Our ineluctable destiny is, sooner or later, to find God, for He is our only reality. Reincarnation, then, is a reassuring doctrine for those who wonder, "Will I *ever* make it?" All of us have an infinite number of chances to improve, and to reach perfection.

The story of the fishermen is a symbol of God's everlasting willingness to give men that "one more" chance they need in order to obtain everything they desire from His ocean of abundance. By extension, this story suggests that God's forgiveness—call it, rather, His loving expectation of us—is eternal.

The soul has eternity in which to achieve perfection. One ought never to abandon hope, even if failure dogs him all his life. Through repeated incarnations, he can—indeed, *must*, eventually—succeed. Yogananda put it beautifully, and often emphasized the point: "A saint is a sinner who never gave up."

On the subject of reincarnation, Indian philosophy seems to be at odds with the Christian teachings. In fact, however, this doctrine is denied only in prevailing *interpretations* of the Bible, and not by the Bible itself. Reincarnation is not an *un-Christian* teaching. Nor, for that matter, is it an un-Jewish one. It was taught by some of the great early Christian Fathers, including Origen (A.D. 185–254),* who claimed he'd received it in an unbroken tradition "from apostolic times." It was not until five centuries after Christ, in 553 A.D. at the Second Council of Constantinople, that this doctrine was finally removed from Christian dogma. The anathema pronounced against it was delivered owing to certain political maneuverings, and was less an outcome of theological purism. Scholars have recently discovered that Pope Vigilius, though present in Constantinople at that time, took no part in pronouncing the anathema, and in fact boycotted the Council itself altogether.

Numerous Biblical passages support belief in reincarnation.† The doctrine of rebirth may be found, subsequent to Biblical times, in Jewish as well as in Christian traditions.

* The Encyclopedia Britannica calls Origen "the most prominent of all the Church Fathers with the possible exception of Augustine." Origen wrote, of reincarnation, "Is it not reasonable that souls should be introduced into bodies in accordance with their merits and previous deeds?"

† An example: "Then Job arose, and rent his mantle, and shaved his head, and fell down upon the ground, and worshiped. And said, Naked came I out of my mother's womb, and naked shall I return thither [i.e., into another womb]." (Job 1:20,21)
"But thou, Bethlehem Ephratah, though thou be little among the thousands of Judah, yet out of thee shall he come forth unto me that is to be ruler in Israel; whose goings forth have been from of old, from everlasting." (Micah 5:2)
"For all the prophets and the law prophesied until John. And if ye will receive it, this is Elias, which was for to come. He that hath ears to hear, let him hear." (Matthew 11:13–15)
"And as they came down from the mountain, Jesus charged them, saying, Tell the vision [of his transfiguration, in which he had revealed himself as the Messiah] to no man, until the Son of man be risen again from the dead. And his disciples asked him, saying, Why then say the scribes that Elias must first come? And Jesus answered and said unto them, Elias truly shall first come, and restore all things. But I say unto you, That Elias is come already, and they knew him not, but have done unto him whatsoever they listed. Likewise shall also the Son of man suffer of them. Then the disciples understood that he spake unto them of John the Baptist." (Matthew 17:9–13)
"Him that overcometh will I make a pillar in the temple of my God, *and he shall go no more out.*" (Revelation 3:12)
The above passages present a small selection, only, of many in the Bible that demonstrate support for the doctrine of reincarnation. Christian traditionalists would be wise to question some of the *sources* for their own traditions. Do those sources derive from great saints, who knew God? Or are they merely the deductions of rationalists, whose theological conclusions were founded on reason, not on actual spiritual experience?

Rabbi Manasseh ben Israel (1604–1657 A.D.), Jewish theologian and statesman, wrote, "The belief or the doctrine of the transmigration of souls is a firm and infallible dogma accepted by the whole assemblage of our church [sic] with one accord, so that there is none to be found who dares to deny it. . . . The truth of it has been incontestably demonstrated by the Zohar, and all the books of the Kabalists." And while modern Jews generally reject this doctrine, rabbis familiar with the spiritual traditions of Judaism do not endorse that rejection.

Reincarnation is endorsed in the *Shulhan Oruch*, which is the major book of laws in the Torah. A student for the rabbinate in Israel once sent me several supportive quotations from this book, including these words from the Sha'ar Hatsiyune, letter 6vav: "That soul will be sent time and time again to this world until he does what God wants him to do." The student said that his rabbi, after reading this letter, could no longer deny the doctrine of reincarnation.

Rabbi Abraham Yehoshua, a Hasidic master who died in 1825, spoke of ten lives that he had lived previously, concluding, "And so I was sent forth again and again in order to perfect my love. If I succeed this time, I shall never return again."*

Among famous Westerners who have subscribed to this doctrine, the German philosopher Schopenhauer wrote: "Were an Asiatic to ask me for a definition of Europe, I should be forced to answer him: It is that part of the world which is haunted by the incredible delusion that man was created out of nothing, and that his present birth is his first entrance into life."† Voltaire wrote, "It is not more surprising to be born twice than once." And the British philosopher Hume stated that reincarnation is "the only system to which Philosophy can so much as hearken."

According to the doctrine of reincarnation, earth-life is a school, and as such it contains many grades. The ultimate goal of human experience is graduation from bondage to ego into cosmic consciousness. Steppingstones to this unconditioned awareness are the

* Martin Buber, *Tales of the Hasidim*, New York, Schocken Books, 1948, p. 118.

† *Parerga and Paralipomena.*

removal, first, of all confining attachments and desires; second, the expansion of love; and third, a growing realization that God is the one underlying Reality of the universe.

The "plot" of the cosmic dream—the drama of Creation—embraces not only biological evolution, but also separate egoic evolution. For the ego to reach ultimate perfection requires many lifetimes.

The evolution of awareness begins at the lowest levels of conscious identity. It moves upward automatically at first, through mineral, plant, insect, and lower animal forms until at last it attains the human level.* From this point on, evolution ceases to be automatic. Man's brain and nervous system, being more highly developed, grant him that specificity of awareness which is called the ego. Man has the ability to exercise intelligent discrimination, and has also a certain amount of free will. From this point on, he can either speed up his spiritual evolution, delay it, or temporarily reverse it, by his own use or misuse of freedom.

The results of self-effort are regulated by the law of karma. (Newton's well-known law of action and reaction is a material manifestation of this universal spiritual principle.) According to karmic law, every action, even of thought, engenders an opposite reaction. God's Creation, which is only a dream in the mind of the Creator, maintains its appearance of separateness by the illusion of duality. Brahman, the Supreme Spirit, is in itself one and Indivisible. It manifested Creation by setting a portion of Its consciousness in motion—like waves on the surface of a body of water,† or like the tines of a tuning fork which produce sound by movement in opposite directions from a state of rest in the middle. No movement is complete in itself: it is always offset by an equal movement in the opposite direction.

Karma means simply *action*, or movement. Every action implies movement from a state of rest in the center; it results invariably, sooner or later, in an equal and opposite movement, a reaction *in kind*. Hatred given results in hatred received. Love given attracts

---

* The Hindu scriptures state that to reach the human level requires from five to eight million incarnations in lower life forms.

† "And the Spirit of God moved upon the face of the waters. And God said, Let there be light: and there was light." (Genesis 1:2,3)

love. Anger, kindness, forgiveness, or help freely given to others results in anger, kindness, forgiveness, or help returned—if not from
the same people, then from others, since the "post" to which the
action is tied is the originating ego. The response can be delayed
indefinitely, however, by what Master called "the thwarting cross-
currents of ego."

In time, as the ego acquires wisdom, it sheds bit by bit its bag-
gage of self-definitions, and lets all further actions flow through it
without any personal involvement. At this point, even the fruits of
action cease to affect one. There *is* a reaction, of course, but since the
causative act was not tied to ego-consciousness, its resultant reaction has little or no effect on him, personally. Being inwardly free,
it is usually to his disciples, tied to him as they are by the bonds of
affection, that those benefits revert. The true sage rests unshaken at
the calm center of his being, blissful in the realization that he and the
ever-free Spirit are One.

Spiritually speaking, karma has different levels of manifestation,
depending on how clearly it expresses the divine consciousness.
Love, for example, is a more spiritual karma than hatred, since it
reinforces the awareness of life's essential oneness. Hatred increases
the delusion of separateness from other people, and from God. To
tell a truth is a more spiritual karma than to tell a lie, for truthfulness
develops a refined awareness of *what really is*—of the Divine Reality
behind all appearances.

Karma, then, may be described as the system of rewards and pun-
ishments which helps the ego ultimately to spurn all personal attachments, and thereby to manifest its innate divinity. Suffering is the
karmic result of action performed that is not in tune with a person's
intrinsic divine nature. Fulfillment is the reward for living at least to
some degree in harmony with that nature. To learn all one's lessons
thoroughly requires more opportunities for error and self-correction
than one gets in a single lifetime. Often, indeed, more than one incarnation is needed to learn even *one* important lesson.

Reincarnation explains the enormous inequities of health, intelligence, talent, and opportunity one finds in human life. It is, as David
Hume stated, "the only system to which Philosophy can hearken."

People often object, "If everyone reincarnates, why is it that no one remembers having lived before?" The simple answer is, Many do remember! In the West, of course, if it is children who claim to have such memories, they soon learn from the disapproval of their elders to keep those claims to themselves. Yet even so, a number of well-documented cases in the West have received considerable publicity.* Because my own interest in such matters is somewhat well-known, a number of people through the years have related to me their own experiences with past-life recall.

One lady told me that she had once played a piece on the piano for a four-year-old boy, a student of hers. Matter-of-factly the child announced, "I know that piece. I used to play it on my violin." Knowing that he had studied only the piano, she questioned him. The boy demonstrated correctly the difficult finger positions and arm movements for playing the violin. "He's never seen a violin before," insisted his mother later. "He's never even heard violin music!"

One of the most interesting accounts of this nature ever to come to my attention was sent to me many years ago by a friend in Cuba, where it had been reprinted in the newspapers from an article that had first appeared in France. The account tells that a young French girl, the child of devout Catholic parents, had been using recognizably Indian words, such as "rupee," as soon as she was old enough to speak. Two words that she used repeatedly were, "Wardha," and "Bapu." Her parents, intrigued, began reading books on India. Wardha, they learned, was the village where Mahatma Gandhi had established his ashram. And "Bapu" was the familiar name by which he was known to his intimate friends and disciples. The child claimed that in her last life she had lived in Wardha with Bapu.

One day someone presented her parents with a copy of *Autobiography of a Yogi*, in the latter part of which Yogananda describes his 1935 visit to Mahatma Gandhi in Wardha. The moment the

---

* Books on the subject include *Twenty Cases Suggestive of Reincarnation*, by Dr. Ian Stevenson; *Many Mansions*, by Dr. Gina Cerminara; *Here and Hereafter*, by Ruth Montgomery; and *Reincarnation in the Twentieth Century*, edited by Martin Ebon. There are many others.

child saw Yogananda's photograph on the jacket, she cried gleefully, "Oh, that's Yogananda! He came to Wardha. He was very beautiful!"

People who believe they live only once are compelled to compromise their hopes of perfection. Orthodox believers will try to conduct their lives in such a way as to avoid hellfire after death, but most of them, I suspect, are inclined even so to ask themselves pragmatically, "How bad can I be and get away with it?"

Belief in the principle of rebirth helps one to view progress joyously, without fear and self-doubt.

"Is there any end to evolution?" a visitor once asked Paramhansa Yogananda.

"No end," the Master replied. "Progress goes on until you achieve endlessness."

At Mt. Washington, reincarnation was normal to our way of thinking. We took it quite in stride if ever Master told us, as he sometimes did, about our own or someone else's past lives.

Looking one day at Jan Savage, aged nine, he exclaimed laughingly, "Little Jan is no child. He's still an old man!"

I once told him I had always wanted to live in solitude. His reply was, "That is because you have done it before. Most of those who are with me have lived alone many times in the past." He made such remarks so casually that it rarely occurred to me to press him for more information. A few others expressed deeper interest, however, and sometimes Master responded to them quite explicitly.

A few years after Dr. Lewis lost his mother, Master, knowing Doctor's devotion to her, informed him, "She has been reborn. If you go to . . ." he mentioned some address north of Boston, in New England, "you will find her there." Dr. Lewis made the journey.

"It was uncanny," he told me later. "The child was only three years old, but in many of her mannerisms she seemed exactly like my mother. I observed, too, that she took an instantaneous liking to me. It was almost as though she recognized me."

Mrs. Vera Brown visited a theater one evening with Master and a few of the disciples. A little girl in the row ahead of them captured her interest. "I couldn't take my eyes off her," she later told me. "There was something about the child that just fascinated me. I think it was because she looked so old and wise for her age, and at the same time so sad. Afterwards Master said to me, 'You were fascinated by that little girl, weren't you?' 'Yes, Sir,' I answered. 'I don't know why, but I found myself watching her the whole time we were there.'

"'In her last life,' Master said, 'she died in a German concentration camp. That is why she looks so sad. But her tragic experiences there, and the compassion she developed as a consequence, have made her a saint. That was the wisdom you saw in her that attracted you so.'"

One day Master was given a newborn baby to hold. "I almost dropped it," he told friends later. "I saw suddenly in that little, inno-cent-seeming form, the brought-over consciousness of a murderer."

Discussions on reincarnation sometimes became intensely in-teresting. One day I asked Master, "Did Judas have any spiritual realization?"

"He had some bad karma, of course," Master replied, "but all the same, he was a prophet."

"He *was*?" This variant on the common theme of that disciple's villainy astonished me.

"Oh, yes," Master asserted emphatically. "He had to be, to be one of the twelve. But he had to go through two thousand years of suf-fering for his treachery. He was liberated finally in this century, in India. Jesus appeared to a certain master there, whom he asked to free him. I knew Judas in this life," Master added.

"You did!" Eagerly I pursued the matter. "What was he like?"

"Always very quiet and by himself. He still had a little attachment to money. One day another disciple began to poke fun at him for this tendency, but the Master shook his head. 'Don't,' he said quietly. 'Leave him alone.'"

In 1935 Master visited Stonehenge in England. To his secretary, Richard Wright (Daya Mata's brother), he remarked quietly, "I lived here myself thirty-five hundred years ago."

Sometimes he intrigued us with references, always casual, to the past lives of certain well-known public figures. "Winston Churchill," he told us, "was Napoleon. Napoleon wanted to conquer England. Churchill, as England's Prime Minister, has fulfilled that ambition. Napoleon wanted to destroy England. As Churchill he has had to preside over the disintegration of the British Empire. Napoleon was sent into exile, then returned again to power. Churchill, similarly, was sent out of politics, then after some time came back to power again."

It is an interesting fact that Churchill, as a young man, found particularly interesting the military exploits of Napoleon.

"Hitler," Master continued, "was Alexander the Great." An interesting point of comparison here is that, in warfare, both Hitler and Alexander employed the strategy of lightning attack — *blitzkrieg*, as Hitler called it. In the Orient, of course, where Alexander's conquests were responsible for the destruction of great civilizations, that appellation, "the Great," is quoted with sarcasm.

Master had hoped to reawaken in Hitler the well-known interest of Alexander in the teachings of India and of yoga, thereby to steer the dictator's ambitions toward higher ideals. He actually attempted to see Hitler in 1935, but his request for an interview was denied.

Mussolini, Master said, was Mark Antony. Kaiser Wilhelm was Julius Caesar. Stalin was Genghis Khan.

"Who was Franklin Roosevelt?" I inquired.

"I've never told anybody," Master replied with a wry smile. "I was afraid I'd get into trouble!"

Abraham Lincoln, he informed us, had been a yogi in the Himalayas who died with a desire to help bring about racial equality. His birth as Lincoln was for the purpose of fulfilling that desire. "He has come back again in this century," Master said, "as Charles Lindbergh."

It is interesting to note that the public acclaim that was denied Lincoln, though so richly deserved, came almost effortlessly to Lindbergh. Interestingly, too, after Lindbergh's death a Hawaiian friend of his, Joseph Kahaleuahi, exclaimed, "This is not a small man. This man is like a President."* Charles Lindbergh was noted for his interest in Indian philosophy. Perhaps (one wonders), having fulfilled his desire as a yogi to work for racial equality, and having, as Lindbergh, rejected the acclaim that was his karmic re-

* *Reader's Digest*, December 1974, p. 258.

ward for Lincoln's success, he will once again become a yogi in his next life.*

Of more saintly people, Master said that Therese Neumann, the Catholic stigmatist of Konnersreuth, Germany, was Mary Magdalene. "That," he explained to us, "is why she was granted those visions of Christ's crucifixion."

"Lahiri Mahasaya," he once told me at Twenty-Nine Palms, "was the greatest saint of his time. In a previous life he was King Janaka.† Babaji initiated him in that golden palace in reflection of the fact that he had lived in a palace before."

According to another disciple, Master told someone that Lahiri Mahasaya had also been the great medieval mystic Kabir.

"Babaji," Master told us, "is an incarnation of India's greatest prophet, Krishna."

Master then revealed to us that he himself had been Krishna's closest friend and disciple, Arjuna. ("Prince of devotees," the Bhagavad Gita calls him.) We found it easy to believe that he had been that mighty warrior, for Master's incredible will power, his innate gift for leadership, and his enormous physical strength (when he chose to exert it), all pointed to someone with the tendencies of a mighty, conquering hero. Speaking of that incarnation, Master told me, "That is why, in this life, I am so close to Babaji."

Master knew the value of offsetting abstract teachings with these interesting sidelights. The barriers to memory that exist in the average person's consciousness between this lifetime and his previous ones melt away before the insight of wisdom. But of course Master's real interest, and ours, lay in our attainment of divine enlightenment. We found that familiarity with the law of reincarnation helped us to deepen our determination to escape the monotonous round of death and rebirth, but this was by no means,

---

* For a creative and quite interesting argument that Lincoln reincarnated as Lindbergh, see Richard Salva's *The Reincarnation of Abraham Lincoln: Historical Evidence of Past Lives*. The author unearths hundreds of similarities between the two men.

† Janaka, though a king, was also one of the great masters of ancient India: a *rajarishi*, or royal sage. Durga Mata in her book about Master says that Rajarshi's title means, "king of sages." This is not wholly accurate.

in any of our minds, the central focus of our devotion to Master's teachings.

Belief in reincarnation also provided us with occasional insights into present spiritual difficulties.

Henry Schaufelberger and Ed Harding (another, older, disciple), were distressed for a time to discover a deep-seated, mutual, but apparently irrational animosity between them.

"That is because you were enemies in a former life," Master explained to Henry, who asked him one day for guidance in the matter. This knowledge helped both men to understand the problem, and to overcome it.

The doctrine of reincarnation is closely related, as I have said, to the law of karma. Sometimes people object, "But what can I learn from suffering, if I don't remember what I did in the past that brought it upon me?" The answer is that both the act and its karmic consequences reflect a mental *tendency* that is still carried with him. It is primarily with this tendency that the law deals.

For example, if, out of mercenary greed, I once cheated someone out of his inheritance, and suffer in consequence, in this life, by losing an inheritance, myself, both that first act and my subsequently being cheated will reflect my underlying tendency toward greed. I may have forgotten what I did before, but if I decide now that cheating is something that shouldn't happen to anybody, *and if I resolve never, on my part, to cheat others*, I will have untied at least one knot in my tendency to be avaricious. There may remain other kinks in that tendency to be straightened out: a whole series of them, in fact, developed from that single tendency, and each one in its own way reinforcing it.

If I am wise, therefore, the loss of that inheritance will not only make me reflect on the fact that cheating is wrong; it will inspire me also to trace this question of dishonesty back to its root cause: avarice. I'll conclude that monetary greed is itself a fault, and will try to discover and uproot the seeds of this fault in myself. If I am successful in this effort, a nullifying force-field of non-attachment will be set up that will minimize the karmic consequences of any others of my greedy acts in the past.

The power of karma depends in great measure on the intensity of the thought associated with it.

Suppose I have overcome greed and acquired non-attachment *before* I lose that inheritance. In this case, the money I lose may come back to me unexpectedly from another source. In any case, I will suffer much less.

Patanjali, the ancient exponent of yoga, states in his *Yoga Sutras* that when avarice is fully overcome, one attracts everything in life that he needs. As Patanjali quaintly put it, "One will attract jewels in abundance."*

It should be understood that the karmic law is quite impersonal. We can learn from our karma if we've a will to. It is quite possible, however, *not* to will to. An unwise reaction, for example, to a stolen inheritance would be to try to "get even" with the world in turn, by cheating others. One who takes this course will only reinforce the tendency which attracted his misfortune in the first place. Thus, he will sow seeds of even greater suffering in the future.

Dr. Lewis once asked Master why a certain acquaintance had been born with a club foot. "That," Master replied, "is because in his last life he kicked his mother."

Having a club foot in this life probably didn't stir that man to any noble resolution not to kick his mother in this life, but it must have acted on that tendency indirectly. His mother, after all, was the source of his physical existence. She represented in a very special way to him, therefore, the sacredness of life. When he kicked her, he (in effect) expressed contempt for life itself. His club foot in this incarnation may well have made him, at least in his own eyes, an object of contempt. An unwise reaction to such a self-image would be to hate life more than ever—a tendency that might be continued for many lives until, in sheer desperation, he decided to reform. But if he reacted wisely to this self-image, he might tell himself what a blessing it would be to have a perfect body. Automatically, from this reaction, would come respect for life, which in turn would make it very likely that he would never treat any future mother with such contempt.

* *Yoga Sutras* II:37.

One benefit of the doctrine of reincarnation is that it helps to keep one humble, concerned rather with attuning himself to God's all-ruling will than with imposing on the world his own petty desires. A belief in reincarnation helps one to accept more easily that least popular, but most important of ancient injunctions, "Change thyself."

I once had an interesting dream; indeed, it seemed to me more than a dream. I saw myself in another life, deeply devoted to a particular friend. He took advantage of my love for him, and treated me with an unkindness that fluctuated between condescension and outright contempt. In time, there arose in me a feeling of deep bitterness toward him. As I approached the end of that incarnation, I realized that if I died with this attitude my bitterness would, like a magnet, draw both of us back to similar, but reversed, circumstances. I would have the opportunity to treat him as unkindly as he had treated me. And if I treated him thus, ensuing bitterness on *his* part might very possibly reverse our positions once again. Perhaps only a succession of such "return engagements," gradually diminishing in intensity, would enable us at last to work out our love-hate relationship, even as echoes die out gradually in a valley, or as the ripples caused in a pond by a falling stone subside gradually as they pass back and forth over the pond several times.

"Why take so long?" I asked myself. "Isn't it possible to escape these waves of retribution right now? Whatever the lessons my friend needs to learn, surely *I*, at least, can free myself." Then, from the depths of my heart, I cried, "I forgive him!" At that moment, with a feeling of ineffable relief, I awoke. In that simple act of forgiveness I felt that I had actually freed myself of some karmic burden.

All human life, so the Indian scriptures tell us, is a dream. Its ultimate goal is for us to learn our lessons well, to overcome our attachments to material limitations, and to realize that all things, seemingly so separate and real in themselves, are only manifestations of the one light of God. The highest lesson of all is to learn to love God. The best karma of all is to love Him.

"Sir," Norman said, rather morosely, one day to Master, "I don't think I have very good karma."

"Remember this," Master replied with deep earnestness, "it takes very, *very*, VERY good karma even to *want* to know God!"

Through love of God, and only through that love, can one win final release from physical rebirth, and earn the right to advance to higher spheres of existence. Victory comes not by hating this world, but by beholding God's presence in it everywhere, and by paying reverence to the veriest fool as though to a holy shrine.

"You must be very joyous and happy," Master said, "because this is God's dream, and the little man and the big man are all nothing but the Dreamer's consciousness."

CHAPTER 29

Gardens—Mundane and Spiritual

IT WAS, AS I recall, sometime during August or September of 1949 that Paramhansa Yogananda acquired his last and most beautiful ashram property: twelve acres shaped by Nature into a bowl around a miniature lake. This "SRF Lake Shrine," as Master named it, nestles serenely in the arms of a broad curve formed by Sunset Boulevard as, leaving the town of Pacific Palisades, it makes its final sweep down to the ocean. The property is one of the loveliest I have seen in a lifetime of world travel.

Soon after Master obtained this property, he invited the monks out to see it. Walking its grounds, we were wonderstruck at their beauty. Happily, Master predicted, "This will be a showcase for the work!" Later on he had us don bathing suits and enter the water with him.

"I am sending the divine light all through this lake," he said. Afterward he said to us, "This is holy water now. Whoever comes here in future will receive a divine blessing."

Even today, nearly thirty years after that event, simply to enter those grounds is to feel their spiritual power. Often I have reflected that people in distant lands go on pilgrimages for blessings like these. Holy shrines in India, Palestine, and elsewhere owe their sanctity, as this one does in modern California, to the blessings of God-known saints. In many of those more ancient shrines, however, people thronging there, eager for mere worldly boons, have diluted the spiritual vibrations. At the SRF Lake Shrine the original vibrations are still powerful, as one feels them also in Yogananda's other ashrams. For not only have those places received his blessings (at Mt.

Washington he once told us, "I have meditated on every spot of these grounds"), but since his passing they have been inhabited continuously by sincere devotees.

Soon after acquiring the Lake Shrine, we began the task of preparing it for its public opening one year later. An abundance of trees, shrubs, and flowers were brought in and planted on the steep hillsides. Statues of leading figures in the great world religions were placed in picturesque spots about the grounds, to emphasize Yogananda's teaching of the basic oneness of all religions. ("Where do you want the Buddha to sit?" we inquired one day. Master was standing nearby, directing operations. "The Buddha prefers to remain standing," he replied with a quiet smile.)

In the early months of preparation, swarms of gnats proved an extreme nuisance. The fascination they demonstrated for our eyes, ears, and nostrils was anything but flattering. "Master," I exclaimed in exasperation one day, "what an irony! Why must so much beauty be spoiled by these flies?"

Calmly Master replied, "That is the Lord's way of keeping us ever moving toward Him."

Happily, the Lord found other ways of accomplishing this objective. The gnats, perhaps with Master's blessings, proved only a temporary pest.

One day we were moving a delicate but rather heavy tropical plant into position on the hillside. Our handling of it must have been rough, for Master cried out, "Be careful what you are doing. Can't you *feel*? It's alive!"

His sensitivity to all living things inspired sensitivity from them in return. Not only people and animals, but even plants seemed to respond to his feeling for them. His gardens flourished. Tropical mangoes and bananas grew at Mt. Washington, where the climate is not conducive to their survival.

Shraddha Mata (Miss Sahly) told of watching one day what she called a "rose devotee," which kept turning in its vase to face Master as he moved about the room. When he was sitting in his chair, she noted that the rose was facing him. Twice, however, when he was called to the door, she noted the rose facing in that direction. Several

SRF Lake Shrine Chapel, Pacific Palisades, California.

Outdoor temple at the Lake Shrine.

repetitions of change of directions finally caused this event to surface in her mind.

"Sir," she said finally, "you have a new devotee." She indicated the rose which, now that he was seated again, had turned back toward him.

He looked at it for a moment, then smiled.

"Plants," Master explained, "have a degree of consciousness." Above all, like every sentient being, they respond to love.

Master even felt with certain plants a mysterious personal identity. One day, pointing to an avocado tree that stood by a walkway at Mt. Washington, he told us, "Originally I planted two trees here, one on either side of the path. We had a certain student living here in those days who was deeply devoted. Referring to him once, I told a few of the others, 'One of us will leave this work, and one of these trees also will die. This tree stands for me; that one, for him. The tree that dies will signal which one of us will leave.'

"Well, his tree died. Soon afterwards he left. He had been *very* devoted, too. But—devotion fled. The delusion that took him away was the desire for—money." Master paused momentarily before naming that delusion, to give each of us time mentally to fill in the blank with his own karmic obstacles, and thus to concentrate more on what each one had still to work on.

A pine tree in the eastern part of the grounds at Mt. Washington was dying. In the summer of 1949 Jean Haupt cut it down. Master grieved over the loss of his arboreal friend. "You will see," he remarked quietly to Faye. "The end of that tree marks the beginning of the end of my own life." Strangely worded though his prophecy was, it was to prove true.

Sometimes in his training of us he likened us, too, to plants. Of a certain monk who had been resisting his spiritual counsel, he exclaimed, "What a job one takes on when he tries to improve people! He has to go into their minds and see what they are thinking. The rose in the vase looks beautiful; one forgets all the care that went into making it so. But if it takes so much care to produce a rose, how much more care is needed in developing a perfect human being!"

Like a divine gardener, Master labored unceasingly for our spiritual development. It took patience, love, courage, and considerably greater faith in us than most of us had in ourselves. For where we saw only our own egos struggling to shed their imperfections, he saw our souls struggling to reclaim their divine birthright in God. Some of his disciples justified better than others his faith in them, but he extended to all the same vision of their ultimate perfectibility.

I soon learned that one of the most important things on the path, especially for the newcomer, is to pay attention to how he selects his companions. For even in a spiritual environment there may be a few gossips and grumblers, a few devotees who meditate too little, while others can't seem to get it into their minds that it is they themselves who need changing, not the rest of the world. On the other side, in every truly spiritual organization there are also those who, by their example of selfless service, steadfast cheerfulness, inward focus, and spiritual fervor inspire in others a constant renewal of dedication.

At Mt. Washington I found such inspiration in numerous disciples. Even today I recall them with gratitude. I think of Mrs. Merck (later, Sister Karuna). Well into her eighties, she worked hours every day in the garden. "Ya," she would say sweetly in her thick Swedish accent, "I lahv de flowers. Dey are my shildren!"

I think of Mrs. Royston, also elderly. She it was who told me how Master, years earlier, would run joyously out onto the lecture platform. Her steadfast loyalty and unfailing good spirits epitomized Master's frequent instruction to us: "Be ever even-minded and cheerful."

I think of Mrs. Wright, Daya Mata's mother—at once firm and compassionate. "Great Mother," Master used to call her. (A little sidelight on that story: Master told me, "When her son Richard left here to get married, she defended him. Since then, I have never again called her, 'Great Mother.'")

I think of Mrs. Brown (Meera), whose joyful loyalty to Master was as much a delight as an inspiration. Her joy, by no means callow, was rooted in great inner determination and strength. Mrs. Brown had to contend with prolonged physical suffering; yet she gladly ignored the pain to serve others. To me, as no doubt to many others, she was truly a mother.

Miss Sahly (Shraddha) was the older nun whom I had upbraided like a "young hothead" during that lamentable episode of the committee. As I got to know her better, I found in her a deep, steadfast devotion, one that brooked no nonsense. It reminded me rather of the efficient professional nurse she had once been. But I found her inwardly warm and sympathetic. Her outward severity helped me to keep in mind that the divine quest, though joyful, is at the same time a very serious matter.

Miss Darling (Durga), though sometimes a little sharp-tongued (in this respect, astrology fans would call her "a true Scorpio," her actual sun sign), impressed me with the intensity of her energy and with her complete dedication in everything she did. Master once described to us how, years earlier, she and two of the monks had repainted the main building at Mt. Washington.

"The men," he said, "though larger and much stronger than she, waved their paintbrushes lackadaisically to and fro as if making graceful peace offerings to the building. But Miss Darling fairly attacked the walls! Tirelessly her brush flew, back and forth, back and forth, never stopping to think how difficult the job was. That," Master concluded joyously, "is the kind of spirit it takes to find God!"

At Twenty-Nine Palms he once told me, "The day Miss Darling came here (to Mt. Washington), I said to her quietly, 'You have come.' I knew she belonged with us."

Years later, Laurie, who seemed unable to relate to any realities but her own, told me with contempt in her voice, "The *only* reason Master accepted Durga was because he was in such desperate need of help!" Yes, there still remained normal human weaknesses in most of us, including what I might call feminine prejudices. I knew Faye, also, to express a few of them: for example, against Dr. Lewis, who, though he had his own (perfectly normal) faults, was at the same time deeply devoted to Master. Such aspects of human nature are, I suppose, slow to die, and very difficult to shake off. Swami Sri Yukteswar called them "meannesses of the heart," among which he listed "pride of pedigree," to which I would attribute another frequent monastic failing: "pride of seniority."

Of the nuns, Faye was the one I got the opportunity to know best, and from whom also I drew much inspiration. I found her always fair-minded and gracious. What inspired me most about her was her utter devotion to God and Guru. Her only desire seemed to be to follow Master's will—though I did find, in time, that we differed somewhat in our interpretation of Master's will. That aspect of things, however, I must leave to be told later.

"Is everything all right?" she would ask me when we met in her office to discuss official matters. Ever ready to help us spiritually if she could, she would set organizational problems resolutely aside even when they were pressing, if at any time she sensed a need in us for counseling or encouragement. Into every office discussion she would weave subtle threads of insight and guidance. From her I learned that work and meditation belong not in separate compartments from one another; that rather, when the thought of God is held uppermost, they blend together and become one.

"I feel that you have been close to Master in past lives," she once told me. Our own relationship was more like that of brother and older sister than of junior monk and superior. This relationship, too, as we both realized, was rooted in past lives. I could never express in words the depth of my gratitude for her constant friendship and guidance. I considered it one of the most precious gifts God had given me in this life.

Of the younger nuns I saw very little. Among the monks, few, it turned out, had been in the work as long as the older nuns. ("The spiritual path is harder for men," Master conceded. "But," he added as a consolation, "those who get there become very great.")

Rev. Michael (Brother Bhaktananda) was one of the monks who inspired me. Deeply humble ("He has no ego," Master once said of him), and deeply devoted to God: I almost envied him the unaffected simplicity with which he could sum up the entire spiritual path, stating, "Devotion is the *only* thing."

Joe Carbone (Brother Bimalananda) was another inspiration— and Henry Schaufelberger (Brother Anandamoy), too, who came a year after me. Both men combined sweetness with calm insight in a way that I found deeply appealing. Henry, however—to offer a proper balance in my appraisal—tended also to be judgmental.

Many others there were, besides. I felt it an immeasurable blessing to be living in their midst.

"Of the disciples," Master told a small group of us in the main office one evening, "the first in realization is Saint Lynn. Next comes Mr. Black, and then Sister." James J. Lynn, to whom Master always referred as Saint Lynn, received from Master later on the title and name Rajarshi (royal sage) Janakananda.* Mr. Black was the leader of the SRF center in Detroit, Michigan, and later also founded a spiritual retreat upstate in Vanderbilt, called Song of the Morning Ranch. "Sister" was, as I have indicated before, Master's designation for Sister Gyanamata.

I am standing with Yogacharya Oliver Black during my visit to his SRF center in Detroit, Michigan, in 1955.

At Twenty-Nine Palms, in October 1949, Master said to me, "Those who are with me"—I think he meant, *in tune with me*—"I never have any trouble with. Just a glance with the eyes is enough. It is much better when I can teach that way." He added, "They are saints from before, most of them."

Another time he told me, "Many of the disciples will find freedom in this life." Looking out the window, he saw Mrs. Royston working in the garden. "Even she," he added with an affectionate smile. In

---

* *Janakananda* means "*ananda* (divine bliss) through an ideal balance of outward responsibility and inward spiritual attainment that was perfectly exemplified in ancient times in the life of the royal sage King Janaka."

a lighter vein he continued, "You know, she was even homelier when she first came here!" He went on to praise her highly for her many years of selfless service and devotion.

To a group of us at Twenty-Nine Palms he once said, "Horace is very nearly there. God is satisfied with his devotion." Horace, as the reader may recall, was the spastic devotee who helped James Coller on the occasion of that disastrous yoga lecture in Phoenix.

James, who was present on this occasion, tried to reconcile Master's praise of Horace with his brother disciple as he knew him. "Sir," he said, "it must be a very simple kind of devotion, isn't it?"

"Ah," Master replied with a beautiful smile, "that is the kind God likes! 'He does not reveal Himself unto the prudent and the wise, but unto babes.'"

About James himself Master said several times, "He will be liberated in this life." Once, recalling James's difficulty with organizational discipline, he added jestingly, "I don't know *how*! But God says so, so it must be true."

The disciple who was the most generous with his anecdotes about Master was Dr. Lewis, the first Kriya Yogi in America, and by now highly advanced on the spiritual path. We would sit for hours with Doctor while he regaled us with stories, some of them amusing, some serious, all of them instructive. They helped us to see how the relationship between guru and disciple evolves gradually into one of divine friendship in God.

Toward the end of October of that year Dr. Lewis and several other disciples, including Mrs. Lewis and Norman, accompanied Master to San Francisco to meet Jawaharlal Nehru, India's Prime Minister. Doctor returned to Mt. Washington with tales of their journey, then went on to share with us other reminiscences of his years of association with Master.

"Master," Doctor reported, "asked me to join him one morning in practicing the energization exercises on the hotel porch in San Francisco." Doctor chuckled. "I nearly died of embarrassment! But what good reason can there be, after all, to feel embarrassed about doing a good thing? My self-consciousness had no worthier basis than the fact that our exercises aren't known to most people! Master decided to cure me of this false notion.

"As we were exercising, a policeman walked by on his beat. Master, affecting a guilty conscience, stepped hastily behind a pillar, continuing to exercise there. The policeman glanced at us suspiciously. I was praying for a miracle that would dematerialize me on the spot! But Master went right on exercising as though nothing had happened.

"Minutes later, the policeman returned. Again Master ducked behind the pillar. This time the man, his suspicions thoroughly aroused, came over to us.

"'What's going on here?' he demanded. He probably suspected us of being a pair of crooks planning a crime.

"'Oh, *nothing*, Officer!' Master assured him with an exaggerated air of innocence. 'Nothing at all. We're just exercising. See?' To demonstrate his utter sincerity, he repeated a few movements, then smiled as if in hopeful expectation of a reprieve.

"'Well,' muttered the officer, 'see that you don't get into trouble.' With massive dignity he moved on. By this time I was shaking so hard with suppressed mirth that my embarrassment was completely forgotten."

Master and his little group had visited a Chinese restaurant in San Francisco. The "vegetarian" meal they'd requested had been served with bits of chicken in it. A lady in the group, a prominent member of another religious organization, had stormed angrily into the kitchen and denounced the staff for this "outrage."

"Master," Doctor told us, "considered an uncontrolled temper a far worse 'sin' than the relatively minor one of eating chicken. 'It's not important enough to make a fuss over,' he remarked to the rest of us. Pushing the bits of meat to one side, he calmly ate the rest of his meal."

That night Master and the Lewises had adjoining hotel rooms. "Master kept the door open between us," Doctor said. "I knew he didn't really want us to sleep that night. He himself never sleeps, you know. Not, at least, in the way you and I do; he's always in superconsciousness. And he wants to break *us*, too, of too much dependence on subconsciousness—'counterfeit *samadhi*,' he calls it. So I guess he saw here an opportunity for us to spend a few hours in sharing spiritual fellowship and inspiration with him. We don't get many chances for that anymore, now that the work has become worldwide.

"The problem was, Mrs. Lewis and I were both tired—she especially so. We'd been traveling all day. 'We're going to sleep,' she announced in a tone of finality. That, as far as she was concerned, was that.

"Master, however, had other ideas.

"Mrs. Lewis and I went to bed. Master, apparently submissive, lay down on his bed. I was just getting relaxed, and Mrs. Lewis was beginning to drift peacefully off to sleep, when all at once Master, as though with deep relevance, said:

"'Sub gum.'

"Nothing more. Sub gum was the name of one of those Chinese dishes we'd eaten earlier that day. I smiled to myself. But Mrs. Lewis muttered with grim earnestness, 'He's *not* going to make me get up!' A few minutes passed. We were just drifting off again, when suddenly, in marveling tones:

"'Sub gum *duff*!' Master pronounced the words carefully, like a child playing with unaccustomed sounds.

"Desperately Mrs. Lewis whispered, 'We're sleeping!' She turned for help to the wall.

"More minutes passed. Then, very slowly:

"'*Super* sub gum duff!' The words this time were spoken earnestly, like a child making some important discovery.

"By this time I was chuckling to myself. But though sleep was beginning to seem rather an 'impossible dream' for both of us, Mrs. Lewis was still hanging on fervently to her resolution.

"More minutes passed. And then the great discovery:

"'Super SUBMARINE sub gum duff!'

"Further resistance was impossible! Howling with merriment, we rose from the bed. For the remainder of the night, sleep was forgotten. We talked and laughed with Master. Gradually the conversation shifted to serious matters. We ended up speaking on spiritual subjects, then meditating. With his blessings, we felt no further need for sleep that night.

"I was telling you," Dr. Lewis continued, "that Master never sleeps. I've found this to be true even when he snores! One day, many years ago, he was lying in his room, apparently asleep, and snoring quite loudly. I tiptoed stealthily into the room and tied a string to his big toe, doing my best to make sure he felt nothing. I should add that we were both young then. Master was still snoring peacefully as I crept back to the door. I was about to tie the string onto the doorknob when he stopped snoring long enough to say, 'Aha!'"

Dr. Lewis, finding us keenly receptive to his good humor this evening, related another anecdote. "Master and I were standing on a sidewalk one day many years ago," he said, "when a man riding by on a bicycle noticed Master's long hair, and stuck his tongue out at him derisively. About two feet further on he came to a large mud puddle. Right in the middle of that puddle, the front wheel of his bicycle came off, and he went sprawling!"

Gradually, Doctor's reminiscences grew more serious. "Late in October, 1941," he said, "Master visited us at our summer residence on Plymouth Bay, in Massachusetts. The ocean is extremely cold there at that time of year. Master, however, on his very first night insisted on going out for a moonlight swim. As he was wading out into the water we watched him from the shore, shivering. Pretty soon he was waist deep. 'By now,' I thought, 'he *must* be feeling the cold!'

"Suddenly I saw a blue light forming all around him. My son, standing beside me with his wife, saw it too. Later, when Master returned from his swim, we told him what we had seen.

"Smiling, Master admitted, 'I had to go deep in the Spirit to escape the cold!'

"I saw that blue light around him on another occasion," Dr. Lewis continued, reverting once more to a humorous mood. "This happened years later. We were crossing the Mexican border into California. Master had bought mangoes for everyone; the car was fairly reeking with them! I was certain they'd be confiscated; as you may know, the California customs are strict about that sort of thing. But when the inspector came up to examine our car, he said nothing at all!

Rajarshi Janakananda, Paramhansa Yogananda, and Dr. Lewis.

"'How did we manage that one?' another passenger asked me as we drove on happily into California.

"'I'm sure I couldn't explain the mechanism of it,' I replied. 'All I know is, as we were passing the frontier I saw blue light all around us!'"

Doctor's reminiscences took him back to his early days with Master. "In the early spring of 1923 Master told me, 'Be careful of your health next summer.' Caught up as I was in the bustle of a busy life, I forgot his warning. In midsummer, however, I got my reminder with a vengeance. I was seized by a severe gastrointestinal pain. Days passed, and my agony only increased. At last I prayed fervently to Master.

"It was, as I recall, a Wednesday in July when he came to my rescue. I had gone to my summer home in Plymouth. By this time my endurance had reached a low ebb. Very early that morning—it must have been two or three o'clock—I heard Master's voice in the driveway: 'Doctor! Doctor!'

"What a relief just to hear his voice! He had commandeered a car and come all the way from New York in answer to my prayer.

Entering the house with two students, he drew me aside. In that wonderful, unruffled way of his he promised me that I would be all right. He then gave me a marvelous yogic remedy for use in such cases. My condition improved immediately; soon I'd recovered altogether.

"During those early years in Boston there was a man who'd been condemned to death for a crime of which I, and many others, felt he was innocent. The day before his scheduled execution I happened to be with Master, and mentioned this case to him. Master became very pensive. Silently he retired to a corner of the room, and sat there quietly. After some time he returned to our circle with a smile, and resumed conversing with us. He never mentioned the condemned man. The following morning, however, the news came out in the papers: The governor, at the eleventh hour, had issued a pardon.

"You know, we weren't as familiar in those days with Master's methods as you all are now. We didn't know the wonderful things he could do. For that matter, we didn't know what *any* master can do. By now, people have had years to get to know him better. It was more difficult for us then to have the kind of faith you all have in him. In that episode of the condemned man, for instance, Master never told us he'd done anything to help him. He rarely speaks of the wonderful things he does. It's just that, when things keep on happening around him, you begin to wonder. On that occasion, it was only after the man's reprieve that I began to suspect strongly that Master had played a part in the matter.

"You see, he doesn't want to amaze us with miracles. Love is the force by which he seeks to draw us to God. When I first met him in 1920, he said to me, 'Will you always love me as I love you?'

"'Yes,' I said. I could *feel* his love, you see. 'Yes,' I said, 'I will.'

"But delusion is strong. Sometimes when he talked of the communities we would have someday, and the beautiful buildings, and I saw him living in that little room in Boston, almost in poverty, doubts would assail me. 'When, Sir?' I would ask him. 'When will such great things be possible?' But Master remained serenely confident. 'You will see, Doctor,' he said. 'You'll see.'

"One day a man came to my dental office and told me lie after lie against Master. He spoke quite plausibly. Worse still, I hadn't any facts with which to contradict him. I didn't believe his assertions, but I admit that, inside, I was a little shaken. The man left. Some time passed. Suddenly I heard footsteps outside, resolutely approaching my office. The door opened. Master marched in. Striding straight up to me, he gazed calmly into my eyes. 'Do you still love me, Doctor?' he demanded. He proceeded to repeat word for word all that my earlier visitor had said to me.

"Master, I learned later, had been riding a streetcar four or five miles from my office at that time. He had gotten off at the next stop, and walked all that way with the sole purpose of helping me.

"Master inquired, in conclusion, whether a certain person didn't owe me a sizeable sum of money. 'Yes,' I said, 'he does.'

"'If you go there now, you will get it from him.' I went, and was repaid immediately.

"In how many ways has Master helped me and my family!" Doctor concluded, gratitude shining in his eyes. "When my mother suffered a severe stroke, he prolonged her life. When my daughter, Brenda, then still a child, was stricken with convulsions, Master cured her.

"I was visiting Master at that time. The news reached me by telephone. As soon as Master learned what had happened, he stepped behind a screen. Moments later he reappeared, his face radiant. 'Don't worry, Doctor, she will be all right. And she will never have another seizure.' One worry concerning illnesses of this type is that there may be future recurrences. But in Brenda's case there have been none."

As we left Dr. Lewis late that evening, we thanked him from our hearts for so generously sharing with us his unique experiences.

*   *   *   *   *   *   *

During the fall of 1949 Master asked me, in company with several other monks, to demonstrate the yoga postures before Swami Premananda, an Indian disciple visiting Mt. Washington from Washington, D.C., where he served as the minister of an SRF church. I was at best a mediocre Hatha Yogi; many of the postures I couldn't contort myself into at all. That evening however, in Master's presence, I suddenly found myself able to assume even difficult poses with ease. Indeed, from that day on I became recognized as SRF's Hatha Yoga "expert." I posed for the photographs that illustrated the poses in a series of articles in *Self-Realization Magazine*. If ever anyone was needed to demonstrate the postures, I was the one selected. Master often had me serve lunch when he had guests, and afterwards had me demonstrate the postures to them. Would that expertise might always be acquired so effortlessly!

One day in the fall of 1949 Master, while sitting and chatting with the monks in our dining room, looked at me pensively. "Why don't you grow a beard, Walter?"

"Do you *mean* it, Sir?" I was astonished. Beards were rarely seen in those days. A couple of the other monks, in fact, later began to grow them and Master vetoed their plans with the remark, "I don't want my boys looking like wild men!" (Perhaps his feeling was that one "wild man" in the crowd was enough!)

"Try it," he said.

I was grateful when, soon afterward, he invited me to spend a few weeks with him at Twenty-Nine Palms. Lecturing in Hollywood Church with a slowly emerging stubble had threatened to saddle me with the reputation of being Hollywood's first hobo-minister. Still, whether "wild" or not, by the time the beard had filled out I did at least look somewhat older and more mature.

At Twenty-Nine Palms Master told me privately of his plans to take me with him to India the following summer. Naturally, I was delighted. "I'm sure I could learn Bengali," I said. "I already speak several languages."

"You'll learn it *very* easily," he assured me. He went on to tell me a few Bengali words: *hath* (hand), *chok* (eyes), *mukh* (mouth), *nak* (nose), *kan* (ears). As it turned out, nine years passed before I went to India and got my first opportunity to use those words, but I remembered them easily all that time. I had only to recall the day he'd spoken them to me, and I could hear his voice again mentally, as though speaking in my ear.

This was the first indication I had that he might have bestowed on me a blessing far greater than the mere ability to contort my body into various unusual positions: the ability to recall the words he said to me exactly as he'd spoken them. How else, I asked myself, could I recall his words, tone and all, even when he spoke them in a foreign language?

One day at Twenty-Nine Palms he told me the story of Lahiri Mahasaya's meeting with Babaji. In Hindi he quoted Babaji's words: "Lahiri, *tu agaya* (you have come)." Simple words, to be sure, but to have heard them once only in passing and still be able to recall them clearly enough to confirm them in India nearly a decade later, argues a talent greater, I think, than I possessed naturally.

One day he sang for us a song in Bengali: "*Mukti dete pari; bhakti dete pari koi?*" Though in this case, too, I heard the words once only, they stayed with me until I went to India in 1958, and there verified their accuracy.

The interesting thing is that this power, if such it really was, existed only where Master's words were concerned. The speech of others continued to be recalled in the more or less shadowy manner that is, I suppose, usual in such cases.

At about this time in my life Master began asking me to jot down his words. He intimated strongly that he wanted me someday to write about him. For long hours he would reminisce with me about his life, his experiences in establishing the work, his hopes and plans for its future. He told me countless stories, some of them to illustrate points he was making; others, I imagine, simply because they were interesting, or helped in some general way to round out my understanding of the path and of his life. Many of his meanings reached me not only through the medium of words and stories, but by a kind of osmosis conveyed by a facial expression, a tone of voice, or some even subtler transferral of consciousness.*

Often he talked about various disciples.

"Sir," I inquired one day, "what about the young man whom you initiated in Brindaban during that episode in your book, 'Two Penniless Boys in Brindaban'? Have you ever heard from him again?"

---

* I drew on those notes and recollections for many of the stories in this book, and also for two compilations of his spoken words: *The Essence of Self-Realization* and *Conversations with Yogananda*.

"No," Master replied. "Inwardly, however, he has kept in touch."

"Then it isn't necessary to have outward contact with the Guru?"

"There must be at least one outward contact with him." Master was referring, of course, to a *meaningful* contact, such as happens at the time of initiation.

From other things that he said, and from the fact that he sometimes had disciples initiate people into Kriya Yoga in his stead even while he was alive, I understood that this link with him would be forged by contact with successive generations of disciples who were in tune with him.

One day I asked him, "What are the most important qualities on the spiritual path?"

"Deep sincerity," Master replied, "and devotion. What matters isn't how many years a person spends on the path, but how deeply he seeks God. Jesus said, 'The last shall be first, and the first last.'*

"I once met a lady in the state of Washington. She was eighty years old, and all her life she had been an atheist. At our meeting, by God's grace, she became converted to this path. Thereafter she sought God intensely. For the better part of every day, whenever she wasn't meditating, she would play a recording of my poem 'God! God! God!' She lived only a few years more, but in that short time she attained liberation."

Master also told me stories about several of the more recondite aspects of the path. "There was a young man in India who died," he said. "His body was lying there ready for cremation; the funeral pyre was about to be lit. Just at that moment an old yogi came running out of a nearby forest. 'Don't light your fire!' he shouted. 'I need that young body.' Promptly, he fell to the ground, dead. An instant later the young man leapt up off the pyre and, before anyone could stop him, ran off into the forest. The family had to cremate that old body!"

"Sir," I asked Master one evening, "what about Swami Pranabananda's prediction, in *Autobiography of a Yogi*, that he would be reborn shortly after his death, and go to the Himalayas to live with Babaji?"

* Matthew 20:16.

"He *was* reborn. At the age of six he left home." Master smiled reflectively. "His renunciation at that young age caused quite a stir in his village!"

As Christmas approached, St. Lynn visited Mt. Washington. This was my first opportunity to meet Master's foremost disciple and spiritual heir. I found him gentle, soft-spoken, and remarkably humble. He seemed completely dispassionate, centered in the inner Self. As Master introduced each of us to him, St. Lynn smiled sweetly but said little. I discovered in time that he took almost no interest in small talk. A self-made man of considerable worldly means, he referred hardly ever to his outer life. For all we heard from him personally, he might have been a man of few achievements. Virtually his sole topics of conversation were God, Guru, and meditation. Silently he would come up to us whenever we met him on the grounds, and bless us. He might then offer us a few words of spiritual advice or encouragement. His mind was always inwardly focused on God. To be with him seemed to me like looking out through a window onto infinity.

After Master's passing, Rajarshi Janakananda, as we knew him then, seemed almost to *become* Master. His eyes, by some subtle transformation, were Master's eyes. So perfect was his attunement that our Guru's very thoughts became his thoughts. Master used to say of himself, "I killed Yogananda long ago." Rajarshi Janakananda, similarly, had attained that state of consciousness where nothing of his ego remained. It was as if God and Guru, through him, spoke to us directly.

During the Christmas meditation that year Master led us in singing his chant, "Do not dry the ocean of my love with the fires of my desires, with the fires of my restlessness." Over and over we sang it. "Christ is here," he told us. "Sing it to him." Later he added, "Because you have sung this chant here today, whenever in future you feel delusion pressing in upon you, sing it again, thinking of this occasion, and Christ and Guru will come down themselves to save you. Mark my words, for they are true."

Master spoke for some time, as he'd done the year before, from the depths of his divine communion. He blessed St. Lynn, Dr. Lewis,

Durga, Faye, and several others, telling them that God was greatly pleased with them.

"Walter," he continued then, "you must try *hard*, for God will bless you very much." His words thrilled me so deeply that my meditation the rest of that day was more on what he'd told me than on God.

On Christmas Day we enjoyed our traditional banquet. Master spoke afterward, intimately and lovingly as he had done the year before. During his talk he said, "The ladies in the office gave Faye a Christmas present. They addressed it to, 'Our boss who never bosses.'" Smiling his pleasure at this beloved disciple, he went on to speak fondly of the garden of souls that was growing up around him.

Before the banquet, place cards had been set out on the tables; the affair had been planned as a restricted family gathering. At the last moment, however, numbers arrived uninvited. Room was courteously made for them, some of the renunciates offering their own seats.

In the office afterwards, a few of us were discussing with Master the inconvenience that had been caused by that sudden influx of people. A monk expressed his distress at their presumption. But I had been fortunate to observe another aspect of the episode.

"Sir," I said, "the disciples were vying with one another for the privilege of giving up their seats."

"Ah!" Master smiled blissfully. "Those are the things that please me!"

CHAPTER 30
A Divine Test

I N A VISION when he was a boy, Paramhansa Yogananda saw him-self standing in the marketplace of a small town in the Himalayan foothills. The day was hot, and the marketplace, dusty and crowded with dirty stalls, harassed shoppers, and whining beggars. Dogs ran everywhere. Monkeys stole down from rooftops to snatch at food in the stalls. Donkeys brayed complainingly. People laden with pur-chases bustled to and fro, brows furrowed with anxiety and desire.

No one seemed happy.

Now and again, however, someone in that milling crowd paused before the entranced boy, and gazed high into the distance behind him. Into the gazer's eyes there came a look of intense wistfulness. Then, after a few moments, he would turn away with a weary sigh and exclaim, "Oh, but it's much too high for me!" Lowering his gaze, he returned to the hot and dusty marketplace.

After this sequence had repeated itself several times, Yogananda turned to see what it was that had held so much appeal for those people. And there, rising high above him, he beheld a lofty moun-tain: verdant, serene, beautiful. An absolute contrast it was to every-thing in this hubbub of noise and confusion. On the mountaintop there was a large, exquisitely lovely garden, its lawns green-gold, its flowers many-hued. The boy yearned to climb the mountain and enter that earthly paradise.

Reflecting, then, on the difficulty of the climb, he thought as had the others, "But it's much too high for me!"

Weighing his words, then, he rejected them scornfully. "It may be too high to ascend with a single leap, but at least I can put one foot in front of the other!" Even to fail in the attempt would, he decided, be infinitely preferable to existence in this showcase of human misery.

Step by step, determinedly, he set out. At last he reached and entered the heavenly garden.

For Master, this vision symbolized a predicament common to every person with high aspirations. Indeed, I wonder whether all men do not fret, at least sometimes, at the restrictions the human body places on them with its constant demands for sustenance, rest, and protection. Man longs instinctively for a life freed from competition and worry; freed from hatred and violence; freed from the need for constant care. Few people, alas, even suspect that such a state exists and can be found. Of those, moreover, who do harbor such hopes, most turn away with a sigh, saying, "But it's much too high for me!" How very, very few take up the path in earnest! "Out of a thousand," Krishna says in the Bhagavad Gita, "one seeks Me."

Yet the path is not really so difficult, *for those who will but take it one step at a time.* As Jesus put it, "Sufficient unto the day is the evil thereof."* And as Paramhansa Yogananda often said—a quote I have mentioned earlier in this book—"A saint is a sinner who never gave up."

The spiritual path requires courage, and dedication, and the absolute conviction that only God can ever satisfy the soul's yearning for true happiness. Those who take up the path for what Yogananda called its glamour, expecting only blissful visions and a comfortable, mossy trail strewn with rose blossoms of divine consolation, become discouraged when they find how often God neglects the moss and roses in favor of thorns. For those, however, who cling to their purpose with devotion, taking the path calmly one day at a time, no test is ever too great. Obstructions are seen, then, as blessings, for they provide the strength one needs to reach the heights.

I got an opportunity to learn something about spiritual obstructions during the early months of 1950. My period of testing began with weeks of exceptional inspiration. Encouraged, as it were, by

---

* Matthew 6:34. How is it, I have often asked myself marveling, that so few Christians realize what a delightful, if sometimes incisive, sense of humor Jesus had!

a short, comparatively easy stretch on the journey, I had been racing forward with eager expectation. Now, all of a sudden, I found myself brought joltingly to a halt at the foot of a high cliff.

For some time after the Christmas holidays, my meditations had been blissful. I recall saying to Jean Haupt one day, "If for the rest of my life I never achieve anything more, spiritually, than this, I shall be content." Dangerous words! God doesn't allow His devotees to enjoy for long the luxury of overconfidence.

After a month or so of increasing inner joy, subtle delusions began entering my mind. First came pride in the feeling that this joy separated me from others—not, I believe, in the sense of making me think myself better than they, but in the equally false sense of holding me aloof from their interests, no matter how innocent. This state of consciousness masqueraded as wisdom, but in fact it was born of my spiritual inexperience. For the devotee should learn to see God outside himself as well as inside—outside especially in wholesome activities and in the beauties of this world. The world we live in is God's world, after all. To reject it is, in a sense, to reject Him. Pride follows such rejection, and with pride comes the temptation to take personal credit for whatever inspirations we feel.

Even as I congratulated myself on my growing inner freedom, I felt increasingly uneasy over my spiritual condition. I could see that there was something seriously the matter with me, and that I was not responding as I ought to the blessings I'd been receiving. But where had I erred? My discrimination wasn't developed enough to supply the answer.

It took time for me to realize that I'd been grasping at my blessings too eagerly, as though I'd attracted them by my own efforts alone. I had thought of myself as flying by my own strength, forgetting that, to soar high, the devotee must allow himself to be lifted on breezes of God's grace.

From pride there developed increasing tension in my spiritual efforts. And then, realizing that what I needed was to be more humble, more inwardly receptive, I began trying too urgently, too almost presumptuously, to offer myself up to God's will. I *grasped* at His guidance, as I had been grasping at joy.

"What do You want of me, Lord?" I prayed. "I'll do *anything* for You!" I tried imagining what demands He might make of me, then pictured myself following them to the last letter. In my overeagerness, those imagined demands gradually multiplied until their sheer number defied comprehension. "Don't sit here. Don't go there. Don't eat this. Don't say that." I fell a prey to what the Roman Catholics call "scrupulosity." No longer was there joy in my self-offering. Scarcely even comprehending that I was playing this drama entirely in my own mind, I began to look upon God almost as a tyrant: His demands seemed hopelessly unreasonable! I failed to notice that He'd never actually made any of them!

"Walter is so confused!" Master exclaimed one afternoon to Vera Brown. Several more times that day he shook his head wonderingly. "Walter is *so confused*!" Then, almost as if to reassure himself, he added, "But—he will get there."

At about this time, Master went for seclusion to Twenty-Nine Palms to complete his commentary on the Bhagavad Gita. He took me with him. "I asked Divine Mother whom I should take," he told me, "and your face, Walter, appeared before me. I asked Her twice more, to make sure, and each time your face appeared." I hoped that weeks spent in Master's company would banish the turmoil that had been building within me.

At his desert retreat, it was wonderful to listen to him as he worked on his writings. The ease with which inspiration came to him was extraordinary. He would simply look up into the spiritual eye, then begin speaking, with hardly a pause, while his secretary, Dorothy Taylor, raced to keep up with him on the typewriter. The deepest insights poured from his lips effortlessly.

I got to spend several days at Master's place, listening to him dictate. After that, he instructed me to stay at the monks' retreat and go through the old SRF magazines, clipping out his Gita commentaries and "editing" them.

Editing? I knew this particular assignment had already been given to a senior disciple, Laurie Pratt. "How carefully do you want me to edit, Sir?"

Original letter to me from Paramhansa Yogananda.

Saturday [February] 18th, 1950

29 🌴s [Palms]

Dear Walter,

I am sending all magazines. (1) Cut out first all of Bhagavad Gita articles–gather them on the side; paste only on one side; don't destroy any writing (though different) on back of Gita articles.

(2) Keep editing in pencil the Omar Khayyam articles–put together in a book form, pasting only the back as the pages in a book are.

(3) Have you got glue or paper or knife—if not write and make a list and Jane will bring them to you.

(4) Later you have to cut out all Bible articles and make a book–about the Second Coming of Christ.

(5) Save all the magazines–what is left of them after the Gita, Omar and Bible articles are taken out.

(6) Hand over Radio article and write Bernard to write them henceforth as you are busy editing.

(7) Get up early, meditate a little, exercise and run or walk briskly; then start from 8 A.M. to 6 P.M. Every two hours run for 5 minutes and meditate 15 minutes before lunch–including lunch must be finished in 1 hour).(over)

Work–9 hours a day with deep concentration—meditate two hours deeply at night after dining at 6:30. Sleep 7 hours. Be sure to walk briskly or run for 5 minutes every 2 hours. This will keep strain out. After dinner at night walk on the road and not in jungly brush–for one hour 6 to 7. Then eat and meditate two hours. Adjust routine whatever possible. Not necessary to walk at night. You can work from 7:30 A.M.–if you like. You should take 1/2 hours walk in the morning after quick meditation and breakfast covering (1/2 hour).

Q. Have you got a regular lamp–with strong light for use at night? Perhaps it needs a wick. Write what you need done about lamp. Write to Jane.
Q. Have you finished pasting Omar Khayyam?
Q. How much you have edited? Thorough but fast editing is necessary or nothing will be done. Time is scant.
        With blessing,
        P Yogananda

P.S. Do all work with the thought of God. PY

Original letter to me from Paramhansa Yogananda.

Dear Walter,
1) Please write Virginia Wright–what you need for food:
      (a) milk
      (b) bread
      (c) butter
      (d) Vegetables and fruits I am sending.
      (e) Sending $5 for everything
(2) Please report how much work you do daily–Please work fast—there is much
to do–use kitchen knife and scissors to making cut
      (a) Omar Khayyam
      (b) Then Bhagavad Gita
   I must have them soon–please be day and night busy. Must work fast.
      (2) Give Virginia Miss Wright–Radio Script
      (3) Write Bernard, he has

to prepare Radio Script as you are busy editing now.

Meditate deeply at night and every 2 hours and run around hermitage for 5 to 10 minutes. Keep exercised and body fit for God realization.

Do not procrastinate or act carelessly. Hurry with discretion.

Boundless Blessings through my Self,
P Yogananda

P.S. Have you Butane gas? If not tell Miss Wright. Water plants early morning if not watered. PY

"Just edit," he replied vaguely, gazing at me reflectively. Then with urgency he continued, "Work like lightning. There is no time to be wasted. But"—he spoke sternly—"don't change a word."

Edit, like lightning, and not change a word? To my spiritual confusion was now added the problem that I hadn't the remotest idea what he wanted me to do.

Master instructed me to remain in seclusion and devote myself "with all possible speed" to my job of "editing." Since I'd gone to the desert with high hopes of spending every day with him, it was particularly distressing now to find myself left not only completely alone, but in utter confusion. I was unaccustomed to complete solitude, and felt abandoned. Intense moods began to assail me. At times I would fall into bleak despair, actually collapsing onto my bed and staring helplessly at the ceiling. Every evening I told myself, "This simply *can't* go on for another day!" But it did go on, day after day, for three long months. Each day seemed worse than the day before it.

It was as though two opposing forces were battling within me. Bravely I tried to give strength to the good side by meditating several hours daily, but even the effort to meditate only deepened my sense of hopelessness. During the daylight hours I tried to lose myself in the task I'd been given. My despair, however, at not even knowing what I was supposed to be doing made absorption in the task difficult. My "editing" job seemed to me like the labors of Sisyphus.*

Master once told an audience, "I used to think Satan was only a human invention, but now I know, and add my testimony to that of all those who have gone before me, that Satan is a reality. He is a universal, conscious force whose sole aim is to keep all beings bound to the wheel of delusion." What I felt now was that God and Satan, at war inside me, were beating *me* up in their efforts to get at one another! It was not that I had the slightest wish to return to a worldly life. That desire, with God's grace, since I first set foot on the spiritual path, has never for an instant entered my heart. What

---

* Sisyphus, a cunning king in Greek legend, was condemned in Hades to push a heavy rock repeatedly up a hill, only to have it roll again to the bottom.

was happening, rather, was that, while I longed for inner peace, I found myself unaccountably terrified of it, and of going deep in meditation where alone true peace can be found.

The reader may see in my psychological ferment ample explanation for my feeling of helplessness without this added plea that forces greater than myself were belaboring me. The rational mind, dependent as it is on sensory evidence, would always prefer to reach its conclusions without the intrusion of supra-sensory causes, which to it seem supernatural—that is to say, unreal. Moreover, it is a notorious weakness of the irrational mind to leap eagerly at supernatural explanations for predicaments that it would otherwise be obliged to accept as its own responsibility.

Nonetheless, this much is surely true—that every mental state reflects broader realities of consciousness. Our merriment, for example, demonstrates the already existing potential for merriment in humanity itself; our very consciousness, the potential for consciousness throughout the universe. Living beings *manifest* consciousness, even as a light bulb manifests electricity. Consciousness is a cosmic fact. Man only tunes into, and expresses, limited aspects of consciousness. His thoughts are never solitary cries flung into a cosmic void. Like birds, rather, riding on a wind, his thoughts are supported, and further influenced, by whatever stream of consciousness they enter. Depending on which aspects of cosmic reality man himself tunes in to, he is drawn downward or upward in his spiritual evolution—down toward matter by what is known as the satanic force, or up toward infinity by God's love.

There are beings, both in this world and the next, that act more or less consciously as agents for these divine or satanic forces. Angels, we call those in the first group; demons, those in the second.

A year or so before the period I am describing, I had an experience with an entity in the latter group. The episode sounds almost like a page out of some medieval romance.

I was new on the path, and naively eager for whatever information I could gather regarding it. Boone informed me one day that, according to Master, the stories of possession in the Bible were factual. He went on to describe a strange experience he himself had once had with a demonic entity that had tried to possess him. Intrigued rather than frightened, I decided that it would be interesting to test personally the truth of Boone's assertion.

One night not long afterward, I dreamed that I was at a party. The thought suddenly came to me with striking certainty: "It's time to go meet a disembodied spirit." I left my friends and passed through an empty, well-lit room toward an open door on the far side. I can still see clearly in my mind's eye the bare floorboards and walls, the shining bulb dangling from the ceiling. The next room was dark; here, I knew, I was to meet the disincarnate entity. Momentarily apprehensive, I reached out to switch on the light. Then I rebuked myself, thinking, "Don't be a coward," and pulled back. "How will you learn what this is all about," I asked myself, "if you don't dare face it?" And so, leaving the room dark, I stood in the center of it and called out, "Come!"

Here comes the "gothic" part of my story. The following day Jean Haupt told me that he had been awakened at about the same time of night by a loud, fierce pounding on his door.

"Wh-what is it?" he quailed.

A deep, rough voice loudly demanded, "Who's in there?"

"J-Jean."

"Who?"

"Jean Haupt." By now Jean was thoroughly frightened.

"I don't want you. I want Don Walters!" Whoever or whatever it was stormed noisily out of the building.

Shortly after that, it must have been, when my own strange experience began.

"Come!" As I called out, the floor beneath me began to heave in wave-like movements. An instant later I found myself being drawn out of my body and out the window into a sort of grey mist. A peculiar aspect of AUM, not at all pleasant, resounded loudly all around me. This was evidently not going to be a spiritually uplifting experience! Discrimination, however, was not my strong point that night.

"How interesting!" I thought, going along with events to see where they led.

Presently, some powerful force pitted itself against me; it seemed determined to rob me of my conscious awareness. I struggled to resist, but the opposing will was strong; I wasn't at all sure I would win. I quickly decided I'd better stop playing such a risky game.

"Master!" I cried, urgently.

Instantly the experience ended. The sound ceased. Back again in my body, I sat up in bed, fully awake.

Later that day I asked Master if this had been a true experience.

"Yes, it was. Such things sometimes happen on the path." He added, "Don't be afraid of them."

How could one be afraid, I thought, after such a demonstration of the guru's omniscient protection?

I omitted something in telling this story in the first edition of this book, owing either to my own inability to understand it, or to my fear lest it take my readers or listeners out of their depths of comprehension.

What happened first in our conversation was that Master asked me to describe what had happened. At that point a question arose in my mind; I said, "Sir, didn't you *know* about it?"

As if brushing the question aside, he replied brusquely, "When you are one with God, you *become* God." Was such a thing possible? What he'd said seemed inconceivable! Yet what can be left, once the ego has been demolished? Logically, there can remain only God. Master, in his divine Self, *had* been fully aware of my experience.

The worst of my ordeal at Twenty-Nine Palms, however, was that while it lasted I wasn't even able to call on Master with my accustomed faith in him. Suddenly, without any conscious intent on my part, I found myself plunged into violent doubts. It wasn't that I doubted Master's goodness, or his spiritual greatness, or even my commitment to him as my guru. But the thought suddenly forced itself insidiously upon me: "He lacks wisdom." It was an idea over which I had no control. If Master had said, "The sun is shining in Los Angeles," this doubting serpent inside me would have sneered, "I'll bet it's raining!" There was no question of my *entertaining* these doubts. I would have done anything to be rid of them; they made me utterly miserable.

My doubts began with the commentaries I was supposed to be editing. I found them in bad shape. I didn't realize it at the time, but Master's practice during the early years of his mission had been simply to write an article, then turn it over to his editors and print-ers and never glance at it again. Even I, who knew no Sanskrit, could see plainly that, in their inconsistencies, the Sanskrit names as they were printed showed a woeful lack of familiarity with that language. I didn't realize that the editors had simply not been conscientious enough to catch obvious typographical errors—that, in fact, they'd added not a few eccentricities of their own.

Worse still, in his commentaries Master would sometimes write, "This means so and so," and then turn around—almost, to my mind, as though correcting himself—and say, "On the other hand, it also means . . ." and go on to suggest an interpretation which—again, to my way of thinking—bore little relation to the first one. "Can't he make up his mind?" I marveled. "How is it possible for the same passage to have *both* meanings?"

It was only gradually, over years, that I came to appreciate the subtlety of this way of thinking. I also learned that this multifaceted scriptural commentary is traditional in India. Indeed, I see now that, philosophically, it is a far more sophisticated approach than ours with our preference for limiting every truth to one definition only— as though a definition and the truth it defines were one and the same thing. Reality has many dimensions.

Sri Chaitanya, a youthful saint, lived several centuries ago in India, and followed the path of bhakti (devotion). He moved from Navadweep in Bengal to Puri, in the state of Orissa, to be near the Jagannath temple there. Sarvabhauma, an older man and a famous scholar, decided that this young man, though radiant, needed an in-tellectual foundation for his beliefs. Going to Chaitanya, he offered to give him instruction.

"I'd be happy to learn," the other replied.

Sarvabhauma then, reading from scripture, interpreted a single passage in twenty-five ways: an amazing feat. Chaitanya was properly impressed. After congratulating the older man, however, he said, "Let me see if I can come up with any others." He found eighty more meanings in that passage! Sarvabhauma, faced with that accomplishment, became Chaitanya's disciple.

How different this way of thinking from the Aristotelian "either ... or" method in which I'd been raised! But I came to understand that a deep truth is like the hub of a wheel: the more central it is, the more clearly it relates to the entire wheel of experience.

My dilemma of doubt illustrates more or less typically the problem of every devotee. Before he can attain divine freedom, he must weed out every obstructing tendency he has carried over from the past. Mere intellectual affirmation of victory is not enough: He must also face his delusions in stern hand-to-hand combat. Every seeker has his own special, self-created set of delusions to overcome. Win against them he must, however, if he would attain inner freedom.

"You are doubting now," Master told me one day, "because you doubted in the past." (Out of shame, I hadn't consulted him regarding my dilemma. But he'd known what was on my mind.)

In time I realized that one of the reasons Master wanted me to teach others was that, having entertained doubts myself in past lives, and having already to a great extent conquered them in this one, I needed to reinforce my growing faith by expressing it outwardly, and helping others in their struggles to resolve doubts, themselves. By deepening their faith, I would also pay off my own karmic debt for having ever, myself, doubted.

When I had been at the monks' retreat about a month, Master summoned Henry from Mt. Washington to work on certain projects at his retreat. Henry commuted there daily from our place. After some time, Jerry Torgerson came out and stayed with us also. Jerry, too, of course, worked at Master's place. Later, others came out on weekends; they, too, worked—where else?—at Master's place. It was even more heart-rending for me to see crowds going over to be with Master, while I labored alone, hopelessly, at my incomprehensible task of editing. But Master insisted that I stick to it.

"How much have you edited?" he wrote me in a note that Henry brought back one day. "*Thorough but fast* editing is necessary, or nothing will be done. Time is scant."

Henry's presence was a great blessing for me. During the weeks we spent out there together we became fast friends,* our mutual attunement developing until it often happened that one of us had only to think something for the other to mention it. What rare good fortune, I reflected, to find even one such friend in a lifetime.

As it turned out, the other monks didn't get to spend much time with Master, either, since their work was out of doors, and he, staying indoors, concentrated deeply on finishing his Gita commentaries. Nor was he indifferent to my welfare. Rather, he tried in various ways to reassure me. But it was his way never to intrude on our free will to the point where it would mean fighting our important battles for us. That would have deprived us of the opportunity to develop our own strength.

And so the weeks passed. In April, Mother and Dad visited Mt. Washington. Dad was being posted from Egypt to Bordeaux, France, where eventually he made an important oil discovery at Parentis, and ended his career as an appointee to the French Legion of Honor. Master permitted me to go and receive them. "But you must return after four days," he wrote me, "after seeing your parents—designated by your real Parent, God." Then, referring to his commentaries, he added, "Only three chapters left. Soon we will get together."

Master received me before I left. Looking at my now-flourishing beard, he remarked with a smile, "I can't have you going looking like that!" He had me sit down right then and there, out of doors, called for a comb and scissors, and proceeded with many gleeful chuckles to trim my beard as he wanted it to look. I have tried ever since to keep the beard more or less that length, except for one period in my life when I shaved it off, thinking that now I looked quite old enough. I then decided, however, that it was for more reasons

---

* Reviewing that word, "fast," I am compelled to admit that some other adjective would better serve my meaning, were I able to find it. It has been painful for me in my life to have to accept that no friendship is truly steadfast except God's, and the guru's, in God.

than my youthful appearance that he'd wanted me to grow it, so I let it grow again.

My father, happy as he was to see me, was far from supportive of my new way of life. He shuddered to see my beard, deplored my abandonment of a promising writing career, and altogether rejected my spiritual beliefs. One day he said, "If I were to get the opinions of a few doctors on this teaching about energizing the body by will power, would you accept their verdict?" It wasn't as though he were proposing to consult any of the numerous physicians who were already members of our work. Probably he didn't dream such an animal existed.

"Dad," I remonstrated, "doctors aren't omniscient!"

I attended the morning service with Mother and Dad at Hollywood Church that Sunday. The day before, I had asked Rev. Bernard, who was scheduled to speak, "Do you think you might give a really scientific talk, to impress my father?" "Sure," he'd replied, confidently. Any correspondence, however, between Bernard's and Dad's understanding of science was purely coincidental. Dad came away from church that day convinced that Bernard had taken complete leave of his senses—a judgment that probably, by extension, embraced the whole lot of us, including me.

Here I am on the lawn in front of Mt. Washington headquarters.

It might be conjectured that my parents' visit, coming as it did during my severe trial of faith, made the trial harder than ever for me. In fact, however, that visit helped me to overcome my doubts. For my parents and I, despite our philosophical differences, deeply loved one another. The reality of this underlying bond helped me to see that love is a far better response than reason to that kind of doubt which is quick to condemn, but slow to investigate.

My parents were pleased in the end to see me happy in my new calling. Reflecting on my confusion and unhappiness during college and after it, Mother wrote Master a few weeks later to thank him for the good he had done me.

During my brief visit to Mt. Washington, I found that others of the monks, too, had been passing through inner trials. On my return to Twenty-Nine Palms I said to Master, "Sir, Jean is a little discouraged. Someone told him that Sri Ramakrishna said grace is only a sport of God's. He takes this to mean that a person might meditate for years and get nowhere, whereas God might reveal Himself to any drunkard if He had a mere notion to."

"Ramakrishna would *never* have said that!" Master looked almost shocked. "That is what happens when people without realization try to interpret the saints' teachings. God is no creature of whims! Of course, it may *look* like sport sometimes, to people who can't see the causative influences of past karma. But why would God go against His own law? He responds according to it. Tell Haupt I said this is a serious misunderstanding on his part."

"I will, Sir." I paused. "Master, won't you talk with him? He seems to be having a hard time lately."

"Well," Master answered quietly, "Satan is testing the organization. Haupt is not the only one."

"Is *that* what the trouble has been!"

"Yes." Sadly, Master continued, "Quite a few heads will fall."

"Will it go on for very long, Master?"

"Quite some time." After a pause, he went on, "It all started when that boy, Jan, left Encinitas. Then Smith left. Quite a few more heads will roll." Jan, the nine-year-old who had received a vision of Jesus, had left the work several months later with his mother. Rev. Smith had been the minister of our Long Beach chapel.

It would seem that, in the lives of great world teachers, a sort of housecleaning takes place toward the end of their missions. In this way their work is assured of being carried on as purely as possible after they leave this earth. Jesus Christ told his disciples, "The man who eats my flesh and drinks my blood has eternal life," and again, "The man who eats my body and drinks my blood shares my life, and I share his." He didn't trouble to explain what he meant by those words, or that they'd had a purely metaphorical significance. It was almost as if he were *inviting* people to misunderstand him in order to find out who among his disciples were really in tune with him.

The Bible goes on to say, "Many of his disciples, when they heard him say these things, commented, 'This is a hard teaching indeed; who could accept it?'" Their general reaction is reported next: "From that time many of his disciples withdrew, and walked no more with him."* But the closest disciples of Jesus were in tune with him on an intuitive level. Nothing that he said outwardly could disturb the sublime certitude of that inner knowledge. Their intuitive understanding demonstrated their fitness to promulgate his message after he'd left his body.

One evening at Master's retreat, we were walking together outdoors, just the two of us, when he remarked as if out of the blue, very sternly, "Apart from Saint Lynn, *every man* has disappointed me. And *you MUSTN'T disappoint me!*" His concluding words were spoken with great earnestness. I knew that many of his men

---

* John 6:54–66. Paramhansa Yogananda explained that Jesus, in speaking of his body and blood, was referring to the omnipresent, eternal Spirit with which his consciousness was identified. By "body" he meant all vibratory creation, the Holy Ghost, or *Aum*, which the devotee must absorb into himself ("eat"), until he feels inwardly identified with it. Christ's "blood" is the all-pervading Christ consciousness, which, like blood which sustains the physical body, is the true "life" and sustenance of all creation. The meditating devotee must advance from oneness with *Aum* to oneness with Christ consciousness, and thence to oneness with God the Father beyond creation. I asked Master once, "What stage must a person have attained to become a true master?" He replied, "One becomes a master when he attains Christ consciousness."

disciples had *not* disappointed him spiritually. What, then, could he have meant? Had his meaning something to do with his frequent statement to me, "You have a great work to do, Walter"? I hadn't yet understood clearly what that work would be. And my next question: Had it something to do with the fact of my being a man?

It took me years to understand his admonition that day at Twenty-Nine Palms, and the reason he had delivered it with such intensity.

Men and women, though equally expressions of God, manifest Him differently; thereby they complement one another. In this way they exemplify the dual nature of all manifested existence. Men's energy, Master said, is more naturally outward; women's, more inward. He pointed out that this difference, though of course varying with the individual, is evident even in the sex organs.

He had been disappointed that the men who had come to him as disciples showed no zeal for spreading his mission. Dr. Lewis often spoke disparagingly of ministers who "just get up and blow." Master had had me lecture in the churches, but I always imagined that it must be my bad karma to have to speak in public. I visualized the other disciples—those with good enough karma, as I thought it—sitting at home, meditating.

It was nearly seven years before I came to recognize that people were in fact helped by something I'd said in a sermon or a lecture. One person had been contemplating suicide, but changed his mind after hearing me speak. Another developed faith in God after one of my sermons.

I'm afraid it was Dr. Lewis, primarily, who, by his comments about "blowing," had dampened my enthusiasm for sharing the teachings—that, and also the fact that the women disciples, who served Master more closely and seemed outwardly, at least, closer to him than most of the men, were not given the task of speaking in public. In fact, however, Master had tuned into my most deep-seated desire: to help others, as well as myself, to find God.

Even as I was crossing the country to offer myself as his disciple, two longings had been uppermost in me: to find God, and to help others to find Him. "What a wonderful teaching!" I thought; "I wish everyone in the world could hear, understand, and embrace it!" This thought rose powerfully within me, almost as a part of my longing for God. How could I be satisfied even with finding God, as long as my brothers and sisters everywhere lacked that realization?

Did I really think of everyone on earth as my brother and sister? Yes, to this extent at least: One of my basic motives for seeking God was the dismaying realization that the depths to which anyone can sink are, potentially, depths which everyone must fear. I too could sink that far—not of course in my present realities, but in my humanity. I could become a drug addict, a murderer, a raving lunatic.

I remembered that period of my life when, as a child, my father had read to me from Mark Twain's *Huckleberry Finn*, and how, in my feverish delirium afterward, I had cried out again and again desperately, "I don't *want* to be a drunkard! I don't *want* to be a drunkard!" Man's infinite potential for error as well as for wisdom unites him in consciousness with all men. Everyone in the world is in the same predicament, and shares with all the same need: inner freedom. If I could extricate myself from the universal problem, even to the extent of finding the right path to freedom, I longed to share my discovery with everyone.

This basic instinct in me was dampened by the deprecating comments of more than one of my fellow disciples. My first and only real desire was, after all, to find God. Nothing interested me that might obstruct me in my search for Him. I certainly didn't want to "just get up and blow"!

One day Master commented to a group of us monks about the number of teachers he'd appointed who had allowed public admiration to go to their heads—to the point (absurd as it seems) of considering themselves as knowledgeable as their own guru! Such, alas, is human nature: It likes to preen itself. Master's women editors, also, had presumed to correct not only his word-flow and grammar, but even his teachings. Hearing him describe this danger to those in the ministry, I said to him, "Sir, that's why I don't want to be a public speaker."

He understood that this was an important moment in my life. Speaking gravely and with great emphasis, he lowered his eyes to the floor and averred, "You will *never* fall because of ego!"

There was another aspect, however, to his concern over those who taught in his name or, for that matter, who edited his writings. No one, so far, had shown real enthusiasm for sharing his teachings or his broader mission with others. Everyone seemed more concerned with his or her own spiritual progress. In me Master had found someone at last who really *wanted* to reach out to the whole world with the truths he had come to share.

I heard many years later that an ex-monk had reported to a friend of mine something he'd heard Master say to a small group: "If Walter had come earlier, we would have reached millions!" This, I now suspect, was why he came out onto the stage after my acceptance, and announced with obvious satisfaction, "We have a new brother." It was also why he had me stand up in church the first time I heard him speak there, and introduced me to everyone. My work, as he already knew, was to serve as a spearhead for his teachings. He knew from the beginning that my job would be to introduce his message widely everywhere, without adding "amendments" of my own.

Indeed, through the many thousands of lectures I have given in many countries; through the nearly one hundred books (so far) that I have written; through the over 400 songs and instrumental pieces that have come through me; through his writings that I have edited; through the seven or eight communities I have founded so far; and through the many people—perhaps hundreds of thousands; perhaps even millions—that I have brought to accept discipleship under him, my job has been to bring not only him, but his teachings and mission to the world. Much, of course, remains to be done, but I imagine that few would deny that, with Master's grace, I have been able to make a fair start at getting his work known in the world. And it all really began with those months out at Twenty-Nine Palms.

In my struggle to edit Master's commentaries on the Bhagavad Gita (and, earlier, on the *Rubaiyat of Omar Khayyam*), it turned out that there was enough to correct in the old magazines even without changing their wording. Most of the mistakes were simply typographical errors, or the brainchildren of some editor with a quaint fetish for capitals. But these literary outcastes were so numerous that I could see no practical way of preparing the text for publication without first typing out all the articles afresh, double-spacing for surgery. Master, however, must not have realized what very bad shape they were in. When I suggested to him that I type them out, he said it would take too long.

When, however, I finally submitted the fruits of my labors to the editorial department, having cluttered the margins with as many as six proofreading corrections to a line, it was obvious that my copy would be impossible to work from. Laurie Pratt, the older disciple to whom Master had given the real responsibility for editing, ordered that my work be thrown away altogether, and the whole job typed out, double spaced, from a fresh set of magazines. It was, as I had known all along, the only feasible thing to do.

Why had he had me do all that hard work, so uselessly? Later, I understood. He hadn't much longer left to live, and he wanted to indicate his will for the future of his work, and for our own individual futures. Thus, he had tried in 1925 to start a school for children at Mt. Washington, though he surely knew that parents in America would need first to accept his teaching before they'd consider sending their children to his school. He'd tried to start a yoga university, though he must have known that the time had not yet come for such a venture.

He'd tried to start a "world brotherhood community" in Encinitas, knowing (again, surely) that America was not ready for such a step, nor his renunciate disciples ready to accept it.

And he tried to get me, at the young age of twenty-three, to edit some of his major writings, certainly knowing that I wasn't yet ready for the task.

All this was to help "sow his thoughts in the ether," for future fruition.*

---

* The seeds Master planted in those weeks did indeed bear fruit in time. In 1994 I edited his *Rubaiyat* commentaries, and published them under the title *The Rubaiyat of Omar Khayyam Explained*. And in 2005 (as I explain on p. 501) I wrote *The Essence of the Bhagavad Gita Explained by Paramhansa Yogananda*.

One afternoon at his desert retreat I overheard Master scolding Miss Taylor for not using my work. "If you gave me a million dollars," he cried, "I wouldn't go through what he did to get this job done! Not if you gave me a million dollars!" (As if he'd do *anything* for merely monetary gain!) I smiled, though I was also gratified by the concern he expressed.

That afternoon Laurie Pratt happened to meet me outside Master's house. "My," she exclaimed, "that certainly was a lot of work you did!" Turning to go indoors, she added offhandedly, as if to the air, "Not that it did any good!" Again I smiled, this time wryly. I myself had known it was all useless.

Later that day, Master tried to comfort me for her seemingly unfeeling remark.

"But Sir," I pleaded, "she's quite right! It wouldn't have been possible for anyone to work from my copy."

"You are *defending* her!" Master's expression showed amazement. "But you did *good* work. All those capitals! Why, they'd have made us a laughingstock!"

I was touched by his attempt to reassure me. For me, however, the important thing was that I knew now, more deeply than ever before, that I belonged to him, and that the outward ups and downs of the path didn't really matter so long as I felt his love in my heart. Perhaps, I reflected, he had been keeping me at Twenty-Nine Palms only to help me face important defects in my own character, and not for the sake of his books at all. At any rate, I knew that my months of agony had matured me. Now, I felt nothing but gratitude for them.

There was once—the only time ever—that Laurie Pratt, Master, and I were alone together. It was out of doors at his desert retreat. Master told an amusing story from his early days at the school in Ranchi.

"I used to be a fast runner," he said. "At the school we somehow acquired several dogs that caused us endless problems. No one could catch them. One day I took a gunny sack and chased after them, grabbing each in turn and putting it into the sack. In that way I managed to catch all the dogs. We then took them far away, and succeeded in getting rid of them."

I no longer remember Master's exact words on this occasion. In fact, I couldn't really understand properly what he was saying. He told the story with so much gusto and enthusiasm, using broad gestures and panting in pantomime, laughing, and with a twinkle in his eyes, that his words became obfuscated. His delight in the story was contagious, however, and I laughed with him delightedly.

Laurie, for her part, sat composedly looking into the distance. She seemed mentally quite removed from what Master was saying, untouched by its comedy. Distantly she commented, "Well, well"; and then, "Fancy that!"

Master was obviously directing his story to me. Was he giving me a hint of Laurie's inability to enter into other people's realities, and perhaps her inability also to estimate the validity of those realities if they differed from her own? He must have known that she and I, years later, would have a falling out which resulted in her total condemnation of me.

I wondered at the time, too: Did she even have a sense of humor?

After I'd recovered from my test in that desert, Master looked at me kindly, then reassured me in front of the other monks, "Walter was on his high horse. Now he is coming our way."

CHAPTER 31
The Bhagavad Gita

"A NEW SCRIPTURE HAS been born!" Master spoke ecstatically. His commentary on the Bhagavad Gita had been finished. In three months of unbroken dictation he had completed 1,500 pages. "I told Miss Taylor the pages numbered that many, but she carefully counted them to make sure I was right!"

Master and I were walking around the compound of his retreat. Having finished his manuscript, he had summoned me at last to help him with the preliminary editing.

"A new scripture has been born!" he repeated. "Millions will find God through this book. Not just thousands. Millions! I have seen it. I *know*."

My first task, now that he'd brought me out of seclusion, was to read through the entire manuscript and get an over-all feeling for it. I found the experience almost overwhelming. Never in my life had I read anything so deep, and at the same time so beautiful and uplifting. To think that only recently I had been questioning Master's wisdom! I kicked myself mentally for being such a chump. His book was filled with the deepest wisdom I had ever encountered. Unlike most philosophical works, moreover, this one was fresh and alive, each page a sparkling rill of original insights. With the sure touch of a master teacher, profound truths were lightened occasionally by graceful humor, or with a charming and instructive story, or highlighted with brief touches of new, sometimes startling information. (I was intrigued to learn, for example, that advanced yogis sometimes reincarnate in several bodies at once, in order the more quickly to work out their past karmas.) Best of all, the truths expressed in the book were constantly clarified, as Master himself said exultingly, by "illustration after illustration."

"I understand now," he told me, "why my master never let me read other Gita interpretations. Had I done so, my mind might have been influenced by the opinions expressed in them. But this book came entirely from God. It is not philosophy: the mere *love* of wisdom; It *is* wisdom. To make sure I didn't write any of it from opinion, I tuned into Beda Byasa's* consciousness before beginning my dictation. Everything I wrote came from him.

"There have been many other Gita commentaries," Master continued, "including some that are famous. But none have been so all-rounded in their approach as this one. Swami Shankara's, for example, deep though it was, was limited by the one-sided emphasis he placed on the purely spiritual nature of reality. Scriptures should deal with reality on *every* level. They should help people physically and mentally also, not only spiritually. The more down-to-earth levels of life are what people have to contend with. It is more for ordinary people than for saints, moreover, that scriptures get written."

Again Master said with a blissful smile, "A new scripture has been born!"

"It was God's will," he concluded, "that the Gita be fully explained only now. This was a principal aspect of the mission with which Babaji commissioned me."

Master had told us already that he had been Arjuna in a former life. Small wonder, then, that the task of explaining this scripture authoritatively had been left to him.

The Bhagavad Gita consists of a dialogue between Krishna and Arjuna during which Sri Krishna relates deep, divine truths to his closest disciple. What, I thought, could be more fitting than for the task of interpreting this scripture to have been left to Arjuna himself, in a later incarnation? or for Sri Krishna, in his present form, to have commissioned the undertaking?

My three months of seclusion were over; there now followed two months of concentrated work with Master at his place. I spent many hours in his company, and much time also poring over the

---

* The ancient author of the Bhagavad Gita.

manuscript with Mrs. Nealey, an elderly lady—not a disciple, but a devotee and a trained editor—whom Master had invited to Twenty-Nine Palms to help with the editing.

"I don't like to have you working with her," he told me one day, "but for the present, the work demands it. While you are with her, though, never look into her eyes. That is where the attraction starts."

"Sir!" I protested. "She's an old woman. How could there possibly be any attraction?"

"It makes no difference; that magnetism holds true for all ages." Master paused a moment, then added, "Already she feels a little attached to you—not in a bad way," he hastened to reassure me, "and only very slightly—like a mother for her son. I don't want you to worry about it, but remember, that magnetism is subtle, so be careful."

It puzzled me at first why Master would want anyone to edit his writings for him. They were so manifestly inspired, and—well, I thought, didn't divine inspiration imply perfection on *every* level? Not necessarily, it seemed. Inspiration, Master explained, lies primarily in the vibrations and the ideas expressed.

Logical sentence structure, I gradually realized, like good plumbing, belongs to this physical plane of existence. It is a tool, merely, of thought and communication. Cerebration is slow and ponderous compared to the soul's transcendent intuitions. Many times it has happened that an important scientific discovery appeared full blown in the mind of its discoverer, only to require years of plodding work for him to present his intuitive insight clearly and convincingly to the world.

Great masters usually submit to the laws governing this material universe, which they respect as a part of God's creation. But matter represents inertia, the *tamasic** quality in Nature. To saints whose consciousness has transcended matter, the material way of working must appear slow and cumbersome indeed. As Master told us, he

---

* *Tamas*, the lowest of three *gunas*, or qualities, that infuse the entire universe. The other two are *rajas* or *rajo guna*, the activating quality, and *sattwa*, the elevating or spiritualizing, quality. The three *gunas* represent the progressive stages of manifestation outward from the oneness of Spirit.

preferred to work on a level of vibrations. ("That is how books are written in the astral world."*) In addition to this natural predilection for functioning on non-material levels of reality, great masters often deliberately leave to their disciples the task of translating their teachings onto the material plane, so that they, too, may grow spiritually. As Master once said to me, "By helping me with editing, you yourself will evolve." Master could cope easily and efficiently, when he had a mind to, with mundane problems including those of grammar and literary style. As he once told me, "I did edit one book myself: *Whispers from Eternity*." And this I considered not only one of his finest works, but one of the loveliest books of poetry ever written.[†] In editing his Gita commentaries, Master invited our suggestions, and was content to accept many of them.

On most days, after working on his manuscript, he would sit back and converse with me informally. Occasionally Mrs. Nealey remained in the room with us, joining in the discussion. As usual, Master's teaching on these occasions often took the form of illustrative stories.

* The universe in which souls find themselves after physical death. The astral is the second stage of manifestation, outward from Spirit. In the order of cosmic creation, first comes the causal, or ideational universe, which represents *sattwa guna*. At this stage of manifestation all things exist only as ideas. The next phase is the astral, representing *rajo guna*. At this stage, primordial ideas become clothed in energy. In the third phase, the physical, energy takes on the appearance of solid substance. That all this is an appearance, merely, has been suggested already by modern physics in its discovery that matter *is* energy.

Shapes and colors exist in the astral world, as they do in the physical. There are planets, fields, lakes, mountains, and people on the astral plane. But all things there are seen as varied manifestations of light.

Master once said, "In the astral world, all you need to do is put your vibrations into a book. In this world, Divine Mother disciplined me by forcing me to go over my book many times."

† In 2008 I published a new edition of *Whispers*. Dissatisfied with the one done by Laurie Pratt (Tara Mata) in 1958 (it lacked Master's poetic sense), I planned to reissue his original, 1949 edition. In going over it, however, I found a number of mixed metaphors, and some quaint expressions that no longer worked in today's English. Readers have told me that this new version sounds completely like Master, without those "stumbling blocks." I think that, even though he edited the 1949 edition himself, he still allowed himself to be swept along by intuitive exuberance, which carried him soaring over the rocky terrain of analytical reasoning.

"God rarely wants miracles to be displayed publicly," he told us one day. He went on to relate the story of Sadhu Haridas, a famous miracle-worker in India of the eighteenth century, who, Master said, "remained buried underground for forty days. Afterwards, when his body was exhumed, a group of French physicians examined him, and pronounced him dead. Thereupon, to their amazement, he 'came back to life'!

"One day Sadhu Haridas was seated in a small rowboat with a Christian missionary, who was trying to convert him. 'Why should I follow your Jesus Christ?' demanded Haridas. 'What did he do that I can't do?'

"'The powers he displayed were divine,' retorted the missionary. Glancing at the water surrounding them, he continued, 'He could walk on water.'

"'Is *that* so special?' asked Haridas. Stepping out of the boat, he walked on the water ahead of it. Wherever he went, the boat followed behind him. The missionary, of course, was speechless!

"The maharaja of that state, however, was a great soul. Seeing Sadhu Haridas one day from afar, he said, 'There is something about that man that I distrust.' His courtiers remonstrated, 'But he is a great saint. Look what he has done.' The maharaja replied, 'All the same, there is something about him that I don't like.' He sensed that, by concentrating on miracles, Sadhu Haridas was forgetting God.

"And he was right. Not long afterwards, Haridas forsook his spiritual practices, married, and resumed a worldly life. Finally he saw his error and returned to his disciples. 'I am back,' he announced, simply.

"Years later he declared, 'I have done many wrong things, but now the Beloved is calling me.' Entering *samadhi*, he attained eternal freedom."

"Sir," Mrs. Nealey inquired, puzzled, "how did he rise again so quickly? When a person falls from a high spiritual state, isn't the karmic punishment far greater than for a fallen neophyte?"

Master shook his head. "Mm-mmm. God is no tyrant. If one has been accustomed to drinking nectar, then takes to eating stale cheese, he soon grows dissatisfied with the change, and throws the cheese away, crying for nectar again. God won't refuse him, if he realizes his mistake and longs sincerely again for God's love.

"But you see," Master continued, "one shouldn't display spiritual powers publicly. Not many years ago there was a yogi in India who used to demonstrate, before large gatherings, an ability to swallow deadly poisons without any ill effect. One day he forgot to prepare his mind in advance, and the poison began to take its toll. As he lay dying, he confessed, 'I know this is my punishment for displaying those powers so openly before others.'

"A master may, however, reveal more divine power to his disciples." Master went on to speak of his guru, and of the miracles Sri Yukteswar had occasionally displayed.

"There was a loose tile on the roof of his ashram in Puri," Master recalled with a smile. "I wanted to fix it, as I was afraid it might fall down and hurt somebody. But my master showed not the slightest concern. 'Don't worry about it,' he told me nonchalantly. 'As long as I am alive, it will remain up there.' It stayed there until the day of his death, some twenty years later. On that very day, it fell to the ground!"

One day we discussed the strictness of Sri Yukteswar's discipline in training his disciples. "He didn't want disciples," Master remarked. "Few could take his penetrating insight into their weaknesses—an insight which he never hesitated to reveal! But because I remained loyal to him, I found God. By converting me, he converted thousands."

"Master," I inquired, "might Sri Yukteswar's strictness have been due to his foreknowledge that he wouldn't be returning to this material plane of existence, since his work now is on a high astral plane? Was it not that most of his real disciples were free already, and he was simply being careful not to assume responsibility for any new ones?"

"That's right," Master replied. "He had a few stragglers this time, that's all."

On other occasions Master told us that he himself had in fact attained liberation "many incarnations ago."

"Sir," I asked him one day, "how long have I been your disciple?"

"Well, it has been a long time, that's all I will say."

"But does it always take so long?"

"Oh, yes," Master replied. "Desires for name and fame, etc., take them away many times, until they have learned all their material lessons in this school of life."

Could he, I wondered, have named those two faults because they had been, long ago, my own delusions? Possibly so, for what he predicted for my life now certainly pointed in the direction of attaining them, outwardly. If so, however, there was no answering twinge of recognition in my own heart. Name and fame, which have come to me in service to my Guru with the understanding of truth he awakened in me, I have found only minimally gratifying—the minimal part being that I am of course thrilled to have been of service to him, and to others. Still, at my present stage of life (eighty-two) I can look back and state with confidence that I have *never* done anything from a wish for personal recognition.

In his Gita commentary Yogananda stresses that, once the devotee sincerely longs for freedom, it is only a matter of time before that desire is fulfilled. Compared to the vast number of incarnations that the soul wanders in delusion before turning back toward its source in God, the sincere longing for liberation is hardly a step short of freedom itself.

Talk turned one afternoon to Sri Yukteswar's book, *The Holy Science*. "I find much of it abstruse," I confessed.

"Do you?" Mrs. Nealey showed surprise. "Why, I found it *very* easy to understand!"

Minutes later she left the room. Smiling, Master commented to me, "Even I, when I read that book, have to stop in places and think what it means!"

Conversation turned occasionally to the ways of masters. "People always want miracles from them," Master remarked. "They don't see that in a master's humility lies his greatest 'miracle.' The actions of true masters," he added, "though not easily understood by worldly people, are always wisdom-guided, never haphazard.

"A few years ago a so-called 'master' in India planned to visit this country. He wrote asking me if he might visit Mt. Washington on his way to a religious congress in the Midwest. Well, we prepared an elaborate banquet for him and fifteen of his disciples. We were actually awaiting his arrival when a telegram came from Honolulu. He had traveled all that distance, then suddenly received the 'inspiration' to turn around and go home again." Master chuckled. "No *master* would ever behave that way!"

He went on to discuss a number of other prominent religious figures, some of whom were truly great, and others perhaps less edifying than instructive in the examples they set.

"There was a black preacher named Father Divine, who claimed to be God. He wrote me that if we collaborated together, our success would be enormous. He had a high-backed chair, across the top of which was engraved the word, 'God.'" Master chuckled. "Someone once accused him of fraud. The judge hearing the case died unexpectedly of a heart attack." Laughing, Master concluded, "Father Divine commented sadly, 'I hated to have to do it!'"

Master then turned to more exalted recollections:

"I met a great saint on my trip to India in 1935," he said. "He is still alive. His name is Yogi Ramiah. He is a disciple of Ramana Maharshi, and a fully liberated soul. We walked hand in hand around the grounds at Ramanashram, drunk with God. Oh! If I had spent another half hour in his company, I could never have brought myself to leave India again!'"

(In 1960 I myself spent four days with Yogi Ramiah—Sri Rama Yogi, as he was known then. The visit marked a high point in my spiritual life. I've written about that visit in another book of mine, *Visits to Saints of India*.)

Master then spoke of his work in India, particularly his Ranchi school.

"The trouble with training schoolboys," he said, "is that most of them, when they grow up, return to a worldly life. It does good in the long run, for society needs the uplifting influence of a spiritual education, but when a great work like this is being started, it needs dedicated workers. From this standpoint, what we have here in America is much better. The people who come to us for training

An outdoor class at Master's school in Ranchi, Bihar, India. He believed that education should take place as much as possible in a natural setting.

want to devote their entire lives to God. In this way these teachings can be spread more easily." Here again he emphasized the importance to him of spreading his message. He had not come to America for the sake of only a few.

From time to time he talked of one or another of the disciples, always with a view to instructing me, by their example, in the right attitudes of discipleship—not only for my sake, but to help me in teaching others.

"I was disciplining Michael," Master said one afternoon, referring to one of the monks, "and Dorothy Taylor took pity on him. She felt I was being too hard on him. Michael, touched by her sympathy, began to feel a little sorry for himself. But then I said to him, 'You know, there is a saying in India: She who loves you more than your own mother is a witch! I am your mother. Wouldn't I know what was best for my own child?' After that he was all right."

Referring again to Miss Taylor, Master continued, "She has always been very obliging by nature; she would agree with anyone on almost any matter, simply out of good will. One day I said to her, 'If someone were to come to you and say, "Yesterday I saw Yogananda dead drunk, staggering down Main Street," you would look wide-eyed and reply, "Is that so?" I know you wouldn't believe it. But don't you see that you must be courageous in your convictions? To "stand up" for what you believe in is an important sign of loyalty.'"

Another day, referring again to the need for courage in one's convictions, Master said, "My earthly father, out of a twinge of jealous attachment to me, attempted to criticize Master [Sri Yukteswar] to me one day for something trivial he had heard about him. I looked him straight in the eyes. 'Of all things!' I cried. 'The physical birth you gave me is something, but the spiritual birth my Guru has given me is infinitely more precious! If ever I hear you say one more word against him, I will disown you forever as my father!' After that he always spoke of Master very respectfully."

Referring to the need for attunement with the Guru, Master said to me one day, "Look at Mr. Black, and then look at Saint Lynn. I asked both of them to come and visit our colonies whenever they could, so as to maintain that spiritual contact. Saint Lynn has come out every opportunity he could get, and has spent hours in meditation on the lawn in Encinitas. But Mr. Black never came. He could easily have done so, had he wanted to. He thinks he can get there by himself. But he will find out. Spiritually he is very advanced, but he is bogging down. He knows there is something the matter, but doesn't know what it is. Attunement with Guru, you see, is essential, and it must be on all levels."

Smiling, Master then discussed a certain student, Virginia Scott, whose attunement with him had never, I gathered, been deep on *any* level, though she was one of his "editors." "Whenever I say anything to her, a few days pass, and then back comes a letter, *pages* long, explaining all the ways in which I have misjudged her!"

Other monks came out on weekends, and sometimes for longer visits. To a group of us one day Master told of an amusing occurrence during his months of dictation. Jerry Torgerson had taken a notion to cover the roof of Master's house with concrete. It was an outrageous idea, but Jerry had insisted, over Master's objections, that such a roof would endure forever. "I then told him to finish the job right away," Master continued, "but Jerry said, 'It will be all right. I know what I am doing.'" Master was laughing. "First he put tar paper down on the roof. Then he nailed chicken wire over it. At this point the roof was a complete sieve: Hundreds of nails were sticking through it. 'Hurry up!' I urged. But Jerry saw no reason to rush things.

"Well, presently a huge storm came. Pots and pans were put out frantically in every room. Water dripped everywhere. The house was like a shower bath!

"But there were two rooms in which no water fell: my dictation room, and my bedroom. The roof over these two was as much a sieve as over the rest of the house, but Divine Mother didn't want my work to be interrupted. Only at the very end of the storm, one drop fell into a bucket in the dictation room, and another one onto my bare stomach in the bedroom as I lay relaxing on the bed. That was Divine Mother's way of having a little fun with me!"

Jerry, who was present, said, "I'm sorry I'm so stubborn, Sir."

"Well, that's all right," Master spoke consolingly. "I attract stubborn people!"

"He has great love," Master said to me later of Jerry. "That is what changes people."

Looking at Henry one day, Master told us, "Henry dug the cesspool near this house. He kept digging, digging all day long without ever stopping to see how far he had gone. By evening, to his surprise, he found he had dug a deep hole. That," Master went on approvingly, "is the way to seek God—continuously digging, digging, without looking to see how far one has come. Then suddenly one day he will see: 'I am there!'"

One weekend Mrs. Harriet Grove, the leader of the SRF center in Gardena, California, came out, uninvited, with James Coller to see Master. Not knowing where his retreat was, she found it by pure intuition. ("Turn left here," she told James, who was driving. "Turn right there." Then suddenly: "Stop! This is it." And so it proved to be.)

"This is the afternoon," Master told her when she arrived, "that I usually go out for a ride in the car. But I knew you were coming, so I stayed home."

"Master," James said that weekend, "I have such a great longing for God. Why does He take so long in coming?"

"Ah!" Master replied with a blissful smile, "that is what makes it all the sweeter when He does come! Such is His romance with the devotee."

"Sir," said Debi, anxious for a taste of such longing, "give me the grace of devotion."

"You are saying, 'Give me the money, so I can buy what I want.' But I say, No, first you have to *earn* the money. Then I will give it to you so you can buy what you want."

In the evenings, Master exercised by walking slowly around his retreat compound. Generally he asked me to accompany him. He was so withdrawn from body-consciousness on those occasions that he sometimes had to lean on my arm for support. He would pause, swaying back and forth as if about to fall.

"I am in so many bodies," Master remarked to me one day, as he returned slowly to body-consciousness, "it is difficult to remember which body I am supposed to keep moving."

Boone visited Twenty-Nine Palms for a short time. Accompanying Master and me one evening on our walk, he asked many questions concerning spiritual matters.

"You shouldn't talk to me when I am in this state," Master said finally. The deepest wisdom, he was implying, is beyond words; it must be experienced in the silence of inner communion. But when he did speak, his words during those days were filled with a wisdom rarely to be found in books. At such times he would remind me, "Write my words down. I don't often speak from this level of impersonal wisdom." More and more, from this time onward, he began to speak not as a humble devotee of God, but as one whose consciousness was saturated with the ultimate realization: *"Aham Brahm asmi—*I am Spirit!"

One evening, Master was doing energization exercises by the garage with Boone and me. Boone asked him about a certain saint who had appeared to him once in Encinitas. "Who was he, Master?"

"I don't know to whom you're referring," Master replied.

"It was out in the back garden, Sir, on the bluff above the ocean."

"Well, so many come," Master said. "I often see them. Some have passed on; others are still on this earth."

"How wonderful, Sir!" I exclaimed.

"Why be surprised?" Master replied. "Wherever God is, there His saints come." He paused a minute or two while he did a few exercises. Then he added:

"Yesterday I wanted to know about the life of Sri Ramakrishna. I was meditating on my bed, and he materialized right beside me. We sat side by side, holding hands, for a long time."

"Did he tell you about his life?" I inquired.

"Well, in the interchange of vibration I got the whole picture."

After Master's passing, the first part of this conversation was published, along with many other sayings I and others had recorded, in a book of his sayings called, *The Master Said*. Laurie Pratt, the editor, changed Master's words here to read, "Wherever a devotee of God is, there His saints come." The problem with her version was obvious: I, too, after all, am a devotee of God, yet I make no claim to have been so pestered! Tara was concerned lest readers fault him for a seeming lack of humility. (In fact, I learned in time that his way of speaking to us monks tended to be more impersonal than it was to the nuns.) I can assure the reader, however, that what he actually said was, "*Wherever God is*, there His saints come."

One evening Master was walking around his compound with Boone and me. He was holding onto Boone's arm for support. After a few minutes he stopped.

"Hot!" he remarked, switching from Boone's arm to mine.

Boone at this time was going through a period of temptations that, alas, ended up taking him off the path.

During this time also, Master gave me much personal advice.

"Your life is to be one of intense activity," he told me one evening, "and meditation. Your work will be lecturing, editing, and writing."

"Sir," I protested, "you yourself have written so much already. How can more writing possibly be needed?"

"How can you say that?" My question surprised him. "*Much* yet remains to be written!"

Some months later I addressed him further on this subject. "Master," I said, "Mrs. Nealey has suggested to me that I write a book explaining how I was drawn onto the path—somewhat like Thomas Merton's *Seven Storey Mountain*. It might help many people, she says. Would you like me to write it?"

"Not yet," Master replied. As we discussed the idea further, I understood that he was implying that he did want me to write such a book, in time.

"You have a great work to do," he emphasized again one afternoon, as we were taking a short walk on his retreat grounds. "You must therefore be conscious of how your words and actions affect others." He was trying to get me to combine childlike simplicity with the dignity of one who was centered in the inner Self—a difficult combination, it seemed to me at the time. My inclination was to speak boldly of my failings, and to present myself as having few, if any, virtues—all in the name of humility. This behavior, Master implied, was neither dignified nor necessary to the development of humility. To achieve perfection, one must dwell on the *thought* of it while recognizing it as God's gift, and not as a personal accomplishment. Master set out to correct this flaw in me. As he told me one day, "There must be neither superiority nor inferiority complex. Just tell yourself, 'All is God.'"

"Sir," I asked him one day, "would you prefer for the other monks to call me Walter?" They had been calling me Don.

"They should call you *Reverend* Walter." In dismay (we monks never addressed our ministers as "Reverend"), I tried hastily to change the subject, but Master persisted: "It is not that one disciple is better than another, but in an army there have to be captains as well as privates. You must accept respect from others as proper to your position."

This was, I confess, one piece of advice that I found so difficult to accept that I hastily put it aside, as though he'd never given it.

One day I was sitting in Master's dictation room, waiting while he worked on a few pages of his Gita manuscript. While he wrote, his whole mind gravely focused on the task at hand, I gazed at him lovingly and thought with deepest gratitude how wonderful it was to be his disciple. When the editing work before him was finished, he asked me to help him to his feet. Rising, he held my hands for a moment and gazed with joy into my eyes.

"Just a bulge of the ocean!" he said, softly.

In his Gita commentaries he had compared God to the ocean, and individual souls to its innumerable waves. "God is the Sole Reality manifesting through all beings," he had written. I could see from his loving remark that he wanted my love to expand and embrace the whole Ocean of Spirit, of which his body was but a tiny wave.

CHAPTER 32

"I Am Spirit"

Yet hard the wise Mahatma is to find,
That man who sayeth, "All is Vasudev!"*

THIS PASSAGE FROM Sir Edwin Arnold's translation of the Bhagavad Gita was often quoted by Master as an expression of the supreme truth that God alone exists.

A beautiful story on this subject was told me in 1960 by Yogi Ramiah, the saint of whom Master had said that, had he spent another half hour in the yogi's company, he would not have been able to leave India again:

Namdev [said Yogi Ramiah], a famous saint of Maharashtra, used to worship Krishna in his local temple with so much devotion that the Lord often appeared to him in vision. Namdev was revered by many devotees, who came from great distances to sit at his feet.

In his village there was also another saint, a potter by profession. Like Namdev, this potter was widely reputed to have seen God. One day a large crowd assembled in the temple to celebrate an annual spiritual festival. Many of those present were devotees of Namdev. Partway through the proceedings, the potter, acting on some divine whim, decided to test the spiritual caliber of each of the assembled worshipers.

A potter tests the soundness of his wares by rapping on them with his knuckles. From the sound emitted he can tell whether or not a pot is cracked. With this practice in mind, Namdev's fellow saint went about, slapping the assembled devotees. Because they held him in high esteem, no one complained; it was assumed that this peculiar

---

* Vasudev: Krishna. In this context the reference is to God, the Supreme Spirit. (Bhagavad Gita VII:19)

behavior was intended as some sort of spiritual lesson. When the potter-saint slapped Namdev, however, Namdev was incensed. Wasn't he this man's spiritual equal?

"Why did you hit me?" he demanded indignantly.

Calmly the potter stood up and announced, "There seems to be a crack in this pot!"

Everyone laughed. Later, Namdev, stung to the quick, went into the temple and prayed, "Lord, You know I love You. Why did You allow me to be so humiliated before my own devotees?"

"But what can *I* do, Namdev," said the Lord, appearing to him. "There *is* a crack in that pot!"

"Lord!" cried Namdev, prostrating himself full-length on the floor before the image, "I want to be worthy of You. Won't You show me the way to perfection?"

"For that you need a guru, Namdev."

"But I behold *You*, the Lord of the universe! Of what use would a guru be to me?"

"I can inspire you through visions," the Lord replied. "I can even instruct you. But I can't lead you out of delusion except through the medium of one who knows Me, for such is My law."

"Lord, won't You then at least tell me who my guru is?"

The Lord gave Namdev the name of a certain saint, and that of the village in which he lived. "He will be your guru," the Lord said. He added with a smile, "but don't be surprised if he seems a bit peculiar. That is just his way."

Namdev went to the village named by Krishna, and made inquiries as to the saint's whereabouts.

"That lunatic?" laughed the villagers. "Who would want anything to do with *him*?" It is a practice of some saints, you see, to protect themselves from curiosity seekers by strange behavior. But when Namdev pressed the villagers further, they replied offhandedly, "Oh, you'll probably find him somewhere around the temple. He usually spends his time there."

Namdev went to the temple. No one was in the courtyard, but when he entered the temple he found a wild-looking, disheveled old man carelessly sprawled on the floor. "Surely *this* can't be my guru," he thought anxiously.

A moment later, the question faded from his mind. For to his horror he noticed that the old man's feet were resting on a *Shiva Linga.** Furious at this act of desecration, he strode over and ordered the man at once to shift his feet.

The old man opened his eyes drowsily. "You see, my son," he replied, "my difficulty is that I'm old. This body is no longer so easy for me to move. Would you do me the favor of moving my feet to some spot where there is no *Linga*?"

Namdev hastened to oblige. He was about to set the old man's feet down in a new spot, when he saw directly underneath them another *Shiva Linga*! He shifted them again; a third *Linga* appeared. Yet again: a fourth *Linga*. Suddenly, understanding dawned: This man was indeed his guru! Prostrating himself humbly before him, Namdev prayed for forgiveness.

"I was blind, Gurudeva!"† he cried. "Now I know who you are, and I understand what it is you've been trying to teach me."

With calm majesty then, the old man rose to his feet. "God is everywhere, Namdev," he said. "Realize Him in yourself, and with transformed vision behold Him residing in all things!" The Guru struck Namdev gently on the chest over the heart. Breath left the disciple's body. Rooted to the temple floor, Namdev stood as if transfixed, unable to move a muscle. His consciousness, like rising waters in a lake, burst the frail dam of his body. In fluid light it streamed outward in all directions, embracing temple precincts, the village, the whole of India! Nations, continents, oceans became absorbed by his expanding bliss. At last it included the entire world, solar systems, galaxies! In every speck

---

* An emblem sacred to God in the aspect of Shiva, Destroyer of delusion. The *Shiva Linga*, usually considered an abstract representation of the male phallus, is never literally thought of that way by devout Hindus. Western scholars have erred in claiming that the *Linga* symbolizes male sexuality, and that its worship signifies the worship of sex. In fact, Shiva, in classical mythology, is depicted as the Supreme Renunciate. To Hindus, the *Linga* represents, rather, the universal masculine *principle*, which in human nature manifests through such qualities as strength, determination, and wisdom—as distinct from their feminine counterparts: tenderness, adaptability, and love.

On a more esoteric level, the *Linga* represents also the human spine, through which the life force (*prana*) must flow upward to the brain for the yogi to achieve the state of divine union. The *Shiva Linga*, in fact, depicts in stone a state of expanding awareness that occurs as, in meditation, the life force begins to withdraw from the senses into the spine.

† "Divine Guru," a customary appellation of love and respect for his guru on the part of the disciple.

of space he saw God alone: unending light, bliss infinite! Too deeply absorbed for mere amazement, he realized that all this was *He*!

From that day onward Namdev lived immersed in the divine consciousness. He wandered about the countryside, intoxicated day and night with fathomless bliss.

One day, many months later, he happened to be in the vicinity of his old village. Passing the temple where he had first worshiped God, he entered and sat for meditation. Again the Lord appeared to him as of old, in the form of Krishna.

"My child," said Krishna, "for so many months you have neglected Me—you, who never failed to worship here a single day! I have missed you. Where have you been?"

"My Beloved," cried Namdev, smiling happily at the Lord's playfulness, "how could I think of coming here to see You, when everywhere I gaze I behold Your formless presence!"

Blissfully, then, the Lord replied, "Now there are no cracks in that pot!"

The "crack" in Namdev's "pot" had been his awareness of himself as a separate ego, distinct from all others. In cosmic fact, our egos are nothing but vortices of conscious energy that, within the vast ocean of consciousness, take on the appearance of having a separate reality of their own, like the eddies of water in a brook.

Before this world was formed, when its atoms were drifting about in infinite space, there were no distinctions of the forms and substances that man has come to look upon as reality. There were no trees, mountains, or rivers, no animals, no people—only nebulous gasses. Someday, so astronomers tell us, the material forms we know will once again become gasses. Considering their amorphous past and future, material forms are clearly not real in any fundamental sense. They exist, yes, but their reality is not what it seems.

In the last analysis, as unreal as are all these forms we see around us, so also are our egos. Spiritual evolution reaches its culmination when our separate vortices of ego in the greater stream of consciousness merge at last into Infinity.

If human consciousness were a substance, with weight, shape, and texture—in other words, if it were the product of a mere coalescence of atoms—then consciousness would certainly be as impermanent as those objects are, and would cease to exist after the body's dissolution. Matter itself, however, so modern physics tells us, is insubstantial; it is produced by a subtler reality, energy. This being the case, the progression from subtler to grosser suggests that consciousness, which is the subtlest reality of all, cannot be the outgrowth of the grossest: matter. Yogis nowadays find support for their teachings from a growing number of physicists who also endorse this natural progression; physicists state that, as matter is a manifestation of energy, so energy must in its turn be a manifestation of consciousness.

To our limited minds, the definitions of things and the things themselves seem almost interchangeable. In fact, however, definitions only place limits on our understanding. Infinite consciousness is a state of being in which all definitions cease to exist. Indeed, nothing is left to be defined! Self-definitions, too, are dissolved. As the eddy, when a stream absorbs it, continues to exist as flowing water, so the vortex of emotions and self-definitions simply enters the great flow of consciousness. Self-awareness expands to infinity.

If our egos were dissolved (we ask ourselves) and if our little awareness merged into cosmic consciousness, wouldn't this loss of self-awareness spell the death of *all* awareness, at least as far as we ourselves were concerned?

How cumbersome are the ways of logic! The answer, of course, is, Yes, the loss of self-awareness *does* spell the death of awareness *as far as we ourselves are concerned*. For there remains no "we ourselves" to be concerned! But loss of egoic self-awareness in no way spells for us the loss of awareness itself.

Alfred Lord Tennyson, the great English poet, wrote in his *Memoirs*: "A kind of waking trance—this for lack of a better word— I have frequently had, quite up from boyhood, when I have been all alone. This has come upon me through repeating my own name to myself silently, till all at once, as it were out of the intensity of the consciousness of individuality, individuality itself seemed to dissolve and fade away into boundless being, and this not a confused state but the clearest, the surest of the surest, utterly beyond words—where death was an almost laughable impossibility—the loss of personality (if so it were) seeming no extinction, but the only true life." On another occasion he added, "It is no nebulous ecstasy, but a state of transcendent wonder, associated with absolute clearness of mind."

Great yogis aver that with the complete loss of self-awareness, the seeker's consciousness merges with the ocean of infinite consciousness; *self-consciousness itself becomes infinite.* Physical death alone cannot bring us this state, for at death we shed only the physical body, but keep the astral body and, with it, egoic awareness. Only by meditation and self-transcendence in the vastness of superconsciousness can we win final release from the limitations we impose on ourselves by our egos. In cosmic consciousness we discover that our true Self is infinite. This, and this only, is the real meaning of that expression, so much abused nowadays: Self-realization.

One day at Twenty-Nine Palms, while Master was revising his Bhagavad Gita commentaries, he asked Dorothy Taylor to read sections of it to a group of monks who had come from Mt. Washington. During her reading, Miss Taylor came to a passage that described the state of oneness with God. Once the devotee attains this divine state, Master had said, he realizes that the Ocean of Spirit alone is real. God took on the appearance of the little ego and then, after some time, withdrew that wave into Himself again. In effect, the dream-child wakes up in cosmic consciousness to find himself God once more.

However, Master went on to explain, the enlightened being, after attaining that consciousness, never says, "I am God," for he sees it was the vast Ocean which became his little wave of ego. The wave, in other words, when referring to its little self, would never claim to be the Ocean.

At this juncture Debi, who was present, cried excitedly, "But Sir, if you are one with that Ocean, that means you are God!"

"Why *I*?" Master asked. "Say *'He.' He* is God."

"But still, Sir, you are one with Him, and He is the only reality. That means *you*, too, are God."

"But this body isn't God!"

"You aren't identified with your body, Sir, so one may still say that you are God."

"Well, in that case why do you say, 'You'? *You*, too, are that! In a discussion of this sort, it is less confusing if we say, 'He.'"

"But what's the difference?"

"The scriptures say . . ." Master began.

"It's only your humility, Sir," Debi broke in, "that makes you distinguish between yourself and Him."

"Well, how can there be humility when there is no consciousness of ego?"

Triumphantly Debi cried, "But if you have no ego left, that means you *are* God!"

Master laughingly continued the earlier statement, which Debi had interrupted: "The scriptures say, 'He who knows Brahma becomes Brahma.'"*

"There!" cried Debi. "You said it yourself!"

Master rejoined, still laughingly, "*I* didn't say it. It's the scriptures that say so." Master, that is to say, would not identify those words with the human body that was speaking them. It was in his overarching spirit that he saw himself one with the Infinite. But Debi was unable to make this mental leap from a pure expression of Infinity to Infinity Itself.

"You quoted those scriptures, Sir," he reminded Master relentlessly. "That means you agree with them!"

Recognizing that the distinction was, perhaps, too subtle to be easily grasped, Master concluded, "Well, he who says he *is* God, isn't God. And," he added with a smile, "he who says he isn't, isn't!"

And there the subject rested, amid general laughter.

Liberation from ego does not come with the first glimpses of cosmic consciousness. Present, at first, even in an expanded state of awareness, is the subtle memory: "I, the formless but nevertheless still real John Smith, am enjoying this expanded state of consciousness." The body is immobile in this trance state; one's absorption in God, at this point, is called *sabikalpa samadhi*, or qualified absorption, a condition still subject to change, for on one's return from this lower *samadhi* one assumes once again the limitations of ego.

* *Mundaka Upanishad.*

By repeated absorption in the trance state, however, the ego's hold on all its self-definitions is gradually broken, and finally the realization dawns: "There is no John Smith to go back to. I am Spirit!" This is the supreme state: *nirbikalpa samadhi*, or unqualified absorption—a condition changeless and eternal. If from this state one returns to body-consciousness, he does so no longer with the consciousness of being separate or different from the ocean of Spirit. John Smith no longer exists: It is the eternal Spirit, now, which animates his body, eats through it, teaches through it, and carries on all the normal functions of a human being. This outward direction of energy on the part of one who has attained *nirbikalpa samadhi* is sometimes known also as *sahaja*, or effortless, *samadhi*.

Divine freedom comes only with the attainment of *nirbikalpa samadhi*. Until that stage, the ego can still—and alas, sometimes does—draw the mind back down into delusion again. Only with *nirbikalpa samadhi* does one become what is known as a *jivan mukta*, free even though living in a physical body.

A *jivan mukta*, however, unimaginably high though his state is, is not yet *fully* emancipated. The thought, "I am John Smith," has been destroyed. He can acquire no new karma, since the post of ego to which his karma was tied has been destroyed forever. There remains even now, however, the *memory* of all those prior existences: John Smith in thousands, perhaps millions of incarnations—John Smith the onetime bandit, John Smith the disappointed musician, John Smith the betrayed lover, the beggar, the swaggering tyrant. All those old selves must be made over, their karma spiritualized and released into the Infinite.

"Very few saints on earth have achieved final liberation, becoming *siddhas*, or perfected beings," Master told me one day.

I marveled. "What about all those great saints in your autobiography, Sir? Are they all dead, leaving none to replace them?"

"Great though many of them certainly were, very few had attained final liberation—only Babaji, Lahiri Mahasaya, Sri Yukteswar, and a few others. Many, however, had attained *nirbikalpa samadhi*, the highest state of consciousness. They were true Christs. Two of Lahiri Mahasaya's disciples attained full liberation: Swami

Pranabananda ('the saint with two bodies') and Ram Gopal Muzumdar ('the sleepless saint')."

"What about Swami Keshabananda?"[*]

"Keshabananda was too much attached to miracles. Lahiri Mahasaya often scolded him for it."

"What about your own father, Sir?"

"Oh, no! He was a great soul, but he was still attached to us as his sons."

"And Therese Neumann?"

"She has attained a high state, but isn't yet fully liberated."

"Was Badhuri Mahasaya, 'the levitating saint,' liberated?"

"He was a true master, but no, not he either. It is very difficult to reach complete liberation."

"And Trailanga Swami? I had the impression he was an *avatar*."[†]

"No, an *avatar* comes with a special mission. Trailanga Swami was a *jivan mukta*—a great master, but not yet fully liberated."

"What about Mataji, the sister of Babaji. *She*, surely, is liberated isn't she? Yet you wrote that she was 'almost' as spiritually advanced as her brother."

"Well then, that means she wasn't yet fully liberated." Master paused, then added, "But she must be liberated, by now."

"Sir, why can't a master simply dissolve all his karma the moment he attains oneness with God?"

"Well," Master replied, "in that state you don't really care whether you come back or not. It is just like a dream to you then. You are eternally awake, merely watching the dream. You may go on for incarnations that way, or you may say, 'I am free,' and *be* free right away. It's all in the mind. As soon as you say you are free, then you're free."

Boone, who was present, had evidently missed the central point that the total freedom of which Master was speaking could be attained only *after* one had reached the highest *samadhi*. "But Sir," he objected, "if *I* said I was free, I wouldn't really *be* free, would I?"

---

[*] An advanced disciple of Lahiri Mahasaya mentioned in *Autobiography of a Yogi*.

[†] A "divine incarnation." The term is used to describe one who came into this birth already completely emancipated from all past karma.

"Oh, yes! That is, you would be if you said it in the *consciousness* of freedom. But you've answered your own question: You've said, 'I *wouldn't* be.' The trouble is, the mind is already poisoned by the very delusions it is trying to dispel; it lacks force." Master went on to tell a story to illustrate his point.

"A man who was being troubled by a demon searched the scriptures for a way to dispose of the evil entity. Finding the remedy, he recited certain words over a handful of powder, which he then threw onto the demon.

"'It won't work!' the demon laughed. 'Before you said your incantations over the powder, I got into it myself! How, then, could it affect me?'

"The mind, you see, is like that powder—already infected with the very 'demon' of ignorance it is trying to dispel."

Another time, however, referring to that degree of mental freedom which is a prior condition for even a glimpse of *samadhi*, Master said, "It is only the thought that we are not free that keeps us from actually being free. Merely to break that thought would suffice to put us into *samadhi*! *Samadhi* is not something we have to *acquire*. We have it already!" Master added, "Dwell always on this thought: Eternally we have been with God. For a short time—for the fleeting breaths of a few incarnations—we are in delusion. Then again we are free in Him forever!"

When the soul attains final liberation, it becomes a *siddha* ("perfected being"), or *param mukta* ("supremely free soul"). Even in this state, individuality is not lost, but is retained in the memory of omniscience. The karma of John Smith's many incarnations has been released into the Infinite, but the *memory* of all those lifetimes, now spiritualized, remains an eternal reality in divine memory. The soul, however, once it attains this state of supreme liberation, rarely reactivates its remembered individuality, and *never* does so except at the command of the Divine Will.* When such a supremely free soul returns to this world, it comes only for the sake of humanity. Such an incarnation is called an *avatar*, or "divine incarnation."

---

* God never *forces* anyone to return. The Divine Will, in this case, operates through what Master described as the soul's "desireless desire" to bring liberation to others.

Such, Master told us, was Babaji, the first of our direct line of gurus. Such also were Lahiri Mahasaya—*yogavatar*, Master called him, or "incarnation of yoga"—and Swami Sri Yukteswar, whom Master identified as India's present-day *gyanavatar*, or "incarnation of wisdom."

"Sir," I asked Master one day at his desert retreat, "are *you* an *avatar*?"

With quiet simplicity he replied, "A work of this importance would have to have been started by such a one."

An *avatar*, he told us, descends to worldly birth with a divine mission, often for the general upliftment of mankind as well as the particular salvation of a few disciples. The *siddha*'s effort, by contrast, has necessarily been to unite his own consciousness perfectly with God's. God does not work through *siddhas* in the same way that He works through *avatars*. To *avatars* He gives the power to bring vast numbers of souls to freedom in God. *Siddhas* are given power only to liberate themselves and a few others.

"Master," I said once, "if Yogi Ramiah was fully liberated, did he, like his well-known guru, Ramana Maharshi, have disciples?"

"Oh, yes," Master answered. "He must have had. You must free others before you can become completely free yourself."

When I met this yogi in 1960, and observed how very few disciples he had, I asked him why many more hadn't come to absorb his divine wisdom. His reply was simple: "God has done what He wants to do with this body."

The lowest number that each soul must free before it can itself be raised to the state of *param mukta* is, I believe Master said, six.

Paramhansa Yogananda indicated that he had been sent into the world at a time of extraordinary spiritual need on earth. Debi once told me of a young Hindu friend of his who had come for a year of study in America and who, on his way over by ship, had had a vision of Master. The young man had never heard of Yogananda before. Several months later, Debi brought him to a Sunday service at Hollywood Church. When his friend saw Master, who was lecturing that day, he recognized him immediately as the saint of his vision.

"Sir," Debi inquired later, "my friend has his own guru in India. Why was he granted that vision of you?"

"Because," Master replied, "this work is a special dispensation of God."

An *avatar*, unlike most saints who are still engaged in winning their own final freedom from the coils of *maya*, may appear engagingly human and life-affirming. In his humanity, however, he offers mankind new insights into what it really means, in a spiritual sense, to be a human being. People commonly equate their humanity with weakness, not with strength. "I'm only human," is a common excuse for failure. People don't see that their humanity gives them the best possible reason for success! In the presence of a master, the term "human failing" translates itself to mean "the failure to be *fully* human."

A great woman saint in Kashmir, who lived several centuries ago, had the practice, unusual especially for a woman, of wearing no clothes. "Why don't you wear at least *something*?" demanded her scandalized countrymen. "Why should I?" she replied. "I don't see any men around." One day she learned that another saint, a man, was coming to see her. Hastily she sought clothes to don, for, at last now, a fully Self-realized human being, a true man, was coming to visit.

Though every great master is fully qualified to say with Jesus, "I and my Father are one," many descend occasionally from that absolute state, as Jesus did also, to enjoy a loving "I-and-Thou" relationship with the Lord. The Indian scriptures state that God created the universe "in order that He might enjoy Himself through many." The vast majority of His creatures, alas, have lost conscious touch with the infinite joy of their own being; can God, one asks, really enjoy Himself *through* their suffering? The saints alone, in their joyous romance with the Lord, fulfill this deep and abiding purpose of Creation by letting Him express His joy through their lives. The ending of every life's journey is supernal bliss.

Avatars and other masters often go through years of *sadhana* ("spiritual practice") during their youth, to set an example for others. If they didn't, their disciples might claim that meditation and self-effort are not necessary for God-attainment, or perhaps simply that such practices are not "their path."

"If you want God," Master used to say, "go after Him. It takes great determination and steadfast, deep effort. And remember, the minutes are more important than the years."

A great aid on the path, however, is the constant thought, "I am free already!"

"Memorize my poem '*Samadhi*,'" he once told us. "Repeat it daily. Visualize yourselves in that infinite state; identify yourselves with it. For *that alone* is what you really are!"

CHAPTER 33
"Original Christianity"

How does the concept of *samadhi* agree with the Christian teachings? Most churchgoers, certainly, get no hint on Sunday mornings that the Bible promises them anything like cosmic consciousness. The best they hope for is eternity in the astral world, which they think of as heaven—in India, named *Swarga*—after death, in a body similar to the one they inhabit now.

No one, however, has "a corner" on Christ's teachings, or for that matter on the teachings of any religion. The revelation that God gave to the world through Jesus Christ is the property of mankind, for it is truth itself, and it belongs to no church.

The mass of Christian worshipers is often referred to as "the body of Christ." In fact, however, it is more like Christ's family. For a body is responsive to the brain, whereas few Christians are conscious enough of Christ's presence within them, or faithful enough to his teachings, to give much thought to being *responsive* to him. A body, moreover, is coordinated by the brain, whereas Christians—even those who seriously try to obey Christ—respond to his commandments by rushing off in innumerable, often conflicting, directions. *Family*, then, is certainly the apter metaphor, for even if family members revere their head, they respond to him variously according to their different temperaments and levels of understanding.

A certain lack of coordination, which in a body might be a symptom of functional disorder, is both natural and, to some extent, right in a family. At any rate it shows that its members can think for themselves.

Most Christians in the world are like the family of a great man, some of whose luster reflects on them by association with him. But it is also notorious how many great men have been thoroughly *mis*-understood by their families and close relatives. To be the disciple of a great master gives one an incentive, certainly, to tune in to him, but it in no way *guarantees* that attunement. Jesus accused the Jews of misunderstanding Moses. He even chided his own close disciples for misunderstanding *him*. We must conclude, then, from his own state-ments that Christians have never had a *proprietary* claim on his full, or even his true, meanings. A disciple's understanding of his master's teachings depends on his own *capacity* for understanding, and not on his outward status as a member, nor even as a priest, minister of the Gospel, or other kind of leader in any church.

Many times progress has occurred in human understanding when one civilization was exposed to the different insights of another civi-lization. Islam's great early advances in mathematics were a result of her exposure to Indian civilization—a fact unknown by many scholars. Western civilization took a great leap forward with the Renaissance, owing to fresh exposure to the art and philosophy of Greece. The scattered earldoms of pre-medievel England were al-ternately swayed by invaders from Norway, Saxon Germany, and Denmark. They were molded into a single kingdom by the Norman Conquest of William, his conquest completed by his son Henry.

Religion, today, stands at the threshold of such an opportunity. The energetic influx of teachings from the East has already had a strong impact on Western thinking, causing many people to re-think their position on numerous basic issues. It has reminded them, among other things, of dormant traditions in their faith. The practice of meditation, for example, was once a vital part of Christian ob-servance—particularly in the Eastern Church—and is being revived because of the emphasis given it by teachers from India.

Nor has the influence of Oriental teachings on Christians and on the churches been limited to reminders of forgotten Christian tradi-tions: It has also shown many Biblical teachings in a wholly new light. For truth, like a diamond, is many-faceted. The teachings of Moses and Jesus Christ have received certain traditional emphases in the West, but other perfectly legitimate emphases are possible, and would reflect truths that, elsewhere in the world, have been cherished for centuries. Exposure to those foreign-seeming traditions might prove enormously beneficial to Westerners desirous of deeper insights into their own religious teachings.*

A visitor once asked Paramhansa Yogananda, "You call your temples 'churches of all religions.' Why, then, do you place such special emphasis on Christianity?"

"It was the wish of Babaji that I do so," the Master replied. "He asked me to interpret the Christian Bible and the Bhagavad Gita, or Hindu Bible, and to show that the teachings of both are basically the same. It was with this mission that I was sent to the West."

Many Westerners in this materialistic age have come to doubt the truth of Christ's teachings. Indeed, many of them even doubt that Jesus ever lived. Paramhansa Yogananda, by his example as much as by his teachings, turned agnostics into deeply believing Christians again. His mission, indeed, was not to convert anyone to Hinduism, but to revitalize the Christianity of Christians. He taught, he said, "the original Christianity of Christ."

* * * * * * *

One day in Boston, Massachusetts, Yogananda received a letter criticizing him for "sponsoring" Jesus Christ in the West. "Don't you know that Jesus never lived?" the writer demanded. "He was a myth invented to deceive people." The letter was left unsigned.

Yogananda prayed to be led to the writer. About a week later he was in the Boston Public Library. He saw a stranger there, seated on a bench by one of the windows, and went over, sitting next to him.

"Why did you write me that letter?" he inquired.

---

* At his Sunday worship services Yogananda would present deep truths from the Bible, then compare them to Krishna's teachings in the Bhagavad Gita. He also wrote a long series of articles about Christ's teachings, published in Self-Realization Fellowship's magazine under the title "The Second Coming of Christ." I have presented his teachings in two books of mine: *Revelations of Christ Proclaimed by Paramhansa Yogananda*, and *The Promise of Immortality: The True Teaching of the Bible and the Bhagavad Gita*, which consists of commentaries on parallel passages out of those two great scriptures.

The man started in amazement. "Wh-what do you mean? What letter?"

"The one in which you claimed that Jesus Christ is only a myth."

"But—how on earth did you know I wrote that?"

"I have my ways," the Master replied quietly. "And I wanted you to know that the power which led me to you enables me also to know for certain that Jesus Christ did live in Palestine, and that he was everything that the Bible claims for him. He was a true Christ, a Son of God."

Another time in Boston Yogananda received another remarkable corroboration of his experiences of the reality of Jesus Christ. In meditation he saw Krishna and Jesus walking together on a sea of golden light. To convince himself (as he put it), though more probably to convince skeptics, including sectarian believers who couldn't imagine Jesus and Krishna sharing the same wave, Yogananda asked for objective verification of his vision.

A divine voice replied, "The fragrance of a lotus will remain in the room."

"All that day," Yogananda told us, "a lotus aroma, unknown in the West, lingered on in the room. Many visited me throughout the day. 'What is that wonderful fragrance?' they asked. I knew then I had been given proof positive that what I had seen was true."

In St. Louis one day Master visited a Roman Catholic monastery. The abbot had seen Yogananda in meditation, and knew him for a great saint. The other monks were horrified to see this orange-robed "heathen" in their midst. When the abbot arrived on the scene, however, he hastened over and embraced Paramhansaji lovingly. "Man of God," he cried, "I am happy you have come!"

The saints alone are the true custodians of religion. For they draw their understanding from the direct *experience* of truth and of God, and not from superficial reasoning or book learning. The true saints of one religion bow to the divinity manifested everywhere, including of course to the true saints of other religions.

When Paramhansa Yogananda visited Therese Neumann, the great Catholic stigmatist in Bavaria, Germany, she sent word to him,

"Though the bishop has asked me to see no one without his permission, I will receive the man of God from India."

Yogananda, far from undermining the faith of Christians in their own scriptures, gave many of them renewed faith. One day a Catholic monk, inspired by an interview with him, begged him that in his prayers he be vouchsafed a vision of Jesus. The next day he came back to Yogananda with tears in his eyes. "Last night," he cried, "for the first time in my life, I saw Him!"

Oliver Wendell Holmes said, "To have doubted one's own first principles is the mark of a civilized man." By contrast, to hold any belief dogmatically is like saying, "This much I will have of truth, and no more." Dogmatism is the death of true understanding, and is the very antithesis of enlightened civilization. Again and again throughout history, dogmatism has stood in the way of progress and even of common sense. Consider a few examples:

In 1728 potatoes were introduced into Scotland. The clergy declared them an outrage, unfit for Christian consumption, because no mention is made of them in the Bible.

Again, when umbrellas were first invented, clergymen in many lands denounced them as the work of the Devil—for doesn't the Bible state clearly, "Your Father which is in heaven sendeth rain on the just and on the unjust"? (Matthew 5:45)

Nor is bigotry a monopoly of the West; as Yogananda often remarked, "Ignorance, East and West, is fifty-fifty." In a pilgrim's guide to South Indian temples I discovered this little gem of unreason: "Whosoever dares to spit on the temple grounds will be born for three successive incarnations as a tithiri bird." ("What," I asked an Indian friend of mine, "is a tithiri bird?" "Oh, some despicable creature," he replied vaguely; "something you wouldn't want to be.")

"Other sheep I have," Jesus said, "which are not of this fold." (John 10:16) Might it have been of true devotees in other great religions that he was speaking? We read in the tenth chapter of the Book of Acts: "God has no favorites, but in every nation he who reveres Him and acts righteously is accepted by Him." (Acts 10:34,35)

Christian fundamentalists, who insist that all authority rests in the Bible, quarrel endlessly over what the Bible really means. Luther and Zwingli, leaders of the Protestant Reformation, taught entirely on the basis of scriptural, as opposed to Church, authority. Yet the two of them disagreed on basic scriptural precepts. Their meeting at the Marburg Colloquy in 1529, which had been summoned to resolve these differences, resulted in a doctrinal clash between them. The meeting ended in failure.

It should surprise no one that the Bible means different things to different people. For is it not obvious that it cannot be accepted as authoritative *beyond each person's unique ability to understand*? Jesus said, "Therefore I speak to them in parables: because they seeing see not; and hearing they hear not, neither do they understand." (Matthew 13:13) Even after *explaining* his parable of the sower, he still went on to say, "Who hath ears to hear, let him hear." (Matthew 13:43)

And what is it that determines a person's ability to understand? Far more important than native intelligence is his actual experience of life—especially of the *inner* life. How else can truth be fully absorbed? Truths cannot be *learned*: they must be *recognized*.

A certain American Indian in the nineteenth century, lacking experience with modern machinery, was convinced that a steam locomotive was being operated by a horse cleverly concealed where the boiler appeared to be. Many clergymen, similarly, lacking personal experience of God's love, are equally certain that He is a God of wrath and vengeance.

Jean Danielou, the French cardinal-theologian, wrote, "That which saves is not religious experience, but faith in the word of God." True faith, however, without *some* kind of experience or inner grace, is simply not possible. Reason alone cannot banish doubts for the simple reason that reason dwells in the realm of doubts. Inferences cannot but be tentative. Only the breath of God's love in the soul awakens true faith in His word—as opposed to fanatical belief in it. The deeper the awareness—which is to say, the deeper the *experience*—of that love, the deeper the faith.

The great St. Anselm put it thus: "Who does not experience will not know. For just as experiencing a thing far exceeds the mere hearing of it, so the knowledge of him who experiences is beyond the knowledge of him who hears."

The tendency of spiritually blind theologians and ministers has been to take literally what was meant metaphorically, and to define Reality in terms of their own limited human knowledge of life. A supreme need in Christendom today is a more mystical approach to Truth.

In Calcutta I once met a Christian missionary who had passed through the Holy Land on his way to India. A few months earlier I had visited Galilee myself, traveling in the same direction as he, and with India too as my goal. I feel blessed even today by the experience I had of Christ's presence in the land of his birth. Imagining that this missionary and I shared a common bond in that feeling of blessing, I exclaimed, "Wasn't it wonderful! Jesus seemed so real, I almost expected to see him come walking down out of the hills!" The man stared at me a moment as though I were mad. After a moment, placing his chair conveniently between me and the door, he muttered nervously, "Yes, a beautiful country. Wonderful *history*." Communion with Christ, obviously, had nothing to do with his self-perceived mission in life.

The Roman Catholics, in their centuries-old tradition, have experienced the problems that can arise from individual interpretations of the holy scriptures. Their solution has been to insist that the Pope be their final authority in every such matter. Christ himself, they claim, gave him that authority with the words, "Thou art Peter, and upon this rock I will build my church." (Matthew 16:18) Their argument, however, though spiritually motivated, is fatally flawed. For how do we know that Christ actually *intended* to delegate such authority to them? We have only their word for it, supported by their insistence that, having been given such authority, they *must* have interpreted Christ's meaning correctly. Though this was the argument of Thomas Aquinas, and has been seized upon by Roman Catholics as the entire justification for their belief, it is in fact a perfect argument in a circle!

Paramhansa Yogananda's explanation of that same Bible passage was altogether different. Jesus, he said, was referring to the inner "church" of divine consciousness. He saw that, in Peter, he would be able to "build" this "church," for that disciple had recognized him as the living Christ, and had thereby demonstrated that his spiritual life was founded on the bedrock of divine intuition. Jesus' words—here, as everywhere else—were not meant institutionally. The point I've made here is very important, for Yogananda's interpretation removes the very cornerstone of Catholic theology.

Yet in one important sense the Roman Catholic Church is certainly right: Authority of *some* kind, in spiritual matters, is very much needed, lest the scriptures be misinterpreted in such ways as to reinforce, rather than banish, people's ignorance. It should be the right kind of authority, however, and not a case of the blind leading the blind. *The only valid authority on spiritual matters is true wisdom, based on true spiritual experience.* For such experience, we must look not to the commentaries of learned scholars and theologians, but to Self-realized saints. I repeat: *Only true saints can be the true custodians of religion.*

"The words of the saints," wrote St. Gregory of Sinai, "if they are carefully examined, never disagree; all alike speak the truth, wisely changing their judgments on these subjects when necessary."

Because it is necessary for the same fundamental truths to be presented according to the varying needs of the times, St. Simeon the New Theologian wrote, "A man who does not desire to link himself to the latest of the saints (in time), in all love and humility, owing to a certain distrust, will never be linked with the preceding saints, and will not be admitted to their succession even though he thinks he possesses all possible faith and love for God and for all His saints." All who know God drink from the same fountain. Therefore to reject *any* expression of Him is, to that extent, to reject God Himself.

Yogananda once prayed to Jesus Christ for reassurance that he was interpreting the Gospels correctly. Jesus appeared to him in a vision, along with the Holy Grail, and the Grail passed from his lips to Yogananda's. Jesus then, Yogananda later told us, spoke the following words of heavenly assurance: "The cup from which I drink, thou dost drink." These words were omitted from *Autobiography of* *a Yogi*, no doubt at the editor's insistence,* but Master himself often quoted them during his public sermons and lectures.

To return, then, to the question of Christian corroboration of the state of *samadhi*: It is to the saints that we must look first for guidance.

"The soul, when purified," wrote St. Catherine of Genoa, "abides entirely in God; its being is God."

"The soul must wholly lose all human knowledge and all human feelings," wrote St. John of the Cross, "in order to receive in fullness divine knowledge and divine feelings."

St. Catherine of Sienna stated that Christ had told her in a vision, "I am That I am; thou art that which is not." In other words, the little vortex of her ego had no abiding reality of its own.

St. Veronica Giuliani, the seventeenth-century Capuchin nun, concerning her experience of the supreme ecstasy of mystical union, wrote in her *Diary* that she had received a conviction, far deeper than any intellectual concept or belief, that *"outside of God nothing has any existence at all."*

The great St. Teresa of Avila wrote that, in this state, "the soul is entirely transformed into the likeness of its Creator—it seems more God than soul."

Blessed Henry Suso, describing the enlightened soul, wrote: "In such a person God is the very essence, the life, energy, and vital force. The man himself is a mere instrument, a medium of God."

St. Anselm wrote, "Not all of that joy shall enter into those who rejoice; but they who rejoice shall wholly enter into that joy."

Do not these quotations suggest persuasively that state of oneness with God which is known to Indian yogis as the highest *samadhi*? There are Christian writers (Dom Denys Rutledge, for example, in his pretentious book *In Search of a Yogi*) who claim that to the Christian an absorption of the ego into God would be undesirable. But is this a *Christian*, or merely a quite normal human reaction? Similar, in fact, is an objection one sometimes hears from worldly people to the joys of heaven: "How can heaven be all that wonderful, when it makes no provision for sex enjoyment?" (They

---

* Laurie Pratt it was who changed his words, which I'd quoted exactly, from, "Wherever God is" to "Wherever a devotee of God is" (see p. 380).

forget that, as children, they lived perfectly happily without sex.) But what do such ego-centered writers make of Jesus' own words, "Whosoever will save his life shall lose it: and whosoever will lose his life for my sake shall find it"? (Matthew 16:25) Paul Tillich, the great Protestant theologian, writing from the more expanded vision of a wise man, stated, "Endless living in finitude would be hell. . . . This has nothing to do with Christianity."*

Let us see what Christian saints have said further on the subject of *infinity* as a definition of divine awareness.

Meister Eckhart, a great mystic, said of souls that are merged in God, "By grace they are *God with God*."

"I, *who am infinite*," wrote St. Catherine of Sienna, "seek infinite works—that is, an infinite perfection of love."

St. Bernard wrote, "Just as a little drop of water mixed with a lot of wine seems entirely to lose its own identity, while it takes on the taste of wine and its color . . . so it will inevitably happen that in saints every human affection will then, in some ineffable manner, melt away from self and be entirely transfused into the will of God."

"A man who has attained the final degree of perfection," wrote St. Simeon the New Theologian, "is dead and yet not dead, but infinitely more alive in God. . . . He is inactive and at rest, as one who has come to the end of all action of his own. He is without thought, since he has become one with Him who is above all thought." How closely these words resemble Paramhansa Yogananda's description, in *Autobiography of a Yogi*, of his first glimpse of cosmic consciousness: "The flesh was as though dead, yet in my intense awareness I knew that never before had I been fully alive."

Of St. Simeon's experience of *samadhi*, his disciple, Nicetas Stathos, wrote: "Once, while offering up a pure prayer to God to be drawn into intimate converse with Him, he had a vision: Behold, the atmosphere began to shine through his soul, and though he was inside his cell, it seemed to him that he was lifted up high beyond its confines. It was then the first watch of the night. As this light from above began to shine like an aurora, the building and everything else disappeared, and he no longer believed himself to be in the house

* From his lecture "Symbols of Eternal Life."

at all. Quite outside himself, as he gazed with his whole soul at this light that had appeared to him, it increased bit by bit, making the atmosphere more brilliant, and he felt himself taken, with his whole body, away from the things of earth."

Saints, keenly aware of how impossible it would be to describe the Indescribable, usually speak of it in more or less vague terms. A few, however, have tried to suggest their experience in words.

"Divine darkness," wrote St. Dionysius, "is the unapproachable light in which God is professed to live."

And Basil the Great wrote, "Utterly inexpressible and indescribable is Divine beauty, blazing like lightning. . . . If we name the brightness of dawn, or the clearness of moonlight, or the brilliance of sunshine, none of it is worthy to be compared with the glory of True Light, and is farther removed therefrom than are the deepest night and the most terrible darkness from the clear light of midday."

The Bible, too, describes God in many passages as a great Light. The thirty-sixth Psalm states, "For with thee is the fountain of life: in thy light shall we see light."

St. Paul wrote, "For God, who commanded the light to shine out of darkness, hath shined in our hearts, to give the light of the knowledge of the glory of God in the face of Jesus Christ." (2 Corinthians 4:6)

Christ is spoken of in the Bible as "the only begotten son of God." Does this make us sons of God in a different sense from Jesus? Or has the term "the only begotten" a subtle, mystical meaning? On one side of this argument we have the judgment of orthodox theologians, but on the other that of great saints. Theologians contend that we are *radically* different from Jesus. But great saints have put it as a difference, rather, in the *degree* of Self-awareness. They say that we are, as St. Paul put it, sons by "adoption" only until the Divine Life courses through our veins. When that point is reached, "There is no difference," quoting Meister Eckhart, "between the only begotten son and the soul."

"The disciple is not above his master," Jesus said, "but every one that is perfect shall be as his master." (Luke 6:40) And, "Be ye therefore perfect, *even as your Father which is in heaven is perfect.*" (Matthew 5:48)

"If we are [God's] children," St. Paul wrote, "we share His trea-
sures, and all that Christ claims as his will belong to all of us as well!"
(Romans 8:17) Later in the same chapter Paul speaks of Christ in
relation to his followers as "the eldest of a family of many brothers."

In what way is Jesus Christ the "only begotten son of God"? Not
as a man, certainly. Nor yet as an individual soul. The very word
Christ is a title meaning "The Anointed of God." Christ is part of
the infinite Trinity,* an aspect of God Himself. Jesus was called "the
Christ" because his consciousness was identified with God's presence in all creation. The Christ is the *"only begotten* son" because
Christ consciousness is omnipresent. It is not personal at all in an
egoic sense. "I move my hand," said St. Simeon, "and Christ moves,
who *is* my hand."

"God," St. Paul wrote, "created all things by Jesus Christ."
(Ephesians 3:9) How could God have created the vast universe, with
its billions of galaxies, through a single, little being? That kind of
thinking was possible only in our days of ignorance as a civilization,
when God Himself was regarded as a bearded old Gentleman seated
on a golden throne somewhere high up in the sky. (Who, now, will
attempt to describe anything as "up," in cosmic terms?)

---

* Paramhansa Yogananda explained the Christian Trinity (God the Father, Son, and
Holy Ghost) in a cosmic sense. God the Father, he said, is the Infinite Consciousness from which all things were manifested. God's consciousness was one and un-
divided ("Hear O Israel, the Lord our God, the Lord is One"); apart from that
consciousness there was no substance out of which the universe could have been
made. The universe is His dream. To produce the dream, the Creator had to set
a portion of His consciousness into motion. You, I, our earth, the sun and galaxies,
our thoughts and inspirations, our very longing to be one with Him again—*all* are
products of the vibrations of His consciousness, separate manifestations of the vast
primal vibration of *Aum*, the Holy Ghost.

The Son of the Trinity represents the underlying presence in all vibratory creation
of the calm, unmoving consciousness of the Creator, so called because it reflects
the Father's consciousness. Vibratory creation itself is also known as the Divine
Mother. The devotee must commune first with *Aum*, or the Divine Mother. Uniting
his consciousness with that, he must proceed to realize his oneness with the Son.
Only after achieving union with the Son can he proceed toward oneness with the
Father beyond creation.

The Hindu scriptures name this eternal Trinity, *Sat Tat Aum*. *Sat* stands for the
Spirit, the Supreme Truth, which is God the Father. *Tat* is the *Kutastha Chaitanya*,
the Christ consciousness which underlies all creation. And *Aum* is the Word, the
Holy Ghost, called also the Comforter in the Bible.

"Is it not written in your law, I said, Ye are gods?" (John 10:34) Thus Jesus answered the Jews, when they accused him of blasphemy for telling them, "I and my Father are one." He didn't say, "My Father says so, and you'd better believe it or you'll go to hell!" He said, "*You* are that, too," and went on to explain that the only difference between them and him was that he had been "sanctified" by the Father, a fulfillment they had yet to achieve.

Jesus himself distinguished between his human self and the omnipresent Christ consciousness, with which he was inwardly identified. In both cases he used the pronoun "I," but the meaning differed according to his emphasis.* Speaking impersonally, he said, "I am the way, the truth, and the life: no man cometh unto the Father, but by me." (John 14:6) And again impersonally, "The Father judgeth no man, but hath committed all judgment unto the Son." (John 5:22) His reference here to the Son is to the Christ consciousness with which his own consciousness was perfectly identified. But when someone addressed him as "Good Master," he replied, reflecting then that person's consciousness of him as a man, "Why callest thou *me* good? There is none good but one, that is, God." (Matthew 19:17)

It was in his overarching spirit that Jesus could say truly, "Before Abraham was, *I am*." (John 8:58) It was from a consciousness of omnipresence that he said, "Where two or three are gathered together in my name, there am I in the midst of them." (Matthew 18:20) It was of his infinite Self, not his physical body, that he spoke when he said, "Whoso eateth my flesh, and drinketh my blood, hath eternal life." (John 6:54) It was to rebuke teachers who drew the devotion of their students to themselves, instead of directing it to the Infinite Christ, that he said, "All that ever came before me are thieves and robbers." (John 10:8) Had he been referring, as many Christians imagine, to the prophets before him *in time*, he would not have said also, "Think not that I am come to destroy the law, or the prophets: I am not come to destroy, but to fulfil." (Matthew 5:17)

---

* In the Hindu scriptures, too, the first person singular is often used to describe both the infinite consciousness of a master and the limited, ego-consciousness of an unawakened human being.

"Thou art *That*," say the Indian scriptures—"*Aham brahm asmi* (I am Brahman)." Christians who cannot imagine a higher destiny than eternal confinement in a little body would do well to meditate on the parable of the mustard seed, which Jesus likened to the kingdom of heaven. The mustard seed, he said, though tiny, grows eventually to become a tree, "so that the birds of the air come and lodge in its branches." (Matthew 13:32) Even so, the soul in communion with the Lord expands to embrace the infinity of consciousness that is God.*

And Christians who imagine themselves *inherently* sinful, rather than sinning under the influence of delusion, would do well to meditate on the parable of the prodigal son, whose *true* home was in God. And, if those Christians aspire to heaven, they might ponder these words of Jesus, "No man hath ascended up to heaven, but he that came down from heaven." (John 3:13)

Sectarian Christians have a difficult time explaining the Second Coming of Christ as an objective event in history. Consider these words of Jesus, "When you are persecuted in one town, take refuge in another; I tell you this: *before you have gone through all the towns of Israel* the Son of man will have come." (Matthew 10:23) And consider again these words, when Jesus was discussing his Second Coming: "Verily I say unto you, This generation shall not pass, till all these things be fulfilled." (Matthew 24:34) And how could "all the tribes of the earth see the Son of man coming in the clouds of heaven with power and great glory"? (Matthew 24:30) There would have to be millions of Christs on millions of clouds for all the nations to see him!

To great saints and yogis, these statements are perfectly clear, for to them it is obvious that what he was saying was that, in the cloud-like light of *inner* vision, he would come again at any time, anywhere, to souls whose hearts were pure and, therefore, receptive to his grace.

As Jesus put it, "Blessed are the pure in heart, for they shall see God." (Matthew 5:8)

---

* In what other way that makes sense can this passage be understood? Can anyone imagine an astral world, or universe, growing from a tiny seed "eventually to become a tree"? A literal interpretation, contrary to the very purpose of illustrations, would only obfuscate. It could not clarify.

CHAPTER 34

Kriya Yoga

"**B**LESSED ARE THE pure in heart, for they shall see God." The truth in these simple words has been acclaimed equally by great saints of East and West. It is a truth which every devotee would do well to ponder, for among the followers of all religions it is a common delusion that mere membership in a body of worshipers will be their passport to salvation. Yet Jesus didn't say, "Blessed are my followers, for they shall see God." His message was universal: By the yardstick of inner purity alone is a person's closeness to God determined.

What *is* purity of heart? Jesus defined it effectively, elsewhere, as the capacity to love God with all one's heart, soul, mind, and strength.* And why is this capacity called purity? Simply because we *belong* to God; worldliness is foreign to our essential nature.

How, then, can one achieve such purity? Is self-effort the answer? Is grace? St. Paul said, "By grace are ye saved through faith; and that not of yourselves: it is the gift of God: Not of works, lest any man should boast."† Christian fundamentalists often quote this passage as an argument against self-effort of any kind, and particularly against the practices of yoga. But the Book of Revelation states, "And, behold, I come quickly, and my reward is with me, *to give [to] every man according as his work shall be*."‡ Do these scriptural passages contradict one another? Not at all.

---

* Mark 12:30.

† Ephesians 2:8,9.

‡ Revelation 22:12; italics mine.

St. Paul didn't mean that self-effort is futile, but only that God is above bargaining. Outward "works" in God's name—works, in other words, such as building schools and hospitals—will not *in themselves* win His grace. It depends first of all on a person's *attitude*. Love alone can win Him. Like attracts like, and God *is* Love. But as for those inner efforts which lift the soul up toward God—especially the unconditional offering of trust and love—they are essential, else were the scriptures written in vain. It is to this internal "work" that the Book of Revelation is referring, above.*

To develop love for God, the first prerequisite is that no other desire divert its flow from Him. This, then, is our first spiritual "work": to renounce every desire that conflicts with our devotion. We need not so much *destroy* our desires as rechannel their energies Godward.

And it is in this true labor of love that the techniques of yoga are particularly helpful. Wrong desires, it need hardly be added, could never be transmuted by technique alone. But even as running techniques can be useful to those who hope to excel on the track field, so the techniques of yoga can help devotees to control their physical energies, and redirect them toward God. Yoga practice by itself won't give us God, but it *can* help us very much in our efforts to give *ourselves* to Him. The yoga science helps us, in other words, to *cooperate* with divine grace.

Take a simple example. Devotees naturally want to love God. Many, however, have no clear notion of how to go about developing that love. Too often their efforts are merely cerebral, and end, therefore, in frustration. Yet Jesus hinted at a *technique* when he said, "Blessed are the pure in heart." For, as everyone surely knows who has ever loved, it is in the *heart* that love is felt—not literally in the physical heart, but in the *heart center*, or spinal nerve plexus just behind that physical organ. Christian saints have stressed again and again "the love of the *heart*." And yogis claim that love is developed more easily if, instead of merely *thinking* love, one will

---

* In *The New English Bible*, St. Paul's words, "By grace are ye saved through faith," are rendered, "For it is by his grace you are saved, through trusting him." These words, *through trusting him*, help to emphasize the point that the *right kind* of self-effort *is* needed. For trust implies an active gift, and not a merely passive acceptance.

direct the feeling of love upward from the heart, through the spine, to the brain.

Take another example. Devotees, in their attempt to achieve inner communion with God, often find those efforts thwarted by restless thoughts. Yogis long ago discovered a technique for overcoming this obstacle. The breath, they said, is intimately related to the mental processes. A restless mind accompanies a restless breath. By simple, effective techniques for calming the breath, they learned how to free the mind for deeper divine communion.

Thus, the science of yoga, by its practical application of laws governing man's physical body and nervous system, helps one to become more *receptive* to the flow of divine grace, in much the same way that proficiency at playing the piano enables one to express musical inspiration freely. And divine communion, as St. Paul said, comes not by overtly "pleasing" God, but by making oneself fully *receptive* to His love. Divine Love *wants*, of its own nature, to give of itself.

In Chapter 32 I referred to the ego as a vortex of consciousness, which separates itself from the ocean of awareness by its own centripetal force. Once this vortex is dissolved, I said, self-awareness flows out to embrace infinity. At this point, however, I should explain that to speak of the ego as only one vortex vastly oversimplifies the case. The fact is, egoic awareness gives rise to countless millions of subsidiary vortices: eddies of likes and dislikes, which result in desires, which in turn lead to ego-motivated actions. Every such vortex draws energy to itself, and thereby reaffirms and strengthens the ego from which its energy is derived. Until a desire has been either fulfilled in action, or dissipated by wisdom, it may remain dormant in the subconscious, like a seed, for incarnations.

The stronger a mental tendency, the greater the egoic commitment. The amount of energy diverted toward these myriad commitments is incalculably great. Paramhansa Yogananda used to tell us, "There is enough latent energy in one gram of your body's flesh to supply the city of Chicago with electricity for a week. Yet you imagine yourselves powerless in the face of only a few difficulties!" The reason we are unable to tap more of our energy-potential is that most

of our energy has been already "spoken for"; it is absorbed by countless eddies of prior egoic commitment.

I had an interesting experience a few years ago relative to this ener-
gy-drain. Having, as I thought, seriously overextended myself in my
activities, I had reached a point of utter exhaustion. One evening I had
a class to give. I was visiting my parents. My mother, seeing how really
exhausted I was, urged me, "You *mustn't* punish yourself like this!
Really, this is one evening you simply have to cancel your class."

I couldn't do that, however. I didn't know how to reach all those
students and tell them not to come. Half an hour before leaving
the house, I lay down on my bed to rest. I didn't sleep, however;
instead, I reviewed in my mind as dispassionately as possible all
my reasons for feeling so very tired: the endless activities (daily lectures, classes, a weekly radio program, constant travel); an unceasing
stream of correspondence; constant telephone calls; numerous requests for interviews; incessant demands for personal decisions from
people who could have made just as good decisions on their own.
As I recalled to my mind each of these drains on my energy, my first
reaction was instinctively to reject it: "Oh, no—it's just too much!"

And then, in return, came the dispassionate challenge: "*Is* it? It's
a fact of your life now, whether you like it or not. Why not simply
accept it?" In each case, accepting this advice, I felt as though I had
closed some psychic door through which energy had been pouring
out of me in my anxiety to push the unwanted experience out of my
life. As each door closed, I found more energy welling up within me.

The results were extraordinary. By the end of that half hour my
fatigue had completely vanished, and I was fairly bursting with enthusiasm to give that class! My mother, seeing me now, exclaimed, "What
a wonderful sleep you've had. You look completely refreshed!"

Interestingly enough, the subject of my class that evening was
"Energization." It was perhaps the best class I have ever given on this
subject. Afterwards I still felt so full of energy that I stayed up until
two o'clock the next morning, talking to people after class, reading,
and then meditating.

And the energy that I rechanneled that day must have been only a small fraction of the energy preempted by millions of other vortices that had formed over many incarnations in my subconscious mind!

If only we could channel all our energy in a single direction—if only, for example, we could learn with our whole being to say *Yes* to life instead of mixing every "yes" with a "no" or a "maybe"—our powers of accomplishment would be greater than most people imagine possible. It is important, however, at the same time to channel our energy wisely. For if we use it to achieve goals that are external to our true nature, our very success will bring disappointment in the end.

To understand how to utilize the enormous amounts of energy rightly that would be available to us, once we knew how to access them, we must understand how energy functions in the body.

Energy's main channel is the spine. The spine, like a bar magnet, has its north-south orientation: the north pole being at the top of the head, to which the spiritual eye serves as a conduit; and the south pole, at the base of the spine in the coccyx. In a bar magnet, all the molecules, each with its own north-south polarity, are oriented in one direction. In an unmagnetized bar, the molecules, though similarly polarized, are turned every which way and thereby, in effect, cancel one another out. Most people, similarly, lack the dynamic power one associates with human greatness. They lack it not because they have less energy than the greatest genius, but simply because the "molecules" of their subconscious tendencies—desires and aversions, attachments—pull them in conflicting directions and thereby cancel one another out, even as do the molecules in an ordinary bar of metal.

A steel bar becomes magnetized not by the introduction of any new element, but simply by the realignment of its molecules. Human magnetism, similarly, depends on realigning in a single direction the "molecules" of tendencies and desires, so that they no longer conflict with, but support one another.

Limited power can be achieved, for a time, by directing at least some of our tendencies one-pointedly toward *any* goal. Many modern psychiatrists, in fact, recognizing this truth, recommend that people seek fulfillment by outwardly releasing their subconscious repressions. The deeper realities of human nature, however—and the way our very bodies, reflecting those realities, are made—make it impossible for us to bring *all* our "molecules" of subconscious tendencies into alignment until they all become adjusted to a north-south polarity in the spine. This is to say that every desire and aspiration must flow upward toward the "doorway" to the Infinite, the spiritual eye.

Likes, dislikes, and their resultant attractions and aversions, all of which induce desires and repulsions, are the root cause of our bondage. The progressive stages of involvement with *maya* may be traced through the progressive functions of human consciousness: *mon, buddhi, ahankara*, and *chitta*: mind, intellect, ego, and feeling.

Paramhansa Yogananda illustrated these basic functions by a horse, seen in a mirror. The mirror is the mind (*mon*), which shows us the image as it appears to us through the senses; the mind alone, however, cannot qualify or define that image.

Buddhi (intellect) then defines what is seen, informing our consciousness, "That is a horse."

Ahankara (ego) then appears, declaring, "That is *my* horse." Up to this point we are not necessarily yet bound by the thought of ownership; the identification, though personal, may still remain more or less abstract.

If, then, *chitta* (feeling) comes onto the scene, saying, "How *happy* I am to see my horse!" true ego-bondage begins. *Chitta* is our emotional reaction, including likes and dislikes, desires and aversions. It is the true source of ego-bondage, and the essence of all delusion.

Thus, the ancient classical exponent of the yoga science, Patanjali, defined yoga itself as "the neutralization of the vortices (*vrittis*) of *chitta*."*

Master once told me, "When I applied to the Maharaja of Kasimbazar for permission to transfer my school to his Ranchi property, he asked a group of pundits to test my knowledge of spiritual matters, since my request involved forming a religious institution. I could see those scholars all set for a theological bullfight, so I turned the tables on them. 'Let us talk only,' I said, 'of truths we have actually realized. An ability to quote scripture is no proof of wisdom.' I then asked them a question for which I knew no answer can be found in the scriptures.

---

* "*Yogas chitta vritti nirodh.*" *Yoga Sutras* 1:2. *Chitta* is usually translated "mind-stuff." Paramhansa Yogananda himself, in his autobiography, accepts this translation. But the translation fails in specificity, and I cannot but suspect that his editor supplied it, unnoticed by him, from other recognized translations. Yogananda himself, in a series of classes on Patanjali, and in private discussions with me, defined the word more exactly as I have given it here.

"*Vritti,*" moreover, doesn't mean "fluctuation," or "waves," as it is often translated, but "whirlpool," which more graphically describes drawing feelings inward to a center in the ego.

"'We read,' I said, 'of the four aspects of human consciousness: *mon, buddhi, ahankara,* and *chitta.* We also read that these four aspects have their respective centers in the human body. Can you tell me where in the body each center is located?' Well, they were completely stumped! All they knew was what they had read. I then explained, '*Mon* (mind) is centered at the top of the head; *buddhi* (intellect), at the point between the eyebrows; *ahankara* (ego), in the medulla oblongata at the base of the brain; and *chitta* (feeling), in the heart.'"*

"Blessed are the pure in heart," Jesus said, "for they shall see God." The teachings of the Galilean Master, and those of India's great yogis, were "cut from the same cloth" of Self-realization. Likes and dislikes in the heart manifest as vortices of desire and aversion. Only when these have been dissolved—in short, when the heart has been puri-fied of every downward-flowing tendency in the spine—can Self-realization be attained. The vortex of ego itself is then dissipated with relative ease, for without objective attachments the ego soon loses its centrifugal power, and is dispersed at last by the powerful upward flow of energy which accompanies divine inspiration.

Most efforts to transform oneself involve a laborious struggle to correct an endless array of individual faults—a tendency to gossip; over-attachment to sweets; physical laziness; anger; greed; and a host of other weaknesses. The devotee must of course fight his battles as they present themselves to him. To attempt to win the whole war in this piecemeal fashion, however, would be like trying separately to realign every molecule in a bar of steel. Purely psychological efforts at self-transformation are a never-ending task. Once one has finally succeeded in turning a few mental "molecules" in the right direction,

---

* I have referred earlier to the fact that love is experienced in the heart center. It may be of interest to note also that intense intellectual effort is often accompanied by a slight frown: evidence that energy is being directed to the point between the eye-brows. Again, note how pride tends to draw the head backward: a sign that energy is being focused in the medullary region. That is why we speak of a proud person as "looking down his nose" at others. A bow, on the other hand, which in every culture is a gesture of humility and respect, is suggestive of a release of tension in the medullary region.

there is no guarantee they'll remain that way after one leaves them to work on the next lot.

The way to magnetize a bar of steel is to cause its molecules to turn in a south-north direction. One way of doing so is to place it close to an already-magnetized bar. Spiritually speaking, a person can be magnetized, similarly, by the company and influence of saints, and particularly in close attunement with his own guru. For the guru's special job is to uplift his disciples' consciousness. Because his energy and awareness flow naturally up the spine toward the spiritual eye, attunement with him generates in the disciple a similar upward flow of energy and awareness.

Another way of magnetizing a bar of metal is to introduce into it an electric current flowing in a single direction. The guru's blessings, similarly, can be augmented by the disciple's own efforts. Any disciple, indeed, who relies only passively on the guru's blessings will make only halting progress. Man is, after all, not inert metal; he can and must cooperate in the process of his transformation. Moreover, he can and often does, by disobedience and unwillingness, resist the guru's influence. As Yogananda put it, "The path is twenty-five percent the disciple's own effort, twenty-five percent the guru's effort on his behalf, and fifty percent the grace of God." The guru needs the disciple's cooperation. And the disciple can cooperate best when he understands how this magnetic influence actually works in the body, raising subtle currents of energy through the spine to the brain. Cooperation with the guru's efforts, and with Divine Grace, means doing what one can, personally, to direct energy upwards through the spine.

The correlation between spiritual awakening and this upward flow of energy can be observed to some extent in ordinary human experience as well. Any increase of happiness or inspiration, for example, or any firm resolution to do something wholesome and positive, produces an upward flow of energy through the spine to the brain. One may even find himself standing or sitting more upright, holding his head higher, looking upward, turning the corners of his mouth up slightly in a smile, and feeling lighter on his feet.

On the other hand, accompanying depression or discouragement is a corresponding downward flow of energy, toward the base of the spine and away from the brain. One may even slump forward a little, look downward, depress the corners of his mouth, and actually *feel*, physically, a little heavier.

Spiritual awakening takes place when *all* one's energy flows upward, toward the spiritual eye. Hence the saying of Jesus, "Thou shalt love the Lord thy God with all thy *strength*": that is, "with all thy *energy*." We see here the basic purpose of Kriya Yoga.

This upward flow is obstructed in most people by countless eddies of *chitta*, or feeling. Once these eddies form in the heart, they are distributed along the spine according to their anticipated levels of fulfillment—the lower the level, the more materialistic the desire; the higher the level, the more spiritual. These eddies or *vrittis* of feeling can be dissipated by directing through the spine a strong enough flow of energy to neutralize their centripetal force. Numerous yoga techniques have, for their main objective, the awakening of this energy-flow.

Of all such yoga techniques, so taught Paramhansa Yogananda and his line of gurus, the most effective, because the most central and direct in its application, is Kriya Yoga. Kriya Yoga involves deliberately directing a flow of energy through the spine, thereby realigning in a single south-north direction every "molecule," or tendency. The Kriya technique, so our line of gurus said, was the one taught to Arjuna in ancient times by Krishna. And Krishna, in the Bhagavad Gita, states that he bestowed this technique on humanity in an incarnation long prior to the one in which he taught Arjuna. Of all the techniques of yoga, Kriya is not only the most ancient, but the most central and essential.

Kriya Yoga directs energy lengthwise around the spine, gradually neutralizing there the eddies of *chitta*. At the same time it strengthens the nerves in the spine and brain to receive cosmic currents of energy and consciousness. Yogananda called Kriya the supreme science of yoga. Beside it, other yoga techniques, most of which work on calming the breath and concentrating the mind, though important in themselves (Yogananda also taught a number of them), must be classed as subsidiary.

Other aspects there are to Kriya Yoga that relate to the subjective reactive process, but I do not feel it necessary to burden the reader's mind at this point with this long explanation.

Yogananda often said that Kriya Yoga strengthens one in whatever path—whether that of devotion, discrimination, or service; Hindu, Buddhist, Christian, Judaic, or Moslem—one is inclined by temperament or upbringing to follow.

Once there came to Master's Ranchi school a visitor who for twenty years had been practicing *Bhakti Yoga*, the path of single-minded devotion. Though deeply devoted, he had never yet experienced the Lord's blissful response.

"Kriya Yoga would help you," the Master earnestly suggested to him. But the man didn't want to be disloyal to his own path.

"Kriya Yoga won't conflict with your present practices," Master insisted. "It will only deepen them for you."

Still the man hesitated.

"Let me explain," Master finally said to him. "You are like a man who for twenty years has been trying to get out of a room through the walls, the floor, the ceiling. Kriya Yoga will simply show you where the door is. There is no conflict, in that kind of aid, with your own devotional path. To pass through the doorway you must also do so with devotion."

The man relented at last, and accepted initiation. Hardly a week later he received his first deep experience of God.

"I wasn't sent to the West by Christ and the great masters of India," Yogananda often told his audiences, "to dogmatize you with a new theology. Jesus himself asked Babaji to send someone here to teach you the science of Kriya Yoga, that people might learn how to commune with God directly. I want to help you toward the attainment of actual experience of Him, through your daily practice of Kriya Yoga."

He added, "The time for knowing God has come!"

CHAPTER 35

Organizing the Monks

As often as the heart
Breaks—wild and wavering—from control, so oft
Let him re-curb it, let him rein it back
To the soul's governance.

THESE WORDS OF Lord Krishna in the Bhagavad Gita offer valuable counsel for all stages of the spiritual journey. For it often happens on the path that selfish desires spring up from the subconscious mind with surprising vigor to attack one's devotion. The devotee may be progressing steadily, confident that God is all he wants in life; then all of a sudden, worldly opportunity knocks and he thinks, "Here's my chance—perhaps the only one I'll ever get—to become a great concert pianist!"; or, "to acquire riches and worldly respect!"; or, "to make a great scientific contribution to mankind!"; or, "to marry my soul mate!" I've never seen such desires, if pursued *as an alternative* to selflessly serving God, end in anything but disappointment.

The concert pianist tires of playing for a fickle public. The would-be millionaire soon finds that life without inner peace is truly hell, especially if he has known soul-peace before. The hopeful scientist, particularly if he has high ideals, finds the world either indifferent to his discoveries or anxious to divert them to ignoble ends. And the devotee who forsakes spiritual practices to marry his "soul mate" is soon disillusioned, and, as likely as not, gets divorced after a year or two. (What, indeed, can human love offer to compare with the sweetness of God's love, especially if one has experienced a taste of that love in his heart?)

Among my saddest memories are those of erstwhile devotees who, having left their spiritual calling, have returned to their former brothers and sisters on the path to show off their newly acquired worldly "wealth." With what pride they display their new cars, new suits, new wives! You see in their eyes a will to explain away the good they have lost. You hear in their voices some of the self-conscious laughter of people who boast of getting drunk—as though hoping by noisy affirmation to silence the stern voice of inner conscience. Yet these erstwhile devotees sooner or later lose confidence in the choices they have made, and, too sadly often, in themselves for having made them.

Worst of all, inconstancy to God creates in them a pattern of further inconstancy. They end up rarely succeeding at anything, for they have spurned a quality that is necessary for success in *any* endeavor: steadfastness. Fortunate are those who, having realized their mistake, abandon it and return resolutely to the divine search. I have often admired one such devotee whom others asked how she dared to show herself again in the monastery, having once left it. "Do you expect me," she replied vigorously, "to worship my mistakes?"

Few, alas, are blessed with such power of resolution. Of one fallen disciple, Master said to me, "He hasn't known a day of happiness since he left here. I tried hard to save him, but his mind was set.

"We were together in New York," Master continued, "when one day he told me he wanted to go to Philadelphia.

"'To buy a wedding ring?' I challenged him.

"Well, he couldn't deny it. Instead, therefore, he tried to convince me what an angel the girl was.

"'She isn't at all what you imagine,' I warned.

"'You know nothing about her,' he argued. 'You've never even met her!'

"'I know *everything* about her!' I assured him.

"Well, he wouldn't listen. But—he has since found out." Master's eyes expressed sorrow for his erring disciple. The disciple of whom he was speaking was Richard Wright, who had accompanied him to India.

"All things betray thee, who betrayest Me," wrote Francis Thompson in his beautiful poem, *The Hound of Heaven.*

Master told me many stories about people—students, chance acquaintances, and disciples. One that springs to mind was about Dale Wright, Richard's younger brother. "Every time I tried to help him with advice, he whined to his mother, 'Mommy, he's scolding me!' At last I gave him a toy airplane. He *loved* it! In fact, it settled him in his life direction: When he grew up, he became an aeronautical engineer."

Devotion is the greatest protection against delusion. But that devotee can hardly be found whose devotion *never* wanes, who never experiences times of spiritual emptiness or dryness, or never feels the tug of worldly desire. What is one to do when what Master called the "karmic bombs" of restlessness and desire strike, particularly in the midst of a dry period? In preparation against such a time it is important to fortify oneself with regular habits of meditation, and with loyalty to one's own chosen path. Once the habit of daily meditation has become firmly established, one can cruise steadily through many a storm, succumbing neither to despondency when the way seems hard, nor to over-elation when it seems smooth and easy. Loyalty to one's chosen path nips in the bud the temptation to seek easier, pleasanter pathways to God—perhaps a more "sympathetic" teacher, or practices that make fewer demands of the ego.

"Loyalty is the first law of God," our Guru often said. He was not referring to the superficial, sectarian loyalty of those who feel impelled constantly to prove to others how dedicated they are, and to discredit anyone whose views happen to differ from their own. (Such flag-waving is usually done to conceal subconscious doubts.) Master's reference, rather, was to that calm acceptance of one's own path which admits of no change of heart, which cannot be swayed by any obstacles that one might encounter on the way. This quality, alas, is not stressed in America nowadays, except perhaps as the need for steadfastness to the universal god: Ambition.

Ours is a tradition of pioneers, of men and women who repeatedly affirmed their freedom by pulling up their roots and settling in new territory. Even today, when there are no new lands on this continent to conquer, our youths are urged to court novelty, to follow the will-o'-the-wisp of "fulfillment" wherever it might lead them, and to pay scant heed to such inconvenient considerations as duty and commitment.

"They change jobs, wives, and gurus at a moment's notice," Master lamented. "How can they expect to get anywhere, when they keep changing directions so whimsically?"

"Quite a few heads will fall," he had told me when speaking of the period of testing that began a few months before my trial at Twenty-Nine Palms. I grieved deeply when some of those I most loved left the ashram. I had known for some time that Boone was pulling away, but when Norman left, and then Jean, I was badly shaken.

Poor Norman! He loved God deeply, but moods of despondency came, and he allowed them to undermine his meditative routine to the point where he no longer had the inner peace to resist worldly delusions. But I knew he would always love God, and would continue to seek Him. In fact, now, after the passage of many years, I can say that he did so.

"This is the first time in many lives that delusion has caught Norman," Master remarked sadly, adding, "Divine Mother wants him to learn responsibility. But wherever he is, he is with me."

Norman visited Mt. Washington a few months later. "Do you remember how hard it was for me to get along with Jerry?" he asked me. "That was one of the main reasons I left here. Well, where I work now there are *six* men just like him!"

Over the years I have observed that when devotees try to avoid facing their karmic lessons, they only attract those very lessons again in other forms—often in larger doses!

Jean had great will power, but he didn't concentrate enough on developing devotion. Master always taught us that we should meditate with no other motive than love for God, and the desire to please Him. "Mercenary devotion" he called meditation for personal spiritual gain. "'Lord, I have given You so many Kriyas. Now You have to fulfill Your part of the bargain and give me so much realization.' God never responds to that kind of devotion! He will accept nothing less from us than our unconditional love." When, after two or three years of determined meditative efforts, high spiritual experiences still eluded Jean, he became discouraged. "I didn't come here to rake leaves!" he was reported as saying the day he left. Alas, dear friend, had you forgotten the teachings of the Bhagavad Gita, which say that, to the devotee who offers to the Lord even a leaf, a flower, with deep *love* the Lord Himself responds *in person*?

Of one of the women disciples, who during this period of intense testing left to embrace the path of marriage, Master commented sadly, "The desire for romance had attracted her for years." She had been with Master for many years. Her karmic test must have come to a head shortly before she left, for he added, "Had she remained here just twenty-four hours longer, she would have been finished with that karma forever!"

Particularly awe-inspiring was his warning to one disciple, who later left: "Yours is a very complex karma. If you leave here now, it will take you two hundred incarnations to return to the point you have already reached on the path."

But though Master said that it was not unusual for the fallen devotee to wander in delusion for one or more incarnations, he also said, and the Bhagavad Gita corroborates, that the good karma accrued from yoga practice would bring him back in the end. The masters of India have never seen life in the hell-vs.-heaven terms of orthodox Christian dogmatists. Nor, I am sure (though I cannot speak for all), have the saints of any religion.

"Is it possible, Master," I once asked him, "for the soul to be lost forever?"

"*Never!*" he replied firmly. "The soul is a part of God. How could any part of God be destroyed?"

Most of those who left the work have remained devoted to Master even while pursuing, temporarily, the chimera of a few worldly dreams. They are, after all, his spiritual children, his destined disciples. Of only one who left did I ever know him to say, "He won't be back; he was never in." This was in response to a question of Jerry's: "How long will it be before he returns to you?" But of another disciple (Swami Dhirananda), who for years after leaving Mt. Washington had rejected the guru, Master said, "He will never find God except through this instrument, designated to him by God."

"People are so skillful in their ignorance!" Master exclaimed once in exasperation, after doing his best to help someone. And then, in a discussion with a small group of us, he said, "I see the spiritual path as a foot race. A few devotees are sprinting; others are jogging along slowly. Some are even running backwards!"

"The spiritual life," he told the monks on another occasion, "is like a battle. Devotees are fighting their inner enemies of greed and ignorance. And many are wounded—with the bullets of desire."

Loyalty, devotion, regular meditation, attunement with the guru—armed with these, the devotee will surely win the battle—not easily perhaps, but, in the end, gloriously.

"The more you do what your mind tells you," Master admonished us, "the more you become a slave. The more you do Guru's will, the more you become free."

The difference between those who stayed in the ashram and those who left it seemed to boil down to two alternatives: the desire to live only for God, and the desire to cling still to the little, human self. Jesus said, "Whosoever will save his life shall lose it." Leaving the ashram did not in itself, of course, constitute a spiritual fall. Nor was such a fall, when it occurred, necessarily permanent for this lifetime. It all depended on whether one still put God first in one's life, and on whether one refused to accept even the severest setback as a final defeat. Whatever the circumstances, however, it was an unwise disciple who thought he could leave the ashram with impunity, certain that he would never forget God. "Delusion has its own power," Master often warned us.

I was, as I said, deeply saddened when any brother left—particularly anyone who had inspired me in my own spiritual efforts. Being in charge of the monks now, I determined to do everything in my power to improve the steadfastness of those who were weak, by organizing our routine so that regular spiritual practice would no longer be wanting in any of their lives. Master encouraged me in these efforts. So also did a number of my fellow monks—though, unfortunately, not all of them. Human nature does not easily relinquish outer for inner freedom. I could see in the eyes of a few men the thought, "All right, so Master has put you in charge. That doesn't give you the right to impose your will on us!" When I persisted in trying to organize them, they dubbed me sarcastically, "The monk." It was no joy for me, either, to have to impose rules on them, despite the fact that my purpose was to carry out Master's wishes and to strengthen them in their dedication to the path. My sadness, however, over those we'd lost goaded me to develop a routine that would prove a buttress for others in their times of trial.

"I don't ask your obedience," I told them, "but I know you want to obey Master, and I'd be disobeying him myself if I didn't ask your *cooperation*. At the same time," I added, "I pledge to each of you *my* cooperation in return. Anything that any of you may want from me I will do gladly, as long as it doesn't conflict with our rules." Thus, by placing myself as much as possible in a position of service to them, I gradually won their support. In my own meditations I often sang the chant, "O God Beautiful!" repeating over and over the line, "To the serviceful Thou art service." Daily I filled my mind with the joyous thought that the only work worthy of a devotee is humble service to his Cosmic Beloved.

Ultimately my organizing efforts were successful. Thereafter, partly as a result of those efforts, more and more of the men who came to Mt. Washington remained on the path.

For me personally, however, there was a certain poignancy in these organizational struggles. For I sensed deeply that, the better I succeeded in them, the less Mt. Washington would remain for me the wonderful spiritual home I had found it when I first arrived there. In boarding schools as a child, particularly in this country at Hackley and Kent, I had developed a deep aversion to what I might call "group mentality"—the attitude that Rod Brown and I had chuckled over: "You'd better march in step, son, if you want the whole column to move." To be instrumental in developing this mentality at Mt. Washington, though I knew it was needed, made me feel a little as though I had volunteered for a suicide mission.

It relieved me that Master, too, didn't seem much in tune with the thought of organizing. Sister Gyanamata used to say, "You will never be able to organize the work so long as Master is alive." Sometimes he would speak with longing of the informality of the life of a spiritual teacher in India, "roaming by the Ganges," as he put it, "drunk with God." He preferred the flow of divine intuition to the constriction of rules and regulations. By nature, indeed, I think he might have responded as Ramana Maharshi, the great Indian master, did when disciples complained to him about a certain eminently sensible, but generally inconvenient, rule that his own brother had imposed on the ashram community. The rule read, "Do not use the office as a thoroughfare. Walk around it on your way to the dining room." Ramana Maharshi's reply to the protesters was, "Let us leave this place. It no longer feels like ours!" (Needless to say, the offending rule was quickly abandoned.)

The cultural attitudes of India have never been particularly conducive to rigid organization. "Don't make too many rules," Master told me. "It destroys the spirit." From him I imbibed a principle that has served me well, especially later in life, when I have been responsible for directing the spiritual lives and activities of many people. That principle is, *Never, if possible, put the needs of an organization ahead of those of even one of its members.* Service is the true and only purpose of any spiritual work.

In addition to organizing our routine at Mt. Washington, and to making a few rules (as necessary), I also developed a series of classes in discipleship, the notes for which are still used, I believe, by the monks and nuns; they are thought to have been written by Shraddha Mata. Master worked with me in all these efforts, and often talked about future directions in the work as they related to the monks.

During the last two years of his life Master also spent many hours with the monks, teaching, encouraging, and inspiring them.

"Each of you must individually make love to God," he told us one evening. "Keep your mind at the Christ center, and when you work, all the time think you are working for God and Guru. Always: God and Guru—God, Christ, and Guru. Many come here, then talk and joke all the time—or play the organ [Master glanced meaningly at one of the monks]. They won't get God that way! There are many mice living in the canyon on this property, but they are not develop-

The monks welcome me back to Mt. Washington on my return there from India in April 1960. (*front row, left to right*) Marcel Calet, Henry Schaufelberger, and Rev. Michael (later Brothers Turiyananda, Anandamoy, and Bhaktananda respectively).

ing spiritually! They haven't God. Don't think you can make spiritual progress by merely living here. You yourself must make the effort. Each of you stands alone before God."

One evening he praised the spirit of those disciples (Daya Mata, Virginia Wright, and Miss Darling) who had long served him personally. During their early years at Mt. Washington, especially, they had often followed a full day's work with all-night office labors as well.

"Sir," I inquired, "didn't they get much time to meditate?"

"Well, working near this body as they did, they didn't need so much meditation; they evolved spiritually just the same. But you all must meditate more, because you haven't that outward contact as much as they had."

Often he urged us to be steadfast in our practice of Kriya Yoga. "Practice Kriya night and day. It is the greatest key to salvation. Other people go by books and outer disciplines, but it will take them incarnations to reach God that way. Kriya is the greatest way of destroying temptation. Once you feel the inner joy it bestows, no evil will be able to touch you. It will then seem like stale cheese compared to nectar. When others are idly talking or passing time, *you* go out into the garden and do a few Kriyas. What more do you need? Kriya will give you everything you are looking for. Practice it faithfully night and day."

He added, "After practicing Kriya, sit still a long time; listen to the inner sounds, or practice *Bhakti Yoga* [devotion], or watch the breath in the spine [rising with inhalation; descending with exhalation]. If you eat your dinner and then run, you won't be able to enjoy the meal; your enjoyment will be greater if you rest afterwards. Similarly, after doing Kriya don't jump up right away. Sit still and pray deeply; enjoy the peace that you feel. That is how soul-intuition is developed."

"Give both the good and the bad that you do to God," he told us one evening. "Of course, that does not mean you should deliberately do things that are bad, but when you cannot help yourself because of habits that are too strong, feel that God is acting through you. Make *Him* responsible. He likes that! For He wants you to realize that it is He who is dreaming your existence."

"Sir," Clifford Frederick, one of the men present, addressed him one afternoon, "how can one become more humble?"

"Humility," Master replied, "comes from seeing God as the Doer, not yourself. Seeing that, how can you feel proud of anything you have accomplished? Humility lies in the heart. It is not a show put on to impress others. Whatever you may be doing, tell yourself constantly, 'God is doing all this through me.'"

One of the disciples was being tormented by self-doubt. "As long as you are making the effort," Master consoled him, "God will *never* let you down!"

To Henry one day he said, as he was preparing to go out for a drive, "Whenever you see wrong in the world, remember, it's wrong with you. When you are right, everything is right because you see God there. Perfection is inside."

Vance Milligan, a young black boy, first came to Mt. Washington at the age of seventeen. Being not yet of legal age, he was forced by his mother to leave. As soon as he turned eighteen, however, he returned.

"How does your mother feel now about your being here?" Master asked him.

"This time she says it's all right," Vance replied.

"That's good that you have her consent. Without it you should still have come, but with it is even better.

"Swami Shankara," Master continued, "was only eight when he decided to leave home in search of God. His mother tried to prevent him. Shankara, reluctant to leave without her permission, jumped into a nearby river and allowed himself to be caught by a crocodile. He was highly advanced from past lives, and had the power to save himself. 'Look, Mother,' he cried, 'I'm going to let myself be pulled under if you don't give me your consent. Either way you will lose me!' Hastily she gave her permission for him to leave home. He thereupon released himself from the crocodile, came out of the water, and left home to begin his mission.

"One day, many years later, he cried, 'I taste my mother's milk. She is dying!' Hastening to her side, he helped her in her final moments, then cremated her body with a divine fire shooting out from his upraised hand."

Master continued: "Another born sage who left home at an early age was Sukdeva. He was only six at the time, but he wanted to go in search of his guru. Byasa, his father, the author of the Bhagavad Gita, was fully qualified to be his guru. Sukdeva could see, however, that he was still a little attached to him as his son. As the boy was leaving, Byasa followed him, pleading with him to seek God at home.

"'Keep away from me,' the boy said. 'You have *maya*' — as if to say, 'You have a disease'!

"Byasa then sent him for training to the royal sage, King Janaka."

I mentioned that young black boy, Vance. Vance told me one day, "Master said to me, 'You should mix more with Walter. You don't know what you have in him.'" I was gratified to receive, even indirectly, this personal encouragement from Master, for my self-doubts all too often suggested to me a very different reality.

I asked Master one day, "Sir, in what way ought one to love people?"

"You should love God first," he replied, "then, with His love, love others. In loving people for themselves, rather than as manifestations of God, you might get attached."

Speaking of love another time, he told us, "Human love is possessive and personal. Divine love is always impersonal. To develop devotion in the right way, and to protect it from the taint of possessive, personal love, it is better not to seek God above all for His love until one is highly developed. Seek Him first of all for His bliss."

"Don't joke too much," Master often told us. "Joking is a false stimulant. It doesn't spring from true happiness, and doesn't give happiness. When you joke a lot, the mind becomes light and restless so that it can't meditate."

To one of the younger renunciates* he said one day, "You have devotion, but you are always joking and keeping the others rollicking. You must learn to be more serious."

"I know it, Sir," the young man replied sadly, "but my habit is strong. How can I change without your blessing?"

"Well, *my* blessing is there already. *God's* blessing is there. Only *your* blessing is lacking!"

"It's awfully hard to change my ways, Sir," Jerry lamented one day, "but I'll go on to the end of life."

"That's the spirit," Master said approvingly. "Anyway the wave cannot leave the ocean. It can protrude farther from the surface, but it is still a part of the ocean, and has to return to it at last."

"Never count your faults," he once told us. "Be concerned only that you love God enough. And," he added, "don't tell your faults to others, lest someday in a fit of anger those people raise them

---

* *Renunciate*: This noun form is in common usage in India, but is not to be found in either *Webster's International* or the *Oxford* dictionaries, both of which favor the less euphonic *renunciant*. In Self-Realization Fellowship we used the word *renunciate*, following Master's lead. Sometime in the mid-1950s, however, one of the nuns happened to notice that this form was not listed in the dictionary. *Renunciant* then became adopted. Yet Indian English is quite old enough to be accepted as a legitimate branch of the English language—particularly where, as in this case, the word involves a concept that is *their* specialty, not ours. I opt for the much more pleasant-sounding *renunciate*. Like *initiate* (the noun), *renunciate* is grammatically legitimate. And this, after all, is how new words get accepted into the language. *Renunciate* has only to gain wide circulation for future editions of *Webster's* to give it full recognition.

against you. But tell your faults to God. From Him you should conceal nothing."

Some of the monks grew discouraged at seeing the departure of others. Master once told them, "'Devotees may come, and devotees may go, but *I* go on forever.' *That* must be your attitude." To those who, seeing others fall, doubted their own spiritual chances of success, Master said, "You have to live anyway! Why not live in the right way?"

The American "go-getter" spirit drew praise from him. "'Eventually? Eventually? Why not now!' *That* is the American way that I like. Seek God with that kind of determination, and you will surely find Him!"

Concerning some of the monks who had left, he told me one evening as we were walking about the grounds at SRF Lake Shrine, "Many will have their own centers someday—David, Jan, et cetera, et cetera." I've often wondered whether he wasn't hinting, rather, at my own future path of service to him in separation outwardly from his organization.

My own feeling was that the best possible place to serve the work was at Mt. Washington. One day, however, we were discussing our need for disciples with certain talents, and I mentioned Adano Ley, our center leader in Montreal, Canada. "Why don't we invite him to come here, Master? He is doing very good work there."

"If he is doing good work there," Master replied somewhat indignantly, "why bring him here?"

These statements proved important for me years later, when circumstances forced me, as I've already hinted, to serve him in new ways, away from Mt. Washington and from SRF.

Work qualifications were never in any case the real reason he accepted anyone. We had long needed a printer. One evening I came to Master with what I thought was good news: "We have a new man for the print shop, Sir!"

"Why do you tell me that?" he demanded indignantly. "First see if a newcomer has our spirit; accept him only on that basis. Next, help him to develop that spirit more deeply. Only *then* think where he might fit in the work. Two others have already come and told me we have a new printer. I never ask people first what they can do. I see the spiritual side."

"Believe me, Sir," I replied abashedly, "that's my interest, too. I should have expressed it. This man said to me, 'I'm so glad you all pray here with such devotion.' And I had him in my meditation cave for a long time, chanting and playing Hindu devotional recordings. He loved it."

Master nodded approvingly. "That is what I like to hear."

In fact, however, though he had yet to meet this new man, his response to my words was based on sure intuition. For the man left not many months afterward. Master then remarked to me, "I knew he wouldn't stay."

By the time of that new printer's acceptance, Master had turned over to me the task of accepting new men disciples, while he himself spent much of his time in seclusion, completing his writings. It was difficult for me to face the fact that many who sought admission were simply not ready for our way of life. To me, Mt. Washington offered such a wonderful way of life that I wanted, if possible, to share it with everyone.

One student wrote from an Eastern state that he wanted to come, despite certain difficulties that he was having with his health. Master replied that, since his health was poor, he should not come. But the man wrote back pleadingly, "My doctor assures me I'll be fine as long as I take regular medication." Master was in seclusion when this letter came, so I answered it. The only objection to the man's coming that I knew of was his physical condition; otherwise he seemed to me deeply sincere. Since this objection had been met, I wrote to tell him he could come and give our way of life a try.

When Master returned to Mt. Washington and learned what I had done, he scolded me, "That wasn't my only reason for telling him not to come. It was simply the *kindest* reason. I knew he was not spiritually ready for our way of life." He added, "You will see."

Shortly thereafter the young man arrived. A short week later, he was gone.

I accepted one man who even *I* could see was not ready for acceptance. Despite a sincere desire to live spiritually, he was steeped in worldly habits. It was his strong desire to change that had moved me to take him; I simply hadn't the heart to say no. For several months the newcomer applied himself earnestly, though he shook his head often in wonderment at the change his life had undergone. He didn't stay long, but while at Mt. Washington he did improve greatly. Master was pleased.

"I left it up to your own will to change," he told him one day. Then, referring to the man's rather checkered past, he added, "But it is much easier to be good than bad, really. If one is bad, he is always in terror. But the good man is afraid of nothing and no one. The gods themselves then have to look out for him, for the God of all gods is on his side!"

Because I'd accepted this man, Master did his best to help him. But when he first learned of his acceptance, Master exclaimed to me, "I'm going to have to give you intuition!"

His words may have contained a serious blessing. At any rate, soon thereafter I found I could often tell at a glance whether a man belonged at Mt. Washington or not. Sometimes, even before that man had mentioned anything about coming, I would tell him, "You belong with us." As nearly as I remember, when such a feeling came to me it always proved justified.

Master, in his talks with us, always sought to turn our minds toward God. He urged us to see the Lord manifested in everything and everyone. "Respect one another," he once told us, "as you respect me."

Many hours he spent talking with us, giving us help and encouragement. Above all he urged us to seek our inspiration inwardly, in meditation.

Hearing one of the monks chanting in the main chapel one evening, to the accompaniment of an Indian harmonium, he paused during the course of a conversation downstairs. Blissfully, then, he remarked, "That is what I like to hear in this hermitage of God!"

CHAPTER 36

The Wave and the Ocean

"DIVINE MOTHER ONCE said to me, 'Those to whom I give too much, I do not give Myself.'"

Master was explaining to us the difference between joyful acceptance of divine favors, vouchsafed by God as a sign of His love, and a desire for the favors themselves.

"Seek God for Himself," he told us, "not for any gift that He might give you." Unlike many proponents of spiritual "new thought" who equate progress with the ability to "manifest" increasing material abundance, Paramhansa Yogananda taught us that the true test of spirituality is indifference to everything except God's love. To the sincere devotee, he said, God's lesser gifts are meaningful in one sense only: as demonstrations of His love.

A touching episode, illustrative of this teaching, occurred two or three years after I entered the work. Master, in his travels between Los Angeles and Encinitas, sometimes stopped in the little town of Laguna Beach, at a Scottish tea shop where shortbread was a specialty. One day, going there for this delicacy, he sent Virginia Wright (later, Ananda Mata) in. She returned to report that the last batch had been sold.

Surprised, Master prayed, "Divine Mother, how come?" It wasn't that he was disappointed. Accustomed, rather, to receiving divine guidance in even the slightest details of his life, he wondered whether there might not be some lesson intended in this unexpected denial. All at once, he saw a shaft of light shine down upon the little shop. Moments later, the door opened and the proprietress came out.

"Wait! Wait!" she called. Hastening over to the car with a little package in her hand, she said, "I was saving this order for a local customer. But I want you to have it. I can make more for him."

Master had had no real desire for the shortbread. What touched him deeply about this episode was the divine love it exemplified. The more inconsequential the need to which God responds, the greater, in a sense, the proof of His love. Divine intervention in times of serious need might be attributed to other reasons—perhaps to the wish to see some important work finished. But what motive, save love alone, could there possibly be for intervention in such trivial matters?

Years later, I had a similar demonstration—equally trivial, but showing me that God's love extends even to ordinary devotees. My parents were living in France, relatively near Switzerland. During my school days in Switzerland, I had developed a liking for Swiss chocolate, and had bought it whenever I could. I kept intending to ask my parents to send me some, but the desire was so trivial that I kept on forgetting. One year, a week before my birthday, the thought came to me, "Too bad! Divine Mother, it would have been nice to have some Swiss chocolate for that special day." I dismissed the thought as quite unimportant, and forgot it. I had addressed the thought, however, to Divine Mother. What was my surprise, the very day before my birthday, to receive a box of Swiss chocolate from a congregation member in Hollywood. She had happened to see some of it in a local shop (I hadn't known that it was imported) and, though she didn't know it was my birthday, and didn't know my tastes in the matter, she had thought to send me some. I shared it gratefully with my brother monks. My gratitude went chiefly to the Divine Mother.

To Master, *all* gifts short of divine love itself came under the general heading "lesser gifts." To make religion a matter of "manifesting" an endless succession of worldly goods would be, he implied, to make a religion of materialism. And while he said that we had a right, as children of the Infinite, to God's infinite abundance, he reminded us that this birthright could be *fully* claimed only in cosmic consciousness.

The sincere devotee prefers rather to "manifest" a simple life, and seeks of this world's goods only as many as he needs to sustain him in his spiritual search. If God gives him more than that, he employs it for the welfare of others. And all that he owns he considers God's property altogether, to be returned joyously at a moment's notice to its true Owner.

Even for worldly people, simple living is an important key to happiness. Across the road from Master's retreat at Twenty-Nine Palms there lived a man in a small one-room cabin, by himself. He had no garden, and few modern conveniences indoors. Yet his happiness was a pleasure to observe. He had no debts to burden him. There were no unnecessary chores to pilfer away his precious hours of freedom. Again and again he contentedly played a recording, audible over the nearby countryside, of a popular song that expressed his perfect contentment with life: "I've Got My Home in Twenty-Nine Palms."

Master, gazing toward this man's place one day, remarked, "He is like a king in his palace! Such is the joy of simple living."

Master used to say, "Whenever I see somebody who needs something of mine more than I do, I give it away."

"A few years ago," he told us, "I had a fine musical instrument, an esraj from India. I loved to play devotional music on it. But a visitor one day admired it. Unhesitatingly I gave it to him. Years later someone asked me, 'Weren't you just a *little* sorry to lose it?' 'Never for a moment!' I replied. Sharing one's happiness with others only expands one's own happiness."

Master kept only enough money personally to finance his trips to the different ashrams. Even this amount he often gave away. So strong,

Master playing the esraj.

indeed, was his urge to share with others that he sometimes gave away more than he had. I remember him once asking me to lend him five dollars, so that he might give that money to someone else. When traveling, too, he liked to go simply. He would take with him for his meals only a few nuts, dates, and raisins in a clear plastic box. Generally he ate in the car, to avoid what he termed the "heterogeneous vibrations" of restaurants.

He enjoyed cooking for others, and was also an excellent cook. "It is a form of service," he told me, simply. After preparing an especially tasty dish for us one day, he explained, "I always know just how much spicing to add: I can taste it in the spiritual eye. I never have to sample the food with my tongue." The inimitable ingredient in his cooking, of course, was his vibrations; after eating it, one always felt spiritually uplifted. Although he sometimes fed us sumptuously, however, I noticed that he himself generally ate very little.

He displayed the same indifference to all outward enjoyments. It wasn't apathy; enthusiasm for all aspects of life was a hallmark of his nature. It was clear, however, that he enjoyed things not for their own sake, but because they manifested in various ways the one, infinite Beloved. Often, as he was expressing joy outwardly, I would note in the still depths of his gaze a fathomless detachment.

I once experienced this detachment in a matter that seemed, to me, pressingly important. It was in the summer of 1950. For months I had been looking forward eagerly to our trip to India. Master had said we would be leaving only if and when God gave him the definite guidance to go, but all I heard in his statement was the "when" of it, not the "if." In July, finally, he announced that it was God's will that we not make the voyage that year.

"Will we be going another time, Master?" I asked.

"That is in God's hands," he replied indifferently. "I am not inquisitive about these things. What He wants, I do."

Not inquisitive—about a trip to *India*? Mentally I tightened my belt of expectations, telling myself that it was all the same to me, too. I wasn't completely successful, I'm afraid.

On August 20 of that year Master dedicated the SRF Lake Shrine. The impressive public event was attended by some 1500 people.

The guests of honor were California's Lieutenant Governor, Goodwin J. Knight, and his wife. Present also were many civic dignitaries and other people of worldly prominence. I was impressed to see with what ease, respect, and complete inner freedom Master could mix with all sorts of people: great and humble, famous, and obscure. He gave to each of them his full and loving attention, yet never defined himself in terms of what others expected of him, nor in terms of what he gave to them. He was simply and entirely what he always was: a divine mirror to everyone he encountered, completely devoid of any "complexes" of his own.

After the opening, Master occasionally sponsored evening concerts in the open-air temple by the lake. Large crowds attended, attracted by a series of well-known concert artists and by the beautiful, starlit setting. To Master the concerts were a service to others, based on the fact that divine inspiration often reaches people through the medium of music. Above all, however, he saw these events as a means of drawing people to the spiritual path. For until inspiration becomes rooted in actual God-contact, it is, he reminded us, ever fleeting and uncertain.

Self-Realization Fellowship Lake Shrine dedication ceremony, August 1950. On the far left in the white robe is Rev. Bernard. Next to him is Rev. Stanley, then Dr. Lewis, Master, and me.

One evening he sat chatting with a few of us after a concert. Reflecting on the numbers of visitors who attended these events for merely temporary inspiration, he remarked, "Outsiders come, and see only the surface. Not understanding what this place has to offer them, they go away again. Those who are our own, however, see beneath the surface. *They* never leave."

He was referring, I knew, not only to the casual public, but also to his disciples, not all of whom were discerning enough to recognize the priceless gifts he had to bestow on them.

Not long after the opening of the Lake Shrine, Chuck Jacot, a monk there, was trying to repair a pump that sent water up a little hill, at the top of which stood a statue of Jesus Christ with his hands outheld in blessing. From a point below the statue, water was meant to descend in a graceful cascade. Chuck, a trained plumber, couldn't get the pump to work.

Finally he hit on a spiritual solution; at least, he hoped it would be a solution. Recalling a passage in *Autobiography of a Yogi* that says, "Whenever anyone utters with reverence the name of Babaji, that devotee attracts an instant spiritual blessing," Chuck sat down and called mentally to that great master. Suddenly, to his awe and amazement, Babaji appeared before him in vision, blessed him, and offered him priceless spiritual counsel. Later, when Chuck returned to outward consciousness, he found the pump functioning smoothly, and the water flowing again.

"Logically, that pump just *couldn't* work," he told us. "It hadn't even been primed!"

"I asked Babaji to give Chuck that experience," Master told us later.

Many others have acted upon those words of promise in *Autobiography of a Yogi*, and have received extraordinary blessings.

Pedro Gonzales Milan, who later became our center leader in Mérida, Yucatán (in Mexico), told me of the first time he had read the *Autobiography*. When he came to the above passage, he put the book down, moved to his depths. "If these words be true," he thought, "I must prove them so! Babaji, heed the cry of my heart: Come to me!

"Instantly," he told me, "the room was filled with a glorious light and my heart, with bliss."

I, too, have experienced Babaji's blessings on occasions when I have prayed to him. In 1960, on my second visit to India, I wanted to find a place of seclusion for a few days before returning to Calcutta to resume my activities in our society there. I had no idea where to go, however. Part of my difficulty was that Indians often found a Western swami a novelty. Villagers, especially, would sometimes gather in scores outside any house I stayed at. They waited for hours, if need be, for me to come out.

I was staying in a hotel in Madras at this time, having entered India from Ceylon to the south. One morning I prayed to Babaji, "Please help me to find a *quiet*, secluded place to stay in."

After meditation that morning I went down and ate breakfast in the hotel dining room. A man seated at the table next to mine introduced himself to me. "I have a house," he informed me without any preliminaries, "in a secluded section of the little town of Kodaicanal. I would be honored if you would use it for meditation. I shall be away from there for the next few weeks; no one will bother you. It occurred to me that, since Kodaicanal is in the mountains, its cool climate might be congenial to you. Westerners often go there to escape the heat of the plains."

I took advantage of his offer. The place proved ideal in every respect.

Sometime after the Lake Shrine opening, I attended a concert with Master in another outdoor setting: the famous Hollywood Bowl. Vladimir Rosing, an old friend and student of his, was conducting Johann Strauss's comic operetta, *Die Fledermaus*.

A minister from one of our other ashrams wanted to impress Master with his talent for leadership. This evening, his way of doing so was to order me about.

"Master needs a blanket, Don. Would you please fetch him one?" Or, "Don, be so good as to get Master a glass of water."

I obeyed him eagerly, aware that the real prize in the spiritual life is the opportunity for service, especially to one's guru. It delighted me further when Master, to see if I could be drawn into a competitive attitude, pretended to accept my offerings with a slight sneer of condescension—as though receiving ministration from one of obviously inferior leadership ability. It was quite enough for me that I felt Master's smile in my heart.

After the concert I glimpsed a touching side of his nature. Miss Lancaster (later, Sister Sailasuta), one of the women disciples, had been invited to come along. She had sat separately from us, but joined us on the way out and remarked amusedly on the operetta's worldly theme. Certainly Master would not have attended *Die Fledermaus* on its merits alone; if anything, I imagine he'd have told all of us to give it a miss. But the conductor in this case was a friend of his. Therefore, with solemn loyalty, he replied to Miss Lancaster, "It was a *good* show."

After the Lake Shrine opening we concentrated on completing India Center, a large new building on our church grounds in Hollywood. Well, hardly a *new* building, exactly. Master, pursuing the strategy he had followed in building the church behind it, had bought a large, very old, and very dilapidated structure in some dying neighborhood, and had had it moved, shaking and creaking, onto the church grounds. His obvious purpose was to circumvent some of the cumbersome building code restrictions that applied only to new construction. And so, once again, the neighbors had to put up with an unsightly relic of (one hoped!) better days. And, once again, their dismay turned to pride as we transformed this relic into a beautiful, new-looking hall.

"We," I say? Well, perhaps that pronoun is a euphemism. My own contribution had little to do with the building's ultimate beauty. I dug the ditches, shoveled sand into the cement mixer, and did miscellaneous little jobs that, it was generally understood, would later be conveniently hidden by coats of plaster.

"I've sure learned a lot on this job!" I exclaimed one day to Andy Anderson, our foreman, as the project neared completion. Andy gazed at me for a moment in stunned silence. Obviously wanting to be charitable, he simply couldn't think of anything to say.

During the months while Andy supervised our work at India Center, he developed a deep love for Master. Master, in return, was touched by Andy's devotion, and by his simple, kindly nature. As

The monks working on building India Center in 1951.
(back row) Second from left, Norman Paulsen; far right, Roy Eugene Davis *(middle row)* Second from left, Daniel Boone; next to the right, Leo Cocks; fifth from the left, Rev. Bernard; then to the right, Jean Haupt, Jerry Torgerson, Joe Carbone (Brother Bimalananda), Henry Schaufelberger (Brother Anandamoy), Chuck Jacot. *(front row)* Second from left, Debi Mukerjee; next to the right, me.

Christmas 1950 approached, Andy took pains to buy his guru an appropriate gift. During our luncheon break one day he made a special journey to Mt. Washington and, with great trepidation, went up to the third floor. Placing his gift by Master's door, he fled.

"Oh," he cried, upon his return to India Center, "what a fool I am! I forgot to put my name on that package. Now Master will never know who gave it to him!"

Just then the telephone rang. It was Master asking to speak with Andy. Andy returned a few minutes later, beaming from ear to ear.

"Master just wanted to thank me for my present!"

Andy, like many in the construction trade, rather liked his beer. Sometimes, in fact, he came to work a little "under the influence." One day Master asked him to construct a concrete driveway at Mt. Washington.

"Heavy trucks drive up here," Master explained, "with paper for the print shop. How thick do you suggest we make the driveway to bear all that weight?"

After a few moments' thought, Andy replied, "Four inches would be quite enough, Master."

"Make it six," Master said with a sweet smile.

Andy was about to object, when he saw Master's smile. "All right, Sir." He gulped, swallowing his professional knowledge.

I wondered at the time why two extra inches of concrete should have inspired Master to request them so sweetly. Later I understood. For when the day came for pouring the concrete, it was obvious from the look in Andy's eyes that he was a little tipsy. Not fully conscious of what he was doing, he sprayed too much water on the new driveway, diluting the mixture. If it hadn't been for those extra inches, the cement would have cracked. Master, out of loving respect for Andy, wouldn't allow anyone to replace him. Indeed, it was to compensate for this problem, which he'd foreseen, that he'd requested those extra two inches of concrete. The sweetness of his smile had been due to his compassion for Andy.

India Center was formally opened to the public on April 8, 1951. "The first cultural center of its kind in America," the press called it. A large hall downstairs was dedicated as a "meeting place for men of goodwill of all nations." Upstairs, a public restaurant served delicious vegetarian meals, for which the recipes were Master's own creations. Over the years, both meeting hall and restaurant were to become famous.

India Center (the new name for the property in Hollywood) and the SRF Lake Shrine were, in a sense, Master's parting outward gifts to the world. There was another gift, infinitely more precious to us, his disciples, which he bestowed on us during the last two years of his life.

Great masters have the power to assume onto their own bodies the karma of others, much as a strong man might generously take onto his own body blows that were intended for a weaker person. Masters can sustain a considerable number of such karmic "blows" without themselves suffering any noticeable ill effect. Occasionally, however—especially toward the end of their lives, in order to help their disciples through years of spiritual effort without the Guru's physical presence—they assume large amounts of karma. At such times their own bodies may suffer temporarily.

It was such a gift that Master now bestowed on us. His legs became affected. The result was that, for a time, he couldn't walk. It was primarily an "astral disease," he explained to us, and described a frightening array of demonic entities that were wreaking havoc on his body, especially on his astral body, though the physical body took some of the punishment also.

"I held my mind down to the body during the worst period," he told us, "because I wanted to experience pain as others do."

Faye, with profound sympathy, cried out one day, "Why does Divine Mother treat you like this?"

"Don't you *dare* criticize Divine Mother!" Master scolded. Personal likes and dislikes formed no part of his nature. His only will was to do what God wanted.

Even at the height of his illness, he could still walk when he had to, though sometimes with divine assistance. In August 1951, he was scheduled to speak before a large convocation of members on the former tennis courts at Mt. Washington. Unwilling to publicize his condition, which he viewed as a sacred offering to his disciples for their spiritual growth, he determined to walk when the time came. The car took him as far as the edge of the courts. Someone opened the door, and Master used his own hands to lift his legs and place his feet on the ground. "Instantly, a brilliant light surrounded my body," he told us later. "I was able to walk with ease." We saw him go up onto the lecture platform, stand through his long lecture, then walk back unaided to the car. "Once back in the car," he told us, "my legs became helpless again." (Someone later told me, "As he 'walked,' I noticed his feet weren't touching the ground.")

"Carry my body," Master laughed one day as we bore him up a flight of stairs, "and I'll carry your souls!"

Another time he remarked smiling, "This body is not everything. Some people have feet, but can't walk all over!"

Gradually his condition improved. One afternoon I was helping him into his car. "You are getting better, Sir," I exclaimed thankfully.

"Who is getting better?" Master's tone was impersonal.

August 1951. At the time this photograph was taken, Master was suffering from an illness that had affected his legs, and he was unable to walk. He was scheduled to speak to a large convocation of members. Unwilling to publicize his condition, he determined to walk when the time came. A car took him near the outdoor lecture platform. Master lifted his legs with his own hands, and placed both feet on the ground. "Instantly a brilliant light surrounded my body," he later told us. "I was able to walk with ease." We saw him go up onto the lecture platform, stand through his long lecture, and walk back, unaided, to the car. "Once back in the car," he told us, "my legs became helpless again."

"I meant your body, Sir."

"What's the difference? The wave protruding from the ocean bosom is still a part of the ocean. This is God's body. If He wants to make it well, all right. If He wants to keep it unwell, all right. It is best to remain impartial. If you have health and are attached to it, you will always be afraid of losing it. And if you are attached to good health and become ill, you will always be grieving for the good you have lost.

"Man's greatest trouble is egoism, the consciousness of individuality. He takes everything that happens to him as affecting *him*, personally. Why be affected? You are not this body. You are *He*! Everything is Spirit."

As Master's condition improved, he began to spend more time again with the monks. One day he was conversing with a group of us on the front porch at Mt. Washington when a woman student, Miss Lois Carpenter, passed by us on her way into the building. In one hand she carried a paper bag; evidently it contained something she'd just purchased. Seeing Master, but not wanting to intrude on his discussion with us, she saluted him silently while proceeding toward the door. Master stopped her.

"What have you in that bag?"

"A few dates, Master, for you. I was going to place them by your door."

"Thank you very much. I shall be glad to accept them here."

Master, taking the fruits, passed them out among us. "I had been wanting to give you all something," he explained. "As soon as I saw her with that bag, I knew my wish had been fulfilled."

Early one rather mild autumn evening he was seated in his car, chatting with a few of us before going out for a drive. He was explaining some philosophical point, when, midway through his explanation, he paused and inquired, "Isn't it rather hot today?"

We hesitated, knowing that he had it in mind to give us money for ice cream. He looked at us expectantly. At last I said, smiling, "Well, it *was* hot, Sir, but by now it has cooled off."

"Too bad!" Master laughed playfully. "You've cheated yourselves out of some refreshments!" He returned to his discourse. Several more minutes passed, then he paused again.

"You're *sure* it isn't a bit warm this evening?"

"Well," we replied laughing, "it is if you say so, Sir!"

Decisively he concluded, "I can't keep money and I won't! Here, take these dollars for ice cream. I like having money only so that I can give it away."

I still have the three one-dollar bills he gave us on another evening for ice cream. I replaced them with other dollar bills of my own, and kept the gift he had touched.

One evening he spoke briefly of his recent illness. To our expressions of deep sympathy he said unconcernedly, "It was nothing! When the wisdom dinner from the plate of life has been eaten, it no longer matters whether you keep the plate, or break it and throw it away."

On another occasion he remarked, "I forget myself so much these days that I have to ask others if I've eaten!"

"Man was put here on earth to seek God," he reminded us one evening. "That is the only reason for his existence. Friends, job, material interests: All these, by themselves, mean *nothing*."

"Sir," one of the monks inquired, "is it wrong to ask God for material things?"

"It is all right, if you need them," Master replied. "But you should always say, 'Give me this or that, *provided* it is all right with You.' Many of the things people want end up harming them when they get them. Leave it to God to decide what you ought to have."

On the subject of prayer, he told us, "God answers all prayers, but restless prayers He answers only a little bit. If you tried giving away something that didn't belong to you, your 'generosity' wouldn't mean much, would it? So it is when you try to give your mind to God: You should first own it, yourself. Gain control over your thoughts; give Him your full attention when you pray. You will see, when you pray in that way, that He answers marvelously!"

Whatever Master's topic of conversation—whether some aspect of the spiritual path, or some perfectly ordinary task that he wanted done—if one "listened" sensitively enough one always felt a subtle power emanating from him. If one took this awareness within, one felt blessed with a heightened sense of inner joy and freedom. Sometimes in Master's company, and again years later in India in the ashrams of saints, I observed disciples who were so fascinated by their guru's gestures, words, and facial expressions that they neglected to commune with his magnetizing influence within themselves. Master saw even his own personality quite impersonally, as necessary, simply, to functioning in this physical world.

"Before taking a physical body," he once told me, "I see the personality I am to assume, and feel slightly uncomfortable with it. It is like having to don a heavy overcoat on a hot day. I soon get used to it, but inwardly I never forget that this personality is not my true Self."

At the same time, Master never sanctioned an irresponsible denial of mundane realities. "You should combine idealism with practicality," he once told me. In down-to-earth matters he himself was completely practical. He taught us the importance of meeting every reality on its own level. One minute he might be instructing us in some fine point of meditation, and the next telling us how to keep our rooms tidy. ("Put everything away as soon as you finish with it.")

When he invited guests to lunch, he often had me serve them. After the meal I would demonstrate the yoga postures, then sit in the room while he conversed. Usually, I would write down his remarks. If sometimes I found it difficult to keep up with him, he would notice, and speak more slowly. Occasionally, after the guests had departed, he would keep me with him to discuss my work, particularly as it related to the public, or to correct something I might have said in a private conversation at church, or in a lecture. On one such occasion I expressed astonishment at his complete awareness of things I'd said and done when he was not physically with me.

"I know every thought you think," he once assured me calmly.

Two visitors to Mt. Washington who got to meet Master were, on separate occasions, my mother and my cousin Bet. Mother he received graciously in his upstairs sitting room. Before their meeting I had asked him to give her a special blessing. He'd agreed to do so, but in a manner so separated from our present discussion that I wasn't sure whether my request had really registered with him. What was my gratification, at the end of his interview with her, when he held her hand outside the door, and prayed out loud to God and our line of gurus for the blessing I'd solicited. I've no idea what Mother thought of this unexpected parting, but I touched Master's feet with tears of gratitude, convinced that his blessing could not fail. (Nor, indeed, did it. Years later, she asked me to teach her meditation.)

Bet I introduced to Master as he was leaving for a drive one afternoon. From his remarks about her later, it was clear that she had made an excellent impression on him.

"Would she make a good yogi, Master?"

"Oh, *yes*."

In addition to lecturing in the churches, and to organizing the monks, I wrote letters for Master.

"Sir," I said to him one day, "what letters we are getting from Germany. Such sincerity and devotion! Letter after letter pleads for Kriya Yoga initiation."

"They have been hurt," Master replied with quiet sympathy, "that's why. All those wars and troubles! Kriya is what they *need*, not bombs."

"How wonderful it would be to send Henry there, with his knowledge of German."

"Well, maybe I will send *you* there someday."

Recalling his intention of sending me to India, I replied, "I thought you had other plans for me, Sir. But of course I'll go wherever you send me. I'm familiar with Europe, certainly, having grown up there."

"There is a great work to be done there."

Years later, I founded a work in Italy, with subsidiary meditation groups in other countries including Germany.

"Is this work a new religion?" I asked him one day at his desert retreat.

"It is a new *expression*," he corrected me.

Truth is one: *Sanaatan Dharma* as it is known in India—"the Eternal Religion." The great religions of the world are branches, all, on that one tree.

Sectarianism is divisive. "The one Ocean has become all its waves," Master once told me when I questioned him about his own role in the religious evolution of this planet. "You should look to the Ocean, not to the little waves protruding on its bosom."

CHAPTER 37

The Guru's Reminiscences

"IN THE EARLY days of Mt. Washington, a visitor once inquired of me superciliously, 'What are the assets of this organization?'

"'None!' I replied unhesitatingly, 'Only God.'"

Master was sitting with us downstairs, reminiscing about his early years in America. Toward the end of his life, in addition to counseling us, he spent many hours trying to make us feel a part of that long period of his life before most of us had come to him.

"My reply on that occasion was literally true, too," Master chuckled. "We hadn't *any* money! But it would be just as true today, when our work is financially solvent. For our strength has always been God alone. We might lose everything, materially speaking, but in His love we would still possess all that really mattered.

"Years ago a rich man came here who thought to buy me with his wealth. Knowing we were badly in need of money just then, he tried in certain ways to get me to compromise my ideals. I refused. Finally he said, 'You'll starve because you didn't listen.' Leaving here, he talked against me to a rich acquaintance of his, a student of this work. And *that* was the man whom God chose to give us the help we needed!

"Another time, years later, we were facing another financial crisis: Mt. Washington was threatened with foreclosure. I went out into the desert and meditated all night. 'Divine Mother,' I prayed, 'why did You give me this responsibility? I came to the West to speak of You, not to worry about organizational problems! If You took everything away, it would mean nothing to me but my freedom! Say the word, Mother, and I will walk out into the desert and never once look back!'

"At three o'clock in the morning came Her answer: '*I* am your stocks and bonds. What more dost thou need than that thou hast Me? Dance of death and dance of life—know that these come from Me. My child, rejoice!'

"The next day a check came in the mail for the exact amount of money that we needed."

Master often said, "He is happiest who gives everything to God." He told us an amusing story to illustrate his own preference for simple living, free of all ostentation.

"A wealthy student of mine wanted to buy me a new overcoat. Taking me into a well-known clothing store, he invited me to select any coat I wanted. Seeing one that looked nice, I reached out to touch it. But then, seeing the price tag, I quickly withdrew my hand. The coat was very expensive.

"'But I'd be *happy* to buy it for you,' my friend insisted. He added an expensive hat to match. I appreciated his kindness in giving me these gifts. But whenever I wore them, I felt uncomfortable. Expensive possessions are a responsibility.

"'Divine Mother,' I finally prayed, 'this coat is too good for me. Please take it away.'

"Soon afterwards I was scheduled to lecture at Trinity Auditorium. I sensed that the coat would be taken away from me that evening, so I emptied the pockets. After the lecture the coat was gone. What a relief!

"But then I spotted an omission. 'Divine Mother,' I prayed, 'You forgot to take the hat!'"

Master went on to tell us about someone he'd met long ago in New York. "This man told me, 'I can never forgive myself for taking thirty-five years to make my first million dollars.' 'You still are not satisfied?' I asked. 'No. I will not be satisfied until I have made *forty* million!' Well, before he could make those forty million and settle down to a life of unalloyed happiness, he suffered a complete nervous breakdown. Not long afterward, he died."

When I first wrote these lines, less than a week had passed since the death of Howard Hughes, one of the richest men in the world.

The radio carried his reply to a question, "Are you happy?" "No," the billionaire had answered thinly. "I can't say that I'm happy."

"You don't have to *own* a thing to enjoy it," Master told us. "To possess things is all right, provided your possessions don't possess you, but ownership often means only added worries. It is much better to own everything in God, and cling to nothing with your ego."

Smiling, he continued, "Years ago I visited Radio City Music Hall in New York. Having paid the price of admission, I told myself, 'While I am here, this building is mine!' I walked about, enjoying my beautiful acquisition. When I had enjoyed it as much as I cared to, I gave the building back to the management with thanks, and walked out a free man!"

Master told us of a time when his non-attachment had been tested. "I was standing alone one evening on a dark street corner in New York, when three holdup men came up from behind me; one of them pointed a gun.

"'Give us your money,' they demanded.

"'Here it is,' I said, not at all disturbed. 'But I want you to know that I am not giving it to you out of fear. I have wealth in my heart that makes money, by comparison, mean nothing to me.' They were so astonished! Then, as I gazed at them with God's power, they burst into tears. Returning my money, they cried, 'We can't live this way anymore!' At this point, overwhelmed by the experience, they ran away.

"On other occasions, too, I have changed the hearts of criminals—not I, but God's power through me. One evening during the depression years I lectured to thousands at Carnegie Hall. I spoke out against the way certain rich people were taking advantage of the poor. I actually mentioned a few names. Afterwards, several people urged me, 'Please don't go home alone tonight.'

"'God is with me,' I replied. 'Whom have I to fear?'

"Walking by myself, I entered a dimly lighted part of the station. Just then a man came up behind me brandishing a gun. 'Why did you talk against those people?' he demanded.

"'They deserved it,' I replied. 'God is for the common man as much as for the rich. Both are His children. And He is not pleased when His rich children take advantage of His poor ones.'"

Listening to Master, we chuckled at this point in his story. How incongruous, his ingenuous explanation beside the man's threat of assassination!

Master continued: "Gazing steadily into the man's eyes, I said, 'Why do you live the way you do? You aren't happy. I *demand* that Satan come out of you, and that you change!'

"The man began to tremble. All of a sudden, dropping his gun, he fell to his knees before me. 'What have you done to me?' he cried. 'I was sent to kill you.'

"'You can never win,' I said. 'Pick up your gun and throw it away.' His life was completely transformed by that meeting."

Master told of a similar conversion after another Carnegie Hall lecture. "We had chanted 'O God Beautiful!' for over an hour. Three thousand people had joined me joyfully in singing this chant. Many were in ecstasy. Afterwards, a man burst into my interview room. Flinging a revolver emotionally onto the desk, he cried, 'I ought to kill you for what you've done to me this evening! I can't go back to that way of life anymore.'

"Such is the power of God's love!

"But there have been times," Master continued, "when His power flowed through me in other ways. I follow only His will. One evening in Chicago I visited a park. It was during the depression years, and Chicago, as you know, was notorious at the time for its gangsters. A policeman stopped me as I was about to enter the park, and warned me that it wasn't safe there after dark. 'Even we are afraid to go in,' he said.

"Well, I went in anyway, and took a seat comfortably on a park bench. After some time, a tough-looking man, much larger than I, stopped in front of me.

"'Gimme a dime!' he snarled.

"I reached into a pocket and gave him a dime.

"'Gimme a quarter!' I gave him a quarter.

"'Gimme fifty cents.' I gave him fifty cents.

"'Gimme a dollar.'

"By now, seeing that matters obviously weren't going to improve, I leapt to my feet and, with God's power, shouted:

"'GET OUT!!!'

"The man began to tremble like a leaf. 'I don't want your money!' he mumbled. Backing fearfully away, he repeated, 'I don't want your money! I don't want your money!' Suddenly he turned and fled as though his life depended on it.

"I sat down peacefully once more and watched the moonrise. Later, as I was leaving the park, the same policeman as before saw me and asked, 'What did you say to that man? I saw him with you, and didn't dare to interfere. I know him for a dangerous character!'

"'Oh,' I replied, 'we came to a little understanding.'"

Whether Master protected himself by love, or by sterner measures, depended on the guidance he received inwardly. Perhaps love was what he gave to persons of innate sensitivity who had succumbed to the influences of an evil environment, and sternness to those whose cruelty was self-generated, or who, though not insensitive to finer feelings, suppressed them deliberately. In this last connection he told us of a guest at Mt. Washington during the 1920s. The man's sister was a resident disciple there. She was, in fact, Florina Darling: Durga Mata.

"I was sitting on my bed one morning, meditating," he said, "when God showed me this man coming up the stairs to give me a beating. The man was planning, you see, to boast publicly of what he had done, so as to discredit this work.

"'Give it to him!' the voice said.

"Moments later the man appeared in my doorway. Opening my eyes, I said to him, 'I know why you've come. You may not realize it, but I am very strong; I could easily best you in a fight if I wanted to. But I won't meet you on that level. Still, I warn you: Don't cross that threshold.'

"'Go on, prophet!' he sneered contemptuously. 'What could you do?'

"'I've warned you. You'll be sorry.'

"Ignoring my words, he stepped into the room. The instant he did so, he fell to the floor screaming, 'I'm on fire! I'm on fire!' Leaping up, he ran downstairs and out of the building. I followed quickly behind, and found him rolling about on the front lawn, still crying out, 'I'm on fire! I'm on fire!' When I placed a hand on him he became calm, though he was still terrified of me. 'Don't touch me!' he cried. 'Don't come near me!' He sent his sister into the building for his belongings, and departed at once."

Many were surprised to learn how physically powerful Master was. He was quite short—five feet five or six inches—and, though well built, didn't impress one as being particularly strong. But his strength came primarily from his complete command over the energy in his body.

"In Symphony Hall in Boston," he told us, "I was lecturing once on the merits of the energization exercises, and mentioned the great physical strength one derives from them. I then threw out the challenge: 'Would anyone here like to *try* my strength?'

"Six tall, burly policemen jumped up onto the stage! The audience gasped, certain that I'd fail this test.

"Well, facing those policemen, I placed my back against the wall. Then I asked the men to push on my stomach all together, as hard as they could. They did so. 'Is that the best you can do?' I demanded.

"'Yeah!' they grunted, clenching their teeth.

"Suddenly I arched my back. All six of them went tumbling back into the orchestra pit!"

People who knew only of Paramhansa Yogananda's extraordinary love and compassion, his sweetness, and his childlike simplicity, were sometimes taken aback when they encountered his power. Few realize that power and divine love are opposite sides of the same coin. Indeed, divine love is no gentle sentiment, but the greatest force in the universe. Such love could not exist without power. Great saints would never use their power to suppress or coerce others, but power is, nevertheless, inextricably a part of what it means to be a saint. It took extraordinary power, for example, for Jesus Christ, alone in a crowd, to drive the money-changers from their tradition-sanctioned places in the temple. Worldly people fear this power in the saints, and, fearing it, persecute them. They don't realize that a saint's power is rooted in love, or that it threatens nothing but people's delusions and ignorance-induced suffering.

Yogananda's power was not only a product of his divine awareness; his human personality, too, reflected past incarnations as a warrior and conquering hero. In Calcutta, in his youth, he was approached more than once by people who wanted him to lead a revolution against the British. There was something in his very bearing that bespoke the intrepid warrior.

He told us more than once that in a former life he had been William the Conqueror. Educated as I had been during my early years in the English educational system, I had always thought of William as one

of history's great villains. On learning that that supposed "villain" was my own Guru, I made it a point, needless to say, to study several biographies of William in order to get a broader picture of what he'd really been like.

I found that William the Conqueror was indeed, in every way, a great man. Morally, in an age of widespread profligacy, he was chaste and self-controlled. Spiritually he was deeply religious, and never (so I read) missed a day of mass in his life. He was noble, generous, and forgiving.

He lived, however, in an age when conquest could be accomplished only by a very strong will. He told us he had been given a divine commission, which I have since come to understand was to bring England out of the Scandinavian sphere and under the influence of Roman Christianity. During his lifetime, William promoted the recovery of old monasteries and generally gave great support to the church, endorsing also the concept of chastity for the clergy. William and Archbishop Lanfranc, together, unified the church, and reorganized it from the ground up.

Quite as important in the context of those times, they connected the church administratively, canonically, and liturgically with Rome. His closest friends were spiritual men like Abbot Lanfranc (who in this life, Yogananda stated, was Swami Sri Yukteswar) and Saint Osmund, Bishop of Salisbury. William's occasionally harsh behavior was forced on him by necessity, and never sprang from personal anger (though, consistent with my observation of Master himself on occasion, William's demeanor sometimes appeared very fierce).

I asked Master once (I was thinking of his lifetime as William): "Sir, is an *avatar* [a divine incarnation] always aware of his oneness with God's omnipresence?"

"He never loses his consciousness of inner freedom," Master replied.

William's life, when studied in this light, gains new luster and meaning.

The British historian, E.A. Freeman, wrote in his biography, *William the Conqueror*: "[What we English are today] has largely come of the fact that there was a moment our national destiny might be said to hang on the will of a single man, and that was William [the Conqueror]."

Earlier, Freeman stated: "The Norman conquest . . . has no exact parallel in history . . . largely owing to the character and position of the man who wrought it. The history of England for the last eight hundred years has largely come of the personal character of [that] single man."

Harold Godwinson, on the other hand, though romanticized by those Englishmen who cannot bear the thought that their country was ever justly conquered, was not a noble character at all. He was, moreover, at least half Danish, not pure Anglo-Saxon as many believe; he has erroneously been reported to be the son of a sister of King Canute, but was (if it matters) not of royal birth at all.

England itself was by no means so Anglo-Saxon as relatively recent writers, including Sir Walter Scott, imagined. The north, according to recent DNA testing of old bones, was heavily Scandinavian, and the east came under what was called Danelaw, and must have been more Danish than Anglo-Saxon.

It was William who united the constantly warring earldoms into one kingdom. His legacy, moreover, which bound every native to primary loyalty to his king, saved England the fate of medieval Europe, which saw constant baronial conflicts.

Some months after Master's passing, an inspiration came to me: I suddenly realized that I had been his youngest son, Henry, who later was crowned as Henry I. I had always known with an inner certainty that I had been a king in the past—not that it mattered to me in the present. Leadership had always come to me naturally, however, and in no way caused me to feel important because of it. Rather, I saw it as a means of rendering service to others—of encouraging, and perhaps guiding, them toward their own fulfillment.

I now went to the Los Angeles public library and read up on facts about Henry that were too detailed to appear in a book intended for the general public. It surprised me to see how many parallels there were, even in little matters, between Henry's life and my own.

Henry had been born late enough in William's life to be in a position, after a relatively brief hiatus, to carry on William's mission. The last thirty-three years of Henry's life were years of exceptional peace and prosperity in England. Though he is considered the "least-known" of all English kings, the reason for his obscurity is that he simply worked quietly to establish his father's mission. Albeit known in his lifetime as the most powerful king in Western Europe, he never expressed an interest in enlarging his dominions. All he ever did was conquer back territory that had been lost by his older brothers' ineptitude. The promises he made in his Coronation Charter, though I've read derisive statements to the effect that "of course" he didn't honor them, were honored by him as much as the circumstances permitted. That charter became the basis of the future Magna Carta.

William's first two sons were an embarrassment to his memory. He bequeathed Robert, his oldest, the dukedom of Normandy, knowing that he could not give him the crown of England because of his traitorous nature. (Even as William was lying on his deathbed, Robert, with the aid of the king of France, was staging a rebellion against him.) William Rufus, the second son, was loyal to their father in his fashion, but gave no evidence of understanding William's mission, and dedicated himself wholly to his own power, position, and glory. Perhaps a hiatus in William's mission was necessary for his true spiritual heir, Henry, to develop a deep understanding of it.

A number of specific people in Master's present life had, he said, been with him in that life. Faye (Daya) told me she had been his daughter Agatha. He had sent her to Spain, she said, to marry the heir to the throne, but she had been so desirous of dedicating her life to God that, when her ship arrived in port, she was found in her cabin on her knees, dead.

"Ever since then," she confided to me, "I've had trouble with my knees." I've reflected since then: If indeed Master was not only her father, but her guru, why would dying on her knees in prayer have resulted ever since in *pain* in her knees? Whatever we do to accomplish God's will for us results in blessings for ourselves. Might it not be, then, that she had important lessons to learn in leadership, which she rejected?

I've related earlier that Master told us he was also Arjuna, the disciple of Krishna (who in this life is Babaji). It is interesting to contemplate that both Arjuna in the Bhagavad Gita, and Yogananda in *Autobiography of a Yogi*, expressed themselves with amazement at the divine teachings, as if they themselves were only spiritual neophytes. Both men, however, were already great masters. According to ancient Indian tradition, Arjuna and Krishna had been two great ancient sages, Nara and Narayan.

An interesting story is related about Nara. Satan, to tempt him, materialized before him a beautiful womanly form. Nara promptly materialized a hundred more such forms, and indicated no interest in any of them.

An interesting sidelight on all this is that both Arjuna and William were said to possess bows that only they had the strength to string.

Master said he had also been a leader in Spain, whose mission had been to drive the Moors out of that country, after the Moors had gained a foothold in the Christian West. He didn't tell us who that person was, however.

As an amusing aside, I came upon him one day when he was sitting in the car with Sr. Cuaron from Mexico. Evidently Sr. Cuaron had mentioned something to him about my speaking Spanish, for Master looked at me with a big smile and said, "Cual es su nombre? (What is your name?)" I, smiling also, answered, "Mi nombre es Donald Walters."

One night, the nuns on his floor heard a loud metallic clanking from Master's quarters. The next day he told them that a soldier who had served under him in a former life (perhaps in Spain) had materialized before him and asked for spiritual freedom. How many strange stories one encounters on the spiritual path. I have told hardly a tithe of them.

Master, like William, could be very outspoken when occasion demanded it. It simply wasn't in his nature to be insincere. One time, unable to beg off giving a speech after a high-society banquet, to which he'd been dragged in New York City, he spoke what was in his heart. Sternly he upbraided his listeners for the shallowness of their lives. He didn't condemn them; the indignation he expressed, rather, was on *their* behalf. Graphically he described to them their delusions, and exhorted them to stop wasting another entire incarnation in spiritual sloth. His hearers were stunned. Many wept.

Yet the experience, painful for them though it was, also came to them because of their good karma. For how many people get a chance to hear what they need from a man of true wisdom? Master himself once told Dr. Lewis, "No one's path has crossed mine in this life except for a reason."

Another story that shows how outspoken Master could be concerns a visit he once paid to a certain vegetarian organization. "I was invited to inspect their facilities," he told me. "They believed in raw foods, or, as they called them, 'unfired foods.' They took me around their kitchen, and then into the dining room, where they served me the worst meal I have ever eaten in my life. After this epicurean disaster, they asked me to address them!

"I tried to decline.

"'Oh, but you *must* speak to us,' they insisted. 'Everyone is eager to hear you.'

"'You won't like what I have to say,' I warned. Well, they wouldn't take no for an answer, so at last I stood up.

"'In the first place,' I said, 'I have never in my life tasted worse food. What makes you think there is virtue in preparing meals that are so unpalatable? Enjoyment of what one eats is an aid to the digestion. But you all imagine that what you are eating is healthful. In no way is it so. It is seriously lacking in nutritive balance.'

"Well, by this time they were all greatly agitated! 'You don't know what you are saying,' they shouted.

"'I urge you to take me seriously,' I replied, 'for unless you improve your diet, in fifteen days one of you will die of malnutrition.'

"'You are cursing us!'

"'I'm doing nothing of the kind,' I said. 'You are cursing yourselves by your fanaticism!'

"Well, they wouldn't listen. Fifteen days later one of them died, and soon afterward the whole organization disbanded."

Master usually accepted evil as a regrettable but necessary aspect of the cosmic drama. He fought it especially in people who sought his spiritual aid. "The villain's role on the stage," he used to say, "is to get people to love the hero. Evil's part in the drama of life is, similarly, to spur people on to seek goodness." There were times, however, when he became an avenging angel, particularly when the lives of his own disciples, or of those dear to them, were affected.

The mother of a close disciple was afflicted with cancer of the breast. Finding a sanatorium that advertised a newly discovered and supposedly miraculous cancer cure, she entered it hopefully.

"All that they gave their patients," Master told us, "was water! They took their money, fed them nothing, and simply waited for them to die. When I found out about their scheme, I cried, 'Divine Mother, destroy that place!' Within a month the police came in and closed it. The leaders were all sent to prison."

Master went on to speak of that woman's subsequent death. "I contacted her in the astral world. When I came upon her, she was being led away by an angel, and was marveling at the beauty of the flowers in a field they were crossing. I called to her, but she didn't hear me. Again I called; this time she turned, but at first she didn't recognize me. In the transition of death, you see, she had forgotten. But I touched her, and recognition came. 'I will never again forget you,' she promised. Then, opening her flowing robe, she showed me where the cancer had been. 'See?' she said, smiling. 'It is gone now!'

"Soon thereafter I saw her again, in the sunset."

Master explained to us that after the death of the physical body, the soul remains encased in a subtler body of energy, known as the "astral body." This body is the prototype for the physical body. The astral universe, similarly, forms the prototype for the grosser material universe. When a person dies, he lives on in an astral body, and may, if he is spiritually even slightly developed, inhabit an astral planet with vibrations harmonious to his own. His length of stay there is determined by his karma, and by the strength of his material desires.

In one of the most inspiring chapters of *Autobiography of a Yogi*, Paramhansa Yogananda gives a lengthy description of the astral universe. It is composed, he tells us, of endlessly varied vibrations of light-energy. Compared to this physical world, the astral heavens are inexpressibly beautiful. Not everyone, however, goes to those higher heavens after death. As Jesus put it, "In my Father's house are many mansions."*

Many souls are vibrationally attracted to less exalted, though still harmonious, spheres. Others, having created nothing but disharmony in their own earth-lives, are vibrationally drawn to astral hells. Materialistic people often are only dimly conscious of the astral world between earthly sojourns. People who developed good qualities while on earth, however, especially those who meditated and acquired a measure of soul-awareness, are attracted after death to higher astral worlds.

To Master, death was no "undiscovered country from whose bourne no traveller returns." He told us he spent much of his time in the astral world. Thus, to him, death itself was no tragedy. At the same time, however, he was too warmly human not to feel the reality of people's bereavement, or to offer loving sympathy to them in their grief. Indeed, he sometimes offered far more than sympathy: He actually brought loved ones back "from the grave."

One case involved a lady in Encinitas. Master told me the story:

"A real estate agent in Encinitas, hearing that I had healing power, came to me and requested a healing for his wife, who had been ill for ninety days. I prayed, but God told me not to go to her bedside. Shortly thereafter, she died. Only then was I given the guidance to go there.

"About thirty people were in the room when I arrived. Her husband was weeping and shaking her, almost out of his mind with grief. He wouldn't accept the fact that she was already dead. I motioned him away.

"Putting one hand on the dead woman's forehead, and the other one under her head, I began to invoke the divine power. Five minutes passed. Ten minutes. Suddenly her whole body began to vibrate like a motor. After some time, a deep calmness stole over her. Her heartbeat and breathing returned. Slowly her eyes opened; they

* John 14:2.

held a far-away expression, as though she had just returned from a long journey. She was completely healed."

Another episode concerned a man in Serampore (Sri Ram Pur), a Calcutta suburb. I first heard the story from Master, and then again years later from Sri Tulsi Bose, a childhood friend of his, and a cousin of the man who had died. As Tulsi told me the story, it was because the man was Tulsi's cousin that Master performed this miracle.

"I was passing the house," Master told us, "when I heard a loud outcry within. God told me to go inside. I found a man there stretched out on a bed. Five or ten minutes earlier the doctors had pronounced him dead. The family were all weeping and crying.

"I requested them to leave the room, and remained alone with the dead man for some time, praying. Breath returned to his body at last. His eyes opened. He was fully alive again."

Master was equally at home on all levels of reality. To those who identified with this physical plane of existence and its sorrows, he was compassionate. In the astral world, where physical sufferings are unknown, he was like a sea captain, returning to port as often as he wished. But his own true affinity was with spheres far subtler than either of these: the timeless bliss of divine union. It was amazing to see how effortlessly he entered *samadhi*. For most of us struggling devotees it took time even to touch the hem of superconsciousness. For him, the vastness of cosmic consciousness was always only a breath away.

I remember someone asking his permission one evening to take his photograph. "Just a moment," Master replied, "let me first go into *samadhi*." After two or three seconds, he said, "All right."

"I used sometimes to go to movies," Master told us, "to get away from the unceasing demands of the work. Sitting in the movie theater, I would enter *samadhi*. Later, if people asked me how I liked the movie, I replied, 'Very much!' I had been watching the cosmic 'movie,' with stars and planets whirling through space!"

No environment was wholly mundane to him. Everywhere he saw God. "Do you know where I wrote my poem '*Samadhi*'?" he asked us one day. "It was on the New York subway! As I was writing, I rode back and forth from one end of the line to the other. No one asked for my ticket. In fact," he added with a twinkle in his eyes, "no one even saw me!"

Visitors sometimes boasted of their own high experiences in meditation. Boastfulness would make any discerning person skeptical; true experiences of God, after all, should make one humble. But Master could tell at a glance what level a person had reached in his spiritual development.

"People have a very distorted notion of what the spiritual path is all about," he said. "Visions and phenomena aren't important. What matters is complete self-offering to God. One must be absorbed in His love.

"I remember a man who came forward after a lecture in New York and claimed that he could enter cosmic consciousness at will. Actually, what he meant was that he could travel astrally, but I saw right away that his experiences were imaginary. Still, I couldn't simply tell him so; he wouldn't have believed me. So I invited him up to my room. There I asked him to favor me by going into cosmic consciousness.

"Well, he sat there fidgeting, eyelids flickering, breath heaving— signs, all, of body-consciousness, not of cosmic consciousness! At last he could contain himself no longer.

"'Why don't you ask me where I am?'

"'Well,' I said, to humor him, 'where are you?'

"In rounded tones, as if hallooing from a distance, he replied: 'On top of the dome of the Taj Mahal!'

"'There must be something the matter with your own dome!' I remarked. 'I see you sitting fully here, right in front of me.' He was utterly taken aback.

"I then made a suggestion. 'If you think you can travel all the way to the Taj Mahal in India, why not see if you can go somewhere nearby, to test the validity of your experience?' I suggested that he project himself to the hotel dining room downstairs, and describe what he saw there. He agreed to the test. Going into 'cosmic consciousness' again, he described the dining room as he saw it. He actually believed in his visions, you see. What I wanted to do was demonstrate to him that they were the products of a vivid power of visualization. He described a number of things in the restaurant, including a group of people seated in a corner farther from the door.

"I then described the scene as I saw it. 'In the right-hand corner,' I said, 'there are two women seated at a table by the door.' I described a few more things as they were at the moment. We went downstairs at once, and found the room as I had described it, not as he had. At last he was convinced."

Master often told us stories of his boyhood in India. Years later I wrote and published several of these accounts in a booklet named *Stories of Mukunda*. Here is one that was omitted from that book, as it didn't quite fit the mood of it.

"The first time I fed the poor in India," Master said, "I decided to feed two hundred people. I was just a boy. Everybody wondered how I planned to do it. Another boy, a friend of mine, objected, 'You haven't any money. Neither have I. There's just no way we can feed that many people.'

"'All I need,' I replied, 'is twenty rupees. And that money will come through you.'

"'Impossible!' he cried.

"'It will happen,' I assured him, 'but on one condition: that you take care in no way to antagonize your mother today.'

"Later that day his mother told him to go to his rich aunt's home and deliver something. He was about to refuse, offering some excuse, when he remembered my warning. Docility was hardly his normal attitude, but this time he went without a murmur, and delivered the package.

"When he arrived at his aunt's house, she began scolding him, 'Who is this boy you've been running around with?' Her reference was to me. Like many wealthy people, she tended to harbor suspicions of strangers. My friend grew angry. He was about to leave when she cried, 'Stop! I hear he is planning on doing some good. Take this money and use it.' She gave him twenty rupees.

"The word had already been making the rounds that we were planning to feed the poor. Those twenty rupees bought a sizable amount of rice and lentils. When the neighbors saw this tangible support for our plans, they became enthusiastic. Money came pouring in from all sides. People volunteered their services to help with cooking and serving. Instead of two hundred poor people that day, we fed two thousand!"

Talk turned one evening to the attributes of success. "Will power," Master told us, "is more important to success than knowledge, training, or even native ability. Some people, when you shake them, reply with a groan, 'Don't bother me; I'm sleeping.' Others wake up a little bit, then if you leave them alone for a few minutes they start dozing again. But some people, the moment you speak to them, are wide awake, and keep on going without having to be prodded again. Those are the kind of people I like!

"When I first started on my own in the spiritual life, I settled in a little mud hut with two other boys. One of them was about my size: short and slight. The other was a big, stalwart fellow. One day I said to them, 'Let's lay a cement floor in the main room.'

"'Impossible!' protested the big fellow. 'We don't have the cement; we don't have the equipment; we don't have the know-how; we don't have the money. For a technical job like this you need experience.'

"'If we make up our minds,' I replied, 'we can do it.'

"'Wishful thinking!' he scoffed, and walked away to show what he thought of the scheme.

"That day the other boy and I went around to the neighbors. Bit by bit we gathered donations of materials, and loans of equipment. Two men added careful instructions on how to mix and lay the cement. That whole night we stayed up, mixing and pouring. By the following morning the job was finished. The big fellow returned later to our little hermitage.

"'Well,' I sighed, teasing him, 'I guess you were right.'

"'Aha,' he cried. 'You see? I told you so!'

"I then asked him please to fetch me something from the next room. He opened the door. And there was our new cement floor! We'd even colored it red. He was dumbfounded."

Master went on to emphasize that miracles are possible when man's will is united to God's will.

"Not many miles from our school in Ranchi, there was a high waterfall, above which loomed a rock ledge, dangerous to walk upon. Sometimes I would take the boys across there.

"'Do you believe in God?' I shouted to them over the noise of the water.

"'Yes!' they would all shout back. And so, chanting God's name, we always crossed over in safety.

"One day, several years after I had gone to America, another teacher in the school tried to lead a group of boys across there, repeating the words I had used. One of the boys slipped off the ledge and was drowned. It was because that teacher didn't have inner power. Faith must be rooted in spiritual realization, you see, otherwise it lacks vitality.

"And then, too," Master added, "one's motives must be pure. A few years ago two young boys in India decided that, because they believed in God, He would surely protect them no matter what they did. To prove their point they took a sword, and went out into a nearby forest. One of them kneeled; the other aimed a sweeping blow at his neck with the sword. Well, God didn't consider their presumption deserving of a miracle. The kneeling boy was killed instantly. Had their faith been pure, those children would have had the understanding not to behave so rashly in the first place. A person with pure motives doesn't try to coerce God. When you act in tune with Him, things always turn out well."

On another occasion Master was talking to us about the power of true faith. "One evening I had just returned to Mt. Washington when a sudden, violent wind struck the main building. It was an effect from the evil karma of World War II. People little realize how greatly the very elements are affected by mass consciousness. I told Miss Darling to remove one of her shoes and use it to strike the front porch three times, repeating certain words. She did as I'd said. On the third blow, the wind stopped instantly. In the newspaper the next day there was an item about the violent wind that had started up in Los Angeles, and then, minutes later, abated.

"The mind's potential," Master added, "is considerable, even without the addition of divine power. One day I was traveling in this

country by train. It was a very hot summer day, and the train had no
air conditioning. Everyone was suffering in the heat. I said to those
who were with me, 'See what a little concentration can do. I will
meditate on the thought of icebergs.'

"Minutes later, I held out an arm for them to feel. It was ice cold."

Master often regaled us with amusing anecdotes of his beginnings
in America. "Because of my robe and long hair, people sometimes
thought I was a woman. Once, at a Boston flower exhibition, I wanted to find the men's room. A guard directed me to a certain door.
Trustingly I went in. My goodness! Ladies to the left of me, ladies
to the right of me, ladies everywhere! I rushed out, and once more
approached the guard.

"'I want the *men's* room,' I insisted. Eyeing me suspiciously, he
finally pointed to another door. This time as I entered a man cried
out, 'Not in here, lady! Not in here!'

"In a deep bass voice I answered, 'I know what I am doing!'

"Another time on a train the black conductor kept walking up and
down the aisle, eyeing me. Finally he could restrain his curiosity no
longer. 'Is yo a man,' he asked, 'or is yo a woman?'

"'What do you theenk?'* I demanded in a deep, booming tone.

"I used to wear a beard. On
the ship coming over from India,
a fellow passenger, a Muslim by the
name of Rashid, persuaded me to
shave it off. Americans, he insisted, might accept me if I had *either*
long hair *or* a beard, but definitely
not if I kept both. Since my master
had expressed a wish that I keep my
hair long, I decided to sacrifice the
beard. Rashid volunteered his services as a barber. I placed myself
trustingly in his hands. He lathered

A young Yogananda with beard.

---

* Master spoke English with a pronounced Bengali accent. I've emphasized his pronunciation here because it was part of the charm of the story.

my face, then proceeded carefully to shave off one half of it. At that point, he walked off, abandoning me! And I had no notion of how to shave! I was stranded until, after some hours, he returned, laughing, to complete the job.

"Rashid was a great prankster. But he was also very helpful to me when I began my first lecture tour. He got the halls, prepared the publicity, and acted as my secretary. Still, he did play pranks!

"One evening, however, I got the better of him. He was always avoiding his work, and running after girls. He didn't realize that I knew what he was doing. On this particular evening he'd promised to come in and work with me. When he didn't show up, I knew just where to find him. I went to a nearby park, and there he was, sitting on a bench with a new girl. (He certainly had a way with them!) I crept up stealthily from behind and stood nearby, hidden by a bush. He put his arms around the girl, and was just about to kiss her, when I cried out in a deep, loud voice, 'Rasheeeed!' You should have seen him jump! He came regularly into the office after that, and worked quite docilely!"

We all laughed uproariously at Master's story, which was delivered with suitably droll gestures and expressions.

"But," he concluded, "Rashid, years later, more than made up for all his pranks. He was living in India when I returned there in 1935. He prepared a huge public reception for me in Calcutta, complete with banners and a procession through the streets. I was deeply touched."

I myself got to meet Rashid in Calcutta in 1959. By that time he was much older, but even then it was easy to imagine him as the debonair prankster of his youth.

"When I first came to America," Master continued, "my father sent me money. But I wanted to rely wholly on God, so I returned it. In the beginning, God let me taste a little hardship to test my faith in Him, but my faith was firm, and He never failed me."

Master continued his reminiscences of those years. "A student of this work in Boston told me he wanted to be a renunciate. I said to him, 'Your path is marriage.'

"'Oh, no!' he vowed, 'I'll *never* marry!' Well, a week later he met a beautiful girl and swore to me that he was deeply in love with her!

"'She isn't the one for you,' I warned him.

"'Oh, but she *is*!' he cried. 'She is my soul mate.'

"Well, it wasn't long after that that he returned shamefacedly. 'I want to be a renunciate,' he announced fervently once again. The girl had left him, having enjoyed spending his money.

"'You have yet to meet the right one,' I said.

"Some time later he told me laughingly of a fat, quite unattractive-looking girl who had been showing an unwelcome interest in him.

"'Aha,' I said, 'this sounds like the right one!'

"'No Swami, no!' he cried, horrified. 'You were right before. *Please* don't be right this time!'

"'She sounds like the right one for you.'

"It took him some time, but gradually he discovered what a good nature the girl had beneath her unglamorous exterior, and fell deeply in love with her. Eventually they were married.

"People are so often blinded by outward appearances," Master continued. "Marriage in this country is often a union between a pretty shade of lipstick and a smart-looking bow tie! They hear a little music, fall into a romantic mood, and end up pledging their lives away.

"I remember a couple who came to me in Phoenix and asked me to marry them 'immediately.' I replied, 'I must know the people I marry. I want to meditate on your request. Please come back tomorrow.' At this proposed delay, the man was furious. When they returned the next day, he pressed me, 'Is it all right?'

"'No,' I said.

"He was enraged once again. 'Let's get out of here, *dear*! We can get married by somebody else.'

"They'd almost reached the door when I called out to them. 'Remember my words: You will never be happy together. You will find that out when it is too late. But please, I urge you, at least don't kill each other!'

"They were married elsewhere. Soon afterward they came to Mt. Washington just to show me how happy they were. I said nothing, but inside I thought, 'You don't know what is hidden under that lid!'

"Six months later they returned. This time they knelt humbly before me and confessed, 'We didn't realize how different our natures were. If you hadn't warned us, we would surely have ended up killing each other.' Under the influence of emotional intoxication, you see, they hadn't observed the explosive violence lurking behind their smiles and kisses.

"People must learn to look behind the veil of superficial attraction. Without soul harmony there cannot be true love."

Master saw every human experience, including that of marriage, primarily as an opportunity for inner, spiritual development. Romantic notions of "wedded bliss" were, to him, simply and purely delusions. It wasn't that he denied the satisfactions of a harmonious marriage, but rather that he wanted devotees to see all human experiences as steppingstones to the soul's only true fulfillment, in God. Thus, he recommended to people who sought marriage that they first look for spiritual compatibility in their mates, and only secondarily for mental, emotional, and physical compatibility. He saw marriage not only as a fulfillment, but, much more importantly, as an opportunity for learning essential spiritual lessons in selflessness, loyalty, kindness, respect, and trust.

To devotees who, in the name of dispassion, considered it unnecessary to express these qualities outwardly towards their fellow creatures, he said, "Don't imagine that God will come to you if you behave unkindly to others. Until you know how to win human love, you will never win God's love."

To Master, human experience was, in a sense, part of a process of divine healing. Man's supreme disease, he said, is spiritual ignorance. Master's own life was devoted to healing people on all levels, in keeping with his philosophy that religion should serve humanity's total needs: physical, emotional, and mental, as well as spiritual. Though the supreme "cure" he offered was divine bliss, he healed many whom I knew, including myself, of various physical ailments.

One case of physical healing that stands out in my mind occurred years before I entered the work. Master told us the story:

"It was during the Chicago World's Fair, in 1933. Dr. Lewis telephoned me in Los Angeles to report that a friend of his had a blood clot on the heart and was dying. Could I help him? I sat in meditation and prayed. Suddenly a great power went out from me, like an explosion. At that same instant the man, who had been in a coma, was healed and sat up, fully conscious. A nurse was in the same room at the time—not a spiritual woman at all. She testified later that she'd heard an explosion in the room, and had seen a brilliant flash of light. The man recovered completely."

Master then spoke of the most important kind of healing: the dispelling of soul ignorance. "That is why we have these ashrams," he said, "for those who want to give their lives to God, to be healed of *all* suffering forevermore." He talked on about those earlier years at Mt. Washington.

Looking at us sweetly, he concluded, "How I wish you all had been with me then! So many years had to pass before you came."

CHAPTER 38

His Last Days

Oh, I will come again and again!
Crossing a million crags of suffering,
With bleeding feet, I will come —
If need be, a trillion times —
So long as I know
One stray brother is left behind.
      —from "God's Boatman," by Paramhansa Yogananda

RAINDROPS FALL TO earth, play their countless separate roles, then rise again, to fall in endlessly repeated cycles. Similar is the tale of each soul. Through unnumbered cycles of return we refine our understanding, until we've convinced ourselves to our very depths that the fulfillment we are seeking is ours already — in the bliss of our own being!

Why should it take so long to make such a simple discovery? Why is it so difficult to realize that earthly pleasures are but reflections of our inner joy? Alas, in a house of mirrors one is less inclined to introspect. The reflections are simply too fascinating! If one gives thought to himself, it may be only for the sake of changing those reflections. With human life, similarly, the reflections of our inner joy perceived in outer fulfillments are simply too tantalizing! Many lifetimes pass, usually, before we realize that our fascination has been with mere reflections; that we have been living in an unreal world.

Normally, when a soul achieves final emancipation, ending its long cycle of incarnations, its joy in victory is so overwhelming that it feels no desire to return to this earthly dungeon. Even the spiritual hunger of other seekers cannot suffice to lure it back, for such a soul feels—justifiably, surely—that after untold millions of years in bondage it has earned the right to claim at last its hard-won reward of eternal bliss.

Only a few extraordinary souls, having finally earned soul freedom, postpone the perfect enjoyment of it to return to this darkness and lead other struggling souls out of delusion into the light. Of such rare souls, Paramhansa Yogananda is a shining example. Indeed, even among those few it must be the exception who promises to come back "if need be, a trillion times." Yogananda's compassion simply staggers the imagination.

How many times has he come back already? "I killed Yogananda long ago," he said. My own thought is that he has been coming back for many, many thousands of years. Indeed, I wonder if he and our line of gurus were not, perhaps, designated by God as the saviors of this planet. This, however, is only speculation.

Devotees sometimes ask, "Do souls that have been born on this earth keep reincarnating here?" Master's reply, when I once posed this question to him, was, "No, there are innumerable planets to go to." He added, "If they returned always to the same one, they might find out too quickly!" Divine perception must be earned, in other words. It is not the "plot" of this cosmic drama for wisdom to be thrust upon anyone, uninvited; one must employ personally the sword of discrimination. The house of mirrors must lose its fascination because one has seen through its tricks, rather than merely because, by constant repetition, the reflections have ceased to interest him.

In one respect, however, the soul does tend toward a long repetition of outward associations: in its relationships with other souls.

An example may help here. In the nebulous gasses of infinite space, the atoms drift about at great distances from one another; the average, so I have read, may be as much as seventeen miles: much too far for their gravitational fields to attract one another. But if two atoms happen to drift together, their combined field makes it easier for them to attract a third atom. For three it is still easier to attract a fourth. Thus, an occasional ball of matter keeps on growing until its gravitational field encompasses at last a radius of many millions of miles. At some point in this process a mighty implosion occurs, as nebulous gasses are sucked inward from vast distances. The gravitational force of this huge mass becomes so great that changes occur within the structure of the atoms themselves: A shining star is born.

The soul, similarly, in its gradual progress toward divine wisdom, develops the "gravitational" power by which it attracts and holds the understanding it needs for enlightenment, until at last, in the firmament of living beings, it becomes a veritable "star."

In the same way, too, the soul develops the gravitational pull to form meaningful and lasting relationships with other souls. Gradually, in its outer life, it, and others with whom it is spiritually compatible, form great families of souls that return to earth, or to other planets, to work out their salvation—not only inwardly on themselves, but by interaction with one another. To achieve divine emancipation, it is necessary to spiritualize one's relations with the objective world and with other human beings, as well as with God.

The stronger the family, spiritually speaking, the greater its attractive pull on new souls that may still be wandering in search of an identity of their own. A family evolves with its individual members; at last it, too, becomes a "star" in the firmament of humanity, and begins to produce great souls of Self-realization.

As spiritual "stars," such great families become powerful for the general upliftment of mankind. Like stars, too, they then draw "planets" of less-evolved families into their beneficial auras, vitalizing them with rays of divine truth. Such families are like mighty nations. To them is given the real task of guiding the human race—not in the way governments do, by official ordinances, but by subtler, spiritual influence.

Yogananda's is one such spiritual family. His forms part of a greater spiritual "nation" of which Jesus Christ and Sri Krishna (in this age, Babaji) are also leaders. Yogananda, like William the Conqueror at Hastings, came to America to establish a beachhead—not, in this case, of worldly conquest, but of divine communion. Many have been born and are being born in the West to assist him in his mission. Many others are being attracted to it for the first time by the radiant magnetic influence, the spiritual "gravitational field," it has created.

* * * * * * *

During the last year and a half of Master's life, long-time disciples gathered around him, as though somehow aware that his end was approaching. Some who, for a variety of reasons, had not seen him for years, visited him now. Others who hadn't met him yet, but whose destiny it was to do so in this life, came as if in a hurry to arrive before it was too late.

Recalling Master's panoramic vision, in 1920, of all his destined disciples in America, I asked him in June 1950, "Have you already met most of those you saw in your vision at Ranchi?"

"Practically all," he replied. "I am waiting for only a few more to come."

Among close disciples who visited him during his last year were Señor Cuaron from Mexico, Mr. Black from Detroit (Michigan), and Kamala Silva from Oakland (California).

After Mr. Black's departure, Master remarked to me with loving reminiscence, "Did you see God in his eyes?"

Of Kamala he said to us one day, "Look at that girl. For twenty-seven years she has been in this work. She is very near freedom. After she had been with me a long time, living here at Mt. Washington, I told her she should marry.

"'Oh, no, Master,' she said, 'I don't want to.' But I urged her to, and promised her she would be safe. It was a little past karma she had to work out. I picked out her husband myself.* What a wonderful soul he is—a true *sannyasi*, just like one of you all!"

Señor Cuaron came in 1950, then again in 1951. I first met him moments after someone had delivered a huge, rather shapeless suitcase onto the carpet by the front door of the lobby. I was smiling at the sight of this formless lump when a voice somewhere above me announced, "That's mine." I looked up, and there in human form was the bag's counterpart! I found nothing to smile at, however, except lovingly, in Señor Cuaron's spiritual nature. I soon discovered that he had a heart as large as his body.

---

* Her husband, Edward Silva, was a school teacher in Oakland, California.

Master had great love for him. "I lost touch with you for a few incarnations," Master told him, "but I shall never lose touch with you again." Thereafter Señor Cuaron would lovingly remind Master from time to time of his promise. "Never again," came the loving reassurance.

Mme. Galli-Curci, the famed opera singer, settled near Encinitas. "Has she advanced far spiritually?" I once asked Master, who sometimes discussed with me the spiritual states of the disciples. "She is soaring in God!" he replied blissfully.

Arthur Cometer, who had accompanied Master on his lecture tour across the country in 1924, and had inspected Mt. Washington the first time with Master in 1925, visited the headquarters also during this period. Master spoke of him with warm appreciation.

At about this time also, Jesse Anderson, an elderly disciple in San Jose, California, gave Master a picture of Sri Yukteswar that he had stitched in colored yarn. Retired from work now, and living on a small pension, Mr. Anderson had financed the purchase of the yarn by gathering walnuts from the ground on the roadside, and selling them.

Master was deeply touched by the gift. He had it hung in the hallway at the top of the staircase outside his quarters. Frequently, when passing this picture, he would pause silently, with his palms folded

Jesse Anderson and the picture of Sri Yukteswar he made out of colored yarn.

together in solemn salute to his great guru. Master's reverence for Sri Yukteswar was all the more touching because he himself had long ago outgrown the status of a disciple.

There is a saying, "No man is great in the eyes of his own valet." In the case of saints that saying is falsified, for their own close disciples, who know them best, are the people who regard them the most highly. Sri Yukteswar's nature was stern; he had not been an easy guru to follow. Many a would-be disciple, seeing only his surface personality, had fled at the first crack of his disciplinary whip. But Master had seen the divine consciousness behind the mask.

"One day," he told us, "a group of disciples got fed up with the strictness of his training, and decided to leave him. 'Come,' they said to me, 'we'll follow you. He is too severe for us.'

"'*You* go if you like,' I said sternly. '*I* stay here with my Guru!'"

In Master's case, too, I observed that those disciples who knew him best were invariably those also who held him in the highest esteem.

One such disciple was Sister Gyanamata. Much older than he, the dignified widow of a university professor, and a person who seldom praised anybody, she yet displayed a respect for Master so undeviating, so humble, so profound that the worldly person, visiting the ashram for the first time, might have supposed her the merest neophyte.

In Master's presence, I was told, she always remained standing.

"I was once in the main room of the Encinitas hermitage with Sister and a few others," said Eugene Benvau, a brother disciple, "when Master entered. Sister, though an old woman, stood up immediately with the rest of us. Master never glanced at her, nor did he say a word. Walking over to the window, he gazed out at the ocean. Sister wasn't looking at him, either. But after a while I noticed that both of them were smiling quietly—a sort of inward smile. Several minutes later, Master left the room, having spoken not a word to anyone. But I had a strong feeling that he and Sister had been in silent communication with each other."

"I have only to hold a thought about Sister," Master told us, "and the next day a letter comes from her." A number of her letters to

Master, and to fellow disciples about her relationship with Master, appear in the book *God Alone.**

"Dear Children," she once wrote to some of the younger nuns, "Yesterday you put the question, 'What is the last word in discipleship? What would be the distinguishing mark of the perfect disciple?'

"You know that I am always quiet when in the presence of the Master. This is not a pose, intended to win his approval, nor is it altogether because I know this to be the proper way to behave. It is because I have an inner feeling of stillness. I seem to be listening intently. So his words sink into my mind and heart to be pondered upon, sometimes for years. Because of this, I often get the answer to a mental question in his very words."

She went on to describe how the answer to her sister-disciples' question had come to her this time, too, in Master's words. A lady student, to whom he had given a red rose to be worn during a special ceremony, had protested, "But I don't *want* a red rose. I want a pink one." Master had answered, "What *I* give, *you* take."

"Here is *my* answer," Sister concluded. "The quick, or at least open, mind. The willing hands and feet—these, brought to perfection, would be the last word, the distinguishing mark, the very perfection of discipleship."

Someone once told her of having had a vision of her as she was in a past incarnation. Sister later wrote Master, ending her letter with the words, "Whatever, whoever I have been in the past, in this—the most important incarnation of all—I am Gyanamata, the work of your hands. Please pray for me that I may stand firm and unshaken to the end. With reverence, gratitude, devotion, and love—but not enough. Oh, not enough!"

Ah, what incomparable sweetness! Tears well into my eyes as I type these words. Small wonder, I think, when I recall how Master, paying tribute to her at her funeral, cried out in divine love, "Darling Sister!"

Sister Gyanamata died November 17, 1951, at the age of eighty-two. "I have searched her life," Master said, "and have found there not a single sin, *not even of thought.*"

* Self-Realization Fellowship, 1984.

For the past twenty years Sister had suffered physically. She had borne her burden of ill health heroically, as a priceless gift from God and Guru. Master, speaking about her to a group of us shortly before her funeral, said, "One day when I visited Sister's room I could hear her heart from as far away as the door, wheezing and making a terrible sound. The heart was barely pumping. Seeing me, she said, 'I don't ask you to heal me. All I ask is your blessing.' What faith she had! It saved her instantaneously from death. I had made a covenant with God for her life, and I knew she would not go until I prayed for her release.

"Another time," Master continued, "she and Mrs. Maley were sitting on the porch at Encinitas when a voice they both heard plainly said, 'Tell Paramhansaji I am taking you.' She told me about it afterwards. I replied, 'The next time he speaks to you, tell him it isn't true. I have made a covenant with God for your life. He won't break His word.'

"A few days later she and Mrs. Maley were sitting on the porch again when they heard the same voice, 'I am going to take you soon.' Sister answered, 'Paramhansaji says it isn't true.' At that, the voice fell silent.

"A little while later her doctor, whom I'd never met, came by on his regular visit. As he was leaving I went to intercept him. 'Tell me, Doctor,' I said, 'how do you find Sister?'

"'Oh, all right,' he replied.

"'But tell me,' I said, 'isn't there something you don't understand about her case?'

"'Well, it *is* a little confusing,' he admitted.

"'Don't you think,' I suggested, 'that her trouble might be malnutrition? How would it be to have her placed under observation?'

"'By Jove, perhaps you're right!' he exclaimed. They took her to the hospital, and there discovered that she hadn't enough nourishment left in her body to keep her alive another twenty-four hours. She'd been having sores on her lip, and had been taking nothing but tea—no other nourishment of any kind. They fed her again, and she recovered. But that was what the voice on the porch had meant."

Sister's life was spared repeatedly. At last, after twenty years, Master granted her her release. "Such joy!" she cried with her last breath. "Too much joy! Oh, too much joy!"

"I saw her sink into the watchful state of Spirit, beyond creation," Master said later. Sister's reward for years of perfect surrender to the Guru's will was final liberation.

"She attained God through wisdom," Master told us. "My path has been through joy."

On his return to Mt. Washington, Master spent some time discussing Sister with a group of us. He mentioned again her attainment of complete liberation. The recollection passed through my mind that he had told me at Twenty-Nine Palms the soul must free others before it can itself receive final freedom. Catching my thought, Master said, "She *had* disciples."

"In all the years I have known her," Daya Mata told me during Sister's final hours, "I have never once heard her say anything unkind about anyone." What a beautiful tribute! I reflected that it said something about Daya Mata, too, that she had singled out this quality for special praise. Kindness was the quality in her own personality that she had worked most on developing.

We all felt, with Sister's passing, that the time was fast approaching for Master, too, to leave this world. He himself hinted as much. To Dr. Lewis he remarked one day, "We have lived a good life together. It seems only yesterday that we met. In a little while we shall be separated, but soon we'll be together again."

His next life on earth, Master told us, would be spent in the Himalayas. Having devoted so much of his present life to public service, he planned to remain for many years of that incarnation in deep seclusion. "In my later years," he told us, "I will gather about me those who are close to me now." To most of his close women disciples he said, "You will come as men in that life." Only to Mrs. Brown, as far as I know, did he say that she would come again as a woman. Two hundred years would elapse, he told us, before his next incarnation. (As was the case with Jesus Christ, some teachers would later claim to be his reincarnation. My answer to those who think of studying under such persons is, "Master himself said differently.")

During his last months, especially, he found his greatest earthly joy in those disciples who had lived up to his divine expectations of them. Often he praised Saint Lynn and Sister Gyanamata. He also spoke well of Daya Mata, of Mrs. Brown, and of others. Of Merna Brown (Mrinalini Mata) he said, "She has wonderful karma! You will see what she will do for the work." She had been a saint, he told us, in more than one past life. Of Corinne Forshee (Mukti Mata) he exclaimed to me once, "She is a *wonderful* soul!" Of Virginia Wright (Ananda Mata) he never spoke in my hearing, but it was clear from the way he treated her that she had pleased him deeply. Another disciple who, I know, had pleased him greatly was Jane Brush (Sahaja Mata). In my years of work with her in the editorial department I never saw her anything but cheerful, even-tempered, and kind.

Master showed himself much pleased also with Henry's spirit. Henry (Brother Anandamoy) had one trouble after another. First he broke a rib; next he had a rash of some sort which made his life miserable; then he broke another rib. Minor misfortunes seemed to plague him. One day, when he found himself afflicted anew with something, Master said to him, "Always more troubles, isn't it so? But that's good! You have lots of work to do, that's why you get them. God wants to make you strong. We produce more than D.D.s here. Our ministers win their spirituality in the fires of testing."

To Oliver Rogers (Brother Devananda) he remarked one day, "You have clear sailing!" On hearing this remark, several of the other monks wondered, "What about *me*?" Master caught their thought.

"And you will *all* have clear sailing," he went on with an attempt to be reassuring, "if you are faithful to the end."

Afterward, some of them exulted, "Did you hear Master? He promised *we'd all* have clear sailing!"

I didn't disillusion them with a gentle reminder that his promise had come, in their case, with a condition.

Mr. Rogers told us of an amusing occurrence in his recent work for Master. Master, as I've said earlier, placed great emphasis on the importance of positive thinking. It was his positiveness that was partly responsible for his extraordinary creativity: By visualizing clearly the things he wanted to accomplish, he succeeded where few others could have done so. Sometimes, however, his mental projections were so clear to him that their subsequent manifestation on this material plane may have struck him as a mere signature to a finished painting.

"Master asked me to paint a room," Mr. Rogers said. "One or two days later, before I'd even had time to buy the paint, I found Master in the room conversing with Saint Lynn, both of them in a state of inner joy. Seeing me, Master began praising me to Saint Lynn, ending with the remark, in a tone of childlike wonder, 'And he painted this whole room all by himself!' Saint Lynn looked at the unpainted walls, the ceiling, then at me. We smiled at each other, but said nothing."

Before coming to Mt. Washington, Mr. Rogers had been a professional house painter. "In heaven," Master told him, "you will be creating beautiful astral flowers simply by wishing for them."

"Sir," I said to Master one day, "after you are gone, will you be as near to us as you are now?"

"To those who *think* me near," he replied, "I will be near."

His last months passed quickly. Far *too* quickly, for in our hearts we knew that the end was approaching.

"It will be very soon, I feel," Daya Mata remarked to me one day in her office.

"But surely," I protested, "Master will return once more, first, to India." He was planning to go again that year, and had mentioned to me how sad the Indian disciples were that he had missed going there the last two years.

"Do you think so?" Gazing at me calmly, she said no more. Her presentiment, however, proved correct.

One day Master visited an antique shop to purchase a few canes. In whatever he did, he assumed the consciousness appropriate to that activity. Now, therefore, since he was conducting business, he bargained carefully. But once the transaction was over he ceased to play the role of conscientious buyer saving money for his monastery. Gazing about him, he noted marks of poverty in the shop. Sympathetically, then, he gave the owner much more money than he'd saved by bargaining with him.

"You are a gentleman, Sir!" exclaimed the man, deeply touched. To show his appreciation, he gave Master a particularly fine antique umbrella.

When Master returned home, he sighed, "What a poor-looking floor that man had in his shop! I think I'll buy him a new carpet."

How perfectly he manifested in his life the truth that, to the man of Christ consciousness, all men are brothers.

The last issue of *Self-Realization Magazine* to come out during Master's lifetime contained an article titled "The Final Experience." It was the last in a series of Master's commentaries on the New Testament Gospels that had been running continuously for twenty years. In this issue Master expanded on the words: "And when Jesus had cried with a loud voice, he said, Father, into thy hands I commend my spirit: and having said thus, he gave up the ghost."* Surely the perfect timeliness of this article was more than a coincidence. It appeared in the March 1952 issue. Master passed away on March 7, 1952.

As a further interesting note, the writing of the first edition of the account in these pages about Master's passing coincided closely with the season of Christ's passing. The day before I wrote it was Good Friday, 1976.

Several days before the end, another disciple posed Master a question similar to the one I'd asked him two years earlier: "Have all your disciples of this life come to you yet, Sir?"

"I am waiting for two or three more to come," Master replied.

In that week two more disciples arrived: Leland Standing (later, Brother Mokshananda) and Mme. Erba-Tissot, a well-known and highly successful lawyer from Switzerland who, not long afterwards, gave up her profession to organize centers for Master's work in Europe. There was, I believe, one other who came at this time, but I don't recall that person's name.

We had been impressed by Leland's spirit from months of correspondence with him. Master had written him at last, suggesting that he come to live at Mt. Washington. Leland met Master short-

* Luke 23:46.

ly after his arrival there. "You have good spirit," Master told him. "Remember, loyalty is the greatest thing."

Master had been staying at his Twenty-Nine Palms retreat. He returned to Mt. Washington on March 2 to meet His Excellency, Binay R. Sen, India's recently appointed Ambassador to the United States. On the evening of his return, he embraced each of us lovingly, and blessed us. To some he gave words of personal help, to others, encouragement to be stable in their spiritual efforts, to still others the advice to meditate more. Afterwards I got to see him briefly upstairs, alone.

Many times over the past three and a half years Master had scolded me, mostly for my slowness in understanding him perfectly, sometimes for not weighing in advance the possible consequences of my words. I knew that he often said, "I scold only those who listen, not those who don't," but in my heart there lingered a certain hurt. Try as I would, I couldn't rationalize it away. For some months I had been hungering for a few words of approval from him.

Now, alone with me, he gazed into my eyes with deep love and understanding, and said, "You have pleased me very much. I want you to know that." What a burden lifted from my heart at these few, simple words!

On Tuesday, March 4, the Ambassador and his party visited Mt. Washington. I served Master and his guests in his upstairs interview room. During their visit Mr. Ahuja, India's Consul-General in San Francisco, remarked to Master, "Ambassadors may come, and ambassadors may go. You, Paramhansaji, are India's real Ambassador to America."

Thursday evening, March 6, Master returned from a ride in the car. He had asked Clifford Frederick, who was driving, to take him onto Rome Drive, behind Mt. Washington. There, gazing at the main building, he remarked quietly, "It looks like a castle, doesn't it?"

The monks had just finished their group practice of the energization exercises when Master's car entered the driveway. As we gathered around him, he touched each of us in blessing, and then spoke at length about some of the delusions devotees encounter on the path.

I am presenting a box of *singharas* (an Indian savory) to Master on the occasion of the visit of India's Ambassador, Binay R. Sen, and his wife to Mt. Washington, three days before Master's *mahasamadhi*.

"Don't waste your time," he said. "No one can give you the desire for God. That is something you must cultivate yourselves.

"Don't sleep a great deal. Sleep is the unconscious way of contacting God. Meditation is a state beyond sleep—superconsciousness, as opposed to subconsciousness.

"Don't spend too much time joking. I myself like to laugh, but I keep my sense of humor fully under control. When I am serious, nobody can tempt me to laugh. Be happy within—grave, but ever cheerful. Why waste your spiritual perceptions in useless words? When you have filled the bucket of your consciousness with the milk of peace, keep it that way; don't drive holes in it by joking and idle speech.

"Don't waste time on distractions—reading all the time and so on. If reading is instructive, of course it is good. But I tell people, 'If you read one hour, then write two hours, think three hours, and meditate all the time.' No matter how much this organization keeps me busy, I never forego my daily tryst with God."

In the basement, minutes later, Master saw a box of green coconuts that had just arrived from Abie George's brother in Florida. "Back at the car Divine Mother was trying to tell me these coconuts had come, but I didn't listen—I was talking too much!" Master, laughing genially, opened a coconut and drank from it. But his enjoyment seemed to me somehow tinged with unreality. I looked into his eyes, and saw them deep, still, completely untouched by what he was doing. In retrospect it seems like the heartiness of one who knew he was bidding us goodbye, but didn't want us to know that he was doing so.

Catching my glance, he became all at once almost grave.

"I have a big day tomorrow," he said. Walking toward the elevator, he paused at the door, then repeated, "I have a big day tomorrow. Wish me luck."

The following day, March 7, he came downstairs to go out. He was scheduled to attend a banquet that evening at the Biltmore Hotel in honor of the Indian Ambassador. "Imagine!" he said, "I've taken a room at the Biltmore. That's where I first started in this city!"

Then again he repeated, "Wish me luck."

Master had asked me to attend the banquet with Dick Haymes, the popular singer and movie actor. Dick had recently become a disciple, and had taken Kriya initiation from me.

Years ago Master had said, "When I leave this earth, I want to go speaking of my America and my India." And in a song about India that he had written, to the tune of the popular song "My California," he paraphrased the original ending with the words, "I know when I die, in joy I will sigh for my sunny, grand old India!" Once, too, in a lecture he had stated, "A heart attack is the easiest way to die. That is how I choose to die." This evening, all these predictions were to prove true.

Master was scheduled to speak after the banquet. His brief talk was so sweet, so almost tender, that I think everyone present felt embraced in the gossamer net of his love. Warmly he spoke of India and America, and of their respective contributions to world peace and true human progress. He talked of their future cooperation. Finally he read his beautiful poem, "My India."

Throughout his speech I was busy recording his words, keeping my eyes on my notebook. He came to the last lines of the poem:

> Where Ganges, woods, Himalayan caves and men dream God.
> I am hallowed; my body touched that sod!

"Sod" became a long-drawn-out sigh. Suddenly from all sides of the room there came a loud cry. I looked up.

"What is it?" I demanded of Dick Haymes, seated beside me. "What happened?"

"Master fainted," he replied.

Oh, no, Master! You wouldn't faint. You've left us. You've left us! the forgotten playwright in me cried silently. *This is too perfect a way for you to go for it to mean anything else!* I hastened to where Master lay. A look of bliss was on his face. Virginia Wright was stooped over him, trying desperately to revive him. Mr. Ahuja, the Consul-General, came over to me and put an arm around my shoulders to comfort me. (*Never, dear friend, will I forget that sweet act of kindness!*)

They brought Master's body to Mt. Washington and placed it lovingly on his bed. One by one we went in, weeping, and knelt by his bedside.

"Mother!" cried Joseph. "Oh, Mother!" Indeed, Master had been a mother to us all—ah, and how much more than a mother! Miss Lancaster gave me an anguished look.

"How many thousands of years it took," marveled Laurie Pratt, gazing upon him in quiet awe, "to produce such a perfect face!"

Later on, after we'd left the room, Faye remained alone with Master's body. As she gazed at him, a tear formed on his left eyelid, and slowly trickled down his cheek. Lovingly she caught it with her handkerchief. She would always preserve it.

In death, as in life, he was telling his beloved disciple, and through her the rest of us, "I love you always, through endless cycles of time, unconditionally, without any desire except for *your* happiness, forever, in God!"

right: "The Last Smile," Paramhansa Yogananda the night of his *mahasamadhi*.

The banquet at the Biltmore Hotel, in honor of Binay R. Sen, India's Ambassador. In this room, a short time after this photo was taken, Master entered *mahasamadhi* (a yogi's final conscious exit from the body).

At the head table *(circled, left to right)* are Mr. M. R. Ahuja, Consul General of India; Ambassador Binay R. Sen; Mrs. Sen; and Master. I am seated in the center of the room.

PART III

CHAPTER 39

Spiritual Service

"To those who *think* me near, I will be near."

How often since Paramhansa Yogananda's lips were sealed in death have we, his disciples, experienced the fulfillment of that deathless promise. Truly, his was not death at all, but *mahasamadhi*, "the great *samadhi*": a perfected yogi's final, conscious exit from the body as he merges with the Infinite.

One of the first proofs we received of our Guru's victory over death came from Forest Lawn Memorial-Park, in Glendale, California, where the casket containing his body had been kept unsealed for twenty days pending the arrival of two disciples from India. On May 15 of that year Mr. Harry T. Rowe, Mortuary Director of Forest Lawn, sent Self-Realization Fellowship a notarized letter:

"The absence of any visual signs of decay in the dead body of Paramhansa Yogananda offers the most extraordinary case in our experience. . . . No physical disintegration was visible. . . . This state of perfect preservation of a body is, so far as we know from mortuary annals, an unparalleled one. . . . The appearance of Yogananda on March 27, just before the bronze cover of the casket was put into position, was the same as it had been on March 7. He looked on March 27 as fresh and as unravaged by decay as he had looked on the night of his death."

The casket was closed and sealed after twenty days, when word came that the two Indian disciples would not be able to make the journey. Later, one of them reported that Master, after his *mahasamadhi*, had appeared to him in his physical form and embraced him lovingly. Others in America, too, received this grace of his physical resurrection.

Most of us were grief-stricken for a time at Master's passing. But Mrs. Royston told me of going one day with a few of the nuns to his crypt at Forest Lawn. "The others were standing in front of the crypt," she said, "weeping. But I didn't at all feel we'd lost him. I called to him silently, and suddenly felt him standing beside me. I heard him say quite distinctly, 'I'm not in *there!*' He seemed surprised that disciples schooled in his teachings should be paying so much attention to his mere physical form!"

What about our own lives after his passing? If this book were primarily an autobiography, I'd feel it necessary to recount details of the many years I have lived since then. After all, Master left his body when I was still only twenty-five years old. Now I am eighty-two. My purpose in writing this book, however, has been primarily to tell what it was like to live with him. I prefaced that account with my own search for truth because my search led inevitably to the quest for God, and to its necessary next step: that of seeking guidance from a guru.

As I said before, my longing even as I crossed the country to meet him was twofold: to find God, and to share with others whatever truths I learned from my Guru.

It was towards the fulfillment of this deep-seated desire that Master directed all his training of me. "No more moods, now," he said, "otherwise, how will you be able to help people?" Another time he scolded me for speaking rather too lightly to a church member (though not in Master's or anyone else's hearing), showing me thereby that he kept close tabs on me spiritually, as well as encouraging me to be more inward when dealing with the public. And when I balked at public teaching, he replied lightly, "You'd better learn to like it. That is what you will have to do."

The "great work" he had told me I must do was something he never, to the best of my knowledge, spoke of to anyone else. He may have spoken of it to Rajarshi, who once said to me, "Master has a great work to do through you, Walter, and he will give you the strength to do it." But Rajarshi might just as easily have been "channeling" Master. As for myself, I never took Master's words lightly, nor as a compliment. They were, to me, a sacred commission.

I always assumed, however, that my "great work" would be within the secure confines of his organization. Indeed, my complete loyalty to him precluded my even thinking of serving him apart from Self-Realization Fellowship.

The fact, however, that he spoke to me only in private about my future service to him created problems for me in the years to come. When once I mentioned to Daya Mata Master's statement that I had a "great work" to do, she replied (quite naturally), "Yes, we all have a great work to do."

Though he had told me my work was writing, she tried once to get me to accept a job as pressman in the print shop. (I managed to avoid that one by warning her, truthfully, that past experience had shown me that any machinery I touched would almost certainly break down. The very fact, however, that she tried to push me in that direction shows that she didn't really believe Master had ever given me any commission at all.) Writing books would have seemed to her an unthinkable deviation from the actual needs of the work, as she defined them. And even had I written books, they would never have been published by the editorial department, who themselves, as it turned out, took forty years to edit and publish their own version of Master's Bhagavad Gita commentaries.

I was, in fact, deeply disappointed in that version, for I had worked with Master on the manuscript, which I considered the greatest spiritual work I had ever read. To me, their editing style was stilted, lacking the freshness and spiritual power of the original. Their version, moreover, contained more than one outright philosophical error.

In 2006 I published, from memory, my own version of Master's commentaries. Some years earlier, in a dream, I had asked him what I could do to edit those writings as he had told me to do. "I don't have access to the archives containing

The commentaries as taught by Paramhansa Yogananda, published by Crystal Clarity Publishers, 2006.

your manuscript," I lamented. Still in my dream, he answered me, "Don't overlook the possibility of a skylight."

When it came time for me to do what work I could on it, I was amazed to find that I remembered every stanza—not word for word, but concept for concept. Only today, as I write these words, an unsolicited message has come to me from someone in India stating, "This is really the best Gita I have ever read."

After Master's *mahasamadhi*, I expanded my work with the monks to reorganizing the letter-writing and related departments in the main office; organizing the centers; organizing the lay-disciple order; and helping in various other aspects of the work. My work with the monks had pleased Master, but he'd hinted that this was not what he had in mind for me.

My sister disciples—unfortunately for me—didn't see service to Master at all in the light I did. Feminine nature tends, as I've indicated already, to be less outwardly expansive than the masculine. The nuns kept asking one another, with increasing exasperation, "Why doesn't he just wait to be told what to do?" For me, this would have been impossible, especially considering the fervor with which Master had spoken to me about the things he wanted me to do!

Tensions built up gradually over the years. In SRF, the women ran the show—understandably so, no doubt, since the core of them had come much earlier than most of the men. (As a humorous aside, I remember Rev. Michael saying once, "This must be the only place on earth where the women have all the desires, and the men have to fulfill them!") Yet I mentioned earlier an obstacle on the spiritual path, one of the "meannesses of the heart" that Sri Yukteswar listed as "pride of pedigree." In the monastic life, as I said, this obstacle frequently translates as, "pride of seniority." Often Daya Mata countered my ideas with the statement, "You weren't with Master as long as I was." Perhaps this, partly, was the reason behind Master's statement, quoting Jesus, "The last shall be first."

*   *   *   *   *   *   *

I first went to India in 1958. There I found myself lecturing, for virtually the first time, to audiences consisting mostly of people who were not familiar with either Master's name or his teachings. It was a priceless opportunity to learn how to apply his message creatively to general audiences.

In the autumn of 1959 I was invited to address, at the end of their school day, the student body of a men's college in Simla, a hill station in the Himalayas. I set out by foot from the house where I was staying. Misjudging the distance, I arrived twenty minutes late. The student-body president, on whose recommendation I'd been invited to speak, met me on the street below the hilltop campus, literally trembling with apprehension.

A photograph of me taken in Patiala, 1959.

"I don't know how they'll receive you, Swamiji. The problem isn't only that you've arrived late. It's that we have just concluded a protest rally against China's latest incursions onto Indian soil. The students ended by signing a petition to the Government *in blood!*" He paused, cocking an ear up the hill. "Just listen to them!"

From the hilltop, sounds of tumult were clearly audible: hundreds of voices shouting in protest; the thunder of feet stamping on the floor impatiently.

"Swamiji," my host pleaded, "please allow me to cancel the talk."

"But I can't do that," I remonstrated. "It would mean breaking my word to them."

"I'm only afraid that they may treat you badly for keeping your word!"

Willing to face anything, I climbed the hill, hoping for the best. During the principal's hurried and somewhat nervous introduction of me, a number of students glanced meaningly at the exit. Obviously, the circumstances were far from ideal for a lecture on the benefits of yoga and meditation!

Instead, therefore, I launched into a vigorous speech on the subject uppermost in their minds: China's incursions. One secret of success in lecturing is to get the audience saying, "Yes!" from the beginning. I restated their case for them, perhaps better than they'd heard it stated that day. Right off, I sensed a flicker of interest mounting toward approval. Once I had their support, I gradually introduced a suggestion that warfare, hatred, and other kinds of social disharmony are due primarily to disharmony in man himself. We ourselves, I suggested, though we perhaps hate no one, might yet feel that we hadn't as much inner peace as we'd like. The first thing, then, if we would attract peaceful treatment from others, was to change, not them, but *ourselves.*

By this time the students were eager for more. I went on to speak about yoga and meditation. At the end of my talk they plied me with questions. Many wanted to know how they could study yoga. At last the principal had to plead with them repeatedly to cease asking further questions, as the last buses would shortly be leaving for their villages.

In India, by psychically "listening" to my audiences as I spoke to them, and reflecting back to them the truth as they were able, in their own higher natures, to understand it, I learned how to reach people on their own levels of spiritual development, and get them to take up meditation. After a lecture at Mahindra College, Patiala, in 1959, the professors told me that never in the history of their college had so much interest been awakened by a speaker. Response to my talks and classes in the auditorium of the public library of Patiala was, people said, "unprecedented" for that city. A few weeks later, in New Delhi, thousands enrolled in my yoga classes. I became known in northern India as the "American yogi."

I had entered the ministry reluctantly, years earlier. Now, the more I tried to serve God *through* others, the more clearly I experienced His blessings in everything I did.

Before the first of my class series in New Delhi, I invited our local YSS members* to my hotel room to discuss plans. There weren't many members. They came cautiously, sat cautiously, and cautiously suggested that we rent a small schoolroom where I might address them and perhaps a few friends. I felt, however, that Master wanted me to make his message known to thousands.

"Let us rent a large tent,"† I said.

"A large . . . *what*!?" They gulped apprehensively. "For how many people?"

"About eighteen hundred," I replied. Their look intimated that they thought I'd taken complete leave of my senses. At last, however, they gave in. The tent was set up on a large, empty lot in what was then Main Vinay Nagar (now its name has, I think, been changed to Sarojini Nagar), an outlying district of New Delhi.

The day of my introductory lecture I was meditating in a nearby home. At four o'clock—the announced time of the talk—one of the members came over to fetch me.

"It's a good crowd, Swamiji," he announced lugubriously. "About a hundred people."

---

* Members of SRF through their Indian branch, Yogoda Satsanga Society (YSS).

† *Shamiana* is the Indian word, and was in fact the word I used.

A hundred people—in a tent large enough for eighteen hundred! Later I was told that one member, of particularly timorous disposition, had already begun pacing up and down outside the tent, moaning, "Our reputation will be ruined!"

"Master," I prayed, laughing inwardly, "I had the feeling we'd get at least eighteen hundred people. That wasn't my *desire*. If no one had come, it would have been the same to me." But then, recalling people's tendency to be late, I told this man, "Let us wait a little."

Seven minutes later he returned. "There are two hundred there now, Swamiji. Hadn't we better start?"

"Not yet," I replied. He left, wringing his hands.

At four-fifteen, smiling with relief, he returned. "About six hundred people are there now. Shall we begin?"

Fifteen minutes was a long enough wait. I rose to my feet. During the brief time it took us to reach the tent, crowds more arrived. By the time I'd reached the dais, the tent was full to overflowing. Two thousand people heard me that day. Most of them later enrolled for my classes.

At the end of my lecture I announced, "During this week of classes it would be easier, for those who might want private interviews with me, if I were housed nearby. Would anyone here like to invite me to stay in his home?" Afterwards fifty or more people approached me to extend invitations. Dismayed, I realized I'd have to refuse all of them but one. "Master," I prayed, "whose invitation should I accept?" Then all at once, seeing one man, I was attracted by the look in his eyes. (I can still see that look in my mind.) "I'll stay with you," I said.

Later Sri Romesh Dutt, my host for that week, confided to me, "I read Paramhansaji's *Autobiography of a Yogi* years ago, and wanted very much to receive Kriya Yoga initiation. But I didn't know where to get it. At last I read in the newspaper about your recent lectures in Patiala, a hundred miles away. I decided to request time off from my office and go there to seek initiation from you. But my wife said to me, 'Why go all that distance? If you have faith, Swamiji will come to New Delhi and give initiation here. Not only that, *he will stay in our home!*' Truly, Swamiji, your visit to our humble dwelling is an extraordinary proof of God's grace!"

The Jagannath Temple in Puri, Orissa, one of the most sacred temples of the Hindus. We were among the first Westerners ever allowed to enter the temple.

I stand with Sri Rama Yogi, a great disciple of Sri Ramana Maharshi. Of Sri Rama Yogi Master said, "If I had spent another half hour in his company, I could never have brought myself to leave India again." I stayed four days with Sri Rama Yogi at his ashram outside the city of Nellore, in South India.

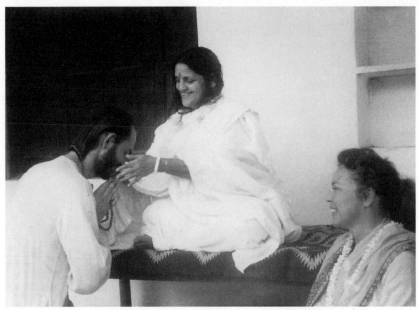

Daya Mata and I on a visit to the great Indian saint, Sri Anandamayee Ma, at her ashram in Benares. Anandamayee Ma has just given me a *rudraksha mala*, or garland of prayer beads, which I still use in my meditations.

Taken in the courtyard of the home of Dewan Balkishen Khosla, in Patiala, Punjab, where I was a guest. I gave a series of lectures and classes in Patiala in November 1959.

Lecturing and speaking to people around India, I gradually came to understand how also to carry out Master's charge to me to write books. For years I had puzzled over what I might say in writing that would convey freshly to people his depth of philosophical and spiritual insight. My usefulness, whether as a teacher or a writer, was to acquaint people with *his* message. *He* was the master. I was only a disciple doing my best to serve him as a lucid instrument.

Yet he had said to me, "*Much* yet remains to be written." To what, I wondered, had he been referring? After two or three years in India, I began to understand how I might "reach out" through writing, as I had been doing through lectures, by "listening" psychically, as it were, to people's needs. I decided to show them how even the worldly fulfillments they sought could be achieved best if they included in their lives a quest for spiritual values.

Master himself, I reflected, had written on numerous subjects of general, and not only overtly spiritual, interest. Perhaps I could expand on points at which he, often, had only hinted. Taking his teachings as the hub, so to speak, of a wheel, I decided I would try to show that many spokes led out in all directions from that center.

One of the principal goads to my own spiritual search had been the spreading evil, in modern times, of nihilism. Many people, influenced by the materialistic sciences, found it difficult to accept moral and spiritual values. Idealism they discarded as "sentimental." Of the college-trained intellectuals I'd encountered, even in India, many insisted that truth is only relative, that no higher natural law exists, and that an act can be justified only in terms of how honestly it expresses the nature with which one was born. A number of people, unable to surrender their moral sense altogether, embraced communism with its materialistic ethic, simply because communism at least makes a show of believing in *something*.

All too often, especially in the West, the educated people I encountered who accepted spiritual values were unable to counter the materialistic challenges of science, and therefore swept those challenges under the carpet rather than acknowledge that they existed. Those people's beliefs, albeit positive, lacked intellectual integrity.

Trained as I was in Master's teachings, and familiar with the clear insights they offered as correctives to the confused thinking of our age, I determined to give people an *honest* basis for spiritual faith.

I ended up devoting sixteen years of my life (though not exclusively) to writing a book named, *Crises in Modern Thought* (since then renamed, *Out of the Labyrinth*). Another book I wrote years later on a related theme was, *Hope for a Better World!*

My new way of thinking was directed toward attuning myself to *people's* needs, rather than to the institution's demands or expectations of me. This approach, unfortunately, set me at odds with the senior nuns in Master's work, whose concern centered entirely on the needs of the organization itself. Tara insisted that, in every situation, the first question we ask ourselves be, "What is best for the work?" To me, the work itself meant addressing the needs of those who came to us for help. I suppose it was natural that tensions built up between our two very different ways of looking at Master's mission.

In 1960 I was elected to the board of directors and appointed SRF's first vice president. These promotions were, I suppose, justified in light of the positions I had held in the work already. There was also, however, another way of looking at these promotions. Was I being "bumped upstairs," in a last ditch effort to make me "shape up" and embrace those senior nuns' priorities? If such was by any chance the case, it was a failure. I continued to follow my own understanding of the meaning and purpose of Master's work. Considering my sheer inability to view the work as they did, they felt themselves left with no other option, I suppose, than to denounce me as a traitor.

In 1953 I had written a manual of guidance for our centers. Nine years later, when the differences between our points of view finally came to a head, the board of directors (of which I was now the male member) had not yet even taken the time to discuss that manual. Our centers worldwide still lacked the necessary guidance. The needs of our dedicated centers were not considered important compared to the board members' own priorities: essential matters such as — well, what?

Daya Mata justified to me what I viewed as her obsession with micromanagement by saying, "Master told me to keep the reins in my hands." I might have answered, "Yes, but he didn't tell you also to be the horse!" Micromanagement, especially as she practiced it, meant delegating no authority, and complete indifference, amounting to disdain for, anything that lay outside her own immediate sphere of interest.

For years, I was on a committee of which the purpose was to make all basic decisions. It was a sort of junior board of directors. The talk was endless; the accomplishments, minimal. One year we were supposed to plan that summer's convocation of the SRF members. When it came to a discussion of the public event, or "open house," at the SRF Lake Shrine, I thought to show the committee what could be accomplished by delegating authority. "I have a group of congregation members at Hollywood Church," I said. "They would be happy to take on this responsibility. Why don't I just plan this event with them?"

Well, the others—all women—were happy to be relieved of this onerous burden. At the end of the next church service, I announced, "If anyone here would like to help put on the convocation open house at the Lake Shrine, please stay after service." About twenty people remained.

To them I said, "Here are the aspects of the event that we'll need to cover: chairs; food; hosts and hostesses." I listed a few others. I then asked for volunteers to supervise each aspect. Later, during the week, I phoned the person in charge of each function to make sure everything was well in hand.

The event itself went like clockwork. I walked around to make sure everyone was at his post. When it came time to move chairs, I spoke to the person in charge of that operation; hundreds of chairs were put into place.

Later, Shraddha Mata, a member of the board of directors, exclaimed to me, "It all went beautifully!"

"Yes," I replied. "And you know, it took almost no effort."

"No effort for you, maybe," she answered, "but plenty of work for the people who did all the planning."

"Do you know what?" I countered. "I did it all myself!"

I had hoped to show our committee how much more can be accomplished by delegating authority—not by abdicating one's responsibility, but by sharing it with others, as they show an ability to shoulder a load. Delegation indicates respect for others. Refusal to delegate shows a want of such respect. And doesn't lack of respect equate with pride?

In 1958 I reminded Daya Mata of Master's frequent public exhortations to people to buy land and band together in intentional communities.

"When do you think we'll be ready to start them?" I asked her.

To my surprise, she replied, "Frankly, I'm not interested."

Her rejection of that idea, and the support she had in that rejection from the other senior nuns, actually led to their editing out an important part of Master's "Aims and Ideals." He had listed one of those aims as, "To spread a spirit of world brotherhood among all peoples *and to aid in the establishment, in many countries, of self-sustaining world brotherhood colonies for plain living and high thinking.*" What they did was omit the entire italicized part of that aim, so that it read only, "to spread a spirit of brotherhood among all nations." Laurie Pratt (Tara Mata) once actually spoke to me laughingly about Master's "impracticality" in harboring this fantastic notion. She also, in a phone conversation with me, scoffed at his repeated statement, "We are not a sect," and in summation commented, "I know he said we are not a sect. Well, we *are* a sect!" Master loved Tara deeply, but I suspect she began to think of her ability to edit his writings as giving her the right also to "edit" his ideas and intentions.

When Master had acquired Mt. Washington, which to him was the point from which he would be able really to launch his mission, he himself related to us humorously Laurie's only comment: "Now your troubles begin." And she once told me, "My idea in those days [the mid-1920s] was that Master would gather up a few disciples, then withdraw with us to the Himalayas."

Master loved Daya dearly also, and was deeply grateful for her many years of devoted service to him. He didn't list her, however, among his most advanced disciples. One day, when he named those disciples to us monks (Saint Lynn, Mr. Black, and Sister Gyanamata, in that order), he responded to a thought that arose in several of our minds, saying, "And Faye? Well, she still has her life to live."

Near the end of his life, I asked him, "Sir, after you leave us, should I go to Faye for guidance?" His reply was both hesitant and equivocal. I wondered afterward why he had so spoken. Many years later, when destiny forced the two of us apart in our service to him, I understood.

The women and I simply saw Master's mission differently. Despite his frequent statement, "Self-Realization has come to change the world!" they clung determinedly to a narrowly circumscribed concept of what he'd brought. Fairly recently, indeed, I heard that it was being put about that Master had come to the West to start a monastery. My own conviction, however, backed by his frequent, and fervent, declarations, has always been that he came to effect a fundamental change in the whole of society: in the way people live, think, work, and worship. His women disciples saw his mission in terms of their control over it. I myself saw it in terms of the *inspiration* we could share.

I would never have gone my own way, though I confess that often, in my enthusiasm, my frustration became agonizing to me. Things finally came to a head when I tried to develop an ashram in New Delhi, where I'd encountered such a gratifying public response. My hopes were high for getting Master's work in India "off the ground" after it had been virtually asleep for forty years. What I intended to do—and Daya Mata gave those intentions her blessings—was to re-launch it in New Delhi. The encouraging response I'd had here resulted finally in my getting an appointment with Jawaharlal Nehru himself, the Prime Minister of India. At that appointment I asked for permission to build on what had been set aside as government land. Seventeen hundred other societies had tried to get land there; all had been rejected. My own application was, to my intense gratification, accepted. Getting Nehru's blessing amounted to a veritable miracle.

By this time, however, the senior nuns at Mt. Washington had come to view me as not only a maverick, but a troublemaker. To make a long story short, we ended up parting ways—not by my will, but (I am sure) by God's. To put it briefly, I was thrown out on my ear.

The difference between them and me was due partly to the fact that those senior nuns, entrenched as they were in an authoritarian position and attitude, saw no need for equality between men and women. Daya once said to me, "Let's face it, women are more spiritual than men." The senior nuns became "*matas*" (mothers), but the men, even today, have never been advanced beyond the status of "brothers." Any difference between the masculine and the feminine point of view had to be, according to the senior nuns, to the detriment of the masculine; the monks were—I imagine they still are—second-class citizens. As for the instructions Master had given me personally, the "*matas*" could never believe that our Guru had said anything to me that he hadn't shared with them in much greater depth. Over the years, it has become clear to me why he gave me only in private his instructions concerning my future role in his work.

Daya Mata visited India in 1961, and came also to Delhi and Patiala. Crowds came to hear her, owing to the groundbreaking work I had done there months earlier, and to my group's promotion of her visit. In her view, however, and in that of her party, the interest that was shown in her arrival bore no relationship to my and our prior efforts.

To balance the picture of my dismissal, bleak as it seemed to me at the time, I can say truthfully that it was the best thing that ever happened to me. From my obligatory separation has come all the work I have done to spread my Guru's work: the books, the 15,000 photographs, the year-round television and radio programs, the schools, the ceremonies, the music, the seven communities I have started (of which the total resident membership is approximately one thousand), where there is complete equality between the sexes in all management positions. I write of the things I have done, but I am keenly aware not only that I have done them for my Guru, but that it is he who has accomplished them through me. I have felt his guidance in every decision, both large and small, of my life. Even the music and the song lyrics have all come by his blessing.

Let me include here the lyrics of one of those songs. Its name is, "Love Is a Magician"*:

> Love is all I know:
> Sunrays on the snow
>> Of a winter long
>> In darkness, without song.
> Oh, my heart's afire,
> Burning all desire.
>> Only You remain,
>> And life again.
> Too long I did stray,
> Flung lifetimes away,
>> Imagined You did not care.
>>> I know now Your smile
>>> Was mine all the while;
>> I listened, and love was there.
> I can't breathe for love!
> All the stars above
>> Call to me, "Come home!
>> Life's waves all end in foam."
> Only love can heal
> All the pain I feel.
>> What a fool was I
>> To turn away!

And so, before explaining a little more the subject of communities, and by trying to interest you, my readers, in this activity, I would like to make the following humble suggestions:

If you seek true fulfillment, shun delusion as you would a disease. *Maya* will never give you what you want. If you are seeking truth, shun everything that is even remotely suggestive of falsehood. If you seek to *experience* truth, seek God, not abstractions. If you want that experience, seek the guidance of one who knows Him. And if you seek that guidance, consider the beauty of a teaching that offers, not mere dogma, but practical common sense, based on modern man's understanding of the universe and on the deep experience of God's love, instead of mere definitions of that love. This is what Paramhansa Yogananda brought to the world.

* I sang this song on *The New Path* audiobook that I recorded, and also on several of my albums: *Windows on the World*, *An Evening in Italy*, and *I've Passed My Life as a Stranger, Lord*.

And though I always say that what I want most deeply is to convert you to your own highest Self, I don't hesitate to add that, if you are still seeking your own path to truth, it may well be worth your while to explore the possibilities offered by this new dispensation, which is, truly, a new path to God.

CHAPTER 40
A New Way of Life

L ORD KRISHNA IS depicted in legend as a boy playing his flute by the banks of the River Jamuna, calling his playmates away from worldly pursuits to the divine search within. All men hear in their souls, whether consciously or unconsciously, this call to divine awareness. Every time a bird's song charms them with the reflection of how sweet life might be, were it tuned to simpler melodies, it is this higher call they hear. They hear it when a sunset reminds them of Nature's beauties overlooked in the frenzied struggle for success; when a starlit night speaks to them of Vastness and Silence, routed — alas! — by noisy self-preoccupation. How well they are able to heed the call depends on how ensnared they are by desires. The less they think of serving themselves, the more they will expand their consciousness to infinity.

Modern society, alas, is committed to an almost diametrically opposite principle. It firmly believes that the more one owns, and the more experiences one has of outward diversity, entertainment, and excitement, the happier he will be. Consumerism is propounded as a moral value: "Spend more, so that there will be more jobs, and more things produced, which will enable you to spend even more."

It is not wrong *per se*, of course, to possess the conveniences modern civilization makes available to us, with its highly developed methods of mass production and distribution. What is wrong is the amount of energy that gets directed toward these outward goals at the expense of inner peace and higher awareness. What is wrong is that the quest for possessions tends to dupe people into thinking that *getting* is more important than *giving*, and self-aggrandizement more important than service; that one's commitments need be honored only as long as they continue to serve one's own ends; that the most valid opinions and ideas are those which have gained the widest circulation; and that wisdom, fulfillment, and happiness can be mass-produced, like the parts of a car. What is wrong, finally, is that people are losing touch with themselves, thereby *losing* their happiness, not gaining more of it.

Giving a lecture in the dome of the Crystal Hermitage during a celebration in 2008.

Probably there has never been an age in which so many people felt alienated from their fellow men, and from life itself; so unsure of themselves and of their neighbors; so nervous, fearful, and *un*happy.

Consumerism, elevated as it has been in modern times to the status of a moral law, sets aside as old-fashioned some of the fundamental teachings of the ages—as if the ability to build airplanes and TV sets qualified us to say that we know better how to live life than Jesus, Krishna, Buddha, or Lao-tzu. Were a prophet of modern consumerism to give us his Sermon on the Mount, he might start with, "Blessed are they who dig in and get theirs, for they shall get more than the other fellow." At least, however, we have had time to observe the results of this sort of philosophy, and they are not pleasing.

Human nature has not changed. Those who ignore its guiding principles pay all the usual penalties, whether as restless and unhappy camel drivers or as restless and unhappy jet airplane pilots, or corporate executives.

It is not that what we have nowadays is wrong. The solution lies not in reverting to primitivism, or to any other culture that imagination may enhalo for us in a romantic glow. Those cultures had their problems, too. We are living today. What is needed is a change in our *priorities*. We need, as every age has needed, to subordinate material to human and spiritual ends. The principles taught by Paramhansa Yogananda will, if adopted, correct the spiritual imbalances of our times.

One of the pressing needs nowadays is for what Yogananda called "world brotherhood colonies"—places that can facilitate the development of an integrated, well-balanced life, setting an example to all mankind of the advantages of such a life. Cooperative communities ought not to be isolationist, like medieval villages, nor in any sense a step backwards in time, but an integral part of the age in which we live.

Cooperative spiritual communities are needed especially as a means of fostering deeper spiritual awareness. Paramhansa Yogananda used the simile of a young sapling, which requires protective hedging against herbivorous animals until it grows large and strong enough to stand exposed to them. The devotee, too, he said, requires the protection of a spiritual environment until he develops the strength in himself to be able to move through the world unaffected by its swirling currents of worldly desire.

People today who recognize the need in society, and in themselves, for a more spiritual way of life need hardly have pointed out to them the difficulties involved in such development. For every affirmation of spiritual values, the world cries out a thousand times from all sides that opulence is the answer to all human needs. The result is spiritual confusion. In a recent survey, children in America were asked who their heroes were. The largest number named actors in their favorite television programs. The next largest chose prominent athletes. Then came well-known politicians. Only two percent chose famous writers or scientists. *None* chose people for their spiritual qualities.

When Dr. Radhakrishnan was vice president of India, he said to me, "A nation is known by the men and women its people look up to as great." By this standard alone it must be clear that America's spirituality, though potentially indeed enormous, requires careful cultivation.

Cooperative spiritual communities, or "world brotherhood colonies," provide a vital solution to one of the most pressing needs of our times—an opportunity for those who want to develop spiritually to satisfy that desire in a supportive environment, and thereby to set for the rest of the world a dynamic example that spiritual principles *really work*, that they are practical.

One of the fundamental needs of our age is for putting down roots again. We have extended ourselves too far outward from the Self within, and from the natural rhythms of the planet on which we live. Even in our outward, human associations we have lost touch with reality.

The average person in America today moves over fourteen times in his life—not to new homes in the same community, but to different communities altogether. Loneliness has become chronic. Friendships tend to be of the cocktail party and patio barbecue variety, and not the deep bonds that people form as a result of trials and victories shared. We know people to smile with, but not to weep with, not to confide in, not to go to for help in times of physical, emotional, or spiritual distress.

Small, spiritual communities offer a viable alternative to the depersonalizing influences of our times. People living and working together, sharing together on many levels of their lives—suffering, growing, learning, rejoicing, winning victories together—develop a depth in their outward relationships as well that helps them, inwardly, to acquire spiritual insight.

Small, cooperative communities offer more than a simple opportunity to demonstrate to the world the value of already-fixed teachings and techniques. Throughout history, the greatest advances have always come from the cross-pollination that occurs when relatively small groups of people with similar ideals have

Joy Is Within You. The symbol stands at the entrance of Ananda Village.

interrelated with one another. We see it in the golden era of Greek philosophy in Athens; among the small bands of early Christians; among the artists and writers of the Italian Renaissance in Florence; in the golden age of music in Germany; and in the days of England's great colonial power.

Again and again, cultural advances have been defined by small groups of people who had the opportunity to relate to one another meaningfully; people whose relationship was one of friendship, of give and take; people with an opportunity to know to *whom* they were talking, and not only to know what they were talking about. On a mass level, such interrelationship is impossible: Nobody can know well more than a handful of people. But elitist cliques like that of England's aristocracy during her colonial days are no longer feasible. Ours is an egalitarian society. The solution now is for small groups of people to set themselves in a position, not of superiority to the rest of society, but somewhat apart from it in meaningful relationships to one another.

It is already happening. During the late 1960s and early 1970s many people went out into the country, bought land, and formed small cooperative communities. To be sure, thousands failed, but a few were remarkably successful. And the lessons those few learned in the process are making it increasingly easy for other, similar communities to get started.

Among the successful communities, there is developing a consciousness of community *with one another*, of sharing in an experiment of national, even of international, dimensions. New definitions are slowly emerging, and are being shared among them—definitions of more fulfilling marriage; of education in how to live, and not only in how to earn a living; of friendship in mutual sharing; of cooperation for mutual well-being; of business as a service; of life's true goals; of success in countless departments of life: definitions that are meaningful for people who live in cities as well as in the country. It is a movement of potentially tremendous importance to modern civilization as a whole.

The communitarian ideal was given its modern impetus, more than most people realize, by Paramhansa Yogananda through his lectures and writings, and by the sheer power of his thought, which, he said, he was "sowing in the ether."

To further his ideals, I myself founded in 1969 what has become one of the handful of successful new communities in America, Europe, and now (I hope), India. Its name is Ananda. *Ananda*, a Sanskrit word, means "Divine Joy." Ananda communities are places for spiritual seekers, whether married, single, or monastic, who feel a need to integrate their work with a life of meditation and of service to God. The members of Ananda are all disciples of Paramhansa Yogananda. Taking his teachings as our basis, we study how to relate them to every aspect of our lives.

Our first community, called Ananda Village, is situated on nearly 1,000 acres of land in the Sierra Nevada foothills of Northern California. The community presently comprises several hundred full-time residents; a meditation retreat open to the public; three "how-to-live" schools (from preschool through high school—and, more lately, a college-level institute); a farm; various supporting businesses; private homes for families: in short, the essentials of a complete spiritual village.

Ananda's most obvious inspiration was Yogananda's "world brotherhood colonies" ideal.

In 1967, by a series of extraordinary events, I discovered and purchased sixty-seven acres of beautiful, wooded land in the foothills of the Sierra Nevada mountains. There, with the aid of a few friends, I began to construct what finally became Ananda World Brotherhood Village.

Then, in the spring of 1968, finding a growing interest among my friends in forming a spiritual community, I wrote and published a small book, *Cooperative Communities—How to Start Them, and Why*, to explain the sort of community I had in mind.

The difficulties I faced at the beginning were twofold: financial of course, and perhaps primarily; secondly, the fact that, because my ideas were still "in the air," many people with substantially different ideas tried to deflect my energies toward helping them to fulfill *their* ideas.

One person offered me $70,000—enough money to get the community off to a good start—on the condition that I build the kind of community *he* wanted. But I saw that our ways were not compatible. He wanted a maximum of rules; I wanted a minimum. Even if I failed, I decided, I must go on as I felt Master wanted me to. Indeed, success or failure alike mattered little to me. I only wanted to serve my Guru.

The financial crises, especially, that we faced were considerable. They included two attempts to foreclose on us and seize our property; a forest fire that destroyed most of our homes and property; and lawsuits that were intended, as the presiding judge commented, to put us "out of business." God, however, always gave us the money and the help we needed to pull through. One reason He did so, I firmly believe, was because I refused to subordinate the welfare of any individual to the needs, however desperate, of our work.

A man came to me one day in 1970 with $200,000, a sum we certainly could have used—it would have put us well on the road to success—and asked whether I thought he ought to join Ananda and give this money to the community, or to go to India. If, however, he had really wanted to live with us, he wouldn't have proposed this alternative.

"Your place," I told him, "is India."

By placing primary emphasis on spiritual values and on God-contact in meditation, Ananda developed, gradually, as a place of selfless dedication to God, and to God in our fellow man. St. Paul, in his letter to the Galatians (5:22), wrote, "The harvest of the Spirit is love, joy, peace, patience, kindness, goodness, fidelity, gentleness, and self-control." These attitudes are difficult, if not impossible, to develop to any significant degree on one's own, but they evolve naturally in the hearts of those who attune themselves to God.

Often have I felt Master's smile in my heart on seeing his "world brotherhood colony" dream become a material reality. His blessings on the land—an almost tangible aura of peace—are felt by everyone who comes here.

The spiritual energy that is developing here extends far beyond Ananda's boundaries. Thousands in America and abroad find in Ananda's example the inspiration, and also the practical direction, for spiritualizing their own lives. This, indeed, is the broader purpose of cooperative spiritual communities. For although relatively few people may ever live in such places, people everywhere can be helped by examples—augmented by the large numbers involved in a flourishing community—that spiritual principles are both inwardly regenerative and outwardly practical. Every devotee, moreover, can be helped by the realization that he is not alone in his spiritual search.

Thus, Ananda—now in its fortieth year of existence—already provides people in many parts of the world with a sense of spiritual family, a sense which serves them as a bulwark in times of trial, and gives them encouragement and shared inspiration in times of joy.

Often, as I stand and gaze out over the green fields, woods, and rolling hills at Ananda, I am reminded of a poem I wrote in Charleston, South Carolina, not long before I came to Master. Since then I have set it in the legendary golden era of Lord Rama, whose kingdom of Ayodhya, in ancient India, was a place of universal harmony, peace, and brotherhood.

Thus may all men learn to live in peace, brotherhood, and harmony, wherever their paths lead outwardly. For now, as then, true, divine peace is possible only when people place God and spiritual values first in their lives.

June in Ayodhya

Listen! Fair June is humming in the air,
And Ram's Ayodhya sings of lasting peace.
The growing grass nods heavy to the wind,
Patient till cutting time. The hay is stored;
The fields spring up with adolescent plants,
Laughing flowers, berries, and graceful corn.
In the orchards, every hand is quickly busy
To catch the ripest fruits before they fall.
Men's hearts are strong with that perfected strength
That smiles at fences, lays aside old hates,
Nurtures true love, and finds such earnest pleasure
In seeking truth that every private mind
Seems drawn to virtue, like a public saint.
The women's words are soft with kindliness;
The children answer with humility;
Even the men are like so many fawns,
Modest and still, sweet with complete respect.
June in Ayodhya is so roused with joy
The earth can scarcely keep its boundaries,
Swelling with energy and waking strength
Till not a mountain, not a valley sleeps,
Straining to burst, and flood the world with laughter.

Such harmony flows everywhere when men,
With grateful hearts, offer their works to God.
Then brotherhood needs no enforcing laws,
No parliaments, no treaties sealed in fear:

True peace is theirs to whom the Lord is near.

CHAPTER 41

The Final Goal

PARAMHANSA YOGANANDA TAUGHT us above all that the true goal of life is union with God. Devotion, self-offering, self-surrender, oneness in Bliss and Divine Love: these are the entire purpose of life.

I lovingly remember one day when Master played a recording for a small group of us by a famous singer of Bengal, Mrinal Kanti Ghosh. It was a devotional song, "Pashan Hoye":

> How long will You remain, Mother,
> A stone image before my gaze?
> Set fire ablaze in Your eyes
> And come to me, dancing over all Creation!
> O Mother! divine energy fills the universe
> With Your flowing hair!
> Garlanded by thoughts in all minds—
> Dancing! Dancing!
> O Mother! free me this day—
> *This very moment*—from delusion's bonds!
> Countless lives have I lived apart from You.
> At last, now, bring peace into my body temple!

I don't remember all the words, and am not conversant enough in Bengali to understand many of them. But I remember Master telling us afterward, "As I was listening, I too was dancing over all Creation!"

Man's relationship with God is intimate, and infinitely dear. What I've hoped above all in writing this book has been to convince you, dear reader, to live more deeply for God: to love Him so completely that you become wholly absorbed in Him.

God hears our every prayer. Of all aspects of the Divine, that of Mother is the sweetest. As my Guru once said, "Mother is closer than the Father." I, too, prefer to pray to God as my Divine Mother. And I can testify to the truth of what my Guru told us: "When you pray to Her, She will answer!"

How often have even my trivial requests been answered—like the so-unnecessary wish I expressed to Her many years ago (I mentioned that episode in these pages) for Swiss chocolate.

One needn't be formal in prayer. Indeed, God should be approached as one's own Dearest Friend and Beloved!

Many years ago—another example—I felt that Divine Mother wanted me to return to India. I had been absent from there for ten years, but now I had enough money saved to go back and stay there for about two months.

Shortly before my scheduled departure, I was driving my car into San Francisco when the engine threw a rod. I realized I'd have to trade in this car for a newer one. This need, however, placed me in a dilemma. The money for my trip was all the wealth I had. Should I trade in my car and buy a new one? or should I keep my money for the trip Divine Mother wanted me to take? I've always tried to reconcile faith with common sense.

Ananda Village is in the mountains, far from urban conveniences. A car is, for me, a virtual necessity. I wouldn't be able to stay long in India. Without a vehicle, I'd be virtually "stranded" upon my return. What should I do?

I asked Divine Mother for guidance. I knew of no place in which to sit quietly and "tune in." All I could think of was to have a quiet lunch with a few friends in a downtown restaurant. No guidance came.

Finally I said, "Divine Mother, You haven't answered me; perhaps I haven't been silent enough to hear You. Common sense tells me, however, that I must have a car when I return from India. I see no reasonable choice, therefore, but to buy one. If You still want me to take this journey, You'll have to reimburse me!"

I paid $1,100 for a good second-hand car. This money, along with $700 I received for my crippled vehicle, covered the cost. I left the car dealership on a Friday evening. The next Monday morning, at home, I received a letter from someone unknown to me. Enclosed was a check—made out to me, personally—for a thousand dollars. The letter stated, "Please use this money as Divine Mother wants you to."

Now, please ask yourself: How many people in America pray to God as their Divine Mother? Hardly any! Every time I recall this episode, my eyes fill with tears. Many, many times in my life have I found Divine Mother's loving assistance fulfilling my needs, answering my questions! In living for God, I have found the thrill of an unceasing, divine romance.

Let me end this book by writing out—first in Bengali, then in English—a devotional song. Thoughts from it found expression in two of my Guru's favorite chants:

> Amar shad na mithilo,
> Asha na purilo,
> Shakholi phuraejai Ma!
> Amar shad na mithilo.
> Janomer shod,
> Dakhi go Ma Tore,
> Kole tule nite ai Ma!
> Shakholi phuraejai Ma!
> Ei prithibir keu
> Bhalo to bashe na;
> Ei prithibi bhalo bashite jane na:
> Jetai achhe shudhu bhalobashi,
> Sheta jete pran chhai, Ma!
> Shakoli phuraejai Ma!
> Bado daga peye
> Bashana twejeyechi—
> Bado daga shaye
> Kamona bhugeyechi.
> Anek kandeyechi:
> Kandite pari na.
> Bhuk phete bhengejai Ma!
> Shakoli phuraejai Ma!

Amar shad na mithilo. . . .
My desires have not yet been fulfilled;
My hopes, not yet realized.
O Mother! my earthly dreams have all fled away!
Once more I call out from the pain of my heart:
Mother! Take me on Your lap!
O Mother! my earthly dreams have all fled away!
In this world, Mother,
Who is there that truly loves?
In this world they do not know how to love!
There, where true love is,
There alone would my heart dwell forever.
O Mother! my earthly dreams have all fled away!
Long, long have I called You, Dearest One!
How much longer can I keep on calling?
For love of You my heart is breaking!
O Mother! my earthly dreams have all fled away!
Yet my hopes, alas, have not yet been fulfilled. . . .

And so ends my story. As Sister Gyanamata would often say: "God alone! God alone!"

INDEX

About the Author

"*Swami Kriyananda is a man of wisdom and compassion in action, truly one of the leading lights in the spiritual world today.*"

—Lama Surya Das, Dzogchen Center, author of *Awakening the Buddha Within*

SWAMI KRIYANANDA

A PROLIFIC AUTHOR, PLAYWRIGHT, accomplished composer, and artist, and a world-renowned spiritual teacher, Swami Kriyananda refers to himself simply as "a humble disciple" of the great God-realized master, Paramhansa Yogananda. He met his guru at the young age of twenty-two, and served him during the last four years of the Master's life. And he has done so continuously ever since.

Kriyananda was born in Rumania of American parents, and educated in Europe, England, and the United States. Philosophically and artistically inclined from youth, he soon came to question life's meaning and society's values. During a period of intense inward reflection, he discovered Yogananda's *Autobiography of a Yogi*, and immediately traveled three thousand miles from New York to

California to meet the Master, who accepted him as a monastic disciple. Yogananda appointed him as the head of the monastery, authorized him to teach in his name and to give initiation into Kriya Yoga, and entrusted him with the missions of writing and developing what he called "world brotherhood colonies." Recognized as the "father of the spiritual communities movement" in the United States, Swami Kriyananda founded Ananda World Brotherhood Community in 1968. It has served as a model for a number of communities founded subsequently in the United States and Europe.

In 2003 Swami Kriyananda, then in his seventy-eighth year, moved to India with a small international group of disciples, to dedicate his remaining years to making his guru's teachings better known. To this end he appears daily on Indian national television with his program, *A Way of Awakening*. He has established Ananda Sangha, which publishes many of his one hundred literary works and spreads the teachings of Kriya Yoga throughout India. His vision for the next years includes founding cooperative spiritual communities in India, a temple of all religions dedicated to Paramhansa Yogananda, a retreat center, a school system, and a monastery, as well as a university-level Yoga Institute of Living Wisdom.

About Paramhansa Yogananda

"As a bright light shining in the midst of darkness, so was Yogananda's presence in this world. Such a great soul comes on earth only rarely, when there is a real need among men."

—The Shankaracharya of Kanchipuram

BORN IN INDIA in 1893, Paramhansa Yogananda was trained from his early years to bring India's ancient science of Self-realization to the West. In 1920 he moved to the United States to begin what was to develop into a worldwide work touching millions of lives. Americans were hungry for India's spiritual teachings, and for the liberating techniques of yoga.

In 1946 he published what has become a spiritual classic and one of the best-loved books of the 20th century, *Autobiography of a Yogi.* In addition, Yogananda established headquarters for a worldwide work, wrote a number of books and study courses, gave lectures to thousands in most major cities across the United States, wrote music and poetry, and trained disciples. He was invited to the White House by Calvin Coolidge, and he initiated Mahatma Gandhi into Kriya Yoga, his most advanced technique of meditation.

Yogananda's message to the West highlighted the unity of all religions, and the importance of love for God combined with scientific techniques of meditation.

Ananda Sangha Worldwide

A NANDA SANGHA IS a worldwide fellowship of kindred souls following the teachings of Paramhansa Yogananda. The Sangha embraces the search for higher consciousness through the practice of meditation, and through the ideal of service to others in their quest for Self-realization. Approximately ten thousand spiritual seekers are affiliated with Ananda Sangha throughout the world.

Founded in 1968 by Swami Kriyananda, a direct disciple of Paramhansa Yogananda, Ananda includes seven communities in the United States, Europe, and in India. Worldwide, about one thousand devotees live in these spiritual communities, which are based on Yogananda's ideals of "plain living and high thinking."

"Thousands of youths must go north, south, east and west to cover the earth with little colonies, demonstrating that simplicity of living plus high thinking lead to the greatest happiness!" After pronouncing these words at a garden party in Beverly Hills, California in 1949, Paramhansa Yogananda raised his arms, and chanting the sacred cosmic vibration AUM, he "registered in the ether" his blessings on what has become the spiritual communities movement. From that moment on, Swami Kriyananda dedicated himself to bringing this vision from inspiration to reality by establishing communities where home, job, school, worship, family, friends, and recreation could evolve together as part of the interwoven fabric of harmonious, balanced living. Yogananda predicted that these communities would "spread like wildfire," becoming the model lifestyle for the coming millennium.

Swami Kriyananda lived with his guru during the last four years of the Master's life, and continued to serve his organization for another ten years, bringing the teachings of Kriya Yoga and Self-realization to audiences in the United States, Europe, Australia, and, from 1958–1962, India. In 1968, together with a small group of close friends and students, he founded the first "world brotherhood community" in the foothills of the Sierra Nevada Mountains in northeastern California. Initially a meditation retreat center located on sixty-seven acres of forested land, Ananda World Brotherhood Village today encompasses eight hundred acres where about 250 people live a dynamic, fulfilling life based on the principles and practices of spiritual, mental, and physical development, cooperation, respect, and divine friendship.

At this writing, after more then forty years of existence, Ananda is one of the most successful networks of intentional communities in the world. Urban communities have been developed in Palo Alto and Sacramento, California; Portland, Oregon; and Seattle, Washington. In Europe, near Assisi, Italy, a spiritual retreat and community was established in 1983, where today nearly one hundred residents from eight countries live. Ananda Sangha also supports more than hundred meditation groups worldwide. Swami Kriyananda currently lives in Pune, India where work has begun to develop both urban and rural communities.

Contact Information:

    mail: 14618 Tyler Foote Road, Nevada City, CA 95959
    phone: 530-478-7560
    online: www.ananda.org
    email: sanghainfo@ananda.org

FURTHER EXPLORATIONS

If you are inspired by *The New Path* and would like to learn more about Paramhansa Yogananda and his teachings, or about Swami Kriyananda, Crystal Clarity Publishers offers many additional resources to assist you.

Books by Paramhansa Yogananda

Crystal Clarity publishes the original 1946, unedited edition of Paramhansa Yogananda's spiritual masterpiece:

Autobiography of a Yogi
Paramhansa Yogananda

Autobiography of a Yogi is one of the best-selling Eastern philosophy titles of all time, with millions of copies sold. It has been named one of the best and most influential books of the twentieth century. This highly prized reprinting of the original 1946 edition is the only one available free from textual changes made after Yogananda's death.

Yogananda was the first yoga master of India whose mission was to live and teach in the West. His account of his life experiences includes childhood revelations, stories of his visits to saints and masters in India, and long-secret teachings of Self-realization that he made available to the Western reader.

In this updated edition are bonus materials, including a last chapter that Yogananda wrote in 1951, without posthumous changes. This new edition also includes the eulogy that Yogananda wrote for Gandhi, and a new foreword and afterword by Swami Kriyananda, one of Yogananda's close direct disciples.

PRAISE FOR *Autobiography of a Yogi*

"In the original edition, published during Yogananda's life, one is more in contact with Yogananda himself. While Yogananda founded centers and organizations, his concern was more with guiding individuals to direct communion with Divinity rather than with promoting any one church as opposed to another. This spirit is easier to grasp in the original edition of this great spiritual and yogic classic."

—David Frawley, Director, American Institute of Vedic Studies, author of
  Yoga and Ayurveda

THIS TITLE IS ALSO AVAILABLE IN:
52-Card Deck and Booklet
Unabridged Audiobook (MP3 format)

Revelations of Christ

Proclaimed by Paramhansa Yogananda,
Presented by his disciple, Swami Kriyananda

Over the past years, our faith has been severely shaken by experiences such as the breakdown of church authority, discoveries of ancient texts that supposedly contradict long-held beliefs, and the sometimes outlandish historical analyses of Scripture by academics. Together, these forces have helped create confusion and uncertainty about the true teachings and meanings of Christ's life. Now, more than ever, people are yearning for a clear-minded, convincing, yet uplifting understanding of the life and teachings of Jesus Christ.

This soul-stirring book, presenting the teachings of Christ from the experience and perspective of Paramhansa Yogananda, one of the greatest spiritual masters of the twentieth century, finally offers the fresh understanding of Christ's teachings for which the world has been waiting. This book presents us with an opportunity to understand the Scriptures in a more reliable way than any other: by learning from those saints who have communed directly, in deep ecstasy, with Christ and God.

PRAISE FOR *Revelations of Christ*

"This is a great gift to humanity. It is a spiritual treasure to cherish and to pass on to children for generations. This remarkable and magnificent book brings us to the doorway of a deeper, richer embracing of Eternal Truth."

—Neale Donald Walsch, author of *Conversations with God*

"Kriyananda's revelatory book gives us the enlightened, timeless wisdom of Jesus the Christ in a way that addresses the challenges of twenty-first century living."

—Michael Beckwith, founder and Spiritual Director, Agape International Spiritual Center, author of *Inspirations of the Heart*

THIS TITLE IS ALSO AVAILABLE IN:
Unabridged Audiobook (MP3 format)

The Essence of the Bhagavad Gita
Explained by Paramhansa Yogananda
As remembered by his disciple, Swami Kriyananda

Rarely in a lifetime does a new spiritual classic appear that has the power to change people's lives and transform future generations. This is such a book.

This revelation of India's best-loved scripture approaches it from a fresh perspective, showing its deep allegorical meaning and its down-to-earth practicality. The themes presented are universal: how to achieve victory in life in union with the divine; how to prepare for life's "final exam," death, and what happens afterward; how to triumph over all pain and suffering.

PRAISE FOR *The Essence of the Bhagavad Gita*

"The Essence of the Bhagavad Gita *is a brilliant text that will greatly enhance the spiritual life of every reader."*

—Caroline Myss, author of *Anatomy of the Spirit* and *Sacred Contracts*

"It is doubtful that there has been a more important spiritual writing in the last 50 years than this soul-stirring, monumental work. What a gift! What a treasure!"

—Neale Donald Walsch, author of *Conversations with God*

THIS TITLE IS ALSO AVAILABLE IN:
Unabridged Audiobook (MP3 format)
Also available as paperback without commentary,
titled *The Bhagavad Gita.*

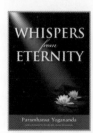

Whispers from Eternity
Paramhansa Yogananda
Edited by his disciple, Swami Kriyananda

Many poetic works can inspire, but few, like this one, have the power to change your life. Yogananda was not only a spiritual master, but a master poet, whose poems revealed the hidden divine presence behind even everyday things.

Open this book, pick a poem at random, and read it. Mentally repeat whatever phrase appeals to you. Within a short time, you will feel your consciousness transformed. This book has the power to rapidly accelerate your spiritual growth, and provides hundreds of delightful ways for you to begin your own conversation with God.

THIS TITLE IS ALSO AVAILABLE IN:
Unabridged Audiobook (MP3 format)

The Wisdom of Yogananda Series

This series features writings of Paramhansa Yogananda not available elsewhere. These books include writings from his earliest years in America, in an approachable, easy-to-read format. The words of the Master are presented with minimal editing, to capture his expansive and compassionate wisdom, his sense of fun, and his practical spiritual guidance.

How to Be Happy All the Time
The Wisdom of Yogananda Series, Volume 1
Paramhansa Yogananda

Yogananda powerfully explains virtually everything needed to lead a happier, more fulfilling life. Topics include: looking for happiness in the right places; choosing to be happy; tools and techniques for achieving happiness; sharing happiness with others; balancing success and happiness, and many more.

PRAISE FOR *How to Be Happy All The Time*
"*The most important condition for happiness is even-mindedness, and here the author of* Autobiography of a Yogi *brings some of this sense to a treatise on how to be happy under virtually any condition. From identifying habits, thoughts, and practices which steal from happiness to understanding simplicity is the key and sharing happiness with others,* How to Be Happy All The Time *is a fine starting point for reaching contentment.*"
—*Bookwatch*

Karma and Reincarnation
The Wisdom of Yogananda Series, Volume 2
Paramhansa Yogananda

Yogananda reveals the truth behind karma, death, reincarnation, and the afterlife. With clarity and simplicity, he makes the mysterious understandable. Topics include: why we see a world of suffering and inequality; how to handle the challenges in our lives; what happens at death, and after death; and the origin and purpose of reincarnation.

Spiritual Relationships
The Wisdom of Yogananda Series, Volume 3
Paramhansa Yogananda

Topics include: how to cure bad habits that spell the death of true friendship; how to choose the right partner and create a lasting marriage; sex in marriage and how to conceive a spiritual child; problems that arise in marriage and what to do about them; the divine plan uniting parents and children; the Universal Love behind all your relationships.

How to Be a Success
The Wisdom of Yogananda Series, Volume 4
Paramhansa Yogananda

This book includes the complete text of *The Attributes of Success*, the original booklet later published as *The Law of Success*. In addition, you will learn how to find your purpose in life, develop habits of success and eradicate habits of failure, develop your will power and magnetism, and thrive in the right job.

How to Have Courage, Calmness, & Confidence
The Wisdom of Yogananda Series, Volume 5
Paramhansa Yogananda

Absorb the power of the Master's words, practice his simple suggestions, and you will feel a new energy filling you, giving you the power to meet every challenge with joyful confidence, calmness, and courage. Topics include: dislodge negative thoughts & depression; cure nervousness; systematically eliminate worry from your life; uproot fear and thoughts of failure—even in the midst of trying circumstances; overcome anger, sorrow, over-sensitivity, and other troublesome emotional responses; and learn to strengthen the heroic element in yourself.

Books by Swami Kriyananda

Religion in the New Age
Swami Kriyananda

Our planet has entered an "Age of Energy" that will affect us for centuries to come. We can see evidence of this all around us: in ultra-fast computers, the quickening of communication and transportation, and the shrinking of time and space. This fascinating book of essays explores how this new age will change our lives, especially our spiritual seeking. Covers a wide range of upcoming societal shifts—in leadership, relationships, and self-development—including the movement away from organized religion to inner experience.

In Divine Friendship
Swami Kriyananda

This extraordinary book of nearly 250 letters, written over a 30-year period by Swami Kriyananda, responds to practically any concern a spiritual seeker might have, such as: strengthening one's faith, accelerating one's spiritual progress, meditating more deeply, responding to illness, earning a living, attracting a mate, raising children, overcoming negative self-judgments, and responding to world upheavals.

Connecting all of these letters is the love, compassion, and wisdom of Swami Kriyananda, one of the leading spiritual figures of our times. The letters describe in detail his efforts to fulfill his Guru's commission to establish spiritual communities, and offer invaluable advice to leaders everywhere on how to avoid the temptations of materialism, selfishness, and pride. A spiritual treasure that speaks to spiritual seekers at all levels.

Meditation for Starters
Swami Kriyananda

Have you wanted to learn to meditate, but just never got around to it? Or tried "sitting in the silence" only to find yourself too restless to stay more than a few moments? If so, Meditation for Starters is just what you've been looking for, and with a companion CD, it provides everything you need to begin a meditation practice. It is filled with easy-to-follow instructions, beautiful guided visualizations, and answers to important questions on meditation such as: what meditation is (and isn't); how to relax your body and prepare yourself for going within; and techniques for interiorizing and focusing the mind.

Awaken to Superconsciousness
Meditation for Inner Peace, Intuitive Guidance, and Greater Awareness
Swami Kriyananda

This popular guide includes everything you need to know about the philosophy and practice of meditation, and how to apply the meditative mind to resolving common daily conflicts in uncommon, superconscious ways. Superconsciousness is the source of intuition, spiritual healing, solutions to problems, and deep and lasting joy.

PRAISE FOR *Awaken to Superconsciousness*

"*A brilliant, thoroughly enjoyable guide to the art and science of meditation. [Swami Kriyananda] entertains, informs, and inspires—his enthusiasm for the subject is contagious. This book is a joy to read from beginning to end.*"

— *Yoga International*

ALSO AVAILABLE IN THIS SERIES:
Music to Awaken Superconsciousness (CD)
Meditations to Awaken Superconsiousness, spoken word (CD)

Affirmations for Self-Healing
Swami Kriyananda

This inspirational book contains fifty-two affirmations and prayers, each pair devoted to improving a quality in ourselves. Strengthen your will power; cultivate forgiveness, patience, health, enthusiasm, and more. A powerful tool for self-transformation.

PRAISE FOR *Affirmations for Self-Healing*

"*[This book] has become a meditation friend to me. The inspiring messages and prayers, plus the physical beauty of the book, help me start my day uplifted and focused.*"

—Sue Patton Thoele, author of *Growing Hope*

THIS TITLE IS ALSO AVAILABLE IN:
Unabrideged Audiobook (MP3 format)

Audiobooks and Music

We offer many of our book titles in unabridged MP3 format audiobooks. To purchase these titles and to see more music and audiobook offerings, visit our website: www.crystalclarity.com. Or look for us in the popular online download sites.

 ## Metaphysical Meditations
Swami Kriyananda

Kriyananda's soothing voice guides you in thirteen different meditations based on the soul-inspiring, mystical poetry of Paramhansa Yogananda. Each meditation is accompanied by beautiful classical music to help you quiet your thoughts and prepare for deep states of meditation. Includes a full recitation of Yogananda's poem *Samadhi*, which appears in *Autobiography of a Yogi*. A great aid to the serious meditator, as well as to those just beginning their practice.

 ## Meditations to Awaken Superconsciousness
Guided Meditations on the Light
Swami Kriyananda

Featuring two beautiful guided meditations as well as an introductory section to help prepare the listener for meditation, this extraordinary recording of visualizations can be used either by itself, or as a companion to the book, *Awaken to Superconsciousness*. The soothing, transformative words, spoken over inspiring sitar background music, creates one of the most unique guided meditation products available.

 ## Music to Awaken Superconsciousness
Swami Kriyananda

A companion to the book, *Awaken to Superconsciousness*. Each of the lush instrumental selections is designed to help the listener more easily access higher states of awareness—deep calmness, joy, radiant health, and self-transcendence. This beautiful recording can be used simply as background music for relaxation and meditation. Or, you can follow the instructions in the liner notes to actively achieve superconsciousness.

Relax: Meditations for Flute and Cello

Composed by Donald Walters

Featuring David Eby and Sharon Nani

This CD is specifically designed to slow respiration and heart rate, bringing listeners to their calm center. This recording features fifteen melodies for flute and cello, accompanied by harp, guitar, keyboard, and strings.

Bliss Chants

Ananda Kirtan

Chanting focuses and lifts the mind to higher states of consciousness. *Bliss Chants* features chants written by Yogananda and his direct disciple, Swami Kriyananda. They're performed by Ananda Kirtan, a group of singers and musicians from Ananda, one of the world's most respected yoga communities. Chanting is accompanied by guitar, harmonium, kirtals, and tabla.

Other titles in the Chant Series:

Divine Mother Chants

Love Chants

*Wellness Chants**

Power Chants

Peace Chants

*Wisdom Chants**

AUM: Mantra of Eternity

Swami Kriyananda

This recording features nearly seventy minutes of continuous vocal chanting of AUM, the Sanskrit word meaning peace and oneness of spirit. AUM, the cosmic creative vibration, is extensively discussed by Yogananda in *Autobiography of a Yogi*. Chanted here by his disciple, Kriyananda, this recording is a stirring way to tune into this cosmic power.

Other titles in the Mantra Series:

*Gayatri Mantra**

*Mahamrityanjaya Mantra**

*Maha Mantra**

* Available starting the summer of 2010.

Crystal Clarity Publishers

WHEN YOU'RE SEEKING a book on practical spiritual living, you want to know it's based on an authentic tradition of timeless teachings, and that it resonates with integrity. This is the goal of Crystal Clarity Publishers: to offer you books of practical wisdom filled with true spiritual principles that have not only been tested through the ages, but also through personal experience. We publish only books that combine creative thinking, universal principles, and a timeless message. Crystal Clarity books will open doors to help you discover more fulfillment and joy by living and acting from the center of peace within you.

Crystal Clarity Publishers—recognized worldwide for its bestselling, original, unaltered edition of Paramhansa Yogananda's classic *Autobiography of a Yogi*—offers many additional resources to assist you in your spiritual journey, including over ninety books, a wide variety of inspirational and relaxation music composed by Swami Kriyananda, Yogananda's direct disciple, and yoga and meditation DVDs.

For our online catalog, complete with secure ordering, please visit us on the web at:

www.crystalclarity.com

To request a catalog, place an order for the products you read about in the Further Explorations section of this book, or to find out more information about us and our products, please contact us:

Contact Information:
  mail: 14618 Tyler Foote Road, Nevada City, CA 95959
  phone: 800-424-1055 *or* 530-478-7600
  online: www.crystalclarity.com
  email: clarity@crystalclarity.com

The Expanding Light

V ISITED BY OVER two thousand people each year, the Expanding Light welcomes seekers from all backgrounds. Here you will find a loving, accepting environment, ideal for personal growth and spiritual renewal. We offer a varied, year-round schedule of classes and workshops. Offerings include: yoga, meditation, spiritual practices, yoga and meditation teacher training, and personal renewal retreats.

We strive to create an ideal relaxing and supportive environment for people to explore their own spiritual growth. We share the non-sectarian meditation practices and yoga philosophy of Paramhansa Yogananda and his direct disciple, Ananda's founder, Swami Kriyananda. Yogananda called his path "Self-realization," and our goal is to help our guests tune in to their own higher Self.

Guests at The Expanding Light can learn the four practices that comprise Yogananda's teachings of Kriya Yoga: the Energization Exercises, the *Hong Sau* technique of concentration, the AUM technique, and Kriya Yoga. The first two techniques are available for all guests; the second two are available to those interested in pursuing this path more deeply.

Contact Information:
mail: 14618 Tyler Foote Road, Nevada City, CA 95959
phone: 800-346-5350
online: www.expandinglight.org
email: info@expandinglight.org